Explainable AI for STEAM Personalization and Ethical Assessment

Jorge A. Ruiz-Vanoye
https://orcid.org/0000-0003-4928-5716
Polytechnic University of Pachuca, Mexico

Francisco R. Trejo-Macotela
https://orcid.org/0000-0003-2133-3456
Polytechnic University of Pachuca, Mexico

Martha Patricia Robles Gutiérrez
https://orcid.org/0009-0000-3143-9831
Polytechnic University of Pachuca, Mexico

IGI Global Scientific Publishing
Publishing Tomorrow's Research Today

Published in the United States of America by
IGI Global Scientific Publishing
701 East Chocolate Avenue
Hershey, PA, 17033, USA
Tel: 717-533-8845 | Fax: 717-533-7115
Website: https://www.igi-global.com E-mail: cust@igi-global.com

Library of Congress Cataloging-in-Publication Data

Names: Ruiz-Vanoye, Jorge A., 1975- editor | Trejo-Macotela, Francisco R., 1976- editor | Robles Gutiérrez, Martha (Martha Patricia), 1965- editor
Title: Explainable AI for STEAM personalization and ethical assessment / edited by: Jorge A. Ruiz-Vanoye, Francisco R. Trejo-Macotela, Martha Robles Gutiérrez.
Description: Hershey PA : IGI Global Scientific Publishing, [2027] | Includes bibliographical references. | Summary: "This book explores the transformative role of Explainable Artificial Intelligence, adaptive algorithms, multimodal learning analytics, intelligent tutoring systems, VR/AR laboratories, IoT-enabled smart spaces, robotics, and ethical automated assessment in shaping the next generation of intelligent and trustworthy learning ecosystems. This book advances the state of knowledge on intelligent, trustworthy, and human-centered learning ecosystems, integrating Explainable Artificial Intelligence (XAI), personalized STEAM education, and ethical automated assessment within Smart Education environments"-- Provided by publisher.
Identifiers: LCCN 2026021820 (print) | LCCN 2026021821 (ebook) | ISBN 9798337396750 hardcover | ISBN 9798337396767 paperback | ISBN 9798337396774 ebook
Subjects: LCSH: Artificial intelligence--Educational applications | Science--Study and teaching
Classification: LCC LB1028.44 .E97 2026 (print) | LCC LB1028.44 (ebook)
LC record available at https://lccn.loc.gov/2026021820
LC ebook record available at https://lccn.loc.gov/2026021821
British Cataloguing in Publication Data
A Cataloguing in Publication record for this book is available from the British Library.

Table of Contents

Detailed Table of Contents

explanations can support trust, learner agency, teacher judgment, and institutional accountability while also revealing the limits of algorithmic interpretation. The chapter distinguishes between different forms of explainability, including model-centered, user-centered, pedagogical, and ethical explanations. It also addresses major barriers such as opacity, bias, data complexity, overreliance on automated systems, and the risk of superficial transparency.

As AI-driven systems become increasingly embedded in STEAM education, questions of trust, transparency, and accountability can no longer remain secondary concerns. This chapter examines how intelligent learning systems shape personalization, assessment, feedback, and learner decision-making, while also raising difficult ethical questions about visibility, fairness, responsibility, and human agency. It argues that trust in AI-supported STEAM environments should not be treated as blind confidence in technological efficiency, but as a carefully built relationship grounded in explainability, evidence, dialogue, and institutional responsibility. The chapter explores the need for transparent algorithmic processes, meaningful teacher oversight, student awareness, and clear accountability structures that identify who is responsible when AI systems influence learning outcomes. Ultimately, it proposes a human-centered approach in which AI supports creativity, inquiry, and equity without weakening the moral and pedagogical role of educators.

While Artificial Intelligence enhances Science, Technology, Engineering, Arts and Mathematics education, reliance on complex "black-box" models undermines transparency, teacher agency, and student trust. This chapter presents a practical, accessible framework for implementing Explainable Artificial Intelligence in STEAM educational tools. Moving beyond theoretical algorithmic advancements, the approach leverages open-source platforms and low-code environments to democratize AI. The text examines how embedding explainability mechanisms into learning analytics

Smart Education relies on non-transparent predictive models for the learners. In STEAM, predicting failure alone is not sufficient for the learners. Educators need transparent insight for educational interventions without demographic bias. This chapter proposes a human-centred framework transitioning AI from purely predictive technologies to prescriptive-assessment engines spanning three layers: Layer 1 uses a stacked ensemble (XGBoost, LightGBM, CatBoost) to predict academic risk via dynamic behavioural metrics (e.g., study hours, attendance) instead of just historical grades. Layer 2 uses explainable AI (SHAP) to deconstruct these predictions, creating a transparent diagnostic profile detailing exactly why a student is at risk. Layer 3 employs an LLM via a RAG pipeline to create personalised, empathetic, and actionable feedback based on the SHAP diagnostic results. The architecture embeds algorithmic fairness and Human-in-the-Loop governance to eliminate socioeconomic proxy discrimination, providing a blueprint for an ethical, scalable learning ecosystem.

This chapter proposes a verifier-guided framework for synthetic educational ecosystems in STEAM learning analytics and illustrates it with a topology-aware prototype for adaptive tutoring and recommendations. Its central claim is that generated educational traces should be used only when their educational meaning, structural fidelity, subgroup behaviour, explanation stability, calibration, privacy, and responsible-use limits can be checked. Quality is treated as a multi-objective problem, and generation follows a conservative cycle: each candidate dataset must pass verifier gates before supporting modelling, benchmarking, or experimentation. The empirical work is bounded: it uses a controlled synthetic environment, not real institutional dropout records; therefore, dropout risk is framed as a future high-stakes

Preface

INTRODUCTION

Artificial intelligence is rapidly transforming education by enabling adaptive learning, automated assessment, intelligent tutoring, predictive analytics, and increasingly personalised learning experiences. Within Science, Technology, Engineering, Arts, and Mathematics education, these developments may offer substantial opportunities to support interdisciplinary learning, creativity, experimentation, and the development of competencies required by contemporary societies and industries. At the same time, the growing influence of algorithmic systems on educational decisions raises fundamental questions concerning transparency, fairness, accountability, privacy, learner autonomy, and the continuing role of human judgement.

Explainable AI for STEAM Personalization and Ethical Assessment addresses these opportunities and challenges through a multidisciplinary examination of explainable artificial intelligence in human-centred STEAM education. The volume brings together conceptual foundations, pedagogical frameworks, technological architectures, empirical studies, and emerging computational methods for designing learning environments that are adaptive and intelligent while remaining understandable, equitable, auditable, and ethically responsible.

The book is grounded in the principle that educational intelligence should not be evaluated exclusively in terms of predictive accuracy or automation efficiency. In educational settings, an intelligent system should also be able to provide meaningful explanations to students, teachers, administrators, and other stakeholders. Such explanations should clarify how recommendations, assessments, risk predictions, feedback, and personalised learning pathways are produced. They should also allow educators to question automated outputs, identify potential bias, intervene where necessary, and retain pedagogical responsibility.

Explainability in education therefore extends beyond the technical interpretation of machine-learning models. It includes pedagogical explainability, which helps learners understand why particular activities or resources are recommended; ethical explainability, which allows institutions to evaluate fairness and accountability; and human-centred explainability, whereby artificial intelligence supports rather than replaces professional judgement, creativity, empathy, and learner agency.

This volume situates these concerns within the broader evolution of STEAM 5.0. In this emerging paradigm, science, technology, engineering, arts, and mathematics are integrated with human-centred values, sustainability, and social responsibility. The responsible use of intelligent systems is similarly placed at the centre of educational development. STEAM 5.0 does not treat technology as an end in itself. Instead, it promotes educational ecosystems in which technological innovation is aligned with human well-being, inclusion, creativity, ethical reasoning, and the development of solutions to complex social and productive needs.

The chapters collectively consider how explainable AI can contribute to personalised learning pathways, adaptive recommendation, intelligent tutoring, automated feedback, smart classrooms, experimental engineering platforms, metaverse-based education, and learning analytics. They also investigate the roles of generative AI, large language models, the Internet of Things, synthetic educational data, algebraic topology, persistent homology, and human-in-the-loop evaluation.

One of the book's central contributions lies in its integration of established educational approaches with emerging computational methods. Several chapters consider how learning trajectories, curricular relationships, and learner–resource interactions can be represented as graphs, geometric structures, and evolving topological objects. These approaches may offer new ways of identifying cycles, transitions, disruptions, prerequisite relationships, and structural patterns that conventional educational analytics may overlook.

The volume also recognises that personalisation may create risks when learners are reduced to profiles, probabilities, or demographic categories. Accordingly, the chapters emphasise fairness-aware design, subgroup evaluation, privacy protection, explanation stability, responsible synthetic-data generation, teacher oversight, and institutional governance. Personalisation should expand educational opportunities without creating opaque classifications, discriminatory recommendations, or unjustified restrictions on learner progression.

The book is organised into five sections. Section 1 establishes the foundations of STEAM 5.0 and human-centred educational ecosystems. Section 2 considers creativity, interdisciplinary competencies, social and productive needs, and the integration of emerging technologies. Section 3 introduces explainable AI, trust, accountability, and human-in-the-loop governance. Section 4 addresses adaptive learning, recommendation systems, personalisation, and explainable feedback.

Section 5 explores immersive environments, intelligent experimental platforms, synthetic educational ecosystems, and topology-aware learning analytics.

Through this structure, the volume moves from educational and philosophical foundations to practical frameworks and advanced computational applications. Its intended audience includes researchers, educators, instructional designers, educational technology specialists, engineers, data scientists, institutional leaders, policymakers, and graduate students interested in the responsible use of artificial intelligence in education.

The chapters have been contributed by scholars from multiple institutions and disciplinary backgrounds. This diversity reflects a central premise of STEAM education: complex educational challenges cannot be addressed through isolated technical or pedagogical perspectives. Meaningful innovation is therefore likely to depend on collaboration among educators, engineers, computer scientists, social researchers, institutional leaders, and the learners affected by intelligent technologies.

Ultimately, this book argues that explainable artificial intelligence should serve as a foundation for educational trust rather than merely as an additional technical feature. Intelligent learning systems must be designed so that their recommendations can be examined, their limitations recognised, their effects evaluated, and their decisions kept subject to meaningful human oversight.

It is our hope that *Explainable AI for STEAM Personalization and Ethical Assessment* may support further research and responsible implementation while encouraging a broader discussion of the educational future being constructed through artificial intelligence. The objective is not simply to make education more automated, but to make intelligent education more transparent, inclusive, creative, accountable, and genuinely human-centred.

CHAPTER OVERVIEW

Chapter 1, Explainable AI-Driven Learning Ecosystems and Emerging Technologies for STEAM Education, analyses the role of explainable AI in addressing opacity and limitations in the interpretability of intelligent educational systems. Drawing on conceptual, documentary, and comparative analysis, the chapter considers models and techniques that may make STEAM learning processes, recommendations, and assessments more transparent and understandable.

Chapter 2, Explainable Artificial Intelligence in Education: Concepts, Taxonomies, and Challenges, introduces the principal concepts and classifications of explainable AI in educational contexts. It distinguishes among model-centred, user-centred, pedagogical, and ethical explanations. The chapter also discusses challenges related to algorithmic opacity, bias, data complexity, overreliance on automated systems, and superficial transparency.

Chapter 3, Trust, Transparency, and Accountability in AI-Driven STEAM Learning Systems, examines the influence of AI on personalisation, evaluation, feedback, and learner decision-making. It proposes that trust should rest on evidence, explainability, dialogue, teacher oversight, student awareness, and clearly defined institutional responsibilities rather than on unquestioned confidence in technological efficiency.

Chapter 4, Implementing Explainable Artificial Intelligence in STEAM Educational Tools: A Practical and Accessible Framework for Transparent and Trustworthy Learning, sets out an accessible framework for incorporating explainability into learning analytics, intelligent tutoring, and other STEAM educational applications. It considers open-source and low-code tools, pedagogical decision-making, student metacognition, fairness, accountability, responsible data use, and alignment with international ethical guidance.

Chapter 5, Human-in-the-Loop Evaluation in Smart Classrooms for Explainable and Ethical AI-Based Education, explores how teacher supervision and iterative human feedback may strengthen automated assessment and learning analytics. It proposes a conceptual architecture in which educators validate, revise, or override AI-generated evaluations. This approach preserves pedagogical responsibility while improving transparency, fairness, and ethical governance.

Chapter 6, Adaptive Learning Systems and Their Impact on STEM Achievement, synthesises recent research on intelligent tutoring, learner modelling, and adaptive recommendation systems. It evaluates their effects on academic performance, engagement, motivation, and self-regulation while identifying limitations in longitudinal evidence, equity analysis, and comparisons among adaptive methods.

Chapter 7, Topological Regularization in Educational Recommendation and Personalized STEAM Tutoring, presents an explainable framework that combines educational graphs, graph-Laplacian smoothness, persistent-homology summaries, prerequisite-aware ranking, ethical auditing, and safe tutoring constraints. The chapter considers how recommendation accuracy may be balanced with curricular coherence, fairness, calibration, stability, and structural validity.

Chapter 8, An Automated, Fairness-Aware Students Feedback System Using SHAP and Generative AI, proposes a three-layer framework that combines ensemble prediction, SHAP-based explanations, and generative AI. The system transforms risk predictions into transparent diagnostic profiles and personalised feedback. It also incorporates fairness controls and human-in-the-loop governance intended to help reduce demographic and socioeconomic discrimination.

Chapter 9, Verifiable Synthetic Educational Ecosystems for Topology-Aware STEAM: Learning Analytics and Adaptive Tutoring, presents a verifier-guided method for generating and evaluating synthetic educational data. It assesses educational meaning, structural fidelity, subgroup behaviour, explanation stability, calibration, privacy, and responsible-use boundaries before synthetic records are used for modelling or benchmarking.

Jorge A. Ruiz-Vanoye
Polytechnic University of Pachuca, Mexico

Francisco R. Trejo-Macotela
Polytechnic University of Pachuca, Mexico

Martha Patricia Robles Gutiérrez
Polytechnic University of Pachuca, Mexico

Chapter 1

Explainable AI-Driven Learning Ecosystems and Emerging Technologies for STEAM Education

Ricardo A. Barrera-Cámara
Universidad Autónoma del Carmen, Mexico

David H. Fuque-Ehuan
http://orcid.org/0009-0005-5032-8076
Universidad Autónoma del Carmen, Mexico

Alejandro Fuentes-Penna
http://orcid.org/0000-0002-4303-3852
El Colegio de Morelos, Mexico

Fernando E. Sánchez-Martínez
http://orcid.org/0000-0003-4458-5402
Universidad Autónoma del Carmen, Mexico

ABSTRACT

The development and integration of artificial intelligence in education, such as the STEAM model, is driving the growth of smart learning environments; unfortunately, many of these systems have shortcomings and limitations in their learning models regarding transparency, interpretability, and the ability to understand decision-making and evaluation processes; this is particularly important for STEAM ecosystems, where results must be understandable, transparent, and justifiable for learning. The objective of this study is to analyze the use and applications of explainable artificial intelligence in the design, development, and use within STEAM educational

DOI: 10.4018/979-8-3373-9675-0.ch001

ecosystems. The methodological approach involves a conceptual, documentary, and comparative analysis of the technologies, applications, approaches, models, and techniques of explainability in STEAM education found in the literature. The incorporation of various mechanisms, techniques, and combinations of models enables transparency and contributes to the understanding of the models and processes that support learning.

INTRODUCTION

The STEAM educational approach (science, technology, engineering, arts, and mathematics) aims to make learning and teaching interdisciplinary in purpose, with the goal of fostering and developing innovation, creativity, and critical and computational thinking to solve complex problems. STEM, the predecessor to STEAM, focused on teaching science, technology, engineering, and mathematics to solve complex problems through innovation.

UNESCO and the OECD argue that STEM education should be promoted from primary through higher education to foster innovation and competitiveness (Organisation for Economic Co-operation and Development, 2019; UNESCO, 2023). In addition, countries such as the United States and Asian nations are implementing strategies to strengthen STEM (Organisation for Economic Co-operation and Development, 2023; UNESCO, 2023).

Artificial intelligence is an emerging technology; as a tool, it enables significant changes in the ways we teach and learn. Learning becomes adaptive and personalized; the teacher takes on the role of a guide and is not replaced by artificial intelligence. Thanks to generative tools, learning time can be reduced; these tools must be used responsibly and ethically to foster innovation and creativity. Artificial intelligence in STEAM must be incorporated in an interdisciplinary and ethical manner into real-world problems, facilitating understanding of those problems and, consequently, strengthening learning in the face of any challenge. Technology must be used to solve environmental problems from a humanistic and ecological perspective, and in the service of humanity.

Based on the above, this chapter demonstrates that STEAM education is closely linked to inclusion, equity, and social responsibility. It is also connected to the Sustainable Development Goals, particularly SDG 4 (education), as well as to the integration of and access to ICTs and artificial intelligence for all, as recommended by UNESCO and the OECD. In Mexico, through the National Strategic Programs, STEAM education and AI can be viewed as a means of linking education to addressing national and social issues.

An opaque or black-box model in artificial intelligence involves algorithms whose behavior or logic is unclear, incomprehensible, or non-transparent to humans, in addition to being complex. The black box receives input and produces output, but the inner workings of the process are unknown. They tend to be more accurate at detecting patterns in large amounts of data, but they may exhibit biases in the training data, and it is not possible to identify the source of an error in the event of failure; furthermore, the lack of transparency undermines people's trust.

Explainable artificial intelligence, or white-box AI, aims to make any AI system transparent so that people can understand how these systems make decisions and provide explanations, thereby strengthening trust and adoption in high-risk areas such as medicine, the justice system, finance, and security. In STEAM education, explainable artificial intelligence allows educators and students to understand these systems (Al-Zahrani et al., 2024), trust them (Feldman-Maggor et al., 2025; Türkmen, 2025), evaluate them transparently (Niu et al., 2025), identify their academic utility (How & Hung, 2019), and generate inclusive resources (Kohnke & Zaugg, 2025) for incorporation into the teaching/learning process.

BACKGROUND

Related Works

An analysis of the capabilities, limitations, and core functionalities of recently developed XAI tools, along with an examination of the perceptions of AIED researchers and AI researchers regarding machine learning in relation to XAI tools, revealed that each group has distinct target users and varying expectations, as well as the need to improve existing tools to enhance reliability and explainability (Fiok et al., 2022).

The XAI-ED framework aims to improve artificial intelligence tools in education in a transparent, reliable, and equitable manner for teachers and students; it also highlights challenges, needs, and opportunities for effectively incorporating explainable artificial intelligence into education (Khosravi et al., 2022). The aspects covered by the XAI-ED framework include stakeholders, benefits, approaches, models, designs, and difficulties/challenges. The study (Meylani, 2025) focuses on reviewing various studies on explainable artificial intelligence in educational contexts, proposes a model that incorporates pedagogical, epistemological, and ethical aspects for future research, and suggests that XIA should foster critical thinking, autonomy, and equity in learning.

A review of research on Explainable Artificial Intelligence reveals a wide variety of machine learning models, techniques, and frameworks (Altukhi et al., 2025). To provide a more comprehensive understanding, the research was grouped and categorized into developed models, evaluation methods and metrics, and user-oriented XIA system design. The aim was to better understand and bridge the gap between technical advancements and users' understanding of XIA.

The report (European Commission, 2025) discusses how responsible human oversight is key to the use of explainable artificial intelligence in education, understanding how it works, and collaboration between humans and artificial intelligence, in addition to proposing recommendations for European Union policies to promote transparency and trust in systems using explainable AI.

The systematic review finds that inclusive education can be improved by incorporating emerging technologies and artificial intelligence into various settings, such as social and cultural contexts (Salas-Pilco et al., 2022) .This benefits students from minority groups by leading to better academic outcomes, boosting their participation, and stimulating students' interest in STEM/STEAM. However, there are also challenges—including pedagogical and technological issues, sociocultural differences, and even technological dissatisfaction—that must be analyzed by education leaders.

Training in 21st-century skills, the integration of technology into courses, and the application of artificial intelligence in STEM education are educational needs identified by elementary school teachers (Bas & Kiraz, 2025). These are essential for the development of 21st-century skills and competencies, particularly in AI-supported STEM education.

Figure 1 illustrates the evolution of STEM and STEAM ecosystems, considering the past, present, and near future of this educational model.

Figure 1. The Evolution of STEM and STEAM Ecosystems.

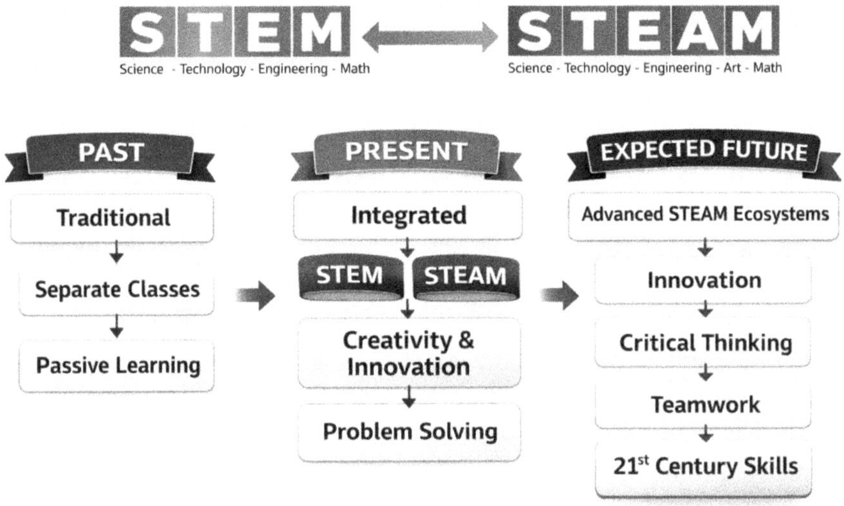

Source. Created by the author.

EXPLAINABLE ARTIFICIAL INTELLIGENCE AS CORE TECHNOLOGY FOR SMART STEAM ECOSYSTEMS

Explainable artificial intelligence is an essential component of smart STEAM environments; this guarantees that the "black box" inherent in various AI models is dependable and transparent. In other words, interdisciplinary AI systems must incorporate transparency, be understandable, and be managed in an ethically responsible manner; this can be achieved by establishing trust requirements and models for AI.

Principles of XAI

NISTIR (Phillips et al., 2021) developed a reference model used to guide the development of policies and strategies, as well as to evaluate and verify a set of principles for XAI that support the development of reliable and secure systems.

These principles were developed through collaboration across disciplines, including information and communication technologies, engineering, and behavioral sciences.

The XAI principles constitute a specific, technical framework focused on the quality of the explanation; there are four such principles (Figure 2):

Explanation. A system must provide or contain evidence, supporting information, or reasons that accompany its results or processes. Explanations are more comprehensive when the context and systems receive the appropriate data and information.

Meaningful. The explanations generated by systems must be clear and understandable to users. However, for individuals, what constitutes an adequate and good explanation or piece of information is influenced by their perceptions, experiences, and prior knowledge acquired or gained over time.

Explanation Accuracy. The explanation adequately reflects the cause that led to a result or accurately describes the system's internal process. The level of detail varies from person to person; some are satisfied with simple explanations, but for others, they aren't enough.

Knowledge Limits. A system should only operate under the conditions for which it was designed and when it achieves sufficient confidence in its result. The system can identify cases that are not suitable for operation and those where responses lack reliability.

Figure 2. Principles of XAI.

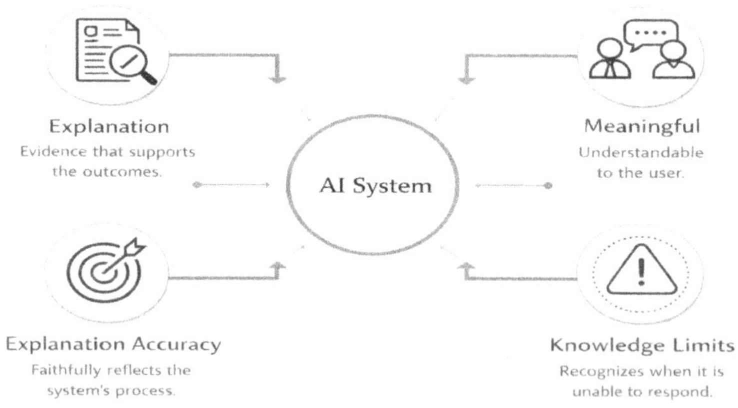

Source. Created by the author.

Trustworthy AI

Ethical and technical principles are fundamental to the framework for trustworthy artificial intelligence known as AI trustworthiness; this framework considers it essential that these aspects be incorporated into every stage of a system's operation (Li et al., 2023).

Technical principles. Their purpose is to make sure the model or system works properly:

Robustness. In machine learning, the system must be prepared to handle unexpected changes and remain stable in the face of them. Robustness is determined by a system's or algorithm's ability to respond to data inputs, inadequate data, unaccounted-for data, or runtime error handling. A lack of robustness affects the system's reliability and security, leading to unexpected or harmful behavior or results.

Generalization. Artificial intelligence models are trained using data, through which they learn and acquire knowledge; this knowledge is applied to small amounts of data and new data, as well as to identifying general patterns. These systems must be audited periodically to avoid bias and maintain reliability.

Explainability. Transparency. AI systems are transparent when it is possible to understand how they arrive at their results, grasp their internal logic, identify the data used, and detect potential errors or biases. Furthermore, this is closely related to explainability.

Reproducibility. The results generated by an artificial intelligence system should be the same when the same process, model, data, or environment is applied.

Ethical principles. These principles are directly and closely linked to human rights, equity, and justice; they must be incorporated as a foundation for artificial intelligence systems:

Algorithmic fairness. Systems must not discriminate; above all, they must eliminate preferential biases and produce fair results.

Privacy protection. Personal data and information must be protected by laws or regulations against any unauthorized use by third parties, including data that allows for identification and location.

Accountability. Anyone involved in any way with artificial intelligence, whether in its design, development, use, or the generation of results, bears some responsibility. Therefore, it is important to periodically assess its ethical implications and impact. Identifying potential flaws would facilitate their correction.

Dependent principles. These are included within other principles or are linked to other principles:

Security. An operational principle is encompassed by robustness; this principle addresses data protection (against potential theft, tampering, or damage) and the protection of infrastructure against potential malicious attacks, enabling individuals to respond effectively and maintain control in such situations.

Safety. This is a security principle considered to be technical in scope; it falls under the concept of robustness, which stipulates that any system should be designed to be fault-tolerant, in order to maintain security and continue to function without causing any harm.

Accuracy. It overlooks fairness, robustness, and transparency as key factors that sustain the trust of end users who make use of artificial intelligence systems. It is designed to measure the performance of artificial intelligence systems without evaluating or determining their reliability.

Limitations of knowledge. AI systems must demonstrate a capacity to know and present that they do not have sufficient information to make any judgment or result. This is linked to the principles of transparency, explainability, reproducibility, and accountability.

Table 1 outlines the main differences between the Trustworthy AI model and the principles-based model of Explainable Artificial Intelligence (XAI); the principles are categorized as technical, ethical, and independent.

Table 1. Comparison of Trustworthy AI Principles and XAI Principles.

Component	Trustworthy AI	XAI Framework
System Lifecycle	Lifecycle-oriented, including governance	Explanation-oriented
Ethical Principles	Algorithmic fairness	–
	Privacy protection	–
	Accountability	–
Technical Principles	Robustness	–
	Generalization	–
	Explainability	Explanation
	Transparency	–
	Reproducibility	–
Dependent or integrated Principles	Security	–
	Safety	–
	Knowledge Limits	Knowledge Limits
	Accuracy	–
Formal Principles of Explanation	Explainability (technical aspect)	Explanation
		Meaningful
		Explanation Accuracy
		Knowledge Limits

Source. Prepared by the author.

Explainability Techniques

Explainability techniques aim to ensure that predictions and explanations are transparent and understandable to people. There is a wide variety of artificial intelligence techniques that are applicable and used in explainable artificial intelligence within STEAM ecosystems; these are related to the type of disciplinary problem:

Science. SHapley Additive Explanations (SHAP): This method aids in predicting student academic performance by considering various factors (George et al., 2025) as well as identifying relevant factors in predictive or complex models (Suaza-Medina et al., 2024); Local Interpretable Model-agnostic Explanations (LIME): A technique used to analyze complex scientific (Mulwa et al., 2024) and educational data for local predictions (Nagy & Molontay, 2024). It facilitates the diagnosis of diseases such as diabetes or Alzheimer's by analyzing patients' tabular and clinical data (Viswan et al., 2024); Fuzzy Hoeffding Decision Tree (FHDT): It makes possible the construction of rules to analyze data incrementally and transparently to identify the variables that affect learning and how predictions are made (Ducange et al., 2021); Bayesian Networks: A technique used to analyze and identify variables such as performance, academic retention, or school dropout rates (Bertolini et al., 2023). This probabilistic technique examines the causal relationships between variables to predict outcomes (Topuz et al., 2024).

Tecnology. DeepLIFT (Deep Learning Important FeaTures): A technique that makes it possible to interpret and identify features, as well as conduct in silico experiments, in order to understand the predictions of deep neural networks) (Tursunalieva et al., 2024); Integrated Gradients: Artificial intelligence models are vulnerable to attacks involving natural language text inputs; these attacks aim to trick the AI model into generating incorrect predictions or results not intended by the model. By using Integrated Gradients with text classifiers, it is feasible to identify these attacks and prevent them from affecting the results or the tasks assigned to the AI model (Moraliyage et al., 2025); CounTEX (Counterfactual explanation with TEXt-driven concepts): This is an XAI model for generating applications using textual concepts that should be present or absent in a prediction presented in natural language in computer vision (Kim et al., 2023).

Engineering. Genetic Programming Symbolic Classifier (GPSC): It supports predictive maintenance by identifying possible equipment failures (Anđelić et al., 2025); furthermore, it is possible to model the behavior of equipment or machines (Anđelić et al., 2023). It is a machine learning technique based on genetic algorithms used for data classification by generating mathematical expressions that produce formulas, which are then analyzed to select the one that classifies best (Anđelić & Baressi Šegota, 2024); Grad-CAM (Gradient-weighted Class Activation Mapping): A deep learning technique used in computer vision to highlight the parts of an image that are most likely to be the subject of a prediction. For example, in the medical field, they help detect and classify gastrointestinal diseases; RISE (Randomized Input Sampling for Explanation): Given an image fed into an AI model, this technique generates a confidence score to determine whether a specific object is the one shown or whether the model is focusing on other elements or objects in the image; it also assists in generating import maps; Layer-wise Relevance Propagation (LRP): A widely used technique for explaining convolutional neural networks, with applications in medical diagnosis, quality control of parts, and document classification. This technique analyzes the final prediction (backpropagation) to identify which input features have the greatest influence on the prediction; Counterfactuals: This technique allows users to modify the input data and, consequently, the results. Users can run simulations or make adjustments to the input data to alter the results obtained, helping them understand the model and achieve specific outcomes. In engineering, it makes it possible to simulate a structure's load-bearing capacity, improve efficiency in industrial processes by adjusting production-related variables, prevent failures, or save energy, as well as simulate how vehicles respond to specific driving and braking conditions.

Arts. Deconvolutional Neural Networks (DeCNN): They perform operations that are the inverse of those used by convolutional neural networks (CNNs), reconstructing low-quality images to generate high-quality ones; they are used to restore works of art or photographs, generate images from text, and analyze works of art; Focus maps: Technique that uses visual maps to highlight the elements that carry the most weight or receive the highest level of attention in the decisions of a given model (Müller, 2025). Examples of applications include art appraisal, museum design, and art creation.

Mathematics. Algebraic circuit complexity: A mathematical framework based on the complexity of algebraic circuits is used to explain models and understand AI through mathematics (Ito et al., 2025), as well as to validate the generated reasoning. Some applications in the field of education include the design of robotic system movements, data analysis, and the analysis of sound waves in digital music; Principal Component Analysis (PCA)/Singular Value Decomposition (SVD): Techniques applied to large datasets in data processing to improve the visualization and interpretation of input data in a model. They are used for image compression, designing recommendation systems, text mining, sentiment analysis, music noise removal, and facial recognition. Information Bottleneck. Technique that compresses input data to filter out noise or unnecessary data, retaining only the data that is relevant to the prediction (Han et al., 2024). It can be used to analyze mathematical equations and optimize functions.

Figure 3 illustrates explainable artificial intelligence techniques in the context of STEAM disciplines.

Figure 3. XAI techniques.

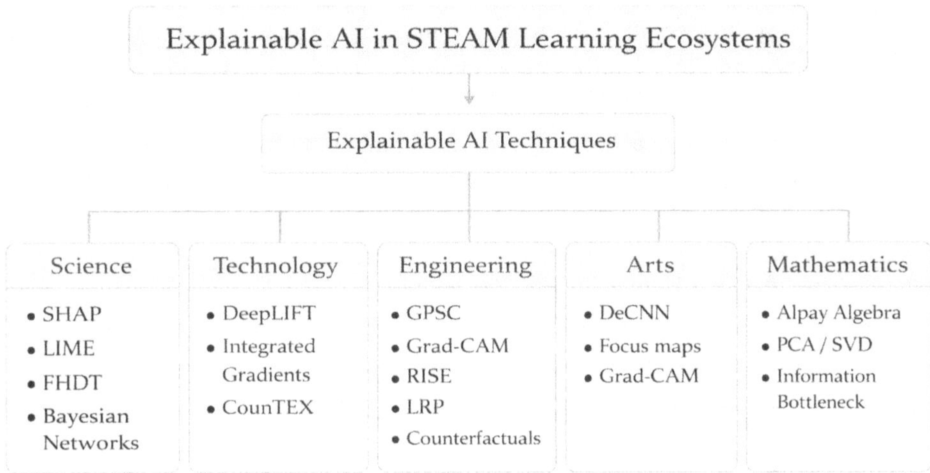

Source. Own work.

Educational and Ethical Benefits

The integration of explainable artificial intelligence into the educational setting offers both educational and ethical benefits.

Educational Benefits

Foster autonomy and control: By understanding the results or suggestions generated by artificial intelligence, students become active agents who take control of their learning through technology; Stimulates self-reflection: When they receive answers, students reflect on how they were generated and how they work, rather than simply using AI as a reference tool, which improves students' critical thinking by sparking curiosity and analysis; Deep learning for problem-solving: Help students use XAI to reliably understand and solve complex problems by applying the reasoning sequence to validate decisions; Critical literacy: students should not merely use technology for its utility; they must be able to detect biases, question, curate, and analyze the effects of results generated by artificial intelligence technologies.

Ethical Benefits

Transparency and trust: XAI fosters trust, transparency, and understanding among students, teachers, and parents regarding the use of AI systems and how they influence teaching and learning processes; Algorithmic fairness: XAI allows the identification and correction of biases in AI that tend to discriminate based on gender, socioeconomic status, or ethnicity. This guarantees fair, equitable, and transparent treatment of students across various processes. XAI identifies and corrects biases in AI that tend to discriminate based on gender, socioeconomic status, or ethnic origin. This ensures fair, equitable, and transparent treatment of students in all processes; Governance and accountability: the decisions or results generated by systems must be explainable; this allows for identifying who is legally and ethically responsible for the decisions made. Without explainability, it is not possible to assume responsibility for the decisions generated; Protection and respect for human dignity: through ethics and fundamental rights, XAI ensures that technology respects human freedom and dignity, contributes to people's well-being, and avoids making decisions that infringe upon their rights.

EMERGING TECHNOLOGIES ENABLING EXPLAINABLE LEARNING ECOSYSTEMS

It consists of a set of technologies and tools that are constantly evolving. They enable the creation of educational environments where people use them seamlessly as part of an educational process, critique them, and evaluate them.

Intelligent Tutoring Systems. Intelligent tutoring systems are computer systems that incorporate artificial intelligence to monitor and personalize learning and provide feedback or suggestions as they collect data on a student's behavior, simulating a human tutor. These systems show favorable results by providing practical guidance for problem-solving in STEM+C models (Science, Technology, Engineering, Mathematics, plus Computer Science, Programming, or Computer Science) (Hieu, 2019). This technology supports learning among students with varying levels of knowledge in computer programming, demonstrating better results among students with advanced knowledge in this academic discipline (Fodouop Kouam, 2024). In mathematics education, it has been shown that its incorporation into the curriculum has yielded significant benefits for students (Son, 2024); furthermore, it makes learning in other disciplines—such as physics, programming, and even mathematics—more adaptive, enabling students to receive personalized feedback on their learning and activities (Villegas-Ch et al., 2025).

Learning analytics. Educational data originating from various sources is processed and analyzed using data mining and artificial intelligence to identify patterns that help improve student learning outcomes. In foreign language learning, combining educational technology with learning analytics contributes to the development of individualized and adaptive learning (Bin Qushem et al., 2025). Online education platforms incorporate learning analytics and offer STEAM courses to students (García-Senín et al., 2022); these technologies make it possible to collect and analyze data and generate information with the aim of understanding students' academic performance to develop strategies that strengthen guided self-learning. The incorporation of learning analytics in medical education promotes and strengthens the use of information technologies, analyzes learning, and enhances self-directed learning as promoted by the STEAM model (Oliva-Córdova et al., 2025).

Educational chatbots. Software programs that use natural language to communicate via audio, video, and text, and rely on artificial intelligence as a key element to simulate human conversation are called chatbots. Chatbots are used in a variety of fields and contexts, including education. Emotions are important in learning courses that combine art with technology. In this regard, an AI-powered chatbot serves as the foundation for designing an emotional learning system that aids in understanding students' emotional responses (Lin, 2022). Chatbots are applied to various domains and contexts, including education. Chatbots act as guides for personalized and self-regulated learning, improving outcomes, increasing classroom engagement, and are also applied to various other educational contexts (Lin & Chang, 2023). The use of technologies such as ChatGPT helps to design lesson plans for arts education aimed at children—that is, STEAM education applied to art instruction; lesson plans developed using artificial intelligence yield better results than those designed using traditional methods (Luo & Tahir, 2025).

Internet of Things. The Internet of Things consists of various devices, sensors, and data collected and analyzed through internet-connected networks that maintain communication and enable the sharing of various resources. When Learning Management Systems, Content Management Systems, and the Internet of Things are combined, they become a powerful tool for science education in elementary and secondary schools. The data generated by the devices and sensors used by students to conduct various experiments is stored on these platforms to be analyzed and used to generate reports that help improve learning or redesign activities or experiments (Kayama et al., 2021). When combined, the Internet of Things (IoT), artificial intelligence, and robotics foster creativity and improve academic performance among students by enabling them to develop prototypes to address real-world problems in robotics education and learning (Valenzuela-Domínguez et al., 2024). The IoT in STEAM promotes project-based learning to design practical solutions to real-world problems that require attention; furthermore, the security of applications developed using the IoT in STEAM education must be examined more closely (Terzieva et al., 2025).

Smart platforms. Digital platform available to a wide range of users, offering a variety of tools and resources that incorporate artificial intelligence, making it possible to manage and support learning by analyzing data generated by students, instructors, and educational resources; create adaptive learning environments; and optimize and automate processes and resources. This technology facilitates the teaching, analysis, and application of data mining to short courses in technological translation that utilize the flipped classroom and blended learning (Kabudi et al., 2021). Platforms with artificial intelligence have also been developed to promote and teach traditional Chinese; these analyze learning and include activities and collaborative spaces useful for STEAM education (Gao, 2025; Jia, 2022; Zhang, 2024). Smart platforms have the ability to personalize, allow access, adapt learning, and guide students in STEM disciplines, including those with disabilities; this leads to better academic outcomes and increased motivation among students (Kohnke & Zaugg, 2025). Through the appropriate design of activities on the adaptive learning platform, the analysis and monitoring of the data generated there, and teachers' assessments and observations, it is evident that the use of the Device-Based Mobile Learning platform fosters greater participation and collaborative work, as well as improved academic outcomes among STEM students (Zhu & Wang, 2023).

Extended reality. Extended reality combines immersive technologies (virtual, augmented, and mixed reality) designed to help the brain to process simulations that blend the digital and real worlds as if they are real experiences or stimuli. Virtual reality: Technology that generates and ldisplays objects or elements within a digital environment as if they were real; when applied to educational settings where teachers require training and professional development, it leads them to increase their interaction and participation in the learning process and gain a deeper understanding of various concepts (Silva-Díaz et al., 2023). The use of virtual reality, project-based learning, and emotional intelligence enables students to create more creative and comprehensive products through their projects (Hsiao et al., 2025); Augmented reality: Augmented reality incorporates graphic objects and sounds into digital representations of the real world; this helps improve understanding of topics such as the translation of geometric figures into the real world (Méndez-Parra & Conde-Carmona, 2025). In geometry, this leads to better conceptual understanding, increased engagement, and improved learning outcomes (Gjoka & Pireva Nuci, 2025). The existence of open-access educational platforms for STEAM education that incorporate this technology provides a variety of learning resources that yield favorable results in teaching and learning processes (Velarde-Camaqui et al., 2024); among secondary-level students, it strengthens critical thinking and skills and increases learning retention (Alkhabra et al., 2023); Mixed reality: The interaction of virtual objects operating within real-world environments in real time is known as mixed reality. This combination fosters creative thinking and enhances practical skills, transforming the way students receive and absorb learning, turning them from consumers of resources into creators of their own educational process (Soroko, 2024). In arts education, it fosters creativity and critical thinking, enhancing the understanding, representation, and interaction with virtual objects (Ojetunde & Ramnarain, 2026).

Educational blockchain. In academic contexts, blockchain technology manages and maintains security in a decentralized and distributed manner, recording all transactions and maintaining a linked ledger as transactions and activities occur, including user authentication (Alshareef, 2022). It also supports the management of academic achievements and records, as well as access to and distribution of various types of resources (Wang et al., 2025); furthermore, reward-based learning in gamified learning environments demonstrates increased student motivation and engagement, contributing to the implementation of the STEAM model (Aljamaan et al., 2025; Lewis & Crawford, 2024).

APPLIED ARCHITECTURES AND TECHNOLOGICAL TOOLS

Layered Architectures

Recent work on explainable learning ecosystems no longer views artificial intelligence as an opaque black box. Instead, scholars propose integrating multilayer architectures within AI-driven decision support systems (AI DSS). Such tiered designs regulate information flow—from raw data to predictive outputs—and generate interfaces that remain intelligible to end users (López-Pernas et al., 2026; Mahamad et al., 2025).

The operational logic of this architecture can be outlined as follows. At the base, a Data Collection Layer acquires multidimensional learning traces, including behavioural metrics from students. These data continuously feed the subsequent processing modules. The Model Layer applies core predictive algorithms—natural language processing (NLP) and deep learning—to produce automated decisions. Examples include forecasting academic performance or early identification of at-risk students.

To ensure that such automated decisions remain transparent, the ecosystem incorporates an Explainability Layer (XAI) that functions as a technical auditor. Cognitive science principles and attention mechanisms are embedded directly into the neural networks. This allows the layer to generate interpretable models (Duan et al., 2024). Yet purely numeric XAI metrics often prove too technical for many stakeholders. A Translation and Personalization Layer, which relies on generative AI, therefore, converts those numerical outputs into multimodal, natural-language representations. In parallel, a personalization engine tailors the depth of explanation to the recipient's role.

The architecture closes with the User Interface (UI) and Delivery Layer. Here, dashboards and learning management systems (LMS) serve as the primary front-end. Through these interfaces, students and instructors receive both the translated explanations and the system's decisions. Such a design fosters a more cohesive and transparent educational environment (López-Pernas et al., 2026; Mahamad et al., 2025).

LMS Integration

The integration of artificial intelligence into LMS platforms, such as Moodle or Canvas, represents the visual layer or front end where algorithmic predictions are realized. This convergence allows machine learning models to be embedded directly into the system's architecture to analyze behavior in real time and serve as early warnings of the risk of academic failure (Mahamad et al., 2025; Osborne & Lang, 2023).

To make this data useful, LMSs present the information through dashboards with visual indicators, such as risk traffic lights (Shoaib et al., 2024). However, simply displaying a label with graphics is insufficient. This is where Explainable AI (XAI) comes in, pairing predictions with graphs that break down the importance of each variable—such as time spent offline or assignment submission—explaining the reasoning behind the calculation and making the data actionable (Jang et al., 2022; López-Pernas et al., 2026).

Finally, the effectiveness of this integration depends on a human-centered design. XAI tools that go beyond simple monitoring to offer concrete recommendations for action have been shown to significantly improve student self-regulation and performance (Afzaal et al., 2021). To achieve this, the LMS must dynamically adapt the depth of its explanations based on the user interacting with the platform, whether they are a teacher, student, or administrator (Duan et al., 2024; Khosravi et al., 2022).

Technology Governance

The implementation of AI ecosystems in higher education goes beyond purely technical challenges, requiring rigorous institutional governance frameworks. Current literature emphasizes that educational AI systems must be governed by the global FATE principles (Fairness, Accountability, Transparency, and Ethics), where explainability (XAI) is established as a non-negotiable requirement to ensure algorithmic transparency for users (Nguyen et al., 2023).

Given this approach, privacy and information security form the first pillar of governance. Predictive systems integrated into LMSs require strict policies regulating the data lifecycle, preventing the overcollection of student information, clicks, or biometrics, and ensuring privacy by design to avoid vulnerabilities and unauthorized uses (Ismail & Aloshi, 2025).

At the same time, a critical challenge is mitigating algorithmic bias. Institutions must conduct ongoing algorithmic audits, as predictive models risk discriminating against certain groups and perpetuating inequalities if the historical training data contains embedded demographic or socioeconomic biases (Bird et al., 2025).

Effective technology governance requires that institutional policies limit automation in high-risk situations. To safeguard student agency and well-being, the integration of AI must consistently maintain a human-centered approach throughout the process. This guarantee that machine-generated predictions are supervised, interpreted, and validated by educators or administrators before any high-impact pedagogical intervention or action is implemented (Holmes et al., 2022; Miah et al., 2025).

Figure 4 presents the original conceptual model proposed for this chapter, which synthesizes and integrates the contributions of the reviewed literature on governance, predictive models, and explainability (Bird et al., 2025; Ismail & Aloshi, 2025; Nguyen et al., 2023).

Figure 4. Conceptual framework for human-centered and ethical AI-LMS integration.

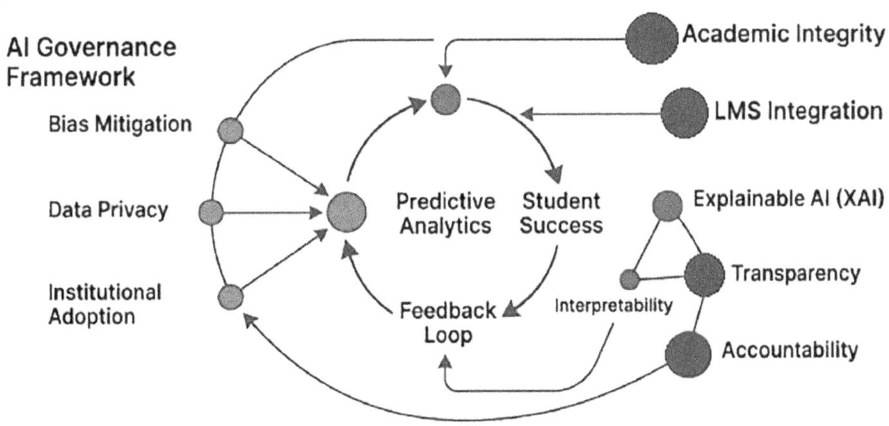

Source. Own elaboration.

EMERGING TECHNOLOGIES ENABLING EXPLAINABLE LEARNING ECOSYSTEMS

It consists of a set of technologies and tools that are constantly evolving. They enable the creation of educational environments where people use them seamlessly as part of an educational process, critique them, and evaluate them.

In fields such as health and the sciences, it is important to predict and address academic performance, where there is a connection between data, the model to be used, the explanation, and the intervention (Mastour et al., 2025). Technological design is based on machine learning with explainable artificial intelligence for learning analytics ecosystems. The data are both academic and non-academic, including academic metrics from students at three educational institutions. For the predictive model, a combination of meta-model stacking with ensemble learning was used, including random forest, AdaBoost, and XGBoost. Various reports were generated for academic and administrative staff to inform the design of educational and intervention strategies. The strategies focused on low-performing courses and students at academic risk. The explainability mechanism is based on the SHAP (SHapley Additive exPlanations) method to explain each variable in the prediction for each student, as well as at the global level, and to provide explanations for interventions and decisions for faculty members. The results show high predictive accuracy. The lessons indicate that explainability is important in educational predictions and decisions; a latent risk is teachers' use of and reliance on XAI; this can lead to biases and inappropriate decisions if teachers do not understand the explanations.

Teaching cyber-physical systems in engineering presents challenges such as high costs, a shortage of expert tutors and teachers, which limits the pool of instructors to those who teach the course, and platforms with limitations in assessment and personalized feedback. At a university in Korea, traditional technology was replaced with the metaverse and digital twins for teaching cyber-physical systems engineering (Yun et al., 2024). Technological design focuses on the use of XAI for intelligent tutoring, based on Jon Radoff's metaverse. The model incorporates self-learning, assesses student learning outcomes, evaluates performance, and provides personalized feedback. The technologies used include Unity, Airsim, PyTorch, and Virtual KIITI 2. Explainability is demonstrated in the evaluation by presenting heatmaps that use XAI algorithms to explain how the assessment is conducted, and the feedback utilizes heatmaps and genetic algorithms to generate personalized feedback. LRP-MD (Layer-wise Relevance Propagation for Multi-Class Object Detection) was applied for achievement assessment. The results indicate that the developed model shows improvements in accuracy compared to other models, enhancing the student's learning model to personalize it based on the tutor's specifications. Feedback via heat maps is very well received by users. As a learning tool, the proposed model is recommended for beginners, but it needs to be improved for more advanced users.

Science learning in secondary schools is analyzed in chemistry and physics courses using data from the PETEL platform, where teachers do not understand how this AI-powered system aggregates data and makes recommendations (Marín Díaz, 2025). Technological design considers data generated by PETEL platform users, uses clusters to classify student groups and profiles; these provide recommendations for teachers, and a random forest is applied for the explainable classifier. Explainability, represented by XAI for clustering through feature (item) importance, is evaluated using SHAP TreeExplainer. For explainability to be accepted, it must be understandable and useful. The results show how student groupings occur and provide explanations that are understandable to teachers. In this regard, the interpretation of the explanations varies depending on each teacher's context. Explainability must take into account teachers' ways of thinking.

CHALLENGES, ETHICAL IMPLICATIONS, AND GOVERNANCE

Despite the proven benefits of artificial intelligence and learning analytics in higher education, their implementation presents a range of technical and socio-technical challenges. The transition to AI-driven campuses requires academic institutions to address critical dilemmas and establish proactive governance frameworks. Below are the three main challenges and their respective mitigation strategies.

Bias

One of the most well-documented risks in educational AI is the perpetuation of algorithmic bias. Predictive models, when trained on institutions' historical data, run the risk of learning and reproducing structural biases related to students' race, gender, or socioeconomic status, which can result in unfair predictions in admissions processes or early warning systems (Baker & Hawn, 2022). To mitigate this, it is imperative to conduct equity audits and apply fairness constraints before the models are deployed in a real-world setting (Van Busum & Fang, 2025).

Privacy

The effectiveness of AI in LMSs depends on the massive collection of data; however, this over-collection of information (clicks, connection time, and even biometric data) poses serious risks of excessive surveillance, cybersecurity vulnerabilities, and the unauthorized secondary use of student data (Dutta & Chauhan,

2025). To address this vulnerability, recent technical approaches suggest moving away from data centralization. Instead, they propose implementing privacy-preserving technologies, such as Federated Learning, which allows algorithms to be trained directly on users' local devices without the need to extract or expose their personal information (Shalabi et al., 2025).

Ethics

The unregulated deployment of AI, particularly generative models, blurs the line between educational support and cognitive replacement, directly threatening academic integrity and student autonomy (Ocen et al., 2025). The primary ethical challenge lies not in banning technology, but in governing it. This is achieved through the development of transparent institutional guidelines that clearly define acceptable use and ensure a human-in-the-loop approach, guaranteeing that high-impact decisions are always supervised by educators (Chan, 2023).

Table 2 summarizes the main ethical and privacy challenges identified in literature, as well as the recommended institutional mitigation strategies.

Table 2. Key Challenges of AI in Higher Education and Institutional Mitigation Strategies.

Challenge	Problem Description	Institutional Mitigation Strategy
Biases	Predictive models can exacerbate historical biases in predictions of academic success and risk (Baker & Hawn, 2022).	Require representative datasets, apply fairness constraints, and conduct ongoing algorithmic audits (Van Busum & Fang, 2025).
Privacy	The extensive collection of biometric data in LMSs poses risks of excessive surveillance and breaches of confidential data (Dutta & Chauhan, 2025).	Integrate privacy-preserving technologies, such as Federated Learning, and establish strict data minimization policies (Shalabi et al., 2025).
Ethics	AI tools threaten academic integrity and student autonomy if they act as unsupervised cognitive substitutes (Ocen et al., 2025).	Develop acceptable use policies and always maintain a human-in-the-loop approach to final decision-making (Chan, 2023).

Source. Own work.

DISCUSSION AND FUTURE RESEARCH DIRECTIONS

As artificial intelligence moves beyond the early adoption phase in higher education institutions, the academic focus must shift from pilot project implementation toward systemic integration and alignment with long-term ethical goals. Below, we discuss two critical areas that will define the next decade of research in this field:

the scalability of AI systems and the transition toward the Industry 5.0 paradigm (Figure 5).

- Scalability. Scaling artificial intelligence in the university setting presents challenges that go far beyond the simple acquisition of technology. Future research must address how institutions can transition from isolated tools to institutionally integrated AI ecosystems. This process of strategic transformation requires the development of clear institutional roadmaps and robust governance models that include ethics committees capable of overseeing large-scale deployments (George & Wooden, 2023). A key challenge in scalability is the infrastructure gap and the interoperability of legacy systems. To address this, IT management strategies must focus on shared architectures and on building staff capabilities to overcome organizational resistance (Sajja et al., 2025; Santos et al., 2024). In this regard, an urgent area of research is determining how to ensure that large-scale systems, such as adaptive learning or predictive analytics, support the massification of education without compromising personalization or exacerbating the digital divide, especially in institutions with limited resources.
- Industry 4.0 / 5.0. The evolution of AI in universities is intrinsically linked to industrial development frameworks. Until now, much of the technological integration has been based on the Industry 4.0 vision, which prioritizes digitization, process automation, big data analysis, and algorithmic efficiency (Abulibdeh et al., 2024; Adel, 2024). However, recent literature calls for a paradigm shift toward Industry 5.0 and its counterpart, Education 5.0.

Figure 5 illustrates the paradigm shift toward human-centered educational ecosystems. The visual content synthesizes the perspectives and future directions proposed in recent literature (Abulibdeh et al., 2024; Adel, 2024; Chigbu & Makapela, 2025; George & Wooden, 2023; Piccarozzi et al., 2024; Sajja et al., 2025; Santos et al., 2024).

Figure 5. Future Trends in Higher Education: The Transition from Industry 4.0 to Industry 5.0.

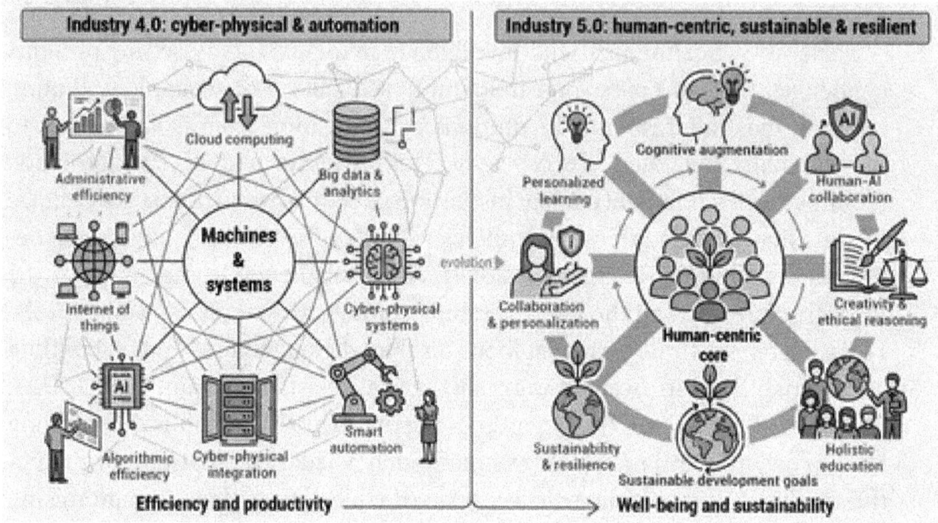

Source. Own elaboration.

Unlike pure automation, Industry 5.0 proposes a human-centered, ethical technological ecosystem aligned with sustainability (Piccarozzi et al., 2024). Future research should explore how AI can act as a collaborative agent that enhances, rather than replaces, human capabilities while keeping teachers and students in the decision-making loop.

Future lines of study should design evaluation frameworks that measure the impact of AI on students' psychological well-being, inclusion, the development of critical skills for the future of work, and its contribution to the Sustainable Development Goals, moving away from metrics based purely on academic performance or administrative efficiency (Chigbu & Makapela, 2025).

Table 3. Proposed research agenda for scaling AI and the transition to Education 5.0.

Research Area	Current Limitation (State of the Art)	Question / Future Research Direction	Support Authors
Infrastructure and Scalability	High dependence on isolated legacy systems and high computational costs.	How can universities develop shared architectures to scale AI without exacerbating the digital divide?	(Sajja et al., 2025; Santos et al., 2024)
Institutional Governance	Implementation of "isolated pilots" without ethical oversight on a large scale.	Which governance models and ethics committees are most effective in managing strategic transformation and mass deployment of AI?	(George & Wooden, 2023)
Human-Centric AI (Industry 5.0)	Excessive focus on automation, efficiency, and massive data analysis (paradigm 4.0).	How can AI systems be designed to act as collaborative agents that augment creativity and human ethical reasoning, rather than replace teachers?	(Piccarozzi et al., 2024)
Wellbeing and Sustainability Metrics	AI impact evaluations are based solely on academic performance and administrative efficiency.	What new assessment frameworks should be designed to measure the impact of AI on students' psychological well-being, inclusion, and the Sustainable Development Goals (SDGs)?	(Abulibdeh et al., 2024; Chigbu & Makapela, 2025).

Source. Own elaboration

CONCLUSIONS

The XAI and Trustworthy AI principles are ethical frameworks designed to ensure that AI systems are no longer "black boxes" in terms of their processes and outcomes, and that they foster trust and fairness when used.

Artificial intelligence that is explainable through its processes helps people understand and trust the results; when applied in STEAM settings, it transforms education by demonstrating that the tools used are equitable and transparent (Khosravi et al., 2022).

FUTURE RESEARCH DIRECTIONS

Undoubtedly, the incorporation of various techniques and algorithms makes the use of explainable artificial intelligence highly beneficial. For this reason, we must delve deeper into existing techniques, improve upon them, and develop new ones. Furthermore, we must develop ethical frameworks related to XAI and AI that complement current ethical models and incorporate them into the various solutions that utilize AI.

INTEREST CONFLICT

The authors declare that they have no conflict of interest in the publication of this chapter.

REFERENCES

Abulibdeh, A., Zaidan, E., & Abulibdeh, R. (2024). Navigating the confluence of artificial intelligence and education for sustainable development in the era of industry 4.0: Challenges, opportunities, and ethical dimensions. *Journal of Cleaner Production*, *437*, 140527. Advance online publication. DOI: 10.1016/j.jclepro.2023.140527

Adel, A. (2024). The convergence of intelligent tutoring, robotics, and IoT in smart education for the transition from industry 4.0 to 5.0. *Smart Cities*, *7*(1), 325–369. DOI: 10.3390/smartcities7010014

Afzaal, M., Nouri, J., Zia, A., Papapetrou, P., Fors, U., Wu, Y., Li, X., & Weegar, R. (2021). Explainable AI for data-driven feedback and intelligent action recommendations to support students self-regulation. *Frontiers in Artificial Intelligence*, *4*, 723447. Advance online publication. DOI: 10.3389/frai.2021.723447

Al-Zahrani, A., Khalil, I., Awaji, B., & Mohsen, M. (2024). AI technologies in STEAM education for students: Systematic literature review. *Journal of Ecohumanism*, *3*(4), 3380–3394. DOI: 10.62754/joe.v3i4.4041

Aljamaan, A., Alsaber, A., Emmanuel, C., & Alkandari, A. (2025). Leveling up learning effectiveness in STEM education through gamification: An empirical study on behavioral intention and digital literacy among undergraduate students in Kuwait. *Frontiers in Education*, *10*, 1586466. Advance online publication. DOI: 10.3389/feduc.2025.1586466

Alkhabra, Y. A., Ibrahem, U. M., & Alkhabra, S. A. (2023). Augmented reality technology in enhancing learning retention and critical thinking according to STEAM program. *Humanities & Social Sciences Communications*, *10*(1), 174. Advance online publication. DOI: 10.1057/s41599-023-01650-w

Alshareef, N. (2022). Investment opportunity of blockchain technology in the education sector of Saudi Arabia: A systematic literature review. *Frontiers in Education*, *7*, 911126. Advance online publication. DOI: 10.3389/feduc.2022.911126

Altukhi, Z. M., Pradhan, S., & Aljohani, N. (2025). A systematic literature review of the latest advancements in XAI. *Technologies*, *13*(3), 93. Advance online publication. DOI: 10.3390/technologies13030093

Anđelić, N., & Baressi Šegota, S. (2024). Achieving high accuracy in Android malware detection through genetic programming symbolic classifier. *Computers*, *13*(8), 197. Advance online publication. DOI: 10.3390/computers13080197

Anđelić, N., Baressi Šegota, S., Glučina, M., & Lorencin, I. (2023). Classification of wall following robot movements using genetic programming symbolic classifier. *Machines (Basel), 11*(1), 105. Advance online publication. DOI: 10.3390/machines11010105

Anđelić, N., Baressi Šegota, S., & Mrzljak, V. (2025). Hybrid explainable AI for machine predictive maintenance: From symbolic expressions to meta-ensembles. *Processes (Basel, Switzerland), 13*(7), 2180. Advance online publication. DOI: 10.3390/pr13072180

Baker, R. S., & Hawn, A. (2022). Algorithmic bias in education. *International Journal of Artificial Intelligence in Education, 32*(4), 1052–1092. DOI: 10.1007/s40593-021-00285-9

Bas, C., & Kiraz, A. (2025). Primary school teachers' needs for AI-supported STEM education. *Sustainability (Basel), 17*(15), 7044. Advance online publication. DOI: 10.3390/su17157044

Bertolini, R., Finch, S. J., & Nehm, R. H. (2023). An application of Bayesian inference to examine student retention and attrition in the STEM classroom. *Frontiers in Education, 8*, 1073829. Advance online publication. DOI: 10.3389/feduc.2023.1073829

Bin Qushem, U., Christopoulos, A., Kaliisa, R., Khalil, M., Salakoski, T., & Laakso, M.-J. (2025). Technology-enhanced learning and learning analytics for personalised STEM learning: A scoping review. *International Journal of Educational Research, 134*, 102827. Advance online publication. DOI: 10.1016/j.ijer.2025.102827

Bird, K. A., Castleman, B. L., & Song, Y. (2025). Are algorithms biased in education? Exploring racial bias in predicting community college student success. *Journal of Policy Analysis and Management, 44*(2), 379–402. DOI: 10.1002/pam.22569

Chan, C. K. Y. (2023). A comprehensive AI policy education framework for university teaching and learning. *International Journal of Educational Technology in Higher Education, 20*(1), 38. Advance online publication. DOI: 10.1186/s41239-023-00408-3

Chigbu, B. I., & Makapela, S. L. (2025). AI in education, sustainability, and the future of work: An integrative review of industry 5.0, education 5.0, and work 5.0. *Journal of Open Innovation, 11*(4), 100645. Advance online publication. DOI: 10.1016/j.joitmc.2025.100645

Duan, X., Pei, B., Ambrose, G. A., Hershkovitz, A., Cheng, Y., & Wang, C. (2024). Towards transparent and trustworthy prediction of student learning achievement by including instructors as co-designers: A case study. *Education and Information Technologies, 29*(3), 3075–3096. DOI: 10.1007/s10639-023-11954-8

Ducange, P., Marcelloni, F., & Pecori, R. (2021). Fuzzy Hoeffding decision tree for data stream classification. *International Journal of Computational Intelligence Systems, 14*(1), 946–964. DOI: 10.2991/ijcis.d.210212.001

Dutta, A., & Chauhan, S. (2025). Artificial intelligence in student privacy and data security. *International Journal of Advanced Research in Computer Science, 16*(3), 146–151. DOI: 10.26483/ijarcs.v16i3.7261

European Education and Culture Executive Agency. (2025). *Explainable AI in education: Fostering human oversight and shared responsibility*. Publications Office of the European Union., DOI: 10.2797/6780469

Feldman-Maggor, Y., Cukurova, M., Kent, C., & Alexandron, G. (2025). The impact of explainable AI on teachers' trust and acceptance of AI EdTech recommendations: The power of domain-specific explanations. *International Journal of Artificial Intelligence in Education, 35*(5), 2889–2922. DOI: 10.1007/s40593-025-00486-6

Fiok, K., Farahani, F. V., Karwowski, W., & Ahram, T. (2022). Explainable artificial intelligence for education and training. *The Journal of Defense Modeling and Simulation, 19*(2), 133–144. DOI: 10.1177/15485129211028651

Fodouop Kouam, A. W. (2024). The effectiveness of intelligent tutoring systems in supporting students with varying levels of programming experience. *Discover Education, 3*(1), 278. Advance online publication. DOI: 10.1007/s44217-024-00385-3

Gao, N. (2025). Design and application of an intelligent teaching platform integrating international Chinese education and STEAM education. In *Proceedings of the 2025 2nd International Conference on Artificial Intelligence and Future Education* (pp. 316–320). Association for Computing Machinery. https://doi.org/ DOI: 10.1145/3785987.3786039

García-Senín, S., Arguedas, M., & Daradoumis, T. (2022). Using learning analytics to support STEAM students' academic achievement and self-regulated learning. *Research on Education and Media, 14*(1), 36–45. DOI: 10.2478/rem-2022-0005

George, B., & Wooden, O. (2023). Managing the strategic transformation of higher education through artificial intelligence. *Administrative Sciences, 13*(9), 196. Advance online publication. DOI: 10.3390/admsci13090196

George, E. B., Senthilkumar, R., Al-Junaibi, F., & Al-Shuaibi, Z.E. Ben George. (2025). Explainable AI methods for predicting student grades and improving academic success. *Journal of Information Systems Engineering & Management, 10*(23s), 117–126. DOI: 10.52783/jisem.v10i23s.3680

Gjoka, A., & Pireva Nuci, K. (2025). Exploring the role of augmented reality in STEAM learning environments: Evidence from geometry education. *Information (Basel), 16*(12), 1113. Advance online publication. DOI: 10.3390/info16121113

Han, S.-I., Nakamura, K., & Hong, B.-W. (2024). Splitting of composite neural networks via proximal operator with information bottleneck. *IEEE Access : Practical Innovations, Open Solutions, 12*, 157–167. DOI: 10.1109/ACCESS.2023.3346697

Holmes, W., Porayska-Pomsta, K., Holstein, K., Sutherland, E., Baker, T., Shum, S. B., Santos, O. C., Rodrigo, M. T., Cukurova, M., Bittencourt, I. I., & Koedinger, K. R. (2022). Ethics of AI in education: Towards a community-wide framework. *International Journal of Artificial Intelligence in Education, 32*(3), 504–526. DOI: 10.1007/s40593-021-00239-1

How, M.-L., & Hung, W. L. D. (2019). Educing AI-thinking in science, technology, engineering, arts, and mathematics (STEAM) education. *Education Sciences, 9*(3), 184. Advance online publication. DOI: 10.3390/educsci9030184

Hsiao, H.-S., Chen, J.-H., Tsai, H.-W., & Chung, G.-H. (2025). Investigating the effectiveness of VR technology on hands-on STEAM learning activities for junior high school students. *Interactive Learning Environments*, 1–19. Advance online publication. DOI: 10.1080/10494820.2025.2580984

Ismail, I. A., & Aloshi, J. M. (2025). Data privacy in AI-driven education: An in-depth exploration into the data privacy concerns and potential solutions. In Keeley, K. L. (Ed.), *AI applications and strategies in teacher education* (pp. 223–252). IGI Global Scientific Publishing., DOI: 10.4018/979-8-3693-5443-8.ch008

Ito, T., Campbell, M., Horesh, L., Klinger, T., & Ram, P. (2025). Quantifying artificial intelligence through algorithmic generalization. *Nature Machine Intelligence, 7*(8), 1195–1205. DOI: 10.1038/s42256-025-01092-w

Jang, Y., Choi, S.-H., Jung, H., & Kim, H. (2022). Practical early prediction of students' performance using machine learning and eXplainable AI. *Education and Information Technologies, 27*(9), 12855–12889. DOI: 10.1007/s10639-022-11120-6

Jia, Z. (2022). Designing an intelligent teaching system of Chinese as a foreign language under the internet background. *Scientific Programming, 2022*, 3610081. Advance online publication. DOI: 10.1155/2022/3610081

Kabudi, T., Pappas, I., & Olsen, D. H. (2021). AI-enabled adaptive learning systems: A systematic mapping of the literature. *Computers and Education: Artificial Intelligence*, *2*, 100017. Advance online publication. DOI: 10.1016/j.caeai.2021.100017

Kayama, M., Nagai, T., Tachi, N., Asuke, T., Taguchi, N., & Futagami, T. (2021). IoT-based learning material and its management system for STEAM in primary and secondary education. In Daniela, L. (Ed.), *The Internet of Things for education: A new actor on the stage* (pp. 145–163). Springer., DOI: 10.1007/978-3-030-85720-2_9

Khosravi, H., Shum, S. B., Chen, G., Conati, C., Tsai, Y.-S., Kay, J., Knight, S., Martinez-Maldonado, R., Sadiq, S., & Gašević, D. (2022). Explainable artificial intelligence in education. *Computers and Education: Artificial Intelligence*, *3*, 100074. Advance online publication. DOI: 10.1016/j.caeai.2022.100074

Kim, S., Oh, J., Lee, S., Yu, S., Do, J., & Taghavi, T. (2023). Grounding counterfactual explanation of image classifiers to textual concept space. In *Proceedings of the IEEE/CVF Conference on Computer Vision and Pattern Recognition (CVPR)* (pp. 10942–10950). IEEE. https://doi.org/DOI: 10.1109/CVPR52729.2023.01053

Kohnke, S., & Zaugg, T. (2025). Artificial intelligence: An untapped opportunity for equity and access in STEM education. *Education Sciences*, *15*(1), 68. Advance online publication. DOI: 10.3390/educsci15010068

Lewis, M., & Crawford, C. (2024). Towards blockchain-based incentives for STEM education. In Stephanidis, C., Antona, M., Ntoa, S., & Salvendy, G. (Eds.), *HCI International 2024 Posters* (Vol. 2117, pp. 123–134). Springer., DOI: 10.1007/978-3-031-61953-3_15

Li, B., Qi, P., Liu, B., Di, S., Liu, J., Pei, J., Yi, J., & Zhou, B. (2023). Trustworthy AI: From principles to practices. *ACM Computing Surveys*, *55*(9), 177. Advance online publication. DOI: 10.1145/3555803

Lin, M. P.-C., & Chang, D. (2023). CHAT-ACTS: A pedagogical framework for personalised chatbot to enhance active learning and self-regulated learning. *Computers and Education: Artificial Intelligence*, *5*, 100167. Advance online publication. DOI: 10.1016/j.caeai.2023.100167

López-Pernas, S., Oliveira, E., Song, Y., & Saqr, M. (2026). AI, explainable AI and evaluative AI: Informed data-driven decision-making in education. In Saqr, M., & López-Pernas, S. (Eds.), *Advanced learning analytics methods: AI, precision and complexity* (pp. 17–39). Springer., DOI: 10.1007/978-3-031-95365-1_2

Luo, Z., & Tahir, R. (2025). ChatGPT-assisted lesson planning for children's STEAM arts education: An experimental study on benefits, challenges, methods, and a prompt framework. *International Journal of Artificial Intelligence in Education, 35*(6), 3696–3745. DOI: 10.1007/s40593-025-00513-6

Mahamad, S., Chin, Y. H., Zulmuksah, N. I. N., Haque, M. M., Shaheen, M., & Nisar, K. (2025). Technical review: Architecting an AI-driven decision support system for enhanced online learning and assessment. *Future Internet, 17*(9), 383. Advance online publication. DOI: 10.3390/fi17090383

Marín Díaz, G. (2025). Integrating exploratory data analysis and explainable AI into astronomy education: A fuzzy approach to data-literate learning. *Education Sciences, 15*(12), 1688. Advance online publication. DOI: 10.3390/educsci15121688

Mastour, H., Dehghani, T., Moradi, E., & Eslami, S. (2025). Explainable artificial intelligence for predicting medical students' performance in comprehensive assessments. *Scientific Reports, 15*(1), 23752. Advance online publication. DOI: 10.1038/s41598-025-07460-1

Méndez-Parra, C., & Conde-Carmona, R. J. (2025). Integración del enfoque STEAM y la realidad aumentada en la enseñanza de la traslación de figuras geométricas. *Revista Virtual Universidad Católica del Norte*, (74), 69–92. DOI: 10.35575/rvucn.n74a4

Meylani, R. (2025). Rethinking explainability in educational artificial intelligence: A critical systematic review of models, applications, and ethical dimensions. *Veredas do Direito, 22*(3), e223553. Advance online publication. DOI: 10.18623/rvd.v22.n3.3553

Miah, M. N. I., Uddin, M. J., & Ahmed, M. W. (2025). Regulating artificial intelligence in education: Analyzing legal and ethical frameworks for the deployment of AI and machine learning models in U.S. educational institutions. *Journal of Computer Science and Technology Studies, 7*(11), 387–404. DOI: 10.32996/jcsts.2025.7.11.37

Moraliyage, H., Kulawardana, G., De Silva, D., Issadeen, Z., Manic, M., & Katsura, S. (2025). Explainable artificial intelligence with integrated gradients for the detection of adversarial attacks on text classifiers. *Applied System Innovation, 8*(1), 17. Advance online publication. DOI: 10.3390/asi8010017

Müller, R. (2025). How explainable AI affects human performance: A systematic review of the behavioural consequences of saliency maps. *International Journal of Human-Computer Interaction, 41*(4), 2020–2051. DOI: 10.1080/10447318.2024.2381929

Mulwa, M. M., Mwangi, R. W., & Mindila, A. (2024). GMM-LIME explainable machine learning model for interpreting sensor-based human gait. *Engineering Reports*, *6*(10), e12864. Advance online publication. DOI: 10.1002/eng2.12864

Nagy, M., & Molontay, R. (2024). Interpretable dropout prediction: Towards XAI-based personalized intervention. *International Journal of Artificial Intelligence in Education*, *34*(2), 274–300. DOI: 10.1007/s40593-023-00331-8

Nguyen, A., Ngo, H. N., Hong, Y., Dang, B., & Nguyen, B.-P. T. (2023). Ethical principles for artificial intelligence in education. *Education and Information Technologies*, *28*(4), 4221–4241. DOI: 10.1007/s10639-022-11316-w

Niu, T., Liu, T., Luo, Y. T., Pang, P. C.-I., Huang, S., & Xiang, A. (2025). Decoding student cognitive abilities: A comparative study of explainable AI algorithms in educational data mining. *Scientific Reports*, *15*(1), 26862. Advance online publication. DOI: 10.1038/s41598-025-12514-5

Ocen, S., Elasu, J., Aarakit, S. M., & Olupot, C. (2025). Artificial intelligence in higher education institutions: Review of innovations, opportunities and challenges. *Frontiers in Education*, *10*, 1530247. Advance online publication. DOI: 10.3389/feduc.2025.1530247

Ojetunde, S. M., & Ramnarain, U. (2026). Enhancing STEM and STEAM education at the grade level through mixed reality applications: A meta-analytical study. *Canadian Journal of Science, Mathematics and Technology Education = Revue Canadienne de l'Enseignement des Sciences, des Mathématiques et de la Technologie*, *26*(2), 19. Advance online publication. DOI: 10.1007/s42330-026-00456-7

Oliva-Córdova, L. M., Tohom, M. F. V., Salazar de la Cruz, R. C., & Martín-Núñez, J. L. (2025). Application of learning analytics in medical education: Enhancing student digital competences within the STEAM framework. *International Journal of Educational Research Open*, *9*, 100511. Advance online publication. DOI: 10.1016/j.ijedro.2025.100511

Organisation for Economic Co-operation and Development. (2019). *OECD skills outlook 2019: Thriving in a digital world*. OECD Publishing., DOI: 10.1787/df80bc12-

Organisation for Economic Co-operation and Development. (2023). *Education at a glance 2023: OECD indicators*. OECD Publishing., DOI: 10.1787/e13bef63-

Osborne, J. B., & Lang, A. S. I. D. (2023). Predictive identification of at-risk students: Using learning management system data. *Journal of Postsecondary Student Success*, *2*(4), 108–126. DOI: 10.33009/fsop_jpss132082

Phillips, P. J., Hahn, C. A., Fontana, P. C., Yates, A. N., Greene, K. K., Broniatowski, D. A., & Przybocki, M. A. (2021). *Four principles of explainable artificial intelligence* (NIST Interagency/Internal Report No. NIST.IR.8312). National Institute of Standards and Technology. https://doi.org/DOI: 10.6028/NIST.IR.8312

Piccarozzi, M., Silvestri, L., Silvestri, C., & Ruggieri, A. (2024). Roadmap to Industry 5.0: Enabling technologies, challenges, and opportunities towards a holistic definition in management studies. *Technological Forecasting and Social Change*, *205*, 123467. Advance online publication. DOI: 10.1016/j.techfore.2024.123467

Sajja, R., Sermet, Y., & Demir, I. (2025). End-to-end deployment of the Educational AI Hub for personalized learning and engagement: A case study on environmental science education. *IEEE Access : Practical Innovations, Open Solutions*, *13*, 55169–55186. DOI: 10.1109/ACCESS.2025.3554222

Salas-Pilco, S. Z., Xiao, K., & Oshima, J. (2022). Artificial intelligence and new technologies in inclusive education for minority students: A systematic review. *Sustainability (Basel)*, *14*(20), 13572. Advance online publication. DOI: 10.3390/su142013572

Santos, A., Martins, J., Pestana, P. D., Gonçalves, R., Mamede, H. S., & Branco, F. (2024). Factors affecting cloud computing adoption in the education context: Systematic literature review. *IEEE Access : Practical Innovations, Open Solutions*, *12*, 71641–71674. DOI: 10.1109/ACCESS.2024.3400862

Shalabi, E., Khedr, W., Rushdy, E., & Salah, A. (2025). A comparative study of privacy-preserving techniques in federated learning: A performance and security analysis. *Information (Basel)*, *16*(3), 244. Advance online publication. DOI: 10.3390/info16030244

Shoaib, M., Sayed, N., Singh, J., Shafi, J., Khan, S., & Ali, F. (2024). AI student success predictor: Enhancing personalized learning in campus management systems. *Computers in Human Behavior*, *158*, 108301. Advance online publication. DOI: 10.1016/j.chb.2024.108301

Silva-Díaz, F., Marfil-Carmona, R., Narváez, R., Silva Fuentes, A., & Carrillo-Rosúa, J. (2023). Introducing virtual reality and emerging technologies in a teacher training STEM course. *Education Sciences*, *13*(10), 1044. Advance online publication. DOI: 10.3390/educsci13101044

Son, T. (2024). Intelligent tutoring systems in mathematics education: A systematic literature review using the substitution, augmentation, modification, redefinition model. *Computers*, *13*(10), 270. Advance online publication. DOI: 10.3390/computers13100270

Soroko, N. (2024). Features of organizing STEAM educational projects using immersive technologies. *Physical and Mathematical Education, 39*(2), 51–59. DOI: 10.31110/fmo2024.v39i2-07

Suaza-Medina, M., Peñabaena-Niebles, R., & Jubiz-Diaz, M. (2024). A model for predicting academic performance on standardised tests for lagging regions based on machine learning and Shapley additive explanations. *Scientific Reports, 14*(1), 25306. Advance online publication. DOI: 10.1038/s41598-024-76596-3

Terzieva, V., Ivanova, M., Djambazova, E., & Ilchev, S. (2025). The role of internet of things and security aspects in STEM education. *Information (Basel), 16*(7), 533. Advance online publication. DOI: 10.3390/info16070533

Topuz, K., Davazdahemami, B., & Delen, D. (2024). A Bayesian belief network-based analytics methodology for early-stage risk detection of novel diseases. *Annals of Operations Research, 341*(1), 673–697. DOI: 10.1007/s10479-023-05377-4

Türkmen, G. (2025). The review of studies on explainable artificial intelligence in educational research. *Journal of Educational Computing Research, 63*(2), 277–310. DOI: 10.1177/07356331241310915

Tursunalieva, A., Alexander, D. L. J., Dunne, R., Li, J., Riera, L., & Zhao, Y. (2024). Making sense of machine learning: A review of interpretation techniques and their applications. *Applied Sciences (Basel, Switzerland), 14*(2), 496. Advance online publication. DOI: 10.3390/app14020496

UNESCO. (2023). *Global education monitoring report 2023: Technology in education: A tool on whose terms?* UNESCO., DOI: 10.54676/UZQV8501

Valenzuela-Domínguez, F. A., Munguía-Martínez, L. F., Meléndez-Tiznado, S., Guzmán-Limón, Z., Benitez, V. H., & Félix-Herrán, L. C. (2024). Design of a two-degrees-of-freedom robotic arm for monitoring applications for teaching robotics and artificial intelligence technology. *Computer Applications in Engineering Education, 32*(6), e22786. Advance online publication. DOI: 10.1002/cae.22786

Van Busum, K., & Fang, S. (2025). Interactive mitigation of biases in machine learning models for undergraduate student admissions. *AI, 6*(7), 152. Advance online publication. DOI: 10.3390/ai6070152

Velarde-Camaqui, D., Celaya-Ramírez, R., Contreras-Fuentes, Y., & Sanabria-Z, J. (2024). Enhancing STEAM education through augmented reality: The EduAR open platform experience. *Frontiers in Education, 9*, 1391803. Advance online publication. DOI: 10.3389/feduc.2024.1391803

Villegas-Ch, W., Buenano-Fernandez, D., Navarro, A. M., & Mera-Navarrete, A. (2025). Adaptive intelligent tutoring systems for STEM education: Analysis of the learning impact and effectiveness of personalized feedback. *Smart Learning Environments*, *12*(1), 41. Advance online publication. DOI: 10.1186/s40561-025-00389-y

Viswan, V., Shaffi, N., Mahmud, M., Subramanian, K., & Hajamohideen, F. (2024). Explainable artificial intelligence in Alzheimer's disease classification: A systematic review. *Cognitive Computation*, *16*(1), 1–44. DOI: 10.1007/s12559-023-10192-x

Wang, X., Younas, M., Jiang, Y., Imran, M., & Almusharraf, N. (2025). Transforming education through blockchain: A systematic review of applications, projects, and challenges. *IEEE Access : Practical Innovations, Open Solutions*, *13*, 13264–13284. DOI: 10.1109/ACCESS.2024.3519350

Yun, S.-J., Kwon, J.-W., Lee, Y.-H., Kim, J.-H., & Kim, W.-T. (2024). A learner-centric explainable educational metaverse for cyber–physical systems engineering. *Electronics (Basel)*, *13*(17), 3359. Advance online publication. DOI: 10.3390/electronics13173359

Zhang, X. (2024). Innovation of teaching methods of international Chinese language education in universities based on artificial intelligence analysis technology. *Applied Mathematics and Nonlinear Sciences*, *9*(1), 20230336. Advance online publication. DOI: 10.2478/amns.2023.2.00336

Zhu, Q., & Wang, M. (2023). Team-based mobile learning supported by an intelligent system: Case study of STEM students. In Wang, M., Ryoo, J., & Winkelmann, K. (Eds.), *Cross Reality (XR) and immersive learning environments (ILEs) in education* (pp. 5–21). Routledge., DOI: 10.4324/9781003457121-2

KEY TERMS AND DEFINITIONS

STEAM Ecosystem: Educational model for solving real-world problems through science, technology, engineering, art, and mathematics.

XAI Principles: Sets of methods and procedures that show how intelligent systems generate and present results in a clear, transparent, and equitable manner.

Chapter 2
Explainable Artificial Intelligence in Education: Concepts, Taxonomies, and Challenges

Mustafa Kayyali
http://orcid.org/0000-0003-3300-262X
Maaref University of Applied Sciences, Syria

ABSTRACT

Explainable Artificial Intelligence (XAI) has become increasingly important as educational systems adopt intelligent tools for personalization, assessment, feedback, and decision-making. Yet in education, explainability is not merely a technical feature; it is a pedagogical, ethical, and institutional necessity. This chapter examines the core concepts, taxonomies, and challenges of XAI in educational settings, with particular attention to STEAM learning and ethical assessment. It explores how explanations can support trust, learner agency, teacher judgment, and institutional accountability while also revealing the limits of algorithmic interpretation. The chapter distinguishes between different forms of explainability, including model-centered, user-centered, pedagogical, and ethical explanations. It also addresses major barriers such as opacity, bias, data complexity, overreliance on automated systems, and the risk of superficial transparency.

INTRODUCTION

The rise of artificial intelligence in education has not arrived as a single dramatic event (Doroudi, 2023). It has entered classrooms, learning platforms, assessment systems, tutoring applications, dashboards, recommendation engines, and institu-

DOI: 10.4018/979-8-3373-9675-0.ch002

tional decision-making processes in fragments, often quietly, sometimes almost invisibly. A student receives a personalized exercise because a system has estimated a weakness in mathematical reasoning. A teacher is shown an alert suggesting that a learner may be at risk of disengagement. A platform adapts the difficulty of a science simulation based on prior responses. An automated assessment tool provides feedback on a written explanation, a coding task, or a design-based project. In each case, an intelligent system is doing more than storing information or delivering content. It is interpreting, classifying, predicting, recommending, and sometimes judging. The question, then, is no longer whether artificial intelligence can be used in education, but whether its decisions can be understood, questioned, trusted, and responsibly governed.

This is where Explainable Artificial Intelligence, commonly referred to as XAI, becomes essential (Minh et al, 2022). In its simplest sense, XAI refers to approaches that make the behavior, outputs, or reasoning processes of AI systems more understandable to human users. Yet in education, this definition is not enough. Explanation is never neutral. A technical explanation that satisfies a data scientist may be meaningless to a teacher preparing tomorrow's lesson (Lee et al, 2022). A visual dashboard that appears transparent to an administrator may confuse a student who wants to know why she was placed on a particular learning pathway. A model may be statistically accurate and still fail educationally if its reasoning cannot be interpreted in relation to human growth, context, emotion, and purpose. Education is not only a field of measurement; it is a field of meaning. Therefore, explainability in education must be understood not merely as a computational requirement, but as a deeply pedagogical and ethical concern.

The growing relevance of XAI is especially visible in STEAM education, where science, technology, engineering, arts, and mathematics are increasingly taught through inquiry-based, project-based, and interdisciplinary learning environments. STEAM learning is rarely linear. Students experiment, fail, redesign, collaborate, improvise, and make connections across concepts and practices (DeWallace-Marenholz, 2025). In such settings, AI systems may support personalization by recommending resources, identifying misconceptions, adapting tasks, or evaluating complex outputs such as designs, models, portfolios, or reflective responses. However, the richer the learning environment becomes, the harder it is to explain how an AI system has reached its conclusions. A conventional quiz score may be easy to interpret, but how should one explain an AI-generated judgment about creativity, collaboration, problem-solving, or scientific reasoning? These qualities are not simple variables; they are layered human performances shaped by culture, language, confidence, prior opportunity, and classroom conditions.

This chapter begins from the assumption that explainability is not a decorative addition to educational AI. It is not a user-friendly label attached after the algorithm has already made its decision. Rather, explainability should be built into the design, deployment, interpretation, and governance of AI systems from the beginning. Without explanation, personalization can become quiet manipulation. Assessment can become opaque sorting. Feedback can become automated correction without dialogue. Learning analytics can become surveillance disguised as support. Even when AI systems are developed with good intentions, their educational value depends heavily on whether students, teachers, and institutions can understand what the system is doing and why it matters.

At the same time, the demand for explainability should not be romanticized. There is a danger in assuming that every AI decision can be fully opened, neatly translated, and made acceptable through a simple visual explanation. Many advanced AI models operate through complex patterns that do not easily correspond to human reasoning. Some explanations are approximate rather than complete. Others may be persuasive without being truthful. A system might produce an explanation that sounds convincing while hiding the real source of bias or uncertainty. This creates a difficult tension: education needs explanations, but not all explanations are equally honest, useful, or educationally meaningful. The challenge is not only to make AI explainable, but to ask what kind of explanation is needed, for whom, under what conditions, and for what purpose.

For teachers, explainability may support professional judgment (Feldman-Maggor et al, 2025). It can help them decide whether to trust an AI recommendation, challenge it, adapt it, or ignore it. For students, explainability can strengthen agency by helping them understand how their learning data is being used and how they can improve. For parents, it may provide reassurance that automated decisions are not arbitrary or unfair. For institutions, it can support accountability, compliance, and responsible innovation. Yet these different users do not need the same explanations. A taxonomy of educational XAI must therefore consider not only technical methods, such as feature importance, rule extraction, counterfactual explanations, or interpretable models, but also the social relationships around explanation. Who is explaining? Who is being asked to trust? Who has the power to question the system? Who benefits when the system is believed?

The ethical dimension is equally important. AI systems in education may reproduce existing inequalities if they are trained on biased data, poorly contextualized indicators, or narrow definitions of success (Bulathwela et al, 2024). A student from an under-resourced background may be labeled "low-performing" without the system recognizing structural disadvantage. A multilingual learner may be misunderstood by an automated writing tool. A creative but unconventional response may be penalized because it does not match expected patterns. In such cases, explainability is not a luxury. It is a form of protection. It allows hidden assumptions to be examined and contested. It gives educators and learners at least some space to resist the silent authority of the machine.

This chapter, therefore, explores the concepts, taxonomies, and challenges of Explainable Artificial Intelligence in education with a particular focus on STEAM personalization and ethical assessment (Otaru, 2025). It examines the conceptual foundations of XAI, including transparency, interpretability, accountability, trust, and human oversight. It also considers different forms of explanation and how they relate to educational users and purposes. Most importantly, it argues that XAI should not be reduced to a technical solution for a technical problem. In education, explainability must serve human learning. It must protect the dignity of learners, support the wisdom of teachers, and keep assessment open to dialogue rather than mechanical closure. The future of AI in education will not be judged only by how intelligent these systems become, but by how responsibly, intelligibly, and humanely they are allowed to act within the fragile space of learning.

UNDERSTANDING EXPLAINABLE ARTIFICIAL INTELLIGENCE IN EDUCATIONAL CONTEXTS

To understand Explainable Artificial Intelligence in educational contexts, one must first move beyond the narrow idea that explanation simply means making a machine "show its work." That phrase sounds reassuring, almost school-like, as if the algorithm were a student solving a mathematics problem on the board. Yet AI systems do not reason in the same way students reason, and they certainly do not explain themselves in the way a teacher explains a concept to a struggling learner. Their operations are often statistical, layered, probabilistic, and deeply dependent on the data from which they learn. They detect patterns, weigh signals, compare cases, and produce outputs that may look authoritative even when their inner logic remains difficult to interpret. This tension lies at the heart of Explainable Artificial Intelligence, or XAI, in education: the need to make intelligent systems understandable without pretending that their complexity can always be translated into simple, tidy human language.

In educational settings, this issue becomes especially delicate because AI does not operate in a neutral space (Schiff, 2022). It enters classrooms, learning platforms, examination systems, student support services, and institutional analytics environments where decisions carry real emotional and academic consequences. A recommendation generated by an AI tutor may affect what a student studies next. A risk prediction may influence how a teacher perceives a learner's motivation. An automated essay evaluation may shape a student's confidence in writing. A dashboard may encourage administrators to intervene in ways that alter a learner's pathway. These are not small matters. Education is full of invisible turning points, and AI can become part of those turning points before anyone has properly asked whether its reasoning is sound, fair, or pedagogically meaningful.

Explainability, then, is not merely a technical preference. It is a condition of educational trust. Teachers are unlikely to rely responsibly on AI-generated recommendations if they cannot understand the grounds on which those recommendations were made. Students may feel confused, reduced, or even quietly judged when systems assign them levels, scores, alerts, or learning routes without a clear account of why. Parents may question whether automated assessment treats their children fairly. Institutions may struggle to justify decisions if algorithmic tools become embedded in admissions, advising, progression monitoring, or academic support. In all these cases, explanation becomes a bridge between computational output and human judgment. Without that bridge, AI risks becoming an opaque authority—efficient perhaps, impressive at times, but educationally brittle.

One of the difficulties is that "explanation" means different things to different people. A software engineer may want to know which features contributed most strongly to a model's prediction. A teacher may want to know whether the system's recommendation fits the student's actual classroom behavior. A student may ask a simpler but more existential question: "Why did it say this about me?" An administrator may need evidence that the system is reliable, auditable, and aligned with institutional policy. A policymaker may worry about bias, privacy, and accountability. Each of these users requires a different kind of explanation, and none of them can be dismissed as secondary. Educational XAI must be plural by design because education itself is plural—crowded with competing needs, different forms of expertise, and unequal degrees of power (Meylani, 2025).

This is why the meaning of XAI in education cannot be borrowed wholesale from computer science. Technical interpretability matters, of course. Tools such as feature attribution, decision rules, counterfactual examples, model simplification, and visual analytics can help reveal how a system behaves. Yet education demands something wider. An explanation must be connected to learning, not just prediction. It must speak to growth, context, misconception, effort, opportunity, and human development. A system might explain that a student was classified as "at risk" because of low quiz scores, reduced platform activity, and delayed assignment submissions. Technically, that may be clear. Educationally, it may still be thin. Was the student absent because of illness? Did the platform fail to capture offline study? Were the quizzes linguistically biased? Did the learner understand the material but disengage because the tasks felt irrelevant? A technically acceptable explanation may still miss the texture of learning.

The classroom complicates everything, in the best and most inconvenient sense (Nokes, 2022). Students are not datasets moving through a pipeline. They are uncertain, playful, anxious, resistant, inventive, distracted, brilliant in uneven ways. A learner may fail a standardized task yet demonstrate insight during a group discussion. Another may produce polished work by relying heavily on external support. Someone else may remain silent for weeks and then reveal, in one unexpected moment, a deep conceptual shift that no analytics dashboard had noticed. Teachers know this. Not perfectly, not always, but through proximity, patience, and repeated encounters. XAI must not attempt to replace such human knowledge with a colder substitute. Its more defensible role is to add another layer of visibility while keeping open the possibility that the machine is incomplete, mistaken, or blind to something important.

The question of explainability becomes even more urgent in personalized learning environments. Personalization is often presented as one of AI's greatest promises: the right content, at the right level, at the right time, for the right learner. It sounds elegant. Yet beneath that elegance sits a difficult question: right according to whom, and based on what evidence? If a system adapts a student's learning pathway, learners and teachers deserve to know whether the adaptation is based on demonstrated mastery, speed of response, error patterns, prior demographic data, engagement metrics, or comparisons with other students. A personalized pathway can empower learners when it helps them understand their own progress. It can also narrow their opportunities if it quietly confines them to what the system predicts they are capable of doing. Explanation is what allows personalization to remain educational rather than merely behavioral.

Assessment presents an equally serious challenge. Educational assessment has always carried a moral burden because it transforms complex human performance into judgments (Yılmaz, 2025). AI intensifies this burden. Automated systems can evaluate essays, code, mathematical solutions, design artifacts, spoken responses, and even patterns of collaboration. In STEAM education, where learning may involve experimentation, creativity, design thinking, and interdisciplinary reasoning, the risk of oversimplification is particularly sharp. How does an AI system explain a judgment about creativity? How does it account for originality that falls outside expected patterns? Can it distinguish between a flawed but promising design and a conventional but technically correct one? These questions are not decorative philosophical puzzles; they affect how learners come to understand their own abilities.

At its best, XAI can make assessment more dialogic. Instead of presenting a score as a closed verdict, an explainable system can show the evidence behind a judgment, identify areas of uncertainty, and invite human review (Fregosi, 2025). It can help students see not only what was marked wrong, but why a particular response was interpreted in a certain way. It can help teachers compare machine-generated feedback with their own professional reading. It can also expose moments where the AI's assumptions do not hold. This last point is crucial. Good explainability does not simply increase trust. Sometimes it should reduce trust. Sometimes an explanation should make a teacher pause and say, "No, this does not fit what I know about this student." That pause is not a failure of XAI; it may be one of its most valuable outcomes.

There is also a political dimension that cannot be brushed aside. Educational data is never innocent. It is shaped by access, language, culture, disability, socioeconomic background, prior schooling, teacher expectations, and institutional design. If AI systems learn from such data without careful scrutiny, they may reproduce old inequalities in a new digital accent. Explainability can help reveal these patterns, but only if it is treated as part of governance rather than as a cosmetic interface feature. A colorful dashboard does not guarantee fairness. A confidence score does not guarantee validity. A simplified explanation does not guarantee truth. In some cases, explanations may even create a false sense of clarity, giving users just enough information to feel reassured while leaving the deeper machinery untouched.

For this reason, understanding XAI in education requires humility. Not the decorative kind, but a practical humility built into design and use (Patil et al, 2025). AI systems should be able to say, in effect, "This is the basis of my output, this is the evidence I used, this is where uncertainty remains, and this is where human judgment is needed." Such humility would be far more educationally honest than the polished certainty often associated with automated systems. Learners need room to question. Teachers need room to override. Institutions need mechanisms for appeal, audit, and revision. Explanation must be tied to action; otherwise, it becomes a performance of transparency rather than transparency itself.

Ultimately, Explainable Artificial Intelligence in education is about preserving the human intelligibility of learning in an age of increasingly complex machines. It asks whether teachers can still exercise judgment when algorithms recommend. It asks whether students can still understand and shape their learning when systems personalize. It asks whether assessment can remain fair when automation enters the scene. And, perhaps most importantly, it asks whether educational institutions are willing to treat AI not as a mysterious oracle, but as a fallible tool that must answer to human purposes. The goal is not to make every algorithm perfectly transparent, as though complexity could be dissolved by better design alone. The goal is more grounded, and maybe more demanding: to ensure that when AI speaks in education, people are not forced merely to listen. They must be able to question, interpret, contest, and respond. That is where explainability begins to matter.

TAXONOMIES OF EXPLAINABLE AI IN EDUCATION: MODELS, METHODS, USERS, AND PEDAGOGICAL PURPOSES

Taxonomies of Explainable Artificial Intelligence in education are useful not because they tidy the field into perfect order, but because they help us notice the many different things people mean when they ask an AI system to "explain" itself (Eldrandaly, 2023). The word sounds singular. Explanation. As if there were one clear object to be delivered, one neat answer that could satisfy everyone involved. Yet educational AI sits inside a crowded human environment, where a student, a teacher, a curriculum designer, a parent, a data scientist, and an institutional leader may all look at the same algorithmic output and ask entirely different questions. Why was this learner placed in the remedial pathway? Why did the automated feedback praise one response and criticize another? Why did the system flag a student as disengaged? Why did the model consider a particular project weak in creativity but strong in technical accuracy? The surface question is the same: why? But the need underneath it shifts from person to person, from context to context, and sometimes from one anxious moment to the next.

A meaningful taxonomy of XAI in education should begin with models, because the kind of AI system being used strongly influences the kind of explanation that can be offered. Some models are interpretable by design. Decision trees, rule-based systems, linear models, Bayesian networks, and certain forms of knowledge tracing can often provide relatively direct explanations of their outputs (Tursunalieva et al, 2024). They may show which rule was triggered, which skill was considered weak, or which observable feature contributed to a prediction. In educational practice, these models have a certain modest dignity. They do not always produce the most spectacular results, and they may lack the seductive power of deep learning systems, but they can sometimes speak in a language teachers can follow. There is value in that. A teacher does not always need a mathematically extravagant model; sometimes what is needed is a system whose reasoning can be inspected before it is allowed to influence instruction.

At the other end are opaque or semi-opaque models: deep neural networks, large language models, ensemble systems, and complex adaptive engines that draw meaning from vast and entangled patterns. These systems may perform impressively in tasks such as natural language feedback, learner modeling, content recommendation, multimodal analysis, or automated assessment. Yet their explanatory capacity is more troubled. They may generate an answer, a grade, a recommendation, or a comment that appears fluent and confident, while the underlying path remains difficult to reconstruct. In such cases, explanation often becomes post-hoc: a secondary account created after the model has already acted. This does not make it useless. But it does mean that educators must treat the explanation with caution. A post-hoc explanation may illuminate something about the system's behavior, but it is not always the same as exposing the system's real reasoning. Sometimes it is a lantern. Sometimes it is a shadow that looks like a lantern.

This distinction between inherently interpretable models and post-hoc explainability methods is one of the most common taxonomic divisions in XAI (Bhati et al, 2025). In education, however, the distinction cannot be merely technical. It has pedagogical consequences. A transparent rule-based tutor that explains why a student made an algebraic error may be pedagogically stronger than a more accurate but opaque system that simply assigns a probability of mastery. Yet the reverse may also be true in certain settings: a complex model may detect subtle patterns of misconception, hesitation, or progress that simpler systems miss. The question, then, is not whether simple models are always better or whether complex models should be rejected. The real question is whether the explanation provided is adequate for the educational decision being made. Low-stakes recommendations may tolerate more opacity. High-stakes assessment, placement, intervention, or progression decisions demand stronger forms of interpretability, scrutiny, and human oversight.

A second taxonomy concerns methods of explanation. These include feature-based explanations, example-based explanations, rule-based explanations, counterfactual explanations, visual explanations, natural-language explanations, and interactive explanations. Feature-based explanations show which variables or indicators influenced the outcome: attendance, quiz performance, time-on-task, revision behavior, collaboration frequency, vocabulary range, or previous mastery estimates. They are useful, but also risky. The phrase "time-on-task," for instance, may look objective, yet it can mean very little without context. A student may spend little time on a platform because the material is too easy, too difficult, inaccessible, boring, or because learning is happening elsewhere. A feature is never just a feature in education; it is a fragment of a larger human story.

Example-based explanations operate differently. They explain an output by showing similar cases, previous responses, model comparisons, or representative learner patterns. For students, this can be helpful when used gently. A writing system might show how a stronger argument develops evidence, or a coding tutor might compare a learner's solution with a structurally similar solution that avoids a logical error (Neshaei et al, 2025). The danger lies in turning comparison into quiet ranking. Learners may feel measured against invisible peers rather than supported in their own development. The explanation must be framed as guidance, not humiliation. Educational design lives in these small tonal differences. A system can be technically correct and still emotionally clumsy.

Counterfactual explanations are especially promising in education because they answer a practical question: what would need to change for a different outcome to occur? Instead of merely saying, "You are predicted to struggle with this unit," a system might explain, "If your performance on proportional reasoning tasks improves and you complete two additional practice activities with fewer recurring errors, the next pathway will open." This kind of explanation can preserve agency. It tells the learner that the prediction is not destiny. Still, counterfactuals must be designed with care. If they suggest changes beyond the learner's control—such as prior achievement, demographic factors, or access-related variables—they become not empowering but cruelly informative. An explanation should not reveal a locked door and call that transparency.

Visual explanations, such as dashboards, heat maps, progress graphs, and skill maps, are common in learning analytics and adaptive platforms (Tretow-Fish & Khalid, 2023). They can make complex patterns easier to grasp, particularly for teachers managing many learners at once. Yet visual clarity can be deceptive. A red warning icon beside a student's name may compress ambiguity into alarm. A progress bar may imply linear growth where learning is actually recursive, uneven, and occasionally invisible. A dashboard may show participation but not curiosity; completion but not understanding; speed but not depth. Visual explanation must resist the temptation to convert all learning into clean geometry. Some of the most important things in education do not fit comfortably into a graph.

Natural-language explanations have gained new importance with the rise of generative AI (Li et al, 2025). These explanations can feel more accessible because they resemble ordinary human communication. An AI tutor may say, "Your answer shows that you understand the main idea, but you need to connect your evidence more clearly to your claim." This is far more approachable than a statistical output. Yet fluency can become a trap. A smooth explanation is not necessarily a valid explanation. Language can create trust too easily. In educational settings, where students may already assume that a system "knows," natural-language XAI must be anchored in evidence, uncertainty, and pedagogical restraint. It should not overclaim. It should not moralize. It should not pretend to know the learner more intimately than it does.

Another important taxonomy organizes XAI by users. Teachers need explanations that support professional judgment. They need to know whether a recommendation fits classroom evidence, whether an alert is urgent, whether a score is reliable, and whether the system has missed relevant context. Students need explanations that support self-understanding and agency. They need to know what the system has inferred, how they can improve, and whether they have the right to question or correct the system's interpretation. Administrators need explanations related to validity, fairness, compliance, and institutional impact. Developers need diagnostic explanations to improve models and detect failure points. Parents or guardians may need explanations that are accessible without being simplistic, especially when AI influences assessment or support pathways. Policymakers need explanations that reveal governance risks, not just technical functionality.

These user categories matter because a single explanation rarely works for everyone. A teacher-facing explanation may include pedagogical indicators and classroom-level patterns. A student-facing explanation must be less technical, more formative, and more sensitive to tone. An administrator-facing explanation may focus on aggregate trends, audit trails, and risk management. A developer-facing explanation may include model behavior, data drift, error distribution, and subgroup performance. Confusing these audiences can damage trust. Give a student a technical feature-importance chart without interpretation, and the explanation becomes alienating. Give a teacher a vague motivational message where professional evidence is needed, and the explanation becomes useless. Give an administrator a polished dashboard without bias analysis, and the explanation becomes a liability dressed as innovation.

The deepest taxonomy, however, may be the one based on pedagogical purpose. Why is the explanation being offered in the first place? Some explanations are diagnostic: they help identify misconceptions, gaps, or learning needs. Some are formative: they guide improvement during the learning process. Some are justificatory: they defend or clarify an AI-supported decision. Some are reflective: they help learners think about their own strategies, habits, and progress. Some are ethical: they reveal uncertainty, bias, data limitations, or possible harm. Some are dialogic: they invite conversation between teacher, student, and system. This last category is often neglected, yet it may be the most educationally mature. Explanation should not always be a message delivered from machine to human. Sometimes it should begin a conversation.

In STEAM learning, pedagogical purpose becomes especially layered (Bertrand & Namukasa, 2023). AI explanations may need to support conceptual understanding in mathematics, inquiry in science, debugging in technology, design iteration in engineering, and expressive interpretation in the arts. The same explanatory method cannot serve all these purposes equally well. A counterfactual explanation may help a student revise an engineering design. A visual explanation may help map collaboration patterns in a project team. A natural-language explanation may support reflective writing in arts-integrated inquiry. A rule-based explanation may help with procedural errors in algebra. A dialogic explanation may help students debate the ethical implications of a scientific model. Taxonomy, in this sense, is not an abstract classification exercise; it is a way of matching explanation to the grain of learning.

The risk, of course, is that taxonomies become too neat. Educational reality rarely respects categories. A teacher may need a model-level explanation and a student-centered explanation at the same time (Nikolova et al, 2026). A student may need both encouragement and technical specificity. An institution may demand accountability while a classroom needs flexibility. XAI in education must remain sensitive to these overlaps. Its classifications should guide design, not imprison it.

A mature taxonomy of XAI in education must therefore recognize four intertwined dimensions: the model being explained, the method used to explain it, the user receiving the explanation, and the pedagogical purpose the explanation is meant to serve. When these dimensions align, explainability can become more than a technical accessory. It can support better judgment, fairer assessment, more thoughtful personalization, and richer learner agency. When they are misaligned, explanation becomes theater: visible but not useful, fluent but not honest, reassuring but not responsible. The challenge for educational AI is not simply to explain more. It is to explain wisely, modestly, and in forms that respect the fragile, unfinished, deeply human work of learning.

EXPLAINABILITY IN STEAM PERSONALIZATION AND ETHICAL ASSESSMENT

Explainability becomes particularly consequential in STEAM education because STEAM learning is rarely a straight road. It bends, loops, hesitates, breaks apart, and returns in unexpected forms (Shernoff, 2024). A learner working through a robotics project, a mathematical modeling problem, a digital artwork, a science investigation, or an engineering design challenge is not simply moving from "unknown" to "known" in a tidy sequence. The process may involve trial, error, intuition, frustration, peer negotiation, aesthetic judgment, and sudden conceptual awakening. Generative and adaptive AI systems promise to support this complexity by personalizing learning pathways, recommending resources, detecting misconceptions, generating feedback, and assessing multidimensional performances. Yet the more deeply these systems enter STEAM environments, the more urgent explainability becomes. Personalization without explanation can become invisible steering. Assessment without explanation can become silent judgment.

In traditional educational settings, personalization often depends on the teacher's capacity to observe learners closely and adjust instruction accordingly. A teacher may notice that one student understands the formula but not its application, while another can build a working prototype yet struggles to articulate the reasoning behind it (Lyu et al, 2026). A third student may appear disengaged during direct instruction but flourish when allowed to sketch, simulate, or experiment. STEAM learning makes these differences especially visible because it draws on multiple forms of intelligence: analytical, spatial, creative, linguistic, technical, collaborative, and embodied. AI-based personalization attempts to respond to such diversity by analyzing learner data and adapting content, pace, difficulty, sequence, or feedback. At its best, this can be powerful. It may prevent students from being trapped in one-size-fits-all instruction. It may offer additional practice when a concept remains fragile, or open more advanced tasks when a learner is ready to move further. It may even give quieter students a more private route into participation.

Still, one must be careful. Personalization is an attractive word, but it can hide a great deal. An AI system may claim to personalize learning while actually narrowing it, guiding students toward what is easiest to measure rather than what is most educationally valuable (Ayeni et al, 2024). If a system recommends simpler science tasks because a student has previously struggled with abstract reasoning, does it support the learner or quietly lower expectations? If it avoids open-ended design challenges because the learner's responses are difficult to classify, is that personalization or containment? If it generates artistic prompts based on prior preferences, does it nurture creativity or reinforce familiar habits? These questions cannot be answered responsibly unless the system can explain the basis of its decisions. Why this task? Why this sequence? Why this feedback? Why this level of difficulty? Why now?

Explainability in STEAM personalization should therefore do more than justify algorithmic choices after the fact (De Bruijn et al, 2022). It should help learners and teachers understand the educational logic behind adaptation. A student should not simply be told, "You have been assigned this activity." A more meaningful explanation might say: "This activity focuses on proportional reasoning because your recent simulation responses showed difficulty connecting scale changes to output changes." Such an explanation does not need to reveal every technical detail of the model. It needs to reveal enough to make the recommendation intelligible, contestable, and useful. The learner can then see a connection between past performance and future action. The teacher can judge whether the recommendation fits classroom evidence. The system becomes less like a hidden gatekeeper and more like a participant in a pedagogical conversation.

In STEAM settings, the explanation must also respect the interdisciplinary nature of learning (Chang & Kidman, 2025). A student's difficulty in a physics-based design task may not come from physics alone. It may involve weak mathematical representation, limited spatial reasoning, unfamiliarity with digital tools, poor group communication, or uncertainty about how to translate an idea into a prototype. If the AI explanation identifies only one dimension, it may distort the learning picture. For example, labeling a student as weak in "engineering design" may be too broad to be useful and too blunt to be fair. A better explanation would distinguish between idea generation, constraint analysis, iterative testing, technical execution, and reflective justification. STEAM learning needs granular explanations because its performances are layered. A bridge that collapses in a student project may reveal a misunderstanding of load distribution, but it may also reveal poor material choice, rushed collaboration, or a creative risk that deserves discussion rather than simple penalty.

Ethical assessment raises the stakes further. Assessment is never merely an act of measurement; it is an act of recognition. It tells learners what counts, what matters, what is seen, and sometimes, painfully, what is ignored. When AI systems assess STEAM work, they enter a space where human judgment has always been difficult (Spyropoulou & Kameas, 2025). How does one assess creativity without domesticating it? How does one measure collaboration without turning peer interaction into surveillance? How does one evaluate a design process when failure may be evidence of productive experimentation rather than incompetence? How does one judge mathematical reasoning when a student's written explanation is linguistically imperfect but conceptually alive? Ethical assessment requires more than scoring accuracy. It requires interpretive fairness.

Explainability can help protect that fairness, but only if it is designed with ethical seriousness (Matta & Bolli, 2023). An AI-generated score should be accompanied by an account of the evidence used to produce it. If a system evaluates a digital portfolio, it should indicate whether the judgment was based on final product quality, revision history, originality, technical complexity, alignment with rubric criteria, peer feedback, or reflective commentary. If it assesses a coding assignment, it should distinguish between syntax errors, algorithmic logic, efficiency, readability, and problem-solving strategy. If it comments on an artistic or design artifact, it should avoid pretending that aesthetic value can be reduced to predictable features. The explanation should show what the system can reasonably evaluate and what remains beyond its competence. This admission of limitation is not weakness. In ethical assessment, it is a form of honesty.

A particularly important issue is the risk of hidden bias. STEAM education is often presented as future-facing and merit-based, yet access to STEAM learning has always been uneven (Nartey, 2026). Students differ in prior exposure to laboratories, coding tools, robotics kits, art materials, high-quality mathematics instruction, stable internet, and supportive mentors. They also differ in language background, cultural expression, confidence, and familiarity with the norms of formal academic performance. If an AI system has been trained on data from privileged or narrowly defined learning contexts, it may treat certain styles of reasoning, communication, or creativity as more legitimate than others. A student who explains a design through narrative rather than formal technical language may be undervalued (Watkins, 2023). A student who collaborates quietly may be perceived as less engaged. A student whose artistic expression falls outside the system's learned patterns may be judged as less coherent or less original.

This is where explainability must become critical rather than decorative. It should reveal not only what the system decided, but also what assumptions may have shaped that decision. It should allow teachers to ask whether the criteria are culturally narrow, whether the data are representative, whether the rubric privileges certain forms of expression, and whether the system performs differently across learner groups. A fair AI system is not one that simply produces identical procedures for all students. Fairness sometimes requires sensitivity to difference, context, and historical disadvantage. In assessment, equal treatment can become unequal if learners begin from unequal conditions and if the assessment tool fails to recognize that uneven terrain.

There is also a danger that AI-generated explanations may sound more authoritative than they deserve. A generative system can produce polished feedback with remarkable ease, but fluency is not the same as fairness, and confidence is not the same as validity. A student may receive a beautifully worded paragraph explaining why their project lacks originality, when in fact the system has misread an unconventional idea. A teacher may see a dashboard flagging weak collaboration because one student contributed fewer written comments online, while most of that student's contribution happened orally during group work. The explanation may be clear, but still wrong. This is a difficult point, and it must be stated plainly: explainability does not eliminate error. It makes error easier to find, discuss, and correct—provided humans remain willing and able to question the system.

For this reason, explainability in STEAM personalization and assessment should be dialogic (Radvila et al, 2025). It should invite response. Students should be able to ask why a recommendation was made, request clarification, challenge feedback, or provide missing context. Teachers should be able to adjust AI interpretations based on classroom knowledge. Assessment systems should include mechanisms for review, appeal, and revision. In project-based STEAM learning, where the process matters as much as the product, learners should have opportunities to explain their own reasoning alongside any machine-generated evaluation (Peters et al, 2024). The student's voice should not arrive after the algorithmic judgment as a defensive footnote; it should be part of the assessment ecology from the beginning.

A humane approach to XAI in STEAM education also recognizes the emotional life of learning (Dignam et al, 2025). Personalized systems can encourage learners when they make progress visible, but they can also discourage them when predictions feel like labels. Ethical assessment can support growth when feedback is specific and constructive, but it can injure confidence when automated judgments appear final, cold, or incomprehensible. A student told repeatedly that they are "below expected level" may begin to inhabit that category. A learner whose creative work is flattened into numerical indicators may conclude that originality is unsafe. Explanation must therefore be careful in tone. It should avoid fatalistic language. It should emphasize possibility, not fixed ability. It should make clear that a prediction is provisional, an assessment is revisable, and a learning pathway is not a cage.

The strongest role of explainability in STEAM personalization is not to make AI dominant, but to make it accountable to learning (Otaru, 2025). The strongest role of explainability in ethical assessment is not to make machine scoring more acceptable, but to ensure that assessment remains open to human interpretation, disagreement, and care. AI can notice patterns that teachers may miss. It can generate timely feedback, support differentiated pathways, and help manage the complexity of STEAM classrooms. But it cannot fully understand the courage of a failed prototype, the quiet intelligence of a hesitant learner, the cultural meaning behind a design choice, or the spark that appears when a student suddenly sees a connection between mathematics and music, biology and art, code and social need.

Explainability keeps that boundary visible. It reminds educators that personalization must not become prediction disguised as destiny, and assessment must not become automation dressed as objectivity (Tınmaz, 2025). In STEAM education, where the aim is not only to produce correct answers but to cultivate inquiry, imagination, ethical reasoning, and problem-solving in uncertain worlds, AI explanations must be generous enough to support growth and modest enough to admit incompleteness. The point is not simply that machines should explain themselves. It is that education should never allow any system, however intelligent, to speak about learners in ways that learners and teachers cannot understand, question, or humanly revise.

CHALLENGES, LIMITATIONS, AND FUTURE DIRECTIONS FOR HUMAN-CENTERED EDUCATIONAL XAI

The promise of Explainable Artificial Intelligence in education is compelling, almost seductive at times (Fiok et al, 2022). It suggests that intelligent systems can become not only powerful but understandable; not only adaptive but accountable; not only efficient but pedagogically sensitive. Yet the path toward human-centered educational XAI is far less straightforward than this promise implies. The difficulty is not simply that AI systems are technically complex. Education itself is complex. Learning resists clean measurement. Teaching depends on judgment, timing, empathy, and interpretation (Tolman & Kremling, 2023). Assessment carries ethical weight. Institutions are shaped by policy pressures, funding constraints, accountability regimes, and social inequalities. When AI enters this landscape, it does not enter an empty room. It enters a crowded, noisy, deeply human space where explanation must do more than decode a model. It must make sense within the fragile ecology of learning.

One of the most persistent challenges is the gap between technical explanation and educational meaning (Galindo Domínguez et al, 2022). Many XAI methods are designed to explain model behavior through variables, feature importance, probability scores, decision paths, or counterfactual scenarios. These tools may be useful to developers and data scientists, but they do not automatically translate into pedagogical understanding. A system may report that "time-on-task," "error frequency," or "interaction density" contributed significantly to a learner's predicted outcome. Such information looks precise. It may even look convincing. Yet a teacher may still ask: What does that actually mean for this student, in this classroom, at this moment? Did the learner spend less time on the task because they understood it quickly, because they were confused, because the platform was inaccessible, or because they were helping a peer offline? A feature can be statistically meaningful and educationally ambiguous at the same time. That ambiguity is not a minor inconvenience; it is the ordinary condition of teaching.

This difficulty becomes sharper when AI systems are used in high-stakes or semi-high-stakes educational decisions. In theory, explainability should make these decisions more transparent. In practice, explanations may be partial, approximate, or even misleading. Post-hoc explanations, for example, often attempt to interpret the behavior of complex models after the model has already produced an output. They may provide useful clues, but they do not always reveal the genuine internal logic of the system. A polished explanation may create the impression of clarity while concealing uncertainty. This is especially dangerous in education because users may mistake explanation for justification. A teacher might assume that because the system can explain why a student was flagged, the flag must be valid. A student might accept an automated assessment because the feedback sounds fluent and confident (Aeni et al, 2025). An institution might use explainability as a shield against criticism, presenting dashboards and documentation as proof of fairness. Yet explanation is not the same as truth. Nor is visibility the same as justice.

Another limitation concerns the uneven distribution of interpretive power. Not all users are equally able to understand or challenge AI explanations. A technically trained administrator may interpret a model report differently from a classroom teacher. A confident student may question an automated recommendation, while a less confident learner may quietly accept it as final. Parents may be told that an AI system supports learning, but may lack the language or access needed to interrogate how. Even teachers, whose professional judgment should remain central, may feel pressured to defer to algorithmic authority, particularly when AI tools are institutionally endorsed or commercially marketed as evidence-based (Galés, 2024). This produces a subtle but serious problem: explainability may exist formally while remaining socially ineffective. An explanation that cannot be acted upon is not empowering. It is just another layer of information placed in front of people who may have no real authority to use it.

Bias remains one of the most troubling limitations of educational XAI. AI systems are trained on data, and educational data is never untouched by history. Patterns of participation, achievement, language use, attendance, disciplinary action, digital access, and assessment performance are shaped by social class, race, gender, disability, geography, language background, and prior opportunity. If these patterns are absorbed into AI models without critical scrutiny, the system may reproduce inequality while appearing neutral. Explainability can reveal some of these patterns, but only if the institution is willing to look. A model may explain that a learner is at risk because of low engagement, but the explanation may fail to show that "engagement" itself is being measured through platform behaviors that privilege students with stable internet access, quiet study spaces, and familiarity with digital tools. A writing assessment tool may explain its score through grammar, coherence, and vocabulary, while undervaluing multilingual expression or culturally different rhetorical styles. The danger is not only that AI may be biased. The danger is that explanation may make biased judgments appear reasonable.

There is also the challenge of explanation overload. Educational users do not need endless information; they need relevant, timely, and usable explanation. Teachers already work under intense cognitive and emotional pressure. Giving them elaborate model reports, complex dashboards, or dense analytics may increase burden rather than support judgment. Students, too, may become confused or discouraged if explanations are too technical, too frequent, or too heavily focused on deficits. Human-centered XAI must therefore resist the assumption that more explanation is always better (Ma, 2024). Sometimes a brief explanation, carefully phrased, is more valuable than a comprehensive technical account. Sometimes the most ethical explanation is not the longest one, but the one that helps the user take a meaningful next step. Good explanation has rhythm. It knows when to speak, when to simplify, when to disclose uncertainty, and when to invite human conversation.

The problem of trust is equally complicated. Many educational technologies are designed as though trust were something to be maximized. But in human-centered XAI, trust should be calibrated, not inflated. Users should neither reject AI systems out of fear nor accept them with blind confidence. The aim is a more mature relationship: cautious reliance, informed skepticism, and the ability to override machine outputs when necessary. This is difficult to achieve because AI systems often arrive surrounded by institutional enthusiasm and commercial rhetoric. They are described as smart, personalized, efficient, scalable, transformative. Such language can create unrealistic expectations. When systems fail, users may become cynical. When systems work well enough most of the time, users may stop questioning them. Both reactions are problematic. A healthier future for educational XAI requires a culture in which error is expected, uncertainty is visible, and human review is not treated as an obstacle to efficiency.

Privacy and data governance add another layer of concern. Explainability depends on data, but educational data is intimate (Gunasekara & Saarela, 2025). It may include academic performance, behavioral traces, written responses, emotional indicators, learning disabilities, attendance records, demographic information, and interaction patterns. The more personalized an AI system becomes, the more it may require detailed learner data. Yet the more data it uses, the greater the risk of surveillance, misuse, and harm. Students may begin to feel that every click, pause, hesitation, draft, or mistake is being watched and interpreted. This can change the atmosphere of learning. Experimentation may become cautious. Failure may feel recorded rather than instructive. In STEAM education, where trial, error, play, and risk-taking are essential, excessive datafication can quietly undermine the very creativity it claims to support. Human-centered XAI must therefore ask not only how to explain data use, but whether certain forms of data collection should happen at all.

A further limitation lies in the institutional readiness required for meaningful XAI. Schools and universities may adopt AI tools faster than they develop the governance structures needed to manage them (Filgueiras, 2024). Procurement decisions may be driven by cost, reputation, or urgency rather than careful pedagogical evaluation. Teachers may receive little training. Students may not be informed of their rights. Bias audits may be absent. Appeal mechanisms may be vague. Responsibility may be dispersed among vendors, administrators, IT departments, academic units, and teachers until no one knows exactly who is accountable. In such conditions, explainability risks becoming a surface feature added to systems that remain institutionally underexamined. A human-centered future cannot depend on interface design alone. It requires policy, training, documentation, ethical review, and a willingness to slow down adoption when the educational risks are not yet understood.

The future direction of educational XAI should begin with participatory design. Teachers, students, parents, accessibility specialists, curriculum experts, and ethicists should not be invited only after systems are built (Gee et al, 2024). They should shape the questions that AI systems are meant to answer. Too many educational technologies begin with what the system can measure rather than what education actually values. A more humane approach would ask: What kinds of learner agency should this system protect? What forms of teacher judgment should it support? What kinds of harm might arise if the system is wrong? Which decisions should remain firmly human? Where should explanation be mandatory, and where might automation be inappropriate altogether? These questions are slower than technical development, but slowness here is not weakness. It is care.

Future XAI systems also need to become more pedagogically adaptive in their explanations (Idrizi, 2024). A single explanation should not be delivered identically to all users. Teachers may need evidence, uncertainty indicators, links to curriculum goals, and suggestions for intervention. Students may need formative guidance, accessible language, encouragement, and room to respond. Administrators may need audit trails, fairness metrics, and policy-level summaries. Developers may need error analysis and model diagnostics. The explanation should fit the user, the decision, and the stakes. Low-stakes learning recommendations may require light explanations. High-stakes assessment or placement decisions require deeper justification, human review, and appeal. This layered approach would prevent XAI from becoming either too shallow to matter or too complex to use.

Another future direction is the development of contestable AI systems. In education, explanation should not be a one-way delivery of reasons from machine to human. It should allow correction. Students should be able to say, "This does not reflect my work." Teachers should be able to annotate, override, or revise AI outputs. Institutions should be able to trace patterns of error and require system improvement. Contestability turns explanation into a living process rather than a static statement. It recognizes that learners are not passive subjects of prediction. They are participants in meaning-making, capable of clarifying context, challenging assumptions, and reshaping the evidence used to judge them.

Human-centered educational XAI must also preserve space for the unmeasurable (Ma, 2024). This may sound unfashionable in an age that loves analytics, but it is vital. Not everything valuable in learning can be captured through data. Curiosity, moral imagination, intellectual courage, aesthetic surprise, quiet persistence, and the slow formation of confidence often escape computational representation. AI may support education, but it should not define the full horizon of what education is. A future built around human-centered XAI must keep reminding itself that explanation is not only about making machines clearer. It is also about keeping education answerable to human beings.

The central challenge, then, is not merely to build more explainable systems. It is to build educational cultures capable of using explanation wisely. This means skepticism without cynicism, innovation without surrender, personalization without confinement, assessment without dehumanization, and accountability without theatrical transparency. The future of XAI in education will depend less on whether machines can generate explanations and more on whether institutions are willing to listen carefully to what those explanations reveal—and just as importantly, to what they fail to reveal. Human-centered XAI should not promise perfect clarity. It should promise something more honest: that when AI participates in learning, its presence can be questioned, its judgments can be revised, its limitations can be named, and the learner remains more than the sum of the system's predictions.

CONCLUSION

Explainable Artificial Intelligence in education stands at the intersection of technological innovation, pedagogical responsibility, and ethical caution. As AI systems become more embedded in learning environments, the need to understand their decisions becomes more urgent. It is tempting to view explainability as a technical matter: a model produces an output, and another tool explains how that output was generated. But education does not work in such a narrow way. A learning recommendation, an assessment score, or an automated feedback message is never just a data point. It enters the life of a learner. It may influence confidence, opportunity, teacher perception, institutional placement, or future academic direction. For this reason, explainability in education must be treated as a human matter before it is treated as a machine matter.

Throughout this chapter, the central argument has been that XAI should be understood not merely as a mechanism for making algorithms more visible, but as a framework for making educational AI more accountable, meaningful, and fair. A transparent system is not automatically a just system. An interpretable dashboard is not automatically a pedagogically useful one. A technically accurate explanation may still fail if it does not speak to the actual needs of teachers and learners. The deeper value of XAI lies in its ability to open AI-supported education to questioning. Why was this recommendation made? What data shaped this prediction? What assumptions sit beneath this classification? Could the system be wrong? Who is allowed to challenge it? These questions are not minor details. They are the foundation of responsible educational technology.

In STEAM education, the need for such questioning becomes even more pronounced. STEAM learning values exploration, creativity, experimentation, design thinking, and interdisciplinary problem-solving. These are not always easy to measure, and they are certainly not easy to reduce to predictable patterns. When AI systems are used to personalize STEAM pathways or assess complex student work, they must be designed with humility. They should support human judgment, not replace it. They should illuminate learning processes, not flatten them. They should help teachers see patterns that might otherwise remain hidden, while still leaving room for professional interpretation, contextual sensitivity, and the subtle knowledge that emerges from human relationships in classrooms. A good teacher often understands things that no dataset can fully capture: hesitation, resilience, curiosity, fatigue, quiet improvement, or the courage behind an imperfect answer.

The taxonomies of XAI discussed in this chapter show that explainability has many layers. There are model-centered explanations that clarify how an algorithm works. There are user-centered explanations that translate outputs into accessible language. There are pedagogical explanations that help learners understand their progress and next steps. There are ethical explanations that reveal risks, biases, and consequences. These categories are useful, but they should not be treated as fixed boxes. In real educational practice, they overlap. A teacher may need a technical explanation to judge reliability, a pedagogical explanation to guide instruction, and an ethical explanation to ensure fairness. A student may need not only to know what the system concluded, but also how to respond, improve, or contest that conclusion. Explanation, then, is not a single message. It is an ongoing relationship between the AI system and the people affected by it.

One of the greatest challenges facing XAI in education is the danger of superficial transparency. Institutions may claim that their AI systems are explainable because they provide simplified summaries, colorful dashboards, or confidence scores. Yet such features can create an illusion of understanding. They may reassure users without actually revealing meaningful information. Worse still, explanations can become tools of persuasion, encouraging teachers and students to accept automated decisions rather than examine them critically. This is why educational XAI must be connected to digital literacy, professional training, governance policies, and ethical review. People cannot use explanations well if they are not supported in understanding their limits. An explanation is only useful when the user has the ability, confidence, and authority to act upon it.

Another major concern is bias. AI systems learn from data, and educational data is often shaped by historical inequality. Patterns of achievement, participation, attendance, language use, assessment performance, and digital access may reflect social conditions rather than individual ability. If these patterns are absorbed uncritically into AI models, the system may reproduce disadvantage while appearing objective. Explainability can help expose such risks, but only if institutions are willing to look beyond technical performance and examine the broader ecology in which AI operates. Accuracy alone is not enough. A system can be accurate in a narrow statistical sense while still being educationally harmful. The real question is whether AI contributes to fairer, richer, and more humane learning experiences.

The future of XAI in education should therefore be guided by a human-centered vision. This means designing systems that respect teacher expertise, protect student agency, and recognize the moral weight of educational decisions. It means involving educators, learners, parents, policymakers, and communities in the design and evaluation of AI tools. It also means accepting that not every educational judgment should be automated, and not every form of learning can be meaningfully captured by data. There are moments in education where ambiguity is not a failure but a sign of depth. A student's unusual solution, a hesitant question, a collaborative breakthrough, or a creative mistake may resist clean classification. XAI must make space for such complexity rather than forcing it into rigid computational categories.

Ultimately, Explainable Artificial Intelligence offers education both a promise and a warning. The promise is that AI systems, when carefully designed and responsibly governed, can help personalize learning, support assessment, reveal hidden patterns, and provide timely feedback. The warning is that without meaningful explanation, these same systems may deepen opacity, dependence, bias, and mistrust. The task ahead is not to reject AI, nor to embrace it with naïve enthusiasm. It is to shape it with care. Educational AI must remain answerable to human purposes. It must be open to scrutiny, correction, and refusal. Most of all, it must serve learning as a deeply human process, not merely an optimized sequence of predictions. In this sense, the future of XAI in education depends not only on better algorithms, but on better questions: questions about fairness, dignity, responsibility, and the kind of education we are willing to build in the age of intelligent machines.

REFERENCES

Aeni, N., Muhalim, M., Ganteng, H., Tahir, M., & Talib, A. (2025). English Education Students' Perceptions of Automated vs Human Assessment in Spoken English Proficiency. AL-ISHLAH. *Jurnal Pendidikan, 17*(3), 5615–5625.

Ayeni, O. O., Al Hamad, N. M., Chisom, O. N., Osawaru, B., & Adewusi, O. E. (2024). AI in education: A review of personalized learning and educational technology. *GSC Advanced Research and Reviews, 18*(2), 261–271. DOI: 10.30574/gscarr.2024.18.2.0062

Bertrand, M. G., & Namukasa, I. K. (2023). A pedagogical model for STEAM education. *Journal of Research in Innovative Teaching & Learning, 16*(2), 169–191. DOI: 10.1108/JRIT-12-2021-0081

Bhati, D., Amiruzzaman, M., Zhao, Y., Guercio, A., & Le, T. (2025). A survey of post-hoc xai methods from a visualization perspective: Challenges and opportunities. *IEEE Access : Practical Innovations, Open Solutions, 13*, 120785–120806. DOI: 10.1109/ACCESS.2025.3581136

Bulathwela, S., Pérez-Ortiz, M., Holloway, C., Cukurova, M., & Shawe-Taylor, J. (2024). Artificial intelligence alone will not democratise education: On educational inequality, techno-solutionism and inclusive tools. *Sustainability (Basel), 16*(2), 781. DOI: 10.3390/su16020781

Chang, C. H., & Kidman, G. (2025). Interdisciplinary learning and pedagogical content knowledge in sustainability education–implications for STEAM education. *International Research in Geographical and Environmental Education, 34*(2), 95–99. DOI: 10.1080/10382046.2025.2476805

De Bruijn, H., Warnier, M., & Janssen, M. (2022). The perils and pitfalls of explainable AI: Strategies for explaining algorithmic decision-making. *Government Information Quarterly, 39*(2), 101666. DOI: 10.1016/j.giq.2021.101666

DeWallace-Marenholz, J. L. (2025). High-Quality Instruction in Practice: Empowering Teachers Through a Co-Created STEAM Learning Lab (Doctoral dissertation, Northeastern University).

Dignam, C., Smith, C. M., & Kelly, A. L. (2025). The heart and art of robotics: From AI to artificial emotional intelligence in STEM education. *Journal of Education in Science, Environment and Health, 11*(2), 151–169. DOI: 10.55549/jeseh.813

Doroudi, S. (2023). The intertwined histories of artificial intelligence and education. *International Journal of Artificial Intelligence in Education, 33*(4), 885–928. DOI: 10.1007/s40593-022-00313-2

Eldrandaly, K. A., Abdel-Basset, M., Ibrahim, M., & Abdel-Aziz, N. M. (2023). Explainable and secure artificial intelligence: Taxonomy, cases of study, learned lessons, challenges and future directions. *Enterprise Information Systems, 17*(9), 2098537. DOI: 10.1080/17517575.2022.2098537

Feldman-Maggor, Y., Cukurova, M., Kent, C., & Alexandron, G. (2025). The impact of explainable AI on teachers' trust and acceptance of AI EdTech recommendations: The power of domain-specific explanations. *International Journal of Artificial Intelligence in Education, 35*(5), 1–34. DOI: 10.1007/s40593-025-00486-6

Filgueiras, F. (2024). Artificial intelligence and education governance. *Education, Citizenship and Social Justice, 19*(3), 349–361. DOI: 10.1177/17461979231160674

Fiok, K., Farahani, F. V., Karwowski, W., & Ahram, T. (2022). Explainable artificial intelligence for education and training. *The Journal of Defense Modeling and Simulation, 19*(2), 133–144. DOI: 10.1177/15485129211028651

Fregosi, C. (2025). How to Explain in XAI?-Investigating Explanation Protocols in Decision Support Systems.

Galés, N. L. (2024). Trust and connection in the artificial intelligence educational ecosystem: From algorithmism to algoritharism. *Revista Catalana de Pedagogia, 26*, 4–37.

Galindo Domínguez, H., Perines, H., Verde Trabada, A., & Valero Esteban, J. M. (2022). Understanding the pedagogical gap between the educational research and the reality of teachers: an analisis of the difficulties and proposals.

Gee, K., Ryndak, D. L., Fisher, M., & Walker, V. L. (2024). Access to the general education curriculum for students with extensive support needs: Experts' perspectives. *Research and Practice for Persons with Severe Disabilities : the Journal of TASH, 49*(1), 3–19. DOI: 10.1177/15407969231219027

Gunasekara, S., & Saarela, M. (2025). Explainable AI in education: Techniques and qualitative assessment. *Applied Sciences (Basel, Switzerland), 15*(3), 1239. DOI: 10.3390/app15031239

Idrizi, E. (2024, May). Exploring the role of explainable artificial intelligence (XAI) in adaptive learning systems. In *Proceedings of the Cognitive Models and Artificial Intelligence Conference* (pp. 100-105). DOI: 10.1145/3660853.3660877

Lee, H., Mojica, G., Thrasher, E., & Baumgartner, P. (2022). Investigating data like a data scientist: Key practices and processes. *Statistics Education Research Journal, 21*(2), 3–3. DOI: 10.52041/serj.v21i2.41

Li, Y., Shan, Z., Raković, M., Guan, Q., Gašević, D., & Chen, G. (2025). When AI explains in natural language: Unveiling the impact of generative AI explanations on educators' grading and feedback practices. *Education and Information Technologies, 30*(17), 24931–24964. DOI: 10.1007/s10639-025-13741-z

Lyu, W., Wang, Y., Yue, M., Sun, Y., Suh, J., Kier, M., & Zhang, Y. (2026, April). Designing AI Peers for Collaborative Mathematical Problem Solving with Middle School Students: A Participatory Design Study. In *Proceedings of the 2026 CHI Conference on Human Factors in Computing Systems* (pp. 1-21). DOI: 10.1145/3772318.3791138

Ma, S. (2024). Towards Human-centered Design of Explainable Artificial Intelligence (XAI): A Survey of Empirical Studies. arXiv preprint arXiv:2410.21183.

Matta, S. S., & Bolli, M. (2023). Trustworthy ai: Explainability & fairness in large-scale decision systems. *Review of Applied Science and Technology, 2*(04), 54–93. DOI: 10.63125/3w9v5e52

Meylani, R. (2025). Rethinking explainability in educational artificial intelligence: A critical systematic review of models, applications, and ethical dimensions. *Veredas do Direito, 22*(3), e223553–e223553. DOI: 10.18623/rvd.v22.n3.3553

Minh, D., Wang, H. X., Li, Y. F., & Nguyen, T. N. (2022). Explainable artificial intelligence: A comprehensive review. *Artificial Intelligence Review, 55*(5), 3503–3568. DOI: 10.1007/s10462-021-10088-y

Nartey, E. K. (2026). *Generative AI in Higher Education: Ethical Governance, Skills, and Employability* (Vol. 2). CRC Press. DOI: 10.1201/9781003502517

Neshaei, S. P., Tolzin, A., Berkle, Y., Leuchter, M., Leimeister, J. M., Janson, A., & Wambsganss, T. (2025). Leveraging Learner Errors in Digital Argumentation Learning: How ALure Helps Students Learn from their Mistakes and Write Better Arguments. *Proceedings of the ACM on Human-Computer Interaction, 9*(2), 1–32. DOI: 10.1145/3711023

Nikolova, N., Kirilova, B., Mihnev, P., Zafirova-Malcheva, T., & Petkova, M. (2026). From Formal to Operational: A Triangulated Analysis of Policy, Practice, and Perception Regarding Digital Competence Development in Mathematics and IT Teacher Education. *Education Sciences, 16*(2), 272. DOI: 10.3390/educsci16020272

Nokes, C. (2022). Effective learning in the modern classroom. Journal for Learning through the Arts, 18(1).

Otaru, B. E. (2025). Leveraging Artificial Intelligence (AI) for personalized and inclusive STEAM education: Strategies for bridging learning gaps among diverse learners. *KONTAGORA JOURNAL OF SCIENCE AND TECHNOLOGY, 18*(1-2), 94–99.

Patil, H. Y., Assumption, M., & Latha, G. H. (2025). Smart Education: A Need of the Hour Using Explainable Artificial Intelligence (XAI). In Personalized Learning Through Adaptive Systems and Intelligent Tutoring (pp. 1-72). IGI Global Scientific Publishing.

Peters, M. A., Jackson, L., Papastephanou, M., Jandrić, P., Lazaroiu, G., Evers, C. W., Cope, B., Kalantzis, M., Araya, D., Tesar, M., Mika, C., Chen, L., Wang, C., Sturm, S., Rider, S., & Fuller, S. (2024). AI and the future of humanity: ChatGPT-4, philosophy and education–Critical responses. *Educational Philosophy and Theory, 56*(9), 828–862. DOI: 10.1080/00131857.2023.2213437

Radvila, V., Bredelytė, A., & Lekutienė, K. (2025). Empowering STEAM educators through AI: A conceptual framework for adaptive, inclusive professional development. *Social Welfare: Interdisciplinary Approach, 15*, 160–174. DOI: 10.15388/SW.2025.15.9

Schiff, D. (2022). Education for AI, not AI for education: The role of education and ethics in national AI policy strategies. *International Journal of Artificial Intelligence in Education, 32*(3), 527–563. DOI: 10.1007/s40593-021-00270-2

Shernoff, D. J. (2024). Computer science, artificial intelligence (ai), and machine learning in STEM/STEAM education. In *Integrative STEM and STEAM Education for Real-Life Learning* (pp. 197–222). Springer International Publishing. DOI: 10.1007/978-3-031-69824-8_9

Spyropoulou, N., & Kameas, A. (2025). AI and the future of teaching in STEAM: Competences, challenges, and opportunities. INTED2025 Proceedings, 4421-4427.

Tınmaz, H. (2025). From Transparency to Trust: A Literature Review on Explainable AI in Educational Systems. *Mersin Üniversitesi Eğitim Fakültesi Dergisi, 21*(3), 999–1018. DOI: 10.17860/mersinefd.1739347

Tolman, A. O., & Kremling, J. (Eds.). (2023). *Why students resist learning: A practical model for understanding and helping students.* Taylor & Francis.

Tretow-Fish, T. A. B., & Khalid, M. S. (2023). Methods for Evaluating Learning Analytics and Learning Analytics Dashboards in Adaptive Learning Platforms: A Systematic Review. *Electronic Journal of e-Learning*, *21*(5), 430–449. DOI: 10.34190/ejel.21.5.3088

Tursunalieva, A., Alexander, D. L., Dunne, R., Li, J., Riera, L., & Zhao, Y. (2024). Making sense of machine learning: A review of interpretation techniques and their applications. *Applied Sciences (Basel, Switzerland)*, *14*(2), 496. DOI: 10.3390/app14020496

Watkins, J. (2023). "That is Still STEM": Appropriating the Engineering Design Process to Challenge Dominant Narratives of Engineering and STEM. *Cognition and Instruction*, *41*(4), 405–435. DOI: 10.1080/07370008.2022.2156512

Yılmaz, O. I. (2025). AI, ethical stress, and emotional labor in educational leadership: Toward a human-centered framework. The New DNA of Education: Innovation, Technology, Equity, and the Cognitive Turn, 77.

Chapter 3
Trust, Transparency, and Accountability in AI-Driven STEAM Learning Systems

Mustafa Kayyali
http://orcid.org/0000-0003-3300-262X
Maaref University of Applied Sciences, Syria

ABSTRACT

As AI-driven systems become increasingly embedded in STEAM education, questions of trust, transparency, and accountability can no longer remain secondary concerns. This chapter examines how intelligent learning systems shape personalization, assessment, feedback, and learner decision-making, while also raising difficult ethical questions about visibility, fairness, responsibility, and human agency. It argues that trust in AI-supported STEAM environments should not be treated as blind confidence in technological efficiency, but as a carefully built relationship grounded in explainability, evidence, dialogue, and institutional responsibility. The chapter explores the need for transparent algorithmic processes, meaningful teacher oversight, student awareness, and clear accountability structures that identify who is responsible when AI systems influence learning outcomes. Ultimately, it proposes a human-centered approach in which AI supports creativity, inquiry, and equity without weakening the moral and pedagogical role of educators.

DOI: 10.4018/979-8-3373-9675-0.ch003

INTRODUCTION

The expansion of artificial intelligence into STEAM learning systems has changed the educational conversation in ways that are both exciting and deeply unsettling. For years, educational technology was often discussed through the language of access, efficiency, engagement, and innovation. Digital platforms promised wider participation, faster feedback, richer simulations, and more flexible learning pathways. Yet AI-driven learning systems introduce something more complex than ordinary technological support. They do not merely deliver content or store grades. They observe learners, interpret patterns, recommend next steps, generate feedback, predict performance, and sometimes quietly shape what students are encouraged to attempt, avoid, repeat, or believe about their own abilities. In STEAM education, where scientific reasoning, creative experimentation, design thinking, mathematical modeling, and technological fluency are closely interwoven, such systems can become powerful companions (KANAROS, 2025). But power in education is never neutral. It always asks to be examined.

Trust, transparency, and accountability therefore stand at the heart of any serious discussion of AI-driven STEAM learning (Spyropoulou & Kameas, 2025). Trust is often treated as a soft value, something desirable but secondary to measurable performance. In reality, it is one of the conditions that makes meaningful learning possible. Students need to trust that a system's guidance is not arbitrary, biased, manipulative, or reductive. Teachers need to trust that AI tools will support rather than undermine their professional judgment. Institutions need to trust that the technologies they adopt will serve educational purposes rather than merely produce attractive dashboards or marketable claims of innovation. Yet trust cannot be demanded simply because a system is advanced, expensive, or statistically impressive. Trust must be earned, and in educational settings it must be earned repeatedly through fairness, openness, reliability, and respect for human dignity.

This is especially important in STEAM learning because the field itself depends on inquiry, uncertainty, exploration, and revision. A student working through a physics simulation, designing a prototype, interpreting environmental data, composing a digital artwork, or solving a mathematical problem is not simply moving toward a correct answer. The student is learning how to think, how to test assumptions, how to tolerate ambiguity, and how to make sense of failure. If AI systems personalize learning too aggressively, they may narrow rather than widen intellectual experience. If they classify learners too early, they may turn temporary struggle into a fixed identity. If they recommend tasks without explaining why, they may create an invisible curriculum, one in which students follow machine-generated pathways without understanding the logic behind them. Such systems may appear efficient, but efficiency alone is a thin educational virtue.

Transparency is therefore not a technical luxury; it is a pedagogical necessity (Winkelmes, 2023). Explainable AI matters because learners and educators need to understand, at least in meaningful terms, how educational decisions are being made. This does not mean that every student must understand the mathematical structure of a machine learning model. Nor does it mean that all algorithmic processes can be made perfectly simple. Rather, transparency requires that AI systems provide intelligible reasons for their recommendations, assessments, classifications, and interventions. Why was a learner given this task? Why did the system identify this misconception? Why was this feedback generated? Why was one form of evidence weighted more heavily than another? Without such explanations, AI-driven education risks becoming a polished form of opacity, where decisions appear authoritative precisely because their inner logic remains hidden.

Accountability adds another layer of urgency. When an AI system misjudges a student's ability, reinforces bias, produces misleading feedback, or shapes assessment outcomes unfairly, who is responsible? The software developer? The institution that purchased the system? The teacher who used it? The administrator who mandated it? The data scientists who trained the model? Accountability cannot be scattered so widely that it disappears. In STEAM education, where AI may influence assessment, progression, confidence, and future academic choices, responsibility must be clearly distributed and actively maintained (Spyropoulou & Kameas, 2025). A human-centered AI learning ecosystem cannot allow machines to make consequential educational judgments while humans retreat behind technical complexity.

This chapter examines trust, transparency, and accountability as interconnected foundations for ethical AI-driven STEAM learning systems. It argues that explainability should not be understood only as a computational feature, but as an educational relationship. A system becomes explainable not merely when it produces a reason, but when that reason can be interpreted, questioned, challenged, and used by teachers and learners to support growth. Similarly, accountability should not be reduced to compliance documents or institutional policy statements. It must be lived through design choices, classroom practices, data governance, assessment protocols, and the everyday willingness to ask whether AI is strengthening or weakening the human purposes of education.

The central concern of this chapter is not whether AI belongs in STEAM education. That question has already become too narrow. AI is entering classrooms, laboratories, assessment platforms, tutoring systems, and creative learning environments with increasing speed. The more important question is what kind of presence it will have. Will it deepen inquiry or flatten it? Will it make learning more equitable or quietly reproduce old hierarchies through new technical language? Will it help teachers see students more clearly, or will it replace rich human understanding with predictive labels? Will it encourage learners to become more reflective, creative, and capable, or more dependent on automated guidance?

These questions do not invite simple answers. They require a careful balance between technological possibility and moral restraint. AI-driven STEAM learning systems may indeed support more responsive instruction, timely feedback, adaptive assessment, and personalized exploration (Otaru, 2025). But these benefits become educationally meaningful only when they are anchored in trust that is justified, transparency that is usable, and accountability that has real force. Without these foundations, AI risks becoming another layer of authority in education—impressive, efficient, and strangely unanswerable. With them, it may become something more valuable: a tool that supports human curiosity without taking possession of it.

RETHINKING TRUST IN AI-DRIVEN STEAM LEARNING ENVIRONMENTS

Trust in AI-driven STEAM learning environments cannot be understood as a simple matter of whether students and teachers "accept" technology. That would be far too thin, almost careless. Trust is not the same as convenience, nor is it the same as enthusiasm. A student may use an AI tutor every evening and still feel vaguely watched by it. A teacher may rely on an adaptive assessment dashboard and still wonder, quietly, whether the system has misunderstood the learner behind the numbers. An institution may invest heavily in intelligent learning platforms and still lack a serious answer to a basic question: why should anyone believe that these systems are educationally trustworthy?

This question matters because AI is no longer sitting at the edge of the classroom as a supplementary device. It is entering the interior of learning (Quevedo Piratova et al, 2025). It recommends pathways, diagnoses misconceptions, generates practice tasks, predicts risk, produces feedback, and sometimes organizes students into categories that may follow them across courses, semesters, or even institutional records. In STEAM education, this influence becomes especially sensitive. Science, technology, engineering, arts, and mathematics are fields built around experimentation, error, interpretation, design, imagination, and disciplined uncertainty. Students do not simply receive knowledge in such spaces; they test, revise, construct, dismantle, visualize, misread, recover, and try again. The process is rarely tidy. It has hesitations in it. It has wrong turns. It has moments where confusion is not failure but the beginning of insight. A trustworthy AI system must understand this educational messiness, or at least be designed humbly enough not to pretend that every pause, mistake, or unconventional answer can be reduced to a clean data signal.

The problem is that many AI-driven learning systems arrive wrapped in a language of confidence (Tariq, 2024). They speak in predictions, scores, levels, recommendations, alerts, and performance bands. Their interfaces often appear calm and authoritative, as though uncertainty has been processed out of existence. Yet underneath this polished surface are models trained on particular datasets, shaped by particular design assumptions, and optimized for particular outcomes. None of this is inherently wrong. All educational tools contain assumptions. A textbook has a worldview. A rubric carries values. A laboratory manual decides what counts as evidence. The difference is that AI systems often conceal their assumptions behind computational sophistication. They can make judgments feel objective even when those judgments are partial, probabilistic, or contextually fragile.

This is where trust becomes complicated. Trust in AI-supported STEAM education should not mean blind reliance on machine-generated outputs (Vasconcelos et al, 2025). It should mean justified confidence, built through transparency, reliability, contestability, and ethical care. A student should be able to understand why an AI system recommends a certain activity or identifies a particular weakness. A teacher should be able to inspect the basis of an automated judgment rather than simply receive it as a finished truth. Administrators should not treat platform analytics as neutral mirrors of institutional reality. They are not mirrors. They are constructed interpretations, sometimes useful, sometimes distorted, sometimes dangerously persuasive.

There is also a quiet emotional dimension here that academic discussions sometimes flatten. Students form relationships with learning technologies, even when those relationships are not personal in the ordinary sense. When an AI tool repeatedly tells a learner that they are "below expected performance," "not ready," or "at risk," the learner may begin to internalize that language. In a mathematics course, for example, a recommendation engine might keep routing a student toward remedial exercises because of earlier mistakes. Technically, the system may be responding to data. Pedagogically, however, it may be narrowing the learner's horizon. The student begins to inhabit a small room built from previous errors. Trust, then, is not only about accuracy. It is about whether the system preserves the learner's sense of possibility.

In STEAM contexts, this point becomes even sharper because creativity and competence often emerge unevenly. A learner may struggle with symbolic notation but excel in spatial reasoning. Another may perform poorly on timed quizzes yet produce astonishing design solutions when given time to prototype. A third may use unconventional reasoning that does not match the expected pathway but still reveals deep conceptual movement. If AI systems are trained to recognize only standardized traces of learning, they may misread difference as deficiency. They may reward compliance with predictable patterns while failing to notice originality, persistence, aesthetic judgment, or collaborative intelligence. A system that cannot see the richness of learning should not be allowed to define the learner too confidently.

Rethinking trust therefore requires moving away from the idea that AI systems become trustworthy merely by becoming more accurate (Reinhardt, 2023). Accuracy is important, of course. No one wants a careless recommendation engine or a feedback tool that hallucinates explanations in physics, chemistry, coding, or mathematical reasoning. But accuracy alone is not enough. A system can be accurate on average and still harmful in specific cases. It can perform well across a population while disadvantaging a subgroup. It can predict likely outcomes while reinforcing the very conditions that make those outcomes likely. It can identify patterns without understanding the lived circumstances behind them. Educational trust has to be more demanding than statistical performance.

A more mature conception of trust would include at least three layers. The first is technical reliability: does the system function consistently, protect data, avoid obvious errors, and provide outputs that are pedagogically sound? The second is interpretive openness: can teachers and learners understand the reasoning behind its recommendations in usable, meaningful language? The third is moral accountability: are there clear human responsibilities when the system causes confusion, misclassification, unfair treatment, or inappropriate intervention? Without the third layer, the first two become brittle. A technically reliable system that no one is responsible for is not trustworthy. It is merely efficient.

Teachers occupy a crucial place in this trust ecology. Too often, AI in education is framed as though trust must be established between the learner and the system alone (Omirali et al, 2025). That is misleading. Teachers mediate trust. They contextualize automated feedback, challenge algorithmic interpretations, notice the student who is more than the dashboard suggests, and translate data into humane pedagogical action. When AI tools bypass teachers or reduce them to supervisors of machine-generated pathways, the trust structure becomes unstable. Students may begin to see the system as the real authority and the teacher as a secondary figure. Or teachers may feel pressured to accept AI recommendations even when their professional intuition raises doubts. Neither scenario serves education well.

For this reason, trustworthy AI-driven STEAM environments should be designed around teacher agency, not teacher replacement (Huang et al, 2025). The teacher should be able to ask: Why did the system recommend this intervention? What evidence supports this classification? Is there uncertainty in the model's judgment? Are there alternative explanations for the student's performance? Can this recommendation be adjusted, rejected, or supplemented? These questions are not signs of resistance to innovation. They are signs of professional responsibility. A classroom where AI cannot be questioned is not technologically advanced; it is pedagogically impoverished.

Trust also depends on the way institutions communicate with students. Learners should know when AI is being used, what kinds of data are collected, how those data influence recommendations or assessments, and whether they can challenge automated decisions. Too often, educational data practices are buried inside policy documents that no student reads and few teachers can explain. This creates a strange moral imbalance: students produce the data, systems interpret it, institutions act on it, yet the learner remains only partially informed. In a genuinely trustworthy STEAM environment, data transparency should not be treated as a legal ritual (Esteves et al, 2022). It should be part of digital and scientific literacy. Students learning with AI should also learn about AI: its strengths, limits, biases, uncertainties, and social consequences.

There is an irony here. STEAM education often aims to cultivate critical thinkers who can examine evidence, question assumptions, and design responsible technologies (Leavy et al, 2023). Yet if students are placed inside AI-mediated learning systems that they are not allowed or equipped to question, the educational message becomes contradictory. We tell students to think critically, then surround them with systems whose judgments appear beyond critique. We invite them to become designers, scientists, engineers, artists, and mathematicians, but we hide from them the design logic of the tools shaping their own learning. That contradiction should make educators uncomfortable. Productively uncomfortable.

Trustworthy AI in STEAM learning must therefore be relational rather than merely functional. It is built among students, teachers, designers, institutions, and communities. It grows when systems are explainable without being simplistic, adaptive without being controlling, data-informed without being data-obsessed, and powerful without becoming unanswerable. It also requires room for doubt. This may sound counterintuitive, but doubt is part of healthy trust. A system that permits questioning can be trusted more than one that demands obedience. A platform that admits uncertainty is more educationally honest than one that performs false certainty. A recommendation that says, in effect, "this may help, but here is why and here is where it might be wrong," respects the learner more than a silent algorithmic command.

Rethinking trust, then, means resisting both naïve optimism and reflexive rejection. AI-driven STEAM learning systems can support remarkable forms of personalization, simulation, feedback, and creative exploration (Le & Taherdoost, 2025). They can help learners encounter concepts through multiple representations, assist teachers in noticing patterns that might otherwise remain hidden, and expand access to forms of guided practice once available only through intensive human tutoring. These possibilities are real. Yet they become educationally defensible only when trust is earned through openness, care, and shared responsibility.

The deepest question is not whether AI can be trusted in education. That question is too broad, too blunt. The better question is: under what conditions does trust become reasonable? The answer lies not in the machine alone, but in the surrounding human architecture. Trustworthy AI requires thoughtful design, visible reasoning, teacher authority, learner voice, institutional honesty, and mechanisms for redress when things go wrong. It requires educators to remember that learning is not simply a sequence of optimized tasks. It is a fragile, living process through which people come to understand the world and themselves a little differently. Any AI system invited into that process must be held to a standard higher than usefulness. It must be worthy of the educational trust it seeks.

TRANSPARENCY AS A PEDAGOGICAL AND ETHICAL REQUIREMENT

Transparency in AI-driven STEAM learning systems is often discussed as though it were a technical feature, something that can be added through a dashboard, a model card, a privacy notice, or a small explanatory sentence beneath an automated recommendation (Tınmaz, 2025). That view is far too modest. In education, transparency is not merely about making a system visible; it is about making its influence understandable, contestable, and pedagogically meaningful. A learning system may display abundant information and still remain opaque. It may produce charts, predictions, skill maps, confidence scores, and behavioral analytics, yet leave teachers and students unsure about the deeper logic through which these outputs were produced. Visibility is not the same as clarity. Information is not the same as understanding.

This distinction matters because AI systems in STEAM education do not simply support learning from the outside. They can enter the very machinery of pedagogical judgment. They may recommend that a student revisit algebraic reasoning before attempting a physics simulation. They may generate feedback on a coding task, identify a misconception in a chemistry problem, assess the originality of a design prototype, or suggest that a learner is at risk of falling behind in a mathematics sequence. These judgments may appear helpful, and often they are. Yet the moment such systems influence what students are asked to do, how they are evaluated, or how teachers interpret their progress, transparency becomes an ethical necessity rather than a decorative ideal.

At the heart of this issue is a deceptively simple question: why did the system decide this? In a traditional classroom, a teacher's judgment can usually be questioned, clarified, or discussed. A student may ask why a solution was marked incomplete (Vonen, 2024). A teacher may explain that the reasoning was sound but the evidence was insufficient, or that the final answer was correct but the method revealed a conceptual gap. This exchange is not just administrative. It is pedagogical. It helps the learner understand the standards of the discipline, the nature of evidence, and the difference between error and misunderstanding. When AI systems make or support similar judgments without explanation, a vital educational conversation is interrupted.

STEAM learning is particularly vulnerable to this interruption because it depends so heavily on process (Belbase et al, 2022). The work of a learner in science, technology, engineering, arts, and mathematics is rarely reducible to a final output. A mathematical proof matters not only because of its conclusion, but because of the reasoning that carries the learner there. An engineering design matters not only because it functions, but because the constraints, trade-offs, failures, and revisions reveal the student's developing judgment. A digital artwork or creative coding project may contain aesthetic decisions that are difficult to measure but central to the learning experience. If an AI system evaluates such work through hidden criteria, students may receive a grade, score, or recommendation without understanding what kind of thinking has been recognized—or ignored.

This is where transparency becomes deeply pedagogical. Explanation helps learners learn from the system rather than merely comply with it. A recommendation that says "practice more geometry" is thin. A recommendation that says "your recent work shows difficulty connecting angle relationships to spatial transformations, especially when diagrams are rotated" is far more useful. It gives the student something to think with. It allows the teacher to intervene intelligently. It transforms a machine-generated output into a possible site of learning. The explanation may still be imperfect, but it opens a door. Silence closes one.

Yet transparency should not be confused with overwhelming disclosure. There is a certain kind of false transparency that buries users under technical language, statistical documentation, or legalistic data policies. It technically reveals information while practically hiding meaning. Most students do not need to know every parameter of a model, and most teachers do not need to inspect the full computational architecture behind an adaptive platform (Fasco, 2025). What they do need is educationally usable transparency: clear accounts of what data were used, what patterns were detected, what assumptions guided the recommendation, how confident the system is, and what human alternatives remain available. Transparency must be calibrated to the audience. Otherwise, it becomes theatre.

There is also a moral discomfort that should not be brushed aside. AI systems often learn from data produced by previous learners, past institutional practices, and existing patterns of performance. These data may carry traces of inequality: uneven access to technology, linguistic differences, disability-related accommodations, cultural variation in expression, gendered participation patterns, or prior educational disadvantage. If the system's operations remain hidden, these inherited inequalities may reappear as apparently neutral recommendations. A student from a less privileged background may be classified as lower-performing not because of limited capacity, but because the system has mistaken unfamiliarity, interrupted schooling, or linguistic difference for weakness. An opaque system can turn social history into personal diagnosis.

Transparency, then, is not only about explanation after a decision has been made (Grant et al, 2025). It also concerns the conditions under which the system was designed, trained, tested, and deployed. What educational values were built into the model? What counts as success? Speed? Accuracy? Persistence? Creativity? Collaboration? Conceptual depth? Completion rates? A system optimized for rapid correct answers may quietly penalize reflective learners who take longer but reason more carefully. A system built around standardized performance may struggle to recognize divergent thinking in arts-integrated STEAM tasks. A platform designed for large-scale efficiency may undervalue the slow, awkward, human texture of inquiry. These choices are never innocent. They decide what forms of learning become visible.

For teachers, transparency protects professional agency. When educators are asked to use AI-generated insights without being given access to the reasoning behind them, they are placed in a strangely diminished position. They become responsible for decisions they cannot fully examine. This is unfair to teachers and dangerous for students. A teacher should not have to choose between rejecting AI altogether and accepting its outputs on faith. The more reasonable position is interpretive partnership. The system provides evidence, patterns, and possible explanations; the teacher brings context, experience, ethical judgment, and knowledge of the learner as a person rather than a data profile. Transparency makes this partnership possible. Without it, AI does not assist professional judgment; it competes with it from behind a curtain.

Students, too, deserve transparency because they are not passive subjects of educational data (Heiser et al, 2026). They are participants in their own formation. When AI systems track their actions, infer their weaknesses, recommend activities, or shape their assessment pathways, students should understand the broad terms of that relationship. This is especially important in STEAM education, where learners are often being prepared to live and work in technologically dense societies. To learn through AI without learning about AI would be a missed educational opportunity, perhaps even a contradiction. Students should be encouraged to ask: What does this system know about me? What does it not know? Can it misunderstand me? Can I challenge it? What kind of evidence does it treat as important? These questions cultivate digital and ethical literacy together.

The ethical dimension becomes sharper when AI systems are used in assessment. Assessment carries consequences: grades, progression, placement, confidence, scholarships, institutional reporting, and sometimes future opportunity. If an AI-supported assessment system cannot explain how it evaluated a student's work, its authority becomes questionable. A student has a moral right to understand the basis of consequential judgment. This does not mean every assessment must be endlessly negotiable, but it does mean that automated or semi-automated judgments should be open to review. In STEAM fields, where reasoning may be exploratory and solutions may be multiple, rigid opacity can be especially harmful (Bhattacharjya, 2025). A student may arrive at an unconventional but valid solution, only to be penalized by a system that recognizes the expected route but not the intellectual merit of an alternative one.

Transparency also requires honesty about uncertainty. AI systems are frequently presented with an air of precision that does not match the probabilistic nature of their outputs. A prediction that a student has an "82% risk" of failing a module may seem mathematically authoritative, yet it is still an estimate based on selected variables, historical patterns, and model assumptions. It is not destiny. It is not prophecy. It should not be treated as a label stamped onto the learner's future. Ethical transparency would make uncertainty visible. It would show confidence levels, limitations, possible sources of error, and the need for human interpretation. Sometimes the most responsible thing a system can say is: "This pattern may indicate difficulty, but further evidence is needed." That kind of humility is not weakness. In education, it is wisdom.

A transparent AI-driven STEAM environment is not one where every mechanism is exposed in raw technical detail, nor one where every decision is slowed by explanation until learning becomes bureaucratic. It is one where the presence of AI is openly acknowledged, its reasoning is made intelligible, its limits are named, and its judgments remain available for human questioning. It is an environment where students are not quietly steered through invisible pathways, where teachers are not reduced to monitors of algorithmic output, and where institutions do not hide behind vendor complexity when difficult questions arise.

The deeper point is that transparency is a form of respect. It respects the student as a thinker capable of understanding and questioning the conditions of learning. It respects the teacher as a professional whose judgment cannot be replaced by analytics. It respects the institution's ethical duty to ensure that educational technologies serve human development rather than merely administrative efficiency. And perhaps most importantly, it respects the fragile nature of learning itself. Learning is not just movement through content. It is a gradual awakening of judgment. When AI systems enter that process, they must not operate like silent machinery beneath the floorboards. They must be visible enough, honest enough, and answerable enough to belong in the educational space they help shape.

EXPLAINABLE AI AND THE VISIBILITY OF LEARNING DECISIONS

Explainable AI enters the discussion of STEAM learning at a very sensitive point: the point where educational decisions begin to move out of human conversation and into computational inference (Le & Taherdoost, 2025). This does not mean that teachers disappear, nor that institutions simply hand the classroom over to machines. The shift is usually subtler than that. An AI system suggests the next activity. A dashboard identifies a learner as struggling. A feedback engine highlights a misconception. A platform predicts that a student may not succeed in a coming assessment. A generative tool proposes a revision pathway, a project idea, a coding correction, or a mathematical explanation. Each of these moments may appear small, even helpful. Yet together they form a new layer of decision-making inside education, a layer that is often powerful precisely because it works quietly.

The visibility of these decisions matters. In a meaningful learning environment, decisions should not fall from above like sealed verdicts. They should be open to interpretation, discussion, revision, and sometimes refusal. This is not only an ethical demand; it is also a pedagogical one. Students learn not simply by receiving outcomes, but by understanding the reasons behind them. A learner who is told that an answer is weak may feel corrected. A learner who understands why the answer is weak can begin to think differently. That difference is enormous. It is the difference between compliance and growth.

In STEAM education, where learning is often experimental, iterative, and uncertain, explainability becomes even more necessary (Saseendran & Thomas, 2025). A student solving an engineering problem may choose an inefficient but inventive design path. Another student working with data may reach a strange conclusion that is not entirely wrong, only insufficiently tested. A student in an arts-integrated coding project may bend the expected rules of form, pattern, or interaction to produce something original. If an AI system reduces such work to a score or classification without explaining what it has recognized, what it has ignored, and where it may be uncertain, then the system does not merely assess learning. It shapes what counts as learning.

This is the quiet danger of invisible learning decisions. They do not always announce themselves as control. They may look like support. They may appear as personalization, guidance, prediction, or efficiency. Yet a system that recommends easier tasks to one learner and more advanced tasks to another is already making a judgment about possibility. A system that repeatedly identifies a student as "at risk" is not only describing performance; it may influence how the student is seen by teachers and how the student comes to see himself or herself. A system that generates feedback in confident language may encourage students to accept its interpretation as final, even when the feedback is partial, poorly contextualized, or blind to the learner's intention. When the logic behind these decisions remains hidden, education becomes less dialogic and more procedural. Something human is thinned out.

Explainable AI should therefore be understood as more than a technical solution to a technical problem (Dwivedi et al, 2023). It is not enough for a system to provide a decorative explanation, a small note attached to an output, or a vague statement such as "based on your previous performance." Such explanations are often too shallow to be useful. They give the appearance of openness without offering real insight. A meaningful explanation should help the learner and teacher understand the relationship between evidence and decision. What data did the system use? Which patterns mattered most? What assumptions shaped the recommendation? Was the decision based on accuracy, speed, persistence, comparison with peers, previous attempts, or some combination of these? Is the system confident, or is it guessing with polished language?

These questions are not minor. They determine whether AI becomes a partner in learning or an obscure authority. A visible learning decision invites the student into reflection. An invisible one asks for obedience. This distinction carries particular weight in STEAM because the disciplines themselves value explanation. Science asks for evidence. Mathematics asks for reasoning. Engineering asks for justification of design choices. The arts ask for interpretive awareness and expressive intention. Technology asks us to understand systems, not merely use them. It would be odd, almost contradictory, to teach students the importance of explanation while relying on educational technologies that cannot explain themselves in educationally meaningful ways.

The best forms of explainable AI in STEAM learning would not simply tell students what to do next (Shernoff, 2024). They would show why a next step might matter. For instance, an AI tutor in physics might not merely say, "Review Newton's second law." It might explain that the student's recent answers suggest confusion between force and velocity, especially in problems involving changing direction. A mathematics platform might not simply mark a solution wrong, but identify that the learner applied a correct procedure in the wrong conceptual setting. A design-based learning system might recognize that a prototype failed not because the idea lacked merit, but because the testing conditions were too narrow. In these cases, explanation becomes a bridge. It connects performance to understanding.

Yet there is a risk of overconfidence here. Explainability can itself become a kind of illusion if the explanation sounds plausible but does not faithfully represent the system's actual reasoning. This is especially relevant with generative AI, where explanations may be fluent, persuasive, and neatly packaged, while still being incomplete or even fabricated. A machine-generated explanation may feel human enough to earn trust too quickly. That is a peculiar danger: not opacity, but false clarity. The learner receives an explanation that satisfies the ear but fails the discipline. For this reason, explainable AI in education must be evaluated not only by whether it explains, but by whether its explanations are accurate, appropriately cautious, and pedagogically useful.

Teacher mediation is crucial here. Explanations should not be designed only for individual learners interacting privately with a platform. They should also support teachers as interpreters of learning. A teacher needs to see whether the AI's diagnosis aligns with classroom evidence, student behavior, prior knowledge, language background, emotional state, and the broader arc of learning. A system may detect repeated mistakes in a coding exercise, but the teacher may know that the student is experimenting deliberately with syntax to understand how errors behave. A system may classify a student's design reflection as vague, while the teacher recognizes an early but promising form of creative reasoning. Explainability strengthens education when it gives teachers something to examine, not when it pressures them to surrender judgment.

There is also a democratic aspect to the visibility of learning decisions. Students should not be treated as silent data sources whose learning pathways are organized by systems they cannot question (Svensson & Warne, 2024). Particularly in STEAM education, where students are being prepared for participation in technological societies, they should have opportunities to understand how algorithmic decisions are made and how such decisions can shape human experience. An explainable AI learning environment can become a site of meta-learning: students learn the subject matter, but they also learn how intelligent systems interpret behavior, classify performance, and generate recommendations. This kind of awareness is no longer optional. It is part of contemporary literacy.

The visibility of learning decisions also helps resist bias. When an AI system's outputs are hidden or unexplained, unfair patterns may remain buried. Certain learners may be repeatedly routed toward remedial content. Others may be rewarded because their ways of writing, reasoning, speaking, or problem-solving resemble the patterns most familiar to the system. Students with disabilities, multilingual learners, and those from underrepresented communities may be misunderstood by systems trained on narrow or historically uneven datasets (Cuba et al, 2026). Explainability does not automatically eliminate bias, but it gives educators and institutions a better chance of noticing it. A visible decision can be questioned. An invisible one quietly becomes normal.

Still, explainability must be handled carefully. Not every explanation should be long. Not every learner needs the same level of detail. A young student, an undergraduate engineering major, a teacher, an administrator, and a system auditor each require different kinds of visibility. The challenge is not to expose everything at once, but to provide layered explanations. A student may need a clear pedagogical reason. A teacher may need evidence patterns and alternative interpretations. An institution may need fairness audits and documentation of model behavior. Regulators may need information about data governance, testing, and accountability structures. Good explainability is not one-size-fits-all. It is responsive to role, context, and consequence.

The deepest purpose of explainable AI in STEAM learning is not simply to make machines more acceptable (Love et al, 2023). That would be a poor ambition. Its real purpose is to preserve the intelligibility of education itself. Learning decisions should remain visible because education is a moral and intellectual relationship, not merely a logistical process. When a student is guided, assessed, corrected, encouraged, or redirected, there should be reasons that can be spoken, examined, and challenged. A system that cannot offer such reasons may still be useful in limited ways, but it should not be granted deep authority over learning.

AI-driven STEAM systems will continue to grow more capable. They will generate richer simulations, more personalized tasks, more detailed feedback, and more predictive analytics. Some of this will be genuinely valuable. But capability without visibility is not enough. The educational worth of these systems will depend on whether their decisions can enter human understanding. Not perfectly. Not always completely. But sufficiently, honestly, and with humility. Explainable AI, at its best, does not remove uncertainty from learning. It makes uncertainty discussable. And that may be one of its most important contributions: it keeps the learner, the teacher, and the system inside a shared space of reason, rather than allowing education to drift into silent automation.

TOWARD RESPONSIBLE, HUMAN-CENTERED STEAM PERSONALIZATION AND ASSESSMENT

Responsible personalization in STEAM education begins with a simple but easily neglected truth: learners are not patterns waiting to be optimized (Kayyali, 2025). They are not merely profiles, clusters, probabilities, or sequences of measurable behavior. They are developing persons, carrying uneven histories of confidence, curiosity, anxiety, language, prior schooling, imagination, and sometimes quiet resistance. AI-driven personalization becomes educationally meaningful only when it recognizes this human thickness. Otherwise, it risks becoming a refined mechanism for sorting students into pathways that look adaptive on screen but feel strangely narrow in practice.

The promise, of course, is not trivial. AI can support forms of personalization that teachers have long desired but could rarely sustain at scale (Dembe, 2024). It can notice recurring errors in mathematical reasoning, generate alternative explanations for a difficult scientific concept, recommend coding exercises based on prior attempts, adapt the complexity of engineering challenges, or provide immediate feedback on a design reflection. In arts-integrated STEAM work, it may help students explore multiple representations, test creative variations, or connect technical decisions with expressive outcomes. Used carefully, such systems can make learning more responsive. They can give students another route into understanding when the first route fails. They can help teachers see patterns that might otherwise remain buried under the ordinary pressure of crowded classrooms and limited time.

Yet personalization has a shadow. When AI systems personalize learning too confidently, they may begin to define the learner rather than support the learner. A student who struggles early with algebra may be repeatedly redirected toward remedial tasks, not because the learner lacks potential, but because the system has learned to protect its prediction (Schwartz, 2025). A learner who writes slowly may be interpreted as disengaged. A student who experiments with unconventional design logic may be marked as inefficient. In such cases, personalization stops being liberating and becomes a soft enclosure. It does not punish loudly. It simply keeps offering the learner a smaller world.

This is why human-centered personalization must be built around possibility, not merely performance. It should ask not only, "What does the learner currently show?" but also, "What might the learner become with different forms of support, challenge, time, and recognition?" STEAM learning depends on this openness. A young scientist may need space to ask an awkward question before arriving at disciplined inquiry. An emerging engineer may learn through failed prototypes that look messy but contain the beginnings of design judgment. A student working in digital art may appear to deviate from instructions while actually discovering a more complex relation between form and function. If personalization is too tightly bound to efficiency, it may tidy away the very experiences through which deep learning grows.

Assessment raises an even sharper set of concerns. AI-supported assessment can offer valuable advantages: faster feedback, richer diagnostic information, adaptive testing, automated analysis of student work, and evidence collected across multiple learning moments rather than a single high-pressure exam. In STEAM fields, where learning often involves process, experimentation, collaboration, and iteration, such tools may help move assessment beyond the rigid final answer (Subramanian et al, 2025). They may capture patterns of revision, persistence, conceptual change, and problem-solving strategy. That is a serious gain. Traditional assessment has often been too blunt to recognize the full intelligence of STEAM learning.

Still, assessment is never just measurement. It is judgment with consequences. It tells students what matters. It shapes teaching priorities. It rewards some forms of thinking and neglects others. It can strengthen confidence or quietly damage it. When

AI enters assessment, the ethical stakes rise because automated systems can make judgments quickly, repeatedly, and at scale. A flawed teacher judgment may affect one moment; a flawed model may reproduce the same misreading across hundreds or thousands of learners before anyone notices. Speed magnifies responsibility.

A responsible model of AI-supported STEAM assessment should therefore be cautious about high-stakes automation. AI can assist assessment, but it should not become an unchallengeable examiner. Its role should be diagnostic, formative, and dialogic wherever possible. Instead of simply assigning a score, the system should help illuminate the learner's reasoning: where a misconception may have emerged, which evidence suggests conceptual growth, what alternative explanation might help, where uncertainty remains. The best assessment does not close the learner down. It opens the next question.

This is especially important in STEAM because evidence of learning is often diverse (Hughes et al, 2022). A student may demonstrate understanding through a written explanation, a simulation, a diagram, a prototype, a performance, a code fragment, a collaborative design discussion, or an iterative portfolio. AI systems that rely only on easily quantifiable traces risk flattening this diversity. Clicks, completion rates, time spent, number of attempts, and answer accuracy may reveal something, but they do not reveal everything. They may miss imagination, frustration, peer learning, ethical reasoning, aesthetic judgment, and the slow internal reorganization that often precedes visible success. Human-centered assessment must resist the temptation to treat what is measurable as what is most meaningful.

The teacher's role becomes central here. In responsible personalization and assessment, teachers are not displaced by AI; they become interpreters, moderators, and ethical guardians of AI-supported evidence. A dashboard may show that a learner is falling behind, but the teacher may know that the student recently changed schools, is working through language barriers, or is intimidated by the platform interface. A system may detect weakness in scientific explanation, but the teacher may recognize that the learner has strong practical understanding and needs support in academic expression. A tool may recommend a lower-level pathway, while the teacher decides that the learner needs challenge, not simplification. These professional judgments are not sentimental additions to data. They are part of what makes education educational.

Students should also be given a stronger voice in personalized AI learning. Too often, personalization is something done to learners rather than with them (Amato et al, 2023). A human-centered approach would allow students to understand, question, and sometimes negotiate their learning pathways. Why has this activity been recommended? What evidence shaped this feedback? Can the learner choose a different route? Can the system explain its uncertainty? Can students set goals that reflect personal interests as well as institutional outcomes? Such questions matter because agency is not a luxury in STEAM education. It is part of the learning itself. Students who are always guided may become efficient followers, but STEAM needs more than that. It needs thinkers who can decide, test, revise, and defend their choices.

Responsible personalization must also be attentive to equity. AI systems may unintentionally reproduce existing inequalities if they are trained on narrow data, designed around dominant cultural assumptions, or evaluated mainly through standardized forms of performance. Learners with disabilities, multilingual students, economically disadvantaged students, and those from underrepresented communities may interact with STEAM tasks in ways that do not fit the system's expected patterns (Otaru, 2025). If the system treats difference as deficiency, personalization becomes another mechanism of exclusion. Equity requires more than equal access to the platform. It requires careful auditing, inclusive design, accessibility, contextual interpretation, and the courage to ask whether the system works differently for different groups.

The most defensible vision is not anti-AI. That would be too easy, and perhaps too nostalgic. AI has real potential to enrich STEAM personalization and assessment when used with restraint and imagination (Ngoc, 2025). It can help teachers manage complexity. It can offer learners timely support. It can create adaptive spaces where students move through concepts at different rhythms. It can make feedback more immediate and, at times, more precise. But these benefits should never be purchased at the cost of learner dignity, professional judgment, or educational breadth.

A human-centered STEAM ecosystem would treat AI as a participant in a wider pedagogical relationship, not as the hidden manager of learning (Torres-Rivera et al, 2025). Personalization would remain flexible, porous, and revisable. Assessment would remain explainable, contestable, and rooted in multiple forms of evidence. Teachers would retain authority to interpret and override. Students would understand how systems shape their pathways. Institutions would audit not only technical performance but also educational consequences. Designers would build tools that admit uncertainty rather than pretending to possess final knowledge of the learner.

The guiding principle is almost modest: AI should help education become more attentive, not more controlling. It should widen the learner's horizon rather than confine it to predictions. It should support assessment that listens more carefully to the complexity of learning. It should make STEAM education more humane, not merely more efficient. Personalization, at its best, is not the art of fitting students into algorithmic pathways. It is the careful work of helping each learner encounter knowledge, difficulty, creativity, and self-understanding in ways that remain open to growth. That openness is where responsible AI must begin—and where it must remain accountable.

CONCLUSION

The future of AI-driven STEAM learning systems will not be determined by technical sophistication alone. It will be shaped by the ethical imagination of those who design, adopt, regulate, teach with, and learn through these systems. This chapter has argued that trust, transparency, and accountability are not decorative principles to be added after innovation has already taken place. They are structural conditions for responsible educational transformation. Without them, even the most advanced AI learning platform may become pedagogically fragile, ethically uncertain, and institutionally dangerous. With them, AI can support forms of learning that are more responsive, more reflective, and more attentive to the complexity of human development.

Trust remains perhaps the most delicate of these conditions. In AI-driven STEAM education, trust should never mean passive acceptance. It should not ask students or teachers to believe that a system is correct simply because it is automated, data-rich, or presented through confident language. Educational trust must be active, questioning, and evidence-based. It grows when learners understand why a recommendation has been made, when teachers can examine and override algorithmic judgments, when institutions communicate honestly about data use, and when systems demonstrate fairness across different learner groups. Trust is not built through promotional claims. It is built through repeated encounters in which the system proves itself worthy of educational responsibility.

Transparency, in this sense, becomes the practical language of trust. If AI systems influence what learners study, how they are assessed, how their progress is interpreted, or how their future pathways are imagined, then those systems must offer explanations that are accessible and meaningful. A black-box system may be technically impressive, but in education, opacity carries a special risk. It can weaken student agency, reduce teacher confidence, and make unfair decisions difficult to detect. Explainable AI must therefore move beyond surface-level justification. It should help teachers and learners ask better questions: What evidence was used? What assumptions are embedded in the model? What alternatives were considered? Where might the system be uncertain? In a healthy STEAM learning environment, explanation should invite dialogue, not close it down.

Accountability is equally essential because educational decisions have consequences that extend beyond a single lesson or assessment. A poorly designed AI system may misread creativity as confusion, interpret non-standard reasoning as weakness, or reward learners who already fit the dominant pattern of the training data. It may also encourage institutions to outsource judgment to platforms that appear objective but carry hidden assumptions. Accountability means refusing to let responsibility dissolve into the machinery. It requires clear governance, regular auditing, teacher oversight, learner rights, data protection, and institutional willingness to correct harm when it occurs. More importantly, it requires a cultural shift: educators and policymakers must stop treating AI as an external force that simply "arrives" in education. These systems are chosen, configured, funded, integrated, and normalized by people. Their effects are therefore human responsibilities.

In STEAM education, the stakes are especially high because students are not only absorbing knowledge; they are learning how to investigate, invent, model, design, test, interpret, and create. These are deeply human activities, even when they involve machines. The promise of AI lies in its ability to support such activities with adaptive resources, dynamic feedback, intelligent simulations, and personalized pathways. Yet the danger lies in allowing personalization to become quiet control. A learner who is constantly guided by algorithmic recommendations may become efficient without becoming independent. A teacher who receives predictive analytics may gain useful insight, but may also begin to see students through categories that are too narrow. A system that optimizes assessment may improve measurement, but may fail to recognize the messy, hesitant, surprising movement through which genuine understanding often emerges.

For this reason, the ethical design of AI-driven STEAM learning systems must begin with a modest but firm principle: technology should enlarge educational possibility, not compress it. It should help students encounter difficulty with support, not shield them from productive struggle. It should assist teachers in seeing patterns, not replace their interpretive wisdom. It should generate feedback that encourages reflection, not merely compliance. It should personalize learning without imprisoning learners inside predictive profiles. Above all, it should remain answerable to the human purposes of education: curiosity, understanding, creativity, justice, participation, and growth.

The chapter therefore points toward a human-centered model of AI integration in STEAM education. Such a model does not reject automation, analytics, or personalization. Instead, it places them within a wider ethical and pedagogical frame. It asks designers to build systems that explain themselves honestly. It asks institutions to adopt technologies carefully, not simply because they are fashionable or commercially persuasive. It asks teachers to remain active professionals rather than passive operators of digital platforms. It asks students to become informed participants in AI-supported learning, capable of questioning the systems that shape their educational experience. And it asks policymakers to create conditions in which innovation and responsibility are not treated as opposing forces.

In the end, the question is not whether AI can make STEAM learning more efficient. It probably can. The deeper question is whether it can help make learning more thoughtful, inclusive, transparent, and humane. That outcome is not guaranteed by algorithms. It must be designed, defended, and continuously revised. AI-driven

STEAM systems will earn their place in education only when they make their reasoning visible, their limitations acknowledged, their consequences accountable, and their benefits genuinely shared. Trust cannot be automated. Transparency cannot be symbolic. Accountability cannot be postponed. These are not barriers to innovation; they are what prevent innovation from becoming careless power.

REFERENCES

Amato, F., Galli, A., Gravina, M., Marassi, L., Marrone, S., & Sansone, C. (2023, May). AI-Powered Learning: Personalizing Education for each Student. In Ital-IA (pp. 478-483).

Belbase, S., Mainali, B. R., Kasemsukpipat, W., Tairab, H., Gochoo, M., & Jarrah, A. (2022). At the dawn of science, technology, engineering, arts, and mathematics (STEAM) education: Prospects, priorities, processes, and problems. *International Journal of Mathematical Education in Science and Technology*, *53*(11), 2919–2955. DOI: 10.1080/0020739X.2021.1922943

Bhattacharjya, M. (2025). Future-proofing education: Developing transdisciplli-nary STEAM models to prepare learners for a workforce in the forthcoming era of automation. *Transdisciplinary Journal of Engineering & Science*, *16*(6), 67–97. DOI: 10.22545/2025/00271

Cuba, M. J., Taylor, J. P., Tariq, A. R., Lee, J. Y., & Avellone, L. (2026). Disproportionate Representation of Multilingual Learners With Intellectual and Developmental Disabilities: A Systematic Literature Review. *Review of Educational Research*, •••, 00346543261426579. DOI: 10.3102/00346543261426579

Dembe, A. (2024). Advancing personalized learning through educational artificial intelligence: Challenges, opportunities, and future directions. *Res Invent J Eng Phys Sci*, *3*(1), 89–101.

Dwivedi, R., Dave, D., Naik, H., Singhal, S., Omer, R., Patel, P., Qian, B., Wen, Z., Shah, T., Morgan, G., & Ranjan, R. (2023). Explainable AI (XAI): Core ideas, techniques, and solutions. *ACM Computing Surveys*, *55*(9), 1–33. DOI: 10.1145/3561048

Esteves, B., Asgarinia, H., Penedo, A. C., Mutiro, B., & Lewis, D. (2022, December). Fostering trust with transparency in the data economy era: An integrated ethical, legal, and knowledge engineering approach. In *Proceedings of the 1st International Workshop on Data Economy* (pp. 57-63). DOI: 10.1145/3565011.3569061

Fasco, P. S. (2025). Cognitive Architecture for Adaptive Problem-Solving and Computational Models of Expert Knowledge Acquisition in Computer Science Education.

Grant, D. G., Behrends, J., & Basl, J. (2025). What we owe to decision-subjects: Beyond transparency and explanation in automated decision-making. *Philosophical Studies*, *182*(1), 55–85. DOI: 10.1007/s11098-023-02013-6

Heiser, R., Underhill, G., & Stritto, M. E. D. (2026). Power, Privacy, and Transparency in Communicating Learning Analytics in Higher Education: A Critical Discourse Analysis. *American Journal of Qualitative Research, 10*(1), 246–265. DOI: 10.29333/ajqr/17463

Huang, Q., Wang, Z., Yang, J., Wu, L., & Hung, W. L. D. (2025). The Influencing Factors of Integrating Artificial Intelligence in Teaching for STEAM Teachers in Primary and Secondary Schools: A Qualitative Study. In International Handbook of Research on STEAM Curriculum and Practice (pp. 432-449). Routledge. DOI: 10.4324/9781003435488-27

Hughes, B. S., Corrigan, M. W., Grove, D., Andersen, S. B., & Wong, J. T. (2022). Integrating arts with STEM and leading with STEAM to increase science learning with equity for emerging bilingual learners in the United States. *International Journal of STEM Education, 9*(1), 58. DOI: 10.1186/s40594-022-00375-7

KANAROS, D. (2025). STEAM Education and Technological Innovation: New Models of Creative Learning. ISPEC JOURNAL OF SCIENCE INSTITUTE, 4(2), 93-103.

Kayyali, M. (2025). The impact of personalized learning on student engagement and achievement in STEAM. In *Integrating personalized learning methods into STEAM education* (pp. 51–78). IGI Global Scientific Publishing. DOI: 10.4018/979-8-3693-7718-5.ch003

Le, N., & Taherdoost, H. (2025, February). Pervasive AI and IoT in STEAM Education: Advancing Future Learning Through Intelligent Systems and Computational Technologies. In *2025 International Conference on Pervasive Computational Technologies (ICPCT)* (pp. 736-741). IEEE. DOI: 10.1109/ICPCT64145.2025.10940569

Leavy, A., Dick, L., Meletiou-Mavrotheris, M., Paparistodemou, E., & Stylianou, E. (2023). The prevalence and use of emerging technologies in STEAM education: A systematic review of the literature. *Journal of Computer Assisted Learning, 39*(4), 1061–1082. DOI: 10.1111/jcal.12806

Love, P. E., Fang, W., Matthews, J., Porter, S., Luo, H., & Ding, L. (2023). Explainable artificial intelligence (XAI): Precepts, models, and opportunities for research in construction. *Advanced Engineering Informatics, 57*, 102024. DOI: 10.1016/j.aei.2023.102024

Ngoc, D. N. T. (2025). Artificial Intelligence Plays a Crucial Role in Integrating Personalized Learning Methods Into STEAM Education. In *Integrating Personalized Learning Methods Into STEAM Education* (pp. 189–210). IGI Global Scientific Publishing. DOI: 10.4018/979-8-3693-7718-5.ch009

Omirali, A., Kozhakhmet, K., & Zhumaliyeva, R. (2025). Digital Trust in Transition: Student Perceptions of AI-Enhanced Learning for Sustainable Educational Futures. *Sustainability (Basel)*, *17*(17), 7567. DOI: 10.3390/su17177567

Otaru, B. E. (2025). Leveraging Artificial Intelligence (AI) for personalized and inclusive STEAM education: Strategies for bridging learning gaps among diverse learners. *KONTAGORA JOURNAL OF SCIENCE AND TECHNOLOGY*, *18*(1-2), 94–99.

Quevedo Piratova, D. A., Sánchez Duarte, M. M., Chiappe, A., & Sáez Delgado, F. M. (2025). Intelligent classrooms: How Ai and Iot can reshape learning spaces. *European Journal of Education*, *60*(1), e70000. DOI: 10.1111/ejed.70000

Reinhardt, K. (2023). Trust and trustworthiness in AI ethics. *AI and Ethics*, *3*(3), 735–744. DOI: 10.1007/s43681-022-00200-5

Saseendran, A., & Thomas, M. V. (2025). Design thinking in science and integrated STEM/STEAM education: Trends, challenges, and future directions from a systematic review. *STEM Education*, *5*(6), 1058–1101. DOI: 10.3934/steme.2025046

Schwartz, R. (2025). Improving Instructional Practices in Algebra I Classrooms by Facilitating a Professional Learning Community and Providing Instructional Performance Feedback (Doctoral dissertation, Fordham University).

Shernoff, D. J. (2024). Computer science, artificial intelligence (ai), and machine learning in STEM/STEAM education. In *Integrative STEM and STEAM Education for Real-Life Learning* (pp. 197–222). Springer International Publishing. DOI: 10.1007/978-3-031-69824-8_9

Spyropoulou, N., & Kameas, A. (2025). AI and the future of teaching in STEAM: Competences, challenges, and opportunities. INTED2025 Proceedings, 4421-4427.

Subramanian, M., Portia, R., Mishra, B. R., & Selvakumar, P. PV, R., & TC, M. (2025). Assessment and evaluation in personalized STEAM education. In Integrating Personalized Learning Methods Into STEAM Education (pp. 103-122). IGI Global Scientific Publishing.

Svensson, Å., & Warne, M. (2024). Staff perspectives on poor mental health in secondary school students: An increasing problem handled with insufficient resources. *Frontiers in Public Health*, *12*, 1292520. DOI: 10.3389/fpubh.2024.1292520 PMID: 38496395

Tariq, M. U. (Ed.). (2024). *AI-driven learning and engagement in higher education*. IGI Global. DOI: 10.4018/979-8-3693-4074-5

Tınmaz, H. (2025). From Transparency to Trust: A Literature Review on Explainable AI in Educational Systems. *Mersin Üniversitesi Eğitim Fakültesi Dergisi, 21*(3), 999–1018. DOI: 10.17860/mersinefd.1739347

Torres-Rivera, A. D., Rendón Peña, A. A., Díaz-Torres, S. T., & Díaz-Torres, L. A. (2025). Ethical integration of AI and STEAM pedagogies in higher education: A sustainable learning model for society 5.0. *Sustainability (Basel), 17*(19), 8525. DOI: 10.3390/su17198525

Vasconcelos, L., de Castro Filho, J. A., Barreto, D., de Castro, J. B., de Souza, M. D. F. C., de Barros Cardoso, L. A., & Maia, D. (2025). Design guidelines for integrating artificial intelligence into preservice teacher EFL and STEAM education. *Journal of Technology and Teacher Education, 33*(4), 753–784. DOI: 10.70725/195498ziigzw

Vonen, M. N. (2024). Teachers' management of students' incorrect answers in oral examinations. *Linguistics and Education, 80*, 101266. DOI: 10.1016/j.linged.2023.101266

Winkelmes, M. A. (2023). Why it works: Understanding the concepts behind transparency in learning and teaching. Transparent design in higher education teaching and leadership, 17-35.

Chapter 4

Implementing Explainable Artificial Intelligence in STEAM Educational Tools:
A Practical and Accessible Framework for Transparent and Trustworthy Learning

Marcos Yamir Gomez Ramos
http://orcid.org/0000-0003-0797-2534
Universidad Politécnica Metropolitana de Hidalgo, Mexico

Laura Araceli Guerrero Herrera
http://orcid.org/0000-0001-5161-3075
Universidad Politécnica de Pachuca, Mexico

Jaime Aguilar-Ortiz
http://orcid.org/0009-0003-5302-1454
Universidad Politécnica de Pachuca, Mexico

ABSTRACT

While Artificial Intelligence enhances Science, Technology, Engineering, Arts and Mathematics education, reliance on complex "black-box" models undermines transparency, teacher agency, and student trust. This chapter presents a practical, accessible framework for implementing Explainable Artificial Intelligence in STEAM educational tools. Moving beyond theoretical algorithmic advancements, the approach leverages open-source platforms and low-code environments to democratize

DOI: 10.4018/979-8-3373-9675-0.ch004

AI. The text examines how embedding explainability mechanisms into learning analytics and intelligent tutors enhances pedagogical decision-making and fosters student metacognition. Additionally, the framework aligns XAI implementation with global ethical standards, including the EU AI Act and UNESCO recommendations, addressing fairness, accountability, and responsible data use. Through illustrative real-world use cases, this work bridges the gap between machine learning research and educational practice, positioning XAI as a foundational enabler of trustworthy, transparent, and human-centered learning ecosystems.

1. INTRODUCTION

The integration of Artificial Intelligence (AI) into educational environments has accelerated significantly in recent years, particularly within Science, Technology, Engineering, Arts and Mathematics (STEAM) education. AI-powered tools such as intelligent tutoring systems, learning analytics dashboards, and adaptive learning platforms, are increasingly deployed to support instructional decision-making, personalize learning pathways and enhance student engagement. These technologies hold considerable promise for addressing long-standing challenges in education, including learner heterogeneity, scalability of instruction, and the provision of timely, meaningful and data-informed feedback. However, this rapid evolution toward data-driven pedagogy is simultaneously constrained by a critical limitation: the reliance on complex machine learning models whose internal logic remains opaque to educators and learners, giving rise to the well-documented "black box" problem (Adadi & Berrada, 2018; Barredo Arrieta *et al.*, 2020; Romero & Ventura, 2010).

While the "black box" issue is often framed as a technical limitation related to model interpretability, in the context STEAM education it represents a deeper epistemic and pedagogical challenge. Education, particularly within scientific and mathematical domains, is fundamentally grounded in the construction, justification and validation of knowledge. When AI systems recommend learning paths, evaluate student competencies, or adapt instructional content without providing a transparent rationale, they separate educational outcomes from the processes of reasoning and understanding that underpin meaningful learning (Adadi & Berrada, 2018; Barredo Arrieta *et al.*, 2020; Floridi *et al.*, 2018). Consequently, educators and learners receive decisions whose underlying logic cannot be readily examined or questioned.

As a result, the opacity of AI systems does not merely limit technical interpretability; it undermines core educational principles, including inquiry, critical thinking, and evidence-based reasoning.

From a pedagogical perspective, this lack of transparency has significant implications for both educators and learners. Teachers' professional autonomy is diminished when they are unable to understand or critically evaluate the recommendations generated by AI systems. For instance, an AI system may flag a student as "at risk" or dynamically adjusts the difficulty of a learning activity, such as prior knowledge, engagement metrics, or time-on-task, educators have limited opportunities to evaluate the recommendation critically. As a result, teachers may become passive implementers of algorithmic decisions rather than informed facilitators of learning (Barredo Arrieta *et al.*, 2020; Siemens & Baker, 2012). This limitation restricts their capacity to make context-sensitive instructional judgments and to integrate AI tools meaningfully into pedagogical practice.

For students, the consequences are equally significant. Automated feedback that lacks interpretability can hinder engagement, reduce trust and limit the development of metacognitive and self-regulatory skills. When learners cannot understand the reasoning behind system-generated feedback or recommendations, they are less able to identify gaps in their knowledge, reflect on their learning strategies, or actively participate in the learning process (Barredo Arrieta *et al.*, 2020; Gunasekara & Saarela, 2025). This not only affects learning outcomes but also challenges the development of learner agency, which is central to STEAM education.

Moreover, the opacity of AI systems raises critical ethical and institutional concerns. The absence of transparency complicates efforts to ensure fairness, accountability and responsible data use, particularly in educational contexts where decisions may have long-term consequences for students' academic trajectories. Biases embedded within data or algorithmics may remain undetected within uninterpretable models, thereby increasing the risk of discriminatory outcomes and undermining institutional compliance with emerging ethical and regulatory standards (Floridi *et al.*, 2018).

In response to these challenges, Explainable Artificial Intelligence (XAI) has emerged as a key paradigm aimed at enhancing the transparency and interpretability of AI systems. XAI encompasses a range of methods and techniques designed to make the behavior, logic and outputs of machine learning models more understandable to human users (Adadi & Berrada, 2018; Barredo Arrieta *et al.*, 2020; Doshi-Velez & Kim, 2017). Although XAI has gained significant traction in high-stakes domains such as healthcare and finance, its adoption in educational technologies remains uneven and, in many cases, largely conceptual. Existing research frequently emphasizes algorithmic explainability or theoretical frameworks. As a result, a persistent gap between technical advancements and the practical realities of implementing explainable system in every educational context.

Addressing this gap requires a shift from a purely technical perspective toward an explicitly applied and pedagogically grounded approach. Rather than conceptualizing explainability as an abstract property of machine learning models, it must be understood as a fundamental design feature of educational technologies. Effective explainability must align with pedagogical objectives, stakeholder needs, and contextual constraints throughout the educational process (Gunasekara & Saarela, 2025; Siemens & Baker, 2012). From this perspective, explainability is not an optional enhancement but a prerequisite for developing AI systems that are both usable and educationally meaningful.

Furthermore, the effective integration of XAI in education depends not only on advances in algorithmic techniques but also on the availability and adoption of accessible technologies. Open-source frameworks, low-code and no-code platforms, and lightweight machine learning tools play a critical role in enabling educational institutions, particularly those with limited resources, to design, deploy and maintain explainable AI systems. These technologies lower technical barriers and democratize access to AI development. They also enable educators, developers, and institutional stakeholders to understand, evaluate, and responsibly implement AI-supported educational tools (Gunasekara & Saarela, 2025; Siemens & Baker, 2012).

Focusing specifically on STEAM education, this chapter examines how Explainable Artificial Intelligence can be integrated into educational tools in a practical, scalable and context-sensitive manner. It explores common AI-driven applications used in STEAM environments, including adaptive learning systems, learning analytics dashboards and recommendation components. The chapter also analyzes how different forms of explanations support instructional decision-making while improving students' understanding of AI-generated feedback. Attention is given to transparency, fairness, accountability, trust, and the responsible use of AI in educational settings (Floridi *et al.*, 2018; Li *et al.*, 2024).

By emphasizing implementation strategies, design considerations and real-world applicability, this chapter contributes to the ongoing discourse on responsible AI in education from a practitioner-oriented perspective. It aims to provide educators, developers and researchers with concrete insights and actionable guidelines for embedding explainability into STEAM educational technologies using accessible tools and frameworks. Ultimately, the chapter positions Explainable Artificial Intelligence not as a supplementary technical feature, but as a foundational enabler of trustworthy, pedagogically coherent, and ethically responsible AI-supported learning environments.

Rather than providing a purely theoretical review of Explainable Artificial Intelligence, this chapter adopts an implementation-oriented perspective that integrates pedagogical, technological, and ethical considerations into a coherent framework for STEAM education. Its principal contribution is the articulation of a practical framework that combines (i) a taxonomy of explainable AI techniques applicable to educational settings, (ii) implementation strategies based on accessible technologies, (iii) stakeholder-centered design guidelines for educators, learners, and developers, and (iv) ethical considerations aligned with emerging principles of trustworthy AI.

By connecting advances in explainable machine learning with authentic educational practice, the chapter provides actionable guidance for designing, deploying, and evaluating transparent AI-supported tools that can be realistically adopted across diverse STEAM learning environments.

2. AI-BASED EDUCATIONAL TOOLS IN STEAM CONTEXTS

The adoption of Artificial Intelligence (AI) in STEAM education has led to the emergence of a wide range of digital tools designed to support teaching, learning and assessment processes. These tools aim to address practical challenges faced by educators, such as managing heterogeneous classrooms, providing timely and personalized feedback and monitoring student progress at scale (Khosravi *et al.*, 2022; Romero & Ventura, 2010).

One of the most prevalent categories of AI-driven educational tools is adaptive learning systems. These platforms dynamically adjust the sequence, difficulty and type of learning activities based on learners' performance, preferences and interaction patterns. In STEAM education, adaptive systems are frequently employed to personalize practice in domains such as mathematics, programming and scientific reasoning. From an operational perspective, these systems rely on computational models that estimate learners' knowledge states or skill levels and use these estimations to select appropriate instructional content (Khosravi *et al.*, 2022). While this approach can significantly enhance learning efficiency and engagement, it also raises critical questions regarding the decision-making processes underlying these adaptations and how such processes can be communicated transparently to both teachers and students.

Another important category comprises Intelligent Tutoring Systems (ITS), which provide step-by-step guidance, contextual hints and real-time feedback during problem-solving activities. Within STEAM domains, ITS are widely applied in areas such as algebra, physics problem-solving, programming exercises and engineering design task (Gunasekara & Saarela, 2025; Romero & Ventura, 2010). Although these systems can deliver highly targeted and individualized support, their internal decision-making mechanism are often complex and difficult to interpret, particularly when machine learning components are used to model student behavior or predict learning outcomes.

Learning analytics dashboards and educational data mining tools represent another significant application of AI in education. These systems aggregate and analyze data from learning management systems and digital learning environments to generate indicators of student progress, engagement and potential risk. In STEAM courses, such dashboards enable instructors to identify students who may require additional support, evaluate the effectiveness of instructional strategies and reflect on patterns of student performance. Increasingly, predictive models and clustering techniques are employed to generate alerts and recommendations (Khosravi *et al.*, 2022; Siemens & Baker, 2012). However, in the absence of adequate explanatory mechanism, these indicators may be misinterpreted or disregarded by educators who lack the means to assess their validity, reliability or pedagogical relevance.

Recommendation systems have also been integrated into educational platforms to suggest learning resources, exercises or project opportunities tailored to individual learners. While these technologies are well-established in commercial domains, their application in education introduces additional challenges related to pedagogical alignment, transparency and fairness. Both teacher and students may question why a specific resource has been recommended and whether alternative options might be more appropriate or beneficial (Gunasekara & Saarela, 2025).

The increasing reliance on data-driven models has undoubtedly enhanced personalization in education; however, it has also intensified concerns related to opacity, interpretability and user control. Many educational institutions adopt these technologies with limited understanding of how the underlying models function or how to interpret their outputs effectively. This limitation is particularly problematic in STEAM education, where fostering critical thinking, systems understanding and reflective problem-solving are central learning objectives (Romero & Ventura, 2010).

Furthermore, the broader technological ecosystem plays a significant role in shaping the implementation of AI-based educational tools. The availability of open-source machine learning libraries, web-based development frameworks, and low-code/no-code platforms has substantially lowered the barriers to developing AI-enhanced applications. Nevertheless, ease of development does not inherently guarantee transparency, interpretability or ethical responsibility. Systems developed without careful design considerations may still operate as opaque or unpredictable "black boxes" (Gunasekara & Saarela, 2025).

For these reasons, the integration of Explainable Artificial Intelligence into AI-based educational tools should be understood as a practical and pedagogical necessity rather than an optional enhancement. In STEAM contexts, where learners are encouraged to critically engage with technology, explainability plays a crucial role in supporting informed use, fostering trust and aligning AI systems with educational objectives. The following sections introduce the foundational concepts of XAI and explore how these principles can be implemented in practice using accessible technologies.

3. FOUNDATIONS OF EXPLAINABLE ARTIFICIAL INTELLIGENCE FOR EDUCATIONAL APPLICATIONS: XAI AS A PEDAGOGICAL ENABLER

Explainable Artificial Intelligence (XAI) refers to a set of methods, techniques and design approaches aimed at making the behavior, internal logic, and outputs of AI systems understandable and interpretable to human users (Adadi & Berrada, 2018; Doshi-Velez & Kim, 2017). Unlike traditional "black box" models, which operate with limited transparency, XAI seeks to provide meaningful explanations that support interpretation, validation and the informed use of AI-driven systems. In educational contexts, particularly within STEAM environments, explainability is not merely a desirable technical feature but a critical requirement, as AI tools directly influence instructional decisions, learning pathways and assessment outcomes.

While XAI has been widely explored in high-stakes domains such as finance and healthcare, its role in education requires a broader conceptualization. In STEAM education, explainability must transcend basic notions of transparency to function as a pedagogical enabler that supports higher-order cognitive processes, epistemic agency, and meaningful engagement with knowledge (Adadi & Berrada, 2018; Barredo Arrieta *et al.*, 2020). Education is fundamentally concerned with the construction and justification of knowledge. Therefore, explanations generated by AI systems should not only clarify how automated decisions are produced but also help learners understand the underlying concepts and reasoning processes that support those decisions.

The effectiveness and utility of explanations in educational settings are inherently dependent on the needs and roles of different stakeholders. Teachers, for instance, require explanations that provide *diagnostic and instructional transparency*. These explanations enable them to evaluate whether AI-generated recommendations are consistent with curricular objectives and pedagogical strategies. Such transparency strengthens professional judgment and allows educators to maintain active oversight of adaptive learning pathways instead of becoming passive recipients of automated recommendations (Floridi *et al.*, 2018, Siemens & Baker, 2012).

Students, on the other hand, engage with explanations as a form of cognitive and metacognitive scaffolding. From a pedagogical perspective, explanations can be situated within the framework of the Zone of Proximal Development (ZPD), where they support learners in bridging the gap between current understanding and potential knowledge acquisition. By clarifying the rationale behind feedback, recommendations, or system-generated hints, XAI can foster self-regulated learning and promote metacognitive reflection. As a result, students are encouraged to engage actively with their own learning processes rather than passively accepting automated outcomes (Gunasekara & Saarela, 2025).

Administrators and institutional stakeholders require a different level of explanation, primarily oriented toward global transparency and system-level interpretability. Their focus lies in monitoring system behavior, identifying potential biases and ensuring that AI deployments comply with institutional policies, ethical standards and fairness requirements. In this context, XAI plays a critical role in enabling accountability, auditability and governance of educational technologies (Siemens & Baker, 2012), (Floridi *et al.*, 2018).

From a technical perspective, XAI methods are commonly categorized based on their relationship to the underlying machine learning models. Intrinsic or inherently interpretable models, such as decision trees, linear models, and rule-based systems, are designed to be understandable by default. Their internal logic provides clear mappings between inputs and outputs. In contrast, post-hoc explanation methods, such as SHAP (SHapely Additive exPlanations) and LIME (Local Interpretable Model-Agnostic Explanations), are applied after model training to approximate and explain the behavior of complex, high-performance models (Lundberg & Lee, 2017; Ribeiro *et al.*, 2016). Additionally, explanations can be differentiated by their scope: *global explanations* aim to describe the overall behavior and logic of a model, while *local explanations* focus on clarifying individual predictions or recommendations. Both types are essential in educational contexts, as they address different interpretive needs across stakeholders.

A central principle in the effective implementation of XAI in education is the adoption of a human-centered explainability approach. An explanation that is technically accurate but pedagogically opaque is unlike to provide meaningful value in educational practice. Therefore, explanations must be designed according to users' cognitive capacities, prior knowledge, and contextual needs. They should also be presented through intuitive interfaces, including visual dashboards, contextual annotations, and interactive visualizations that integrate naturally into existing educational workflows.

In this way, the effectiveness of XAI depends not only on algorithmic sophistication but also on thoughtful interface design and user experience (Gunasekara & Saarela, 2025).

Accessibility represents another critical dimension in the adoption of XAI within educational environments. Many institutions, particularly those operating under resource constraints, lack access to advanced computational infrastructure or specialized expertise in machine learning. However, the emergence of open-source libraries, together with low-code and no-code platforms, has significantly expanded access to explainability features. Although these technologies do not provide the full range of advanced XAI capabilities, they offer sufficient transparency and functionality for a many educational applications. Consequently, they contribute to the democratization of explainable AI within STEAM education.

Despite its potential, it is essential to acknowledge the inherent limitations and challenges associated with XAI. Explanations can sometimes be incomplete, misleading or subject to misinterpretation, particularly when simplifying complex models.

There is also a risk that users may place excessive trust in explanations without critically evaluating their validity. This may create a false sense of understanding or confidence in AI-generated recommendations. Consequently, explainability should be regarded as a mechanism that supports human judgment rather than a substitute for it. Educators should remain actively involved in interpreting AI outputs and use explanations to inform, rather than replace, professional decision-making.

When thoughtfully designed and contextually implemented, XAI has the potential to enhance transparency and foster critical engagement with AI-supported educational processes. It also promotes the ethical and responsible use of AI across diverse educational settings. By bridging the gap between technical systems and human understanding, explainable AI can function not only as a technological enhancement but as a foundational component of pedagogically meaningful, trustworthy and inclusive STEAM learning environments.

4. ACCESSIBLE TECHNOLOGIES FOR IMPLEMENTING XAI IN EDUCATIONAL TOOLS: A TECHNICAL TAXONOMY FOR STEAM CONTEXTS

One of the primary barriers to the adoption of XAI in educational contexts is the widespread perception that its implementation requires advanced technical expertise and specialized computational infrastructure. However, this assumption does not fully reflect the current technological landscape. In practice, many explainability features can be effectively implemented using accessible technològies that are already widely utilized in educational projects, thereby lowering the entry threshold for institutions and practitioners.

Open-source machine learning frameworks, such as scikit-learn, TensorFlow and PyTorch, provide a broad spectrum of models that are either inherently interpretable or compatible with post-hoc explanation techniques. These frameworks are supported by mature ecosystem that include libraries for data visualization, model inspection and analytical interpretation, enabling the generation of feature importance plots, rule-based visualizations and interactive "what-if" analyses (Gunasekara & Saarela, 2025). Such capabilities allow educators and developers to incorporate explainability mechanism without requiring highly specialized expertise in advanced AI methodologies.

In addition to modeling frameworks, web-based development technologies play a crucial role in operationalizing XAI within educational environments. These technologies facilitate the integration of machine learning models into interactive dashboards, learning management systems and standalone educational applications. Interfaces function as the primary medium through which explanations are communicated to users. For instance, learning analytics dashboards can present predictive indicators alongside visual or textual explanations that highlight the variables contributing most significantly to a particular outcome. In this way, the interface becomes not merely a display layer, but a critical component in the interpretability and usability of AI systems.

Low-code and no-code platforms further reduce development barriers by enabling educators, instructional designers and non-specialist developers to construct machine learning workflows and user interfaces through graphical environments. Although these platforms are sometimes perceived as limited in functionality, they can effectively support transparent models and facilitate the visualization of decision logic. In many cases, rule-based systems or simple predictive models developed within these environments are directly inspectable, making them particularly suitable for formative educational contexts where interpretability is prioritized over algorithmic complexity (Gunasekara & Saarela, 2025). This democratization of development tools plays a key role in expanding access to explainable AI across diverse educational settings.

Another important dimension of accessibility lies in the use of lightweight and modular system architectures. These approaches enable the decomposition of educational AI system into smaller, interoperable components, such as prediction modules, explanation modules and interfaces layers. This modularity facilitates experimentation with different types of explanations and allows systems to be adapted to specific pedagogical contexts without requiring a complete redesign. Moreover, modular architectures support scalability and maintainability, making them especially valuable for institutions with limited technical resources.

To better understand the operational differences among explainability techniques, it is useful not only to distinguish between inherently interpretable models and post-hoc explanation methods but also identify the educational scenarios in which each approach is most appropriate. From a practical perspective, educators and developers frequently need guidance on selecting an explanation technique according to the complexity of the underlying model, the intended users, and the pedagogical objectives. Table 1 summarizes these characteristics and provides practical recommendations regarding when each technique is most suitable within STEAM educational environments.

Rather than suggesting a universally superior explainability technique, the comparison presented in Table 1 highlights that the selection of XAI methods should be guided by pedagogical objectives, stakeholder needs, model complexity, and institutional constraints. In practice, educators and developers should view these techniques as complementary rather than mutually exclusive. Many STEAM applications benefit from combining inherently interpretable models with post-hoc explanation methods, thereby achieving an appropriate balance between predictive performance, transparency, and instructional usability.

This comparative framework highlights differences in interpretability levels, methodological characteristics and applicability across STEAM disciplines, including predictive analytics in engineering, adaptive feedback in mathematics, intelligent tutoring in chemistry and programming education.

From a technical and pedagogical perspective, *ante-hoc (intrinsic) models* provide what can be described as *global transparency*, as their internal structure is inherently interpretable. Decision trees, for example, offer a hierarchical representation of decision rules that clearly illustrate that threshold and conditions used to predict outcomes, such as identifying students at risk of failing calculus based on assignment completion rates and quiz performance (Altukhi & Pradhan, 2024; Gunasekara & Saarela, 2025). Similarly, linear and logistic regression models allow for the direct interpretation of feature weights, enabling educators to quantify the relative influence of variables such as "time on task" and "prior knowledge" in determining performance in physics simulations. Rule-based systems provide an even higher degree of transparency by employing explicit "if-then" logic that closely mirrors the step-by-step reasoning processes required in domains such as chemistry equation balancing (Romero & Ventura, 2010).

In contrast, *post-hoc (model-agnostic) explanation methods* are designed to interpret high-performing but inherently opaque models after they have been trained, offering what is typically referred to as *local interpretability*. Techniques such as SHAP (SHapely Additive exPlanations), grounded in cooperative game theory, provide additive feature attribution values that quantify the contribution of each input variable to a specific prediction. This makes SHAP particularly effective for explaining personalized recommendations, such as why a specific advanced robotics resource has been suggested based on a student's prior project history (Lundberg & Lee, 2017; Ribeiro *et al.*, 2016). Similarly, LIME (Local Interpretable Model-Agnostic Explanations) generates local surrogate models around individual predictions, enabling the interpretation of specific outcomes, for example, justifying an AI-generated score for a digital art composition by identifying the visual features that most influenced the evaluation (Gunasekara & Saarela, 2025; Ribeiro *et al.*, 2016).

Table 1. Comparative Analysis of XAI Techniques in STEAM Contexts

Technique Type	Method	Interpretability	STEAM Educational Context & Application	Recommended Use (When to use this technique)
Ante-hoc (Inherently Interpretable)	**Decision Trees**	High	**Predictive Analytics**: Identifying students at risk of falling calculus based on assignment completion rates and quiz scores.	Recommended when educators require transparent and easily interpretable decision rules to support instructional interventions, early warning systems, or classroom discussions where the reasoning process should be directly inspectable.
Ante-hoc	**Linear/Logistic Regression**	High	**Learning Analytics**: Determining the weight of "time on task" versus "prior knowledge" in predicting performance in physics simulations.	Appropriate when the objective is to quantify the relative influence of specific educational variables (e.g., prior knowledge, engagement, time-on-task) and communicate these relationships in a statistically interpretable manner.
Ante-hoc	**Rule-Based Systems**	High	**Intelligent Tutoring**: Providing explicit "if-then" logic for step-by-step guidance in chemistry equation balancing.	Best suited for educational environments where explicit pedagogical logic or curriculum rules need to be represented transparently, such as intelligent tutoring systems, competency assessment, or procedural problem solving.
Post-hoc (Model-Agnostic)	**SHAP (Shapley Values)**	Medium-High	**Personalized Recommendations**: Explaining why a specific advanced robotics resource was suggested based on a student's project history.	Recommended for complex predictive models when educators or developers need reliable feature-level explanations that quantify how individual variables contribute to specific predictions or recommendations.

continued on following page

Table 1. Continued

Technique Type	Method	Interpretability	STEAM Educational Context & Application	Recommended Use (When to use this technique)
Post-hoc	**LIME**	Medium-High	**Assessment Feedback**: Justifying the AI-generated score for a digital art composition by highlighting influential visual features.	Most appropriate for explaining individual student-level predictions or isolated decisions generated by complex machine learning models, especially when localized explanations are sufficient for instructional purposes.
Post-hoc	**Attention Maps**	Medium	**Programming Education**: Visualizing which sections of code, the AI focused on the detect logical errors in a student's Python script.	Particularly useful in deep learning applications involving visual information or programming task, where understanding which regions of an image or code sequence influenced the model's decision supports student reflection and debugging.

Source: Developed by the authors based on Gunasekara & Saarela (2025).

In the context of computer science and programming education, attention-based visualization techniques, such as attention maps, provide an additional layer of interpretability by highlighting which segments of input data are most relevant to the model's decision-making process. These techniques allow learners to visualize which sections of their code a neural network has focused on when detecting logical errors in a Python script, thereby supporting debugging skills and computational thinking (Gunasekara & Saarela, 2025). Although these methods may offer lower global interpretability compared to intrinsic models, they provide valuable localized insights that are highly relevant for specific learning interactions.

Ultimately, accessibility in XAI is not just a technical issue but also an organizational and strategic consideration. The selection of tools and technologies should be guided by factors such as transparency of the development process, availability of documentation, community support and alignment with existing institutional practices. Open-source and widely adopted platforms facilitate knowledge sharing, reproducibility and collaborative development, while reducing dependence on opaque proprietary systems. By prioritizing accessible, interpretable and context-appropriate technologies, educational institutions can foster the responsible adoption of explainable AI and ensure that its benefits are distributed equitably across diverse STEAM learning environments.

5. PRACTICAL IMPLEMENTATION EXPERIENCES AND USE CASES: ARCHITECTURAL STRATEGIES FOR XAI IN STEAM EDUCATION

This section presents a series of illustrative and implementations-oriented examples that demonstrate how XAI can be effectively integrated into STEAM educational tools using accessible and scalable technologies. The practical relevance of XAI becomes particularly evident when theoretical models of explainability are translated into concrete pedagogical applications that directly support teaching and learning processes.

The theoretical foundations of explainability find their greatest value when applied to real-world educational challenges within the STEAM classroom. By transforming algorithmic outputs into actionable and interpretable insights, XAI enables a more nuanced and productive interaction between automated systems and human expertise. Rather than functioning as opaque decision-making engines, AI systems enhanced with explainability mechanisms can actively support pedagogical reasoning, instructional design and student learning processes.

The application scenarios (Table 2) outlined in this framework illustrate how explainability enhances personalized feedback, ensuring that AI-driven interventions remain aligned with both educational objectives and learner needs. These scenarios span a variety of STEAM contexts, including adaptive learning systems, learning analytics dashboards, intelligent tutoring systems, peer-assessment tools, and competency-based dashboards. Each scenario demonstrates how specific XAI approaches, such as feature importance techniques, ruled-based explanations, local interpretability methods, counterfactual reasoning and visual analytics can provide pedagogically meaningful insights.

Table 2. XAI Application Scenarios in STEAM Education

Scenario	Objective	AI Tool Category	Normalized XAI Approach	Pedagogical Benefit
Personalized Content Delivery	Tailoring learning paths to individual mastery levels.	**Adaptive Learning Systems**	Feature Importance (SHAP)	**Transparency**: Students understand why specific remedial or advanced content was assigned.
Early Warning Systems	Identifying students at risk of academic failure.	**Learning Analytics Dashboards**	Decision Trees / Rules	**Instructional Support**: Teachers receive clear justifications (e.g., low engagement in labs) to trigger timely interventions.
Automated Formative Feedback	Providing real-time guidance during complex tasks.	**Intelligent Tutoring Systems (ITS)**	Local Explanations (LIME)	**Scaffolding**: Learners receive "hints" that explain the logic behind a correction in mathematics or coding.
Collaborative Project Evaluation	Assessing group dynamics and individual contributions.	**Peer-Assessment Tools**	Counterfactual Explanations	**Fairness**: Justifies the distribution of grades based on traceable participation metrics in engineering projects.
Skill Gap Analysis	Visualizing mastery across different STEAM competencies.	**Competency-Based Dashboards**	Visual Heatmaps	**Metacognition**: Students can visualize which specific sub-skills (e.g., data visualization vs. statistical analysis) requires more focus.

Source: Developed by the authors based on European Parliament & Council of the European Union (2024) and Naveenkumar (2025).

5.1 Explainable Learning Analytics Dashboard for Teachers

Learning analytics dashboards are among the most widely used AI-driven tools in educational environments, providing insights into student activity, engagement and performance. The integration of explainability into these dashboards significantly enhances their pedagogical value. Instead of presenting only aggregated indicators, such as a generalized "risk level", explainable dashboards incorporate interpretable elements that clarify the factors contributing to a specific prediction.

For example, dashboards can display ranked lists of contributing variables, such as missed assignments, low quiz scores, or reduced engagement in laboratory activities, using either inherently interpretable models (e.g., decision trees) or post-hoc explanations techniques (Romero & Ventura, 2010). This level of transparency enables educators to understand the underlying logic of predictive analytics, thereby supporting more informed and context-sensitive instructional interventions. As a result, teachers are empowered to act not merely on system outputs but on a clear interpretation of the factors influencing those outputs.

Example Box 1. Teacher-Facing Explainable Dashboard Alert

Student Status: At Risk of Academic Underperformance

Why was this alert generated?

This student was flagged as at risk because laboratory participation decreased by 40% during the last four weeks, and the last two quiz scores (58% and 61%) were below the course threshold. In addition, two laboratory reports were submitted after the deadline, indicating a decline in overall engagement.

Recommended instructional action

Review the student's recent performance during the next class meeting, discuss potential learning difficulties, and recommended additional support activities before the next assessment.

This example illustrates how explainable learning analytics dashboard transform predictive alerts into actionable instructional information. Rather than displaying a generic risk indicator, the dashboard communicates the specific variables contributing to the prediction, enabling educators to verify the recommendation, exercise professional judgment, and determine whether additional pedagogical intervention is warranted. In this way, explainability reinforces teacher autonomy while promoting more transparent and evidence-informed instructional decision-making.

5.2 Explainable Recommendations in Adaptive Learning Systems

Adaptive learning systems are designed to tailor instructional content to individual learners based on their performance and interaction patterns. However, without explainability, the recommendations generated by these systems may appear arbitrary or difficult to interpret.

By incorporating XAI mechanisms, adaptive platforms can provide context-sensitive explanations that clarify the rationale behind specific recommendations. For instance, a system may suggest additional practice activities accompanied by an explanation indicating that learners with similar performance profiles have demonstrated improvement after completing those tasks. Such explanations should be concise, accessible and pedagogically aligned, enabling students to understand not only what is recommended but why it is relevant to their learning process.

Example Box 2. Student-Facing Explainable Recommendation

Recommended activity: Practice Set – Logarithmic Functions (Intermediate Level)

Why was this activity recommended?

Your recent quiz results indicate difficulties solving problems involving logarithmic transformations and the application of logarithmic identities. Students with similar learning profiles improved their performance after completing this practice activity. Strengthening these concepts is recommended before progressing to exponential modeling exercises.

Suggested next step: Complete the practice activity and review the accompanying worked examples before attempting the next assessment.

This example illustrates how explainability can be translated into learner-centered messages that communicate both the rationale behind a recommendation and its instructional purpose. Rather than presenting an automated decision without context, the explanation supports self-regulated learning, encourages reflection, and strengthens students' confidence in the personalization process while avoiding unnecessary technical complexity.

5.3 Supporting Student Reflection Through Example-Based Explanations

Example-based explanations represent an effective strategy for supporting student understanding and reflection. These explanations provide representative cases, solutions, or patterns that allow learners to contextualize their own work within a broader set of successful approaches.

Such explanations can be generated using similarity-based methods or case-based reasoning techniques, which identify examples that closely resemble a student's current performance or problem-solving strategy. By comparing their work with these reference cases, students can more concretely interpret feedback, identify errors and refine their approaches. This method not only improves comprehension but also supports metacognitive development, as learners engage in reflective analysis of their own learning processes.

5.4 Explainable Rule-Based and Hybrid Systems in Classroom Tools

Rule-based and hybrid systems offer a particularly effective approach for integrating explainability into classroom tools. These systems combine explicitly defined rules with data-driven components, allowing for a both transparency and adaptability.

For example, a classroom tool designed to monitor project progress may use predefined rules to classify stages of completion while incorporating simple predictive models to identify potential risks or delays. The explicit nature of rule-based logic enables educators and students to inspect, discuss and even modify the rules, transforming explainability into an active component of the learning process.

Hybrid systems, which integrate interpretable model's whit more complex predictive components, provide a balance between performance and transparency. They allow for the gradual introduction of explainability while maintaining sufficient predictive accuracy for practical use.

5.5 Architectural Implementation: Democratization Through Accessible Technologies

The sustainable and scalable adoption of XAI in STEAM education requires a strategic shift away from reliance on high-cost, specialized infrastructure toward the use of accessible and democratized technological solutions. This shift is essential for ensuring that explainable AI can be implemented across diverse educational contexts, including institutions with limited resources.

A key component of this approach is the use of open-source machine learning frameworks, such as *scikit-learn, TensorFlow and Pytorch*. These platforms provide robust support for both interpretable models and post-hoc explanation techniques, enabling the development of explainable systems without dependence on proprietary technologies. Additionally, they support the integration of visualization tools, such as feature importance charts and rule-based diagrams, that can be directly embedded into educational interfaces.

Complementing these frameworks, *low-code and no-code platforms* play a critical role in expanding access to XAI development. These environments enable educators and instructional designers with limited programming expertise to construct machine learning workflows and user interfaces through graphical tools. The models generated in these platforms are often inherently more transparent, making them suitable for classroom use where the interpretability of the system can itself become part of the learning experience (Gunasekara & Saarela, 2025).

Another fundamental strategy for democratization is the adoption of a *modular system architecture*. In this approach, educational AI system is decomposed into distinct components, including:

- The prediction engine (model generation)
- The explanation module (interpretability layer)
- The user interface (interaction and visualization layer)

This modular design enables flexibility and scalability, allowing institutions to replace opaque components with more interpretable alternatives as they become available. It also facilitates the customization of explanation interfaces for different stakeholders, for example, student-facing interfaces that emphasize simplicity and clarity, and teacher-facing dashboards that provide more detailed diagnostic information. Importantly, this approach reduces development complexity and supports iterative improvement without requiring a complete redesign of this system.

5.6 Practical Workflow for Implementing Explainable AI in STEAM Educational Tools

Although explainable AI can be implemented in different ways depending on the educational context and technological infrastructure, a structured implementation process can facilitate the development of transparent, pedagogically meaningful, and trustworthy educational tools. Based on the implementation experiences and design principles discussed throughout this chapter, *figure 1* summarizes a practical workflow that can guide educators, instructional designers, and developers during the design and deployment of XAI-supported STEAM applications.

Step 1. Define the Pedagogical Problem

Clearly identify the educational challenge that the AI system is intended to address, such as improving formative assessment, identifying students at risk, supporting adaptive learning, or recommending personalized learning resources. At this stage, pedagogical objectives should drive technological decisions rather than the reverse.

Step 2. Identify and prepare relevant educational data

Determine which learner date are necessary for the intended application, including academic performance, interaction logs, assessment results, or behavioral indicators. Data quality, privacy, and ethical considerations should be addressed before model development.

Step 3. Select an Appropriate Explainable AI Approach

Choose an interpretable model (e.g. Decision trees, Rule-Based Systems, Linear Regression) whenever sufficient predictive performance can be achieved. When more complex machine learning models are required, incorporate suitable post-hoc explanation techniques such as SHAP or LIME according to the intended educational purpose and stakeholder needs.

Step 4. Design User-Centered Explanation Interfaces

Develop explanations that match the characteristics and information needs of different users. Teachers generally require diagnostic and instructional explanations, whereas students benefit from concise explanations that support reflection and self-regulated learning. Explanations should be integrated naturally into dashboards, tutoring systems, or learning management platforms.

Step 5. Validate Explanations with End Users

Evaluate both the technical correctness and pedagogical usefulness of explanations through pilot studies, usability testing, classroom observations, or structured feedback from teachers and students. Effective explanations should improve understanding without increasing cognitive load.

Step 6. Refine and Iterate the System

Use evaluation results to improve predictive models, redesign explanation interfaces, and adjust educational workflows. Explainability should be considered an iterative design process that evolves together with institutional needs, technological advances, and classroom practices.

Figure 1. Practical Workflow for Implementing Explainable AI in STEAM Educational Tools

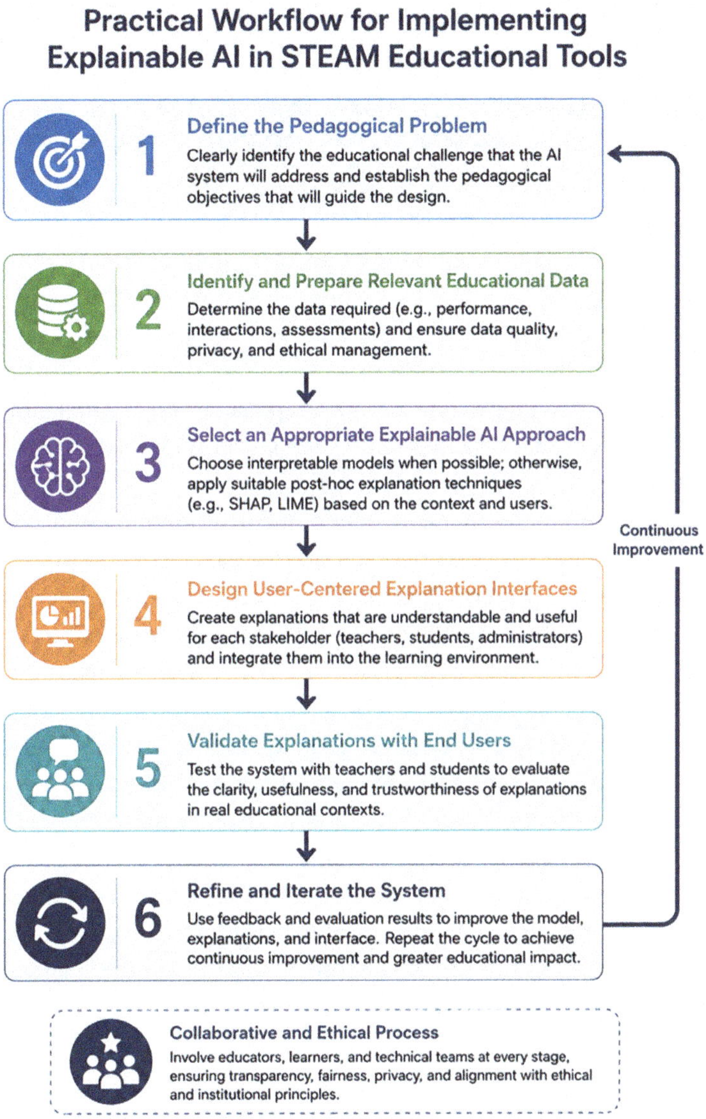

Source: Developed by the authors based on the literature reviewed in this chapter, particularly Adadi and Berrada (2018), Rudin (2019), European Parliament & Council of the European Union (2024), Gunasekara and Saarela (2025), and Naveenkumar (2025).

The proposed workflow should not be interpreted as a rigid sequence but as an iterative design cycle. Feedback obtained during validation may require revisiting previous stages, including data preparation, model selection, or explanation design.

This iterative perspective reflects the dynamic nature of educational innovation and reinforces the importance of continuous collaboration among educators, developers, and institutional stakeholders.

6. ETHICAL AND PEDAGOGICAL IMPLICATIONS AND PRACTICAL APPLICATIONS SCENARIOS IN XAI FOR STEAM EDUCATION

The ethical and pedagogical foundations of Explainable Artificial Intelligence have been discussed in the previous sections. Building upon those principles, this section focuses on their practical implications for the responsible implementation of XAI in STEAM educational environments. Rather than revisiting the conceptual foundations of transparency, the discussion emphasizes how explainability supports concrete educational decisions, ethical governance, and stakeholder-centered applications.

In practice, transparency enables teachers and institutional stakeholders to examine the reasoning behind AI-generated recommendations before acting upon them. Explainability therefore supports informed decision-making, reduces the likelihood of automation bias, and allows educators to determine whether algorithmic recommendations are pedagogically appropriate within their specific instructional context.

Beyond transparency, fairness and bias remain central ethical concerns, particularly when training data reflect historical inequities or systemic imbalances.

Explainability also strengthens accountability by enabling stakeholders to trace automated decisions to understandable and justifiable reasoning. This capability facilitates auditing processes, supports compliance with emerging ethical and regulatory frameworks, including the transparency, human oversight, accountability, and risk management requirements established by the European Union Artificial Intelligence Act and the UNESCO Recommendation on the Ethics of Artificial Intelligence.

Table 3. Ethical Assessment Framework and Regulatory Alignment

Ethical Criterion	XAI Operationalization	Example Indicator in STEAM	Regulatory Reference (EU AI Act / UNESCO)
Transparency	Providing clear, human-understandable logic for AI decisions.	Availability of "Why this?" buttons on recommendation dashboards.	**Art. 13 (EU AI Act)**: Transparency and provision of information to users
Non-Discrimination & Fairness	Identifying and mitigating algorithmic biases in data.	Using SHAP to verify that gender or ethnicity does not influence engineering grades.	**Art. 10 (EU AI Act)**: Data and data governance; preventing biased outcomes.
Human Agency & Oversight	Ensuring teachers retain the final decision-making power.	Explanation-based interfaces that allow teachers to override AI risk flags.	**Art. 14 (EU AI Act):** Human oversight requirements for high-risk AI.
Accountability	Maintaining traceable logs of how decisions were reached.	Audit trails showing the feature weights used in a student's final assessment.	**UNESCO Recommendation (Art. 34)**: Ethical governance and traceability.
Privacy & Data Sovereignty	Explaining logic without revealing sensitive personal data.	Generating explanations based on behavioral patterns rather than personal identity.	**GDPR / EU AI Act Recital 45**: Privacy-preserving transparency.

Source: Developed by the authors based on European Parliament & Council of the European Union (2024) and Zhang (2025).

This ethical assessment framework aligns XAI capabilities with international regulatory standards, offering a structured approach for the responsible deployment of AI-driven tools in academic environments.

From a pedagogical perspective, the ethical principles summarized in Table 3 become meaningful only when they are reflected in everyday educational practice. The following scenarios illustrate how explainability supports instructional decisions, learner reflection, assessment transparency, and equitable educational interventions across different STEAM applications.

However, the effectiveness of explanations depends largely on their design. Poorly constructed explanations may be misleading, excessively complex, or cognitively overwhelming, thereby reducing their educational value. For this reason, explanation design should be aligned with educational objectives, users' prior knowledge, and cognitive load considerations. Well-designed explanations are more likely to be meaningful, understandable, and actionable for different stakeholders.

In parallel, issues related to privacy and responsible data use remain central to the ethical implementation of XAI. Even when the systems are transparent and interpretable, they must adhere to strict data protection standards, ensuring that student information is handled securely and ethically. Transparent communication regarding data collection, processing and usage is essential for maintaining trust among all stakeholders.

Beyond these ethical and pedagogical considerations, the practical value of XAI becomes most evident when it is applied to authentic educational scenarios. The following use cases illustrate how explainability transforms algorithmic outputs into actionable pedagogical insights that enhance both teaching and learning processes.

6.1 Adaptive Learning Systems: Content Transparency

In adaptive learning environments, AI systems dynamically personalize content delivery based on inferred knowledge states and learner performance. By integrating explainability techniques such as SHAP values, these systems can provide feature importance explanations that clearly indicate why a student has been assigned a particular learning activity, such as a remedial module or an advanced calculus exercise (Khosravi *et al.*, 2022).

From a pedagogical perspective, this level of transparency supports self-regulated learning by helping students understand the specific factors influencing their learning pathway. For example, a learner may recognize that additional practice has been recommended because of difficulties with logarithmic functions rather than a generalized lack of ability. This distinction encourages targeted reflection and more effective learning strategies. Such explanations enable students to understand the immediate reasons for the recommendation and encourage targeted learning strategies based on identifiable learning needs.

6.2 Learning Analytics Dashboards: Early Warning Interventions

Learning analytics dashboards designed for instructors often incorporate predictive models to identify students at risk of academic failure. When enhanced with explainability mechanisms, such as decision trees or rule-based systems, these dashboards mode beyond simple risk indicators to provide clear and interpretable justifications for alerts.

Instead of presenting a generic "at-risk" label, the system highlights the specific variables contributing to the prediction, such as decreased laboratory engagement or declining quiz performance (Romero & Ventura, 2010; Siemens & Baker, 2012). These explanations allow instructors to verify the validity of the recommendation before deciding whether intervention is necessary, thereby supporting professional judgment while reducing the risk of automation bias (Khosravi *et al.*, 2022; Siemens & Baker, 2012).

6.3 Intelligent Tutoring Systems (ITS): Scaffolding and Feedback

Intelligent Tutoring System (ITS) leverage local explanation techniques, such as LIME, to provide automated formative feedback during complex problem-solving tasks in domains such as mathematics, chemistry and programming. Rather than simply indicating correct or incorrect answers, these systems generate explanatory "hints" that clarify the reasoning behind corrections (Romero & Ventura, 2010).

Within intelligent tutoring systems, these explanations function as instructional scaffolds rather than simple corrective messages. By identifying and explaining specific errors, such as a logical flaw in a Python script or a miscalculation in a chemical equation, XAI facilitates deeper conceptual understanding. The explanation functions as a cognitive bridge between the learner's current reasoning and the correct solution process. This supports incremental knowledge construction rather than simple error correction (Gunasekara & Saarela, 2025).

6.4 Peer-Assessment Tools: Ensuring Fairness

In collaborative STEAM projects, particularly in engineering and design contexts, AI systems are often used to evaluate group dynamics and individual contributions. In such scenarios, counterfactual explanations play a critical role in ensuring fairness and transparency.

Counterfactual explanations describe how input variables would need to change to produce a different outcome, thereby providing a clear rationale for evaluation results. For example, a system might indicate that a student's individual score would have increased if their contribution to a shared project repository had been higher. This form of explanation allows students to understand the criteria underlying assessment decisions and provides a basis for equitable dispute resolution (Gunasekara & Saarela, 2025).

By making assessment criteria explicit, counterfactual explanations support transparent grading processes and facilitate equitable discussion of evaluation outcomes.

6.5 Competency Dashboards: Skill Gap Visualization

Competency-based dashboards utilize visual explanation techniques, such as heatmaps, to represent student performance across different STEAM competencies. These visualizations enable learners to quickly identify areas of strength and weakness, such as high proficiency in data visualization but lower performance in statistical analysis (Gunasekara & Saarela, 2025).

Such visual representations strengthen metacognitive awareness by allowing students to monitor their learning progress and identify specific skill gaps. As a result, learners can plan targeted learning activities, prioritize areas requiring improvement, and assume greater responsibility for their own development.

7. DESIGN GUIDELINES, LESSONS LEARNED AND ETHICAL-REGULATORY ALIGNMENT

Building upon the pedagogical foundations and practical applications discussed in the previous sections, this section synthesizes a set of implementation guidelines for designing, deploying and governing Explainable Artificial Intelligence in STEAM educational environments. Rather than introducing new conceptual principles, these recommendations translate current evidence into practical design decisions for educators, developers and institutional stakeholders.

Start with pedagogical objectives rather than algorithms. Educational needs, instructional goals and stakeholder roles should be defined before selecting machine learning models or explainability techniques. This approach ensures that XAI supports authentic learning outcomes instead of simply showcasing technological capabilities.

Prioritize simple and actionable explanations. Explanations should communicate only the information required to support educational decisions. Excessively technical descriptions may increase cognitive load and reduce the practical value of XAI in classroom settings.

Adapt explanations to stakeholder needs. Teachers, students and administrators require different levels of explanation depending on their responsibilities. Designing stakeholder-specific explanations increases usability and supports more effective educational decision-making.

Embed explanations within existing educational workflows. Explainability should become a natural component of dashboards, tutoring systems and learning platforms rather than an external feature that users must consult separately. Explanations that are embedded within dashboards, feedback systems, or learning interfaces are more likely to be used effectively, as they become part of the natural interaction between users and AI systems. This integration enhances usability and ensures that explainability supports, rather than disrupts, pedagogical processes.

Select accessible technologies strategically. Open-source frameworks, low-code platforms and lightweight machine learning libraries make XAI feasible for institutions with diverse technological capacities. Technology selection should balance interpretability, predictive performance and available resources.

Treat explainability as an iterative process. Explanations should be continuously evaluated and refined through feedback from teachers and students to ensure that they remain understandable, useful and pedagogically relevant.

Together, these recommendations provide a practical framework for integrating explainability into educational technologies. Their purpose is not only to improve model interpretability but also to support educational decision-making, facilitate responsible AI adoption and promote sustainable implementation across diverse STEAM learning environments.

In addition to these implementation guidelines, XAI must be considered within the broader regulatory landscape governing the use of Artificial Intelligence in education. Recent international frameworks, including the European Union AI Act and UNESCO recommendations, increasingly recognize transparency, human oversight and accountability as essential requirements for trustworthy educational AI systems (European Parliament & Council of the European Union, 2024; UNESCO, 2022; Floridi *et al.*, 2018; Zhang, 2025).

Failure to operationalize these regulatory principles, especially those related to transparency and human oversight, poses significant risks to the integrity of educational systems. For example, Article 14 of the EU AI Act emphasizes the necessity of maintaining meaningful human control over AI-driven processes. Without explainable interfaces, educators are unable to fully exercise their "human-in-the-loop" responsibilities, thereby compromising their professional autonomy and diminishing their capacity to critically evaluate automated decisions (European Parliament & Council of the European Union, 2024).

Accordingly, explainability supports compliance with these regulatory expectations by enabling educators to review, question and justify AI-assisted decisions. In this way, XAI contributes simultaneously to educational practice, institutional accountability and the protection of student rights.

Ultimately, integrating implementation guidelines with ethical and regulatory requirements strengthens the long-term sustainability of XAI in education. Responsible deployment depends not only on technically effective models but also on governance mechanism that ensure transparency, accountability and meaningful human oversight throughout the educational decision-making process.

As summarized in table 4, the successful implementation of Explainable Artificial Intelligence depends on the integration of pedagogical, technical and organizational considerations rather than on the integration of pedagogical, technical and organizational considerations rather than on algorithmic performance alone. These guidelines provide a practical framework that can assist educators, developers and decision-makers in designing, implementing and continuously improving transparent and trustworthy AI-supported educational tools across diverse STEAM learning environments.

Table 4. Design Guidelines for the Practical Implementation of Explainable Artificial Intelligence in STEAM Educational Tools

Guideline	Design Recommendation	Practical Objective
Pedagogical Primacy	Start with learning objectives	Educational alignment
Simplicity	Use concise explanations	Reduce cognitive load
Stakeholder-centered	Tailor explanations	Better usability
Workflow Integration	Embed explanations	Daily adoption
Accessible Technologies	Prefer open-source and modular tools	Feasibility
Iterative Evaluation	Collect user feedback	Continuous improvement.

Source: Developed by the authors based on Adadi and Berrada (2018), Arrieta et al. (2020), European Parliament & Council of the European Union (2024), Gunasekara and Saarela (2025); Pachouly and Bormane (2025), and Zhang (2025).

8. DESIGN GUIDELINES FOR STAKEHOLDER-CENTRIC XAI

The practical implementation of Explainable Artificial Intelligence (XAI) in educational contexts requires adherence to a set of actionable, stakeholder-centered design strategies to ensure its effectiveness, usability and pedagogical relevance.

- ***Pedagogical Primacy***: The design process must begin with clearly defined instructional needs and an explicit understanding of the learner's role, rather than being driven by algorithmic capabilities. This ensures that XAI systems are aligned with educational objectives and contribute meaningfully to learning outcomes.
- ***Role-Specific Design***: The complexity, format and depth of explanations should be tailored to the specific characteristics and needs of each user group. Students benefit from simple, scaffolded explanations that support comprehension and reflection, whereas administrators require more detailed diagnostic information to support monitoring, accountability and audit processes.
- ***Workflow Integration***: Explainability features should be seamlessly embedded within existing educational platforms, such as learning management systems and analytics dashboards, so that they become an integral part of routine educational practices rather than external or optional add-ons.

- ***Iterative Refinement***: The design of explanations should follow a participatory and iterative approach, incorporating continuous feedback from both teachers and students. This ensures that explanations remain accessible, non-overwhelming and practically useful for decision-making in real educational contexts.
- ***Strategic Simplicity***: Explanation design should prioritize clarity and usability over exhaustive technical detail. Overly complex explanations risk being ignored or misunderstood, thereby exacerbating issues of under-trust and reducing the overall effectiveness of XAI systems.

9. CHALLENGES AND FUTURE DIRECTIONS

Despite the significant progress achieved in the development and application of XAI in STEAM education, several critical challenges and open research directions remain. These challenges reflect not only technical limitations but also pedagogical, organizational and societal complexities that must be addressed to ensure the sustainable and responsible adoption of XAI in educational contexts.

9.1 Key Risks and Limitations of XAI in Education

While explainability can enhance transparency, trust, and accountability, the implementation of XAI is not without risks. It is essential to critically examine the limitations of explanations to prevent a false sense of understanding, misplaced trust, and the reinforcement of existing inequities. Table 5 summarizes key risks associated with XAI in STEAM educational tools.

Table 5. Principal Risks and Mitigation Strategies for Explainable AI in STEAM Educational Applications

Risk	Description	Potential Impact in STEAM Education	Mitigation Strategies
Simplified Approximations	Most post-hoc explanations methods provide locally faithful approximations rather than exact representations of complex predictive models.	Educators and students may over-rely on incomplete explanations, leading to misinterpretation of model behavior.	Communicate the scope and limitations of explanations; combine global and local explanations; document assumptions.
Misinterpretation by Non-Technical Users	Explanations may be understood incorrectly due to limited technical background, mathematical literacy, or cognitive load.	Users may draw wrong conclusion about student performance, needs, or potential, resulting in inappropriate interventions.	Design user-centered explanations; use plain language; provide training and contextual guidance for stakeholders.
Over-Trust and Automation Bias	Clear or confident explanations may lead users to over-trust AI outputs, assuming them to be always correct or complete.	Teachers may delegate decision-making to the system; students may accept feedback without critical reflection.	Maintain human-in-the-loop: promote critical AI literacy; include uncertainly indicators in explanations.
Hidden Bias in Training Data and Models	Explainability may reveal influential features without exposing historical, sampling, or structural biases embedded in the training data.	Discriminatory or inequitable outcomes may persist, affecting opportunities in fields such as advanced mathematics or engineering.	Conduct bias audits; use fairness metrics; apply counterfactual analyses; ensure diverse and representative datasets.
Selective or Misleading Explanations	Systems may highlight only certain factors or present explanations designed to justify decisions rather than clarify them.	Loss of transparency; stakeholders may question the integrity or intentions of the system and developers.	Ensure faithfulness of explanations; use model-agnostic validation; follow established XAI evaluation protocols.
Cognitive Overload	Too much information or overly complex explanations can overwhelm users.	Users may ignore explanations or avoid interacting with the system.	Apply progressive disclosure; prioritize key drivers; allow users to customize the level of detail.
Context-Insensitivity	Explanations may not consider classroom context, curriculum goals, or local pedagogical practices.	Recommendations or feedback may not be relevant or actionable within specific STEAM learning environments.	Integrate domain knowledge; involve educators in design; adapt explanations to curriculum and learning objectives.

Source: Developed by the authors based on Adadi and Berrada (2018), Arrieta et al. (2020), European Parliament & Council of the European Union (2024), Gunasekara and Saarela (2025); Pachouly and Bormane (2025), and Zhang (2025).

The risk summarized in Table 5 highlight that explainability should not be interpreted as an inherent guarantee of transparency, fairness, or trustworthy decision-making. Most post-hoc explanation techniques provide simplified representations of complex predictive models rather than exact descriptions of their internal reasoning processes. Consequently, explanations should be understood as decision-support mechanism that facilitate interpretation rather than complete representations of model behavior (Adadi & Berrada, 2018; Arrieta et al., 2020). Moreover, even highly interpretable models cannot eliminate biases originating from data quality, feature selection, or institutional practices, reinforcing the need for critical human oversight throughout the educational decision-making process.

These limitations reinforce the idea that explainability should be understood as one component of a broader framework for responsible educational AI rather than as a standalone solution to issues of transparency and fairness.

Recognizing these risks is essential for implementing Explainable Artificial Intelligence responsible in educational environments. Rather than if explanations automatically improve transparency, fairness, or trust, educators, developers, and institutions should critically evaluate how explanations are generated, communicated, interpreted, and incorporated into pedagogical decision-making. Responsible implementation therefore requires not only technically sound explanation methods but also continuous validation, stakeholder participation, and alignment with educational objectives and ethical principles.

Likewise, the educational value of explanations depends on how they are interpreted and used by different stakeholders. Teachers and students may misunderstand technically sophisticated explanations or develop excessive confidence in AI recommendations when explanations appear convincing but do not adequately communicate uncertainly. Furthermore, explainability alone cannot eliminate biases embedded in training datasets or institutional practices. These limitations reinforce the importance of combining XAI with robust data governance, fairness assessment, human oversight, and continuous pedagogical evaluation throughout the AI life cycle (European Parliament & Council of the European Union, 2024; Floridi et al. 2018; UNESCO, 2022).

One of the most prominent challenges is the persistent tension between model complexity and interpretability, often referred to as the *accuracy-interpretability trade-off*. Highly complex models, such as deep neural networks, tend to offer superior predictive performance but lack transparency, while simpler, inherently interpretable models may sacrifice accuracy for explainability. Addressing this tension requires the development of hybrid approaches and novel methodologies that balance these competing objectives, ensuring that AI systems remain both effective and interpretable without compromising student outcomes (Feldman-Maggor *et al.*, 2025; Rudin, 2019).

Another critical area concerns the *evaluation of explanations*. While numerous XAI techniques have been proposed, there is still a lack of standardized frameworks and metrics for assessing their effectiveness. Future research must integrate both quantitative and qualitative measures to evaluate how explanations influence user understanding, trust, decision-making, and, ultimately, learning outcomes. The development of robust evaluation methodologies that capture both cognitive and pedagogical impacts remains a priority for the field (Doshi-Velez & Kim, 2017; Feldman-Maggor *et al.*, 2025).

The need for pedagogical context adaptation also represents a significant challenge. Explanations that are effective in one disciplinary domain or educational level may not be appropriate in another. For example, the type and complexity of explanations required in engineering education may differ substantially from those needed in mathematics or arts-based STEAM contexts. Consequently, and explanation design must be sensitive to disciplinary norms, learner expertise and instructional objectives, requiring context-aware and adaptable XAI systems.

In parallel, organizational support and professional development are essential for the sustainable AI depends heavily on educators' ability to interpret and act upon AI-generated insights. Therefore, institutions must invest in teacher training and continuous professional development programs that equip educators with the necessary competencies to critically engage with AI systems and integrate them effectively into pedagogical practice (Altukhi & Pradhan, 2024; Pachouly & Bormane, 2025). Without such support, even the most advanced XAI tools may fail to achieve meaningful impact.

From a technological perspective, there is a clear need for the *enhancement of accessible tools and resources*. While existing open-source frameworks and platforms provide a foundation for implementing XAI, there remains a gap in the availability of specialized templates, modular components and user-friendly solutions tailored specifically to educational use cases. Future development efforts should focus on creating reusable and adaptable resources for STEAM applications, including domains such as robotics, programming education and data analysis (Gunasekara & Saarela, 2025). These tools would significantly lower the barriers to adoption and facilitate the broader dissemination of explainable AI.

Finally, the advancement of XAI in education requires a sustained commitment to *ethical and societal research*. Interdisciplinary approaches are needed to explore issues related to governance, accountability, transparency and the long-term societal implications of AI integration in educational systems. This includes examining how explainability influences power dynamics, decision-making authority, and equity in access to educational opportunities. Understanding these broader impacts is essential for ensuring that AI technologies contribute positively to educational ecosystems and do not exacerbate existing inequalities.

Ultimately, explainability should not be interpreted as guarantee of fairness, understanding, or trustworthiness. Rather, it should be regarded as an enabling mechanism that supports more transparent, informed, and accountable educational decision-making when implemented critically, ethically, and in conjunction with appropriate human oversight. As Explainable Artificial Intelligence continues to evolve, future research should focus not only on improving explanation techniques but also on understanding how explanations influence human judgment, instructional practice, and educational equity across diverse STEAM learning environments.

10. CONCLUSIONS

This chapter has presented a practical and implementation-oriented framework for integrating Explainable Artificial Intelligence into STEAM educational tools using accessible technologies. Rather than focusing exclusively on algorithmic explainability, it has combined pedagogical principles, technical implementation strategies, stakeholder-centered design guidelines, ethical considerations, and practical use cases into a coherent. Framework intended to support the responsible adoption of AI in educational practice.

The framework developed throughout this chapter demonstrates that explainability should be considered during the entire design process rather than incorporated as a final technical component. The proposed taxonomy of XAI techniques, implementation workflow, application scenarios, and design guidelines illustrate how transparency can be operationalized in educational systems while remaining aligned with pedagogical objectives and institutional realities.

An additional contribution of this chapter is the emphasis on accessibility. By highlighting the role of open-source frameworks, modular architectures, and low-code technologies, the proposed framework demonstrates that implementing explainable AI does not necessarily require highly specialized infrastructures. This perspective broadens the possibilities for adoption across educational institutions with different technological capacities.

The chapter also emphasizes that explainability is meaningful only when it supports human decision-making. Teachers remain responsible for interpreting AI-generated recommendations within their educational context, while students benefit from explanations that promote reflection, self-regulation, and informed participation in their own learning processes.

At the same time, explainability should not be interpreted as a complete solution to the challenges associated with educational AI. As discussed throughout the chapter, explanations may be simplified approximations, may be interpreted differently by diverse stakeholder, and should therefore be continuously evaluated within authentic educational settings. Responsible implementation requires technical robustness together with ethical reflection, human oversight, and ongoing validation.

Future research should continue developing educationally grounded evaluation frameworks, reusable implementation templates, and context-sensitive explanation strategies that respond to the diversity of STEAM learning environments. Advancing Explainable Artificial Intelligence therefore requires sustained collaboration among educators, computer scientists, instructional designers, and foundational component of transparent, trustworthy, and human-centered educational ecosystems.

Ultimately, the value of Explainable Artificial Intelligence in STEAM educational lies not in making algorithms more visible, but in making educational decisions more understandable, justifiable, and meaningful for everyone involved in the teaching and learning process.

REFERENCES

Adadi, A., & Berrada, M. (2018). Peeking Inside the Black-Box: A Survey on Explainable Artificial Intelligence (XAI). *IEEE Access : Practical Innovations, Open Solutions*, *6*, 52138–52160. DOI: 10.1109/ACCESS.2018.2870052

Altukhi, Z. M., & Pradhan, S. (2024). Systematic literature review: Explainable AI definitions and challenges in education. In *Proceedings of the 45th International Conference on Information Systems (ICIS 2024), 11*. Association for Information Systems. https://aisel.aisnet.org/icis2024/lit_review/lit_review/11

Barredo Arrieta, A., Díaz-Rodríguez, N., Del Ser, J., Bennetot, A., Tabik, S., Barbado, A., Garcia, S., Gil-Lopez, S., Molina, D., Benjamins, R., Chatila, R., & Herrera, F. (2020). Explainable Artificial Intelligence (XAI): Concepts, taxonomies, opportunities and challenges toward responsible AI. *Information Fusion*, *58*, 82–115. DOI: 10.1016/j.inffus.2019.12.012

Doshi-Velez, F., & Kim, B. (2017). *Towards A Rigorous Science of Interpretable Machine Learning*. arXiv. /arXiv.1702.08608DOI: 10.48550

European Commission: Directorate-General for Education, Youth, Sport and Culture. (2022). *Ethical guidelines on the use of artificial intelligence (AI) and data in teaching and learning for educators*. Publications Office of the European Union. DOI: 10.2766/153756

European Parliament and Council of the European Union. (2024). *Regulation (EU) 2024/1689 of the European Parliament and of the Council of 13 June 2024 laying down harmonised rules on artificial intelligence and amending Regulations (EC) No 300/2008, (EU) No 167/2013, (EU) No 168/2013, (EU) 2018/858, (EU) 2018/1139 and (EU) 2019/2144 and Directives 2014/90/EU, (EU) 2016/797 and (EU) 2020/1828 (Artificial Intelligence Act). Official Journal of the European Union, L 2024/1689.* https://data.europa.eu/eli/reg/2024/1689/oj

Feldman-Maggor, Y., Cukurova, M., Kent, C., & Alexandron, G. (2025). The Impact of Explainable AI on Teachers' Trust and Acceptance of AI EdTech Recommendations: The Power of Domain-specific Explanations. *International Journal of Artificial Intelligence in Education*, *35*(5), 2889–2922. DOI: 10.1007/s40593-025-00486-6

Floridi, L., Cowls, J., Beltrametti, M., Chatila, R., Chazerand, P., Dignum, V., Luetge, C., Madelin, R., Pagallo, U., Rossi, F., Schafer, B., Valcke, P., & Vayena, E. (2018). AI4People—An Ethical Framework for a Good AI Society: Opportunities, Risks, Principles, and Recommendations. *Minds and Machines*, *28*(4), 689–707. DOI: 10.1007/s11023-018-9482-5 PMID: 30930541

Gunasekara, S., & Saarela, M. (2025). Explainable AI in Education: Techniques and Qualitative Assessment. *Applied Sciences (Basel, Switzerland), 15*(3), 1239. DOI: 10.3390/app15031239

Khosravi, H., Shum, S. B., Chen, G., Conati, C., Tsai, Y.-S., Kay, J., Knight, S., Martinez-Maldonado, R., Sadiq, S., & Gašević, D. (2022). Explainable Artificial Intelligence in education. *Computers and Education: Artificial Intelligence, 3*, 100074. DOI: 10.1016/j.caeai.2022.100074

Li, M.-J., Li, S.-T., Yang, A. C. M., Huang, A. Y. Q., & Yang, S. J. H. (2024). Trustworthy and Explainable AI for Learning Analytics. *CEUR Workshop Proceedings, 3667*, 3–12. https://ceur-ws.org/Vol-3667/DC-LAK24-paper-1.pdf

Lundberg, S. M., & Lee, S.-I. (2017). A Unified Approach to Interpreting Model Predictions. *Advances in Neural Information Processing Systems, 30*, 4765-4774. arXiv. DOI: 10.48550/arXiv.1705.07874

Naveenkumar, R. (2025). Advancing Modern Education through Explainable Artificial Intelligence: Enhancing Learning Outcomes and Teaching with Transparent AI Systems. *Journal of Computer Based Parallel Programming, 10*(3), 37–49. https://matjournals.net/engineering/index.php/JoCPP/article/view/2821

Pachouly, S., & Bormane, D. S. (2025). Explainable Artificial Intelligence in Education: Transforming Teaching and Learning – A review. *TPM. Testing, Psychometrics, Methodology in Applied Psychology, 32*(S8), 1571–1584. DOI: 10.5281/zenodo.17866084

Ribeiro, M. T., Singh, S., & Guestrin, C. (2016). "Why Should I Trust You?": Explaining the Predictions of Any Classifier. *Proceedings of the 22nd ACM SIGKDD International Conference on Knowledge Discovery and Data Mining*, 1135–1144. DOI: 10.1145/2939672.2939778

Romero, C., & Ventura, S. (2010). Educational Data Mining: A Review of the State of the Art. *IEEE Transactions on Systems, Man, and Cybernetics. Part C, Applications and Reviews, 40*(6), 601–618. DOI: 10.1109/TSMCC.2010.2053532

Rudin, C. (2019). Stop explaining black box machine learning models for high stakes decisions and use interpretable models instead. *Nature Machine Intelligence, 1*(5), 206–215. DOI: 10.1038/s42256-019-0048-x PMID: 35603010

Siemens, G., & Baker, R. S. J. D. (2012). Learning analytics and educational data mining: Towards communication and collaboration. *Proceedings of the 2nd International Conference on Learning Analytics and Knowledge*, 252–254. DOI: 10.1145/2330601.2330661

UNESCO. (2022). *Recommendation on the ethics of artificial intelligence*. https://unesdoc.unesco.org/ark:/48223/pf0000381137

Zhang, J. (2025). Ethics of Artificial Intelligence in Education: Balancing Automation and Human-Centered Learning. *Applied Mathematics and Nonlinear Sciences*, *10*(1), 1–15. DOI: 10.2478/amns-2025-0843

Chapter 5

Human-in-the-Loop Evaluation in Smart Classrooms for Explainable and Ethical AI-Based Education: A Human-Centered Framework for Intelligent Learning

Arturo Austria Cornejo
http://orcid.org/0009-0002-9291-4397
Universidad Politécnica de Pachuca, Mexico

Marco Antonio García Márquez
http://orcid.org/0000-0002-0644-4839
Universidad Politécnica de Pachuca, Mexico

Jazmín Rodríguez Flores
http://orcid.org/0000-0002-3313-0325
Universidad Politécnica de Pachuca, Mexico

ABSTRACT

The integration of Artificial Intelligence in smart classroom environments is transforming teaching, learning, and assessment processes in modern education systems. Intelligent learning platforms, automated evaluation tools, and learning analytics enable personalized learning experiences and data-driven pedagogical decisions. However, the increasing reliance on automated decision-making raises concerns

DOI: 10.4018/979-8-3373-9675-0.ch005

regarding transparency, fairness, and ethical governance in educational contexts. Human-in-the-Loop (HITL) evaluation has emerged as an effective approach to address these challenges by combining the analytical capabilities of artificial intelligence with the pedagogical expertise of educators. This chapter explores the role of Human-in-the-Loop frameworks in supporting explainable and ethically responsible evaluation processes within smart classrooms. A conceptual architecture is proposed in which AI-driven learning analytics and automated assessment systems are supervised and validated by teachers through iterative feedback mechanisms.

1. INTRODUCTION

The accelerated development of digital technologies has significantly transformed educational systems worldwide. Over the past two decades, advances in artificial intelligence, data analytics, cloud computing, and networked educational platforms have reshaped how knowledge is delivered, how learning processes are monitored, and how student performance is evaluated. These technological innovations have led to the emergence of a new paradigm in education known as the smart classroom, an intelligent learning environment that integrates digital infrastructure, advanced analytics, and adaptive learning technologies to enhance both teaching effectiveness and student learning outcomes.

Traditional classroom environments have historically relied on teacher-centered instructional models in which learning activities occur primarily through lectures, printed materials, and periodic assessments. Evaluation processes in such contexts typically involve written examinations, homework assignments, and observational judgment from instructors. Although these approaches have proven effective for decades, they often provide limited insight into the complex dynamics of learning processes. In many cases, assessments focus primarily on final outcomes rather than on the progression of student engagement, comprehension, and interaction throughout the learning process.

The increasing availability of digital educational platforms has fundamentally altered this scenario. Learning management systems (LMS), virtual classrooms, online collaboration tools, and digital assessment platforms generate large volumes of data related to student learning activities. These datasets capture information such as frequency of participation, time spent interacting with educational resources, engagement with collaborative activities, and performance on various forms of assessment. As a result, educators now have access to a wide range of information that can potentially provide a deeper understanding of student learning behavior.

Artificial intelligence technologies have emerged as essential tools for transforming these large datasets into meaningful educational insights. Machine learning algorithms can identify patterns in student interaction data, detect potential learning difficulties, and recommend instructional interventions. Intelligent tutoring systems can adapt instructional content based on individual student performance, while predictive analytics models can estimate the likelihood of academic success or failure based on historical patterns.

Despite these benefits, the growing integration of artificial intelligence in education also introduces significant challenges. One of the most widely discussed concerns is the increasing reliance on automated decision-making processes within educational evaluation systems. Many AI-driven systems analyze large datasets and generate recommendations or evaluation scores without providing clear explanations of how these conclusions were reached. This lack of transparency can create skepticism among educators and students, who may question the reliability or fairness of automated evaluation outcomes.

Another critical issue involves algorithmic bias and fairness. Machine learning models are often trained using historical data that may reflect existing social or institutional inequalities. If these biases are embedded in training datasets, automated evaluation systems may unintentionally produce biased or discriminatory outcomes. In educational contexts, where evaluation results can significantly influence academic opportunities and future career prospects, ensuring fairness and accountability in automated systems becomes essential.

Furthermore, education involves a range of qualitative factors that cannot easily be captured through quantitative data analysis alone. Human educators consider contextual elements such as student motivation, creativity, collaboration, and personal development when evaluating academic performance. These aspects of learning are often difficult for automated systems to interpret accurately.

For these reasons, many researchers argue that artificial intelligence should not replace human decision-making in educational evaluation but rather support it. One promising approach to achieving this balance is the Human-in-the-Loop (HITL) paradigm. Human-in-the-Loop systems integrate human expertise into automated decision-making processes, allowing artificial intelligence to function as a decision-support tool while maintaining human supervision and accountability.

In educational contexts, HITL evaluation frameworks allow AI systems to analyze educational data and generate preliminary assessments, while instructors review, interpret, and validate these results. This hybrid approach combines the computational efficiency of artificial intelligence with the pedagogical expertise of human educators. By maintaining human oversight in the evaluation process, HITL systems help ensure transparency, fairness, and contextual interpretation of assessment outcomes.

The integration of Human-in-the-Loop frameworks within smart classroom environments represents a promising direction for the development of responsible and trustworthy AI-driven educational systems. By enabling collaboration between intelligent algorithms and human educators, these frameworks support more accurate, ethical, and interpretable evaluation processes.

This chapter explores the role of Human-in-the-Loop evaluation in smart classrooms and proposes a conceptual framework for integrating human expertise with AI-driven learning analytics. The chapter examines the evolution of smart educational environments, the role of artificial intelligence in educational assessment, and the importance of human oversight in automated decision systems. Additionally, the chapter introduces a hybrid evaluation model that combines machine intelligence with teacher judgment in order to enhance the reliability and transparency of educational assessment processes.

A key original contribution of this chapter lies in the integration of Human-in-the-Loop evaluation, explainable artificial intelligence, and smart classroom learning analytics into a unified educational assessment framework specifically designed for intelligent learning ecosystems. Unlike conventional explainable AI approaches that focus primarily on interpreting algorithmic outputs after automated decisions have been generated, the proposed framework incorporates continuous human pedagogical supervision directly within the evaluation workflow. Furthermore, in contrast to fully automated educational assessment systems that rely exclusively on predictive algorithms, the proposed model preserves contextual human judgment as a central component of decision-making. The framework also extends beyond the traditional functionality of learning management systems by integrating adaptive analytics, ethical governance principles, explainability mechanisms, and iterative human feedback processes into a collaborative architecture intended to improve transparency, fairness, interpretability, and pedagogical reliability in AI-assisted educational evaluation.

2. SMART CLASSROOMS AND INTELLIGENT LEARNING ECOSYSTEMS

The concept of the smart classroom has emerged as a response to the rapid digital transformation occurring within educational systems worldwide. Educational institutions are increasingly integrating advanced digital technologies in order to improve learning outcomes, enhance student engagement, and enable data-driven decision-making within teaching environments. Smart classrooms represent a convergence of several technological developments, including artificial intelligence, Internet of

Things (IoT) devices, cloud computing infrastructures, and learning analytics platforms that collectively support intelligent learning ecosystems (Holmes et al., 2022).

Traditional classroom environments have historically relied on static pedagogical structures characterized by teacher-centered instruction and periodic evaluation mechanisms. In such settings, learning activities often take place within a limited technological infrastructure where student performance is primarily assessed through written examinations and assignments. While these approaches have proven effective for many decades, they often fail to capture the complex dynamics of modern learning processes that increasingly occur through digital platforms and collaborative environments (Luckin et al., 2016).

The emergence of digital educational technologies has significantly altered this scenario. Learning management systems, virtual classrooms, digital collaboration platforms, and interactive educational tools generate vast amounts of data related to student learning activities. These datasets capture multiple dimensions of the learning process, including participation patterns, interaction with instructional materials, collaborative engagement with peers, and performance across different forms of assessment. The availability of such data has created new opportunities for educational researchers and instructors to analyze learning behaviors and improve instructional design through evidence-based approaches (Siemens & Baker, 2012).

Smart classrooms extend beyond the simple integration of digital technologies within educational environments. Instead, they represent intelligent systems capable of continuously collecting, processing, and interpreting learning-related data in order to support adaptive educational processes. These environments incorporate sensors, digital interfaces, and advanced analytics tools that enable educators to observe student engagement and performance in real time. As a result, instructors can obtain insights that were previously unavailable through traditional classroom observation alone.

A key characteristic of smart classrooms is their ability to facilitate personalized learning experiences. Personalized learning refers to instructional approaches that adapt educational content, pace, and feedback mechanisms according to the individual needs and abilities of each student. Artificial intelligence technologies play a crucial role in enabling such personalization. Machine learning algorithms can analyze patterns in student performance and recommend learning resources that target specific knowledge gaps or conceptual difficulties (Zawacki-Richter et al., 2019).

Another important aspect of smart classroom environments is their capacity to support real-time feedback and adaptive instruction. Digital learning platforms can continuously monitor student interactions with educational content and identify indicators of engagement or disengagement. For example, systems may detect when students repeatedly struggle with a specific concept or when participation levels decline. These insights allow instructors to intervene early and provide targeted support before academic difficulties escalate into more serious learning challenges (Holmes et al., 2022).

Despite these advantages, the implementation of smart classroom technologies also presents several challenges. One major concern relates to the ethical management of educational data. The collection of detailed information about student behavior and performance raises important questions regarding privacy, consent, and data governance. Educational institutions must therefore establish clear policies regarding how student data are collected, stored, and analyzed in order to ensure compliance with ethical standards and regulatory frameworks.

Another challenge involves the interpretation of educational analytics results. While artificial intelligence can identify statistical patterns within large datasets, these patterns do not always correspond directly to meaningful pedagogical insights. Teachers must therefore interpret data analytics results within the broader context of their professional expertise and knowledge of student behavior. This requirement highlights the importance of integrating human expertise into intelligent educational systems.

Consequently, smart classroom ecosystems should not be understood as fully automated environments in which artificial intelligence replaces human instructors. Instead, they should be conceptualized as collaborative systems in which technology supports educators in making more informed decisions about teaching strategies and student evaluation. Within this perspective, artificial intelligence functions as a tool that enhances human capabilities rather than substituting them.

The integration of artificial intelligence with human-centered pedagogical practices represents a key element in the development of sustainable smart classroom ecosystems. By combining advanced technological infrastructures with professional educational expertise, smart classrooms can provide more responsive and adaptive learning environments capable of addressing the diverse needs of modern learners.

3. ARTIFICIAL INTELLIGENCE IN EDUCATIONAL ASSESSMENT

Artificial intelligence has become an increasingly influential component in the design of modern educational assessment systems. By applying machine learning algorithms and data analytics techniques to educational datasets, AI-driven systems can evaluate student performance, detect learning patterns, and provide personalized feedback. These capabilities have attracted considerable attention among researchers and educators seeking to improve the scalability and effectiveness of assessment processes in both traditional and online learning environments (Baker & Inventado, 2014).

One of the earliest applications of artificial intelligence in education involved automated essay scoring systems. Natural language processing algorithms can analyze written text and evaluate linguistic features such as grammar, vocabulary usage, coherence, and argument structure. Although automated essay scoring systems cannot fully replicate the nuanced judgment of human instructors, they provide a valuable tool for managing large-scale evaluation tasks and generating preliminary feedback for students (Shermis & Burstein, 2013).

In addition to text-based evaluation systems, artificial intelligence has also been applied to the assessment of structured assignments such as programming exercises, mathematical problem sets, and scientific simulations. Intelligent grading systems can automatically analyze student submissions, identify errors in problem-solving processes, and provide immediate feedback that helps learners correct misunderstandings. These systems are particularly valuable in large-scale online courses where thousands of students may submit assignments simultaneously.

Another emerging area of AI-driven educational assessment involves predictive learning analytics. Predictive models use historical educational data to forecast future student performance or identify individuals who may be at risk of academic failure. By analyzing patterns in engagement, attendance, and assessment results, predictive systems can detect early warning signals that indicate potential learning difficulties. Instructors can then implement intervention strategies aimed at supporting students before their academic performance declines significantly (Siemens & Baker, 2012).

Despite these advantages, the increasing reliance on automated evaluation systems has raised several important concerns. One major issue involves the transparency of algorithmic decision-making processes. Many machine learning models operate as complex statistical systems whose internal mechanisms are difficult for humans to interpret. When evaluation outcomes are generated by such systems, students and educators may struggle to understand how the final assessment was determined.

This lack of interpretability is particularly problematic in educational contexts where assessment outcomes can influence important academic decisions such as course grades, graduation eligibility, and admission to advanced programs. Without clear explanations of how algorithmic decisions are made, automated evaluation systems may be perceived as unreliable or unfair.

Another concern involves the potential presence of algorithmic bias within AI-based educational systems. Machine learning models are typically trained using historical datasets that may reflect existing inequalities within educational institutions. If such biases are embedded within the training data, automated assessment systems may inadvertently produce unfair outcomes that disadvantage certain groups of students (Selwyn, 2019).

These challenges highlight the need for responsible AI design in educational contexts. Researchers increasingly emphasize the importance of transparency, fairness, and accountability when developing AI-driven evaluation systems. Explainable artificial intelligence (XAI) techniques have been proposed as a means of improving the interpretability of machine learning models. By providing explanations of how algorithmic decisions are generated, XAI approaches enable educators to better understand and validate the outputs produced by intelligent systems.

However, technical explainability alone is not sufficient to address all concerns associated with automated educational evaluation. Human expertise remains essential for interpreting algorithmic results within their pedagogical context. Teachers possess contextual knowledge about student learning histories, classroom dynamics, and individual circumstances that cannot easily be captured through computational models.

For this reason, many scholars argue that artificial intelligence should function as a decision-support system rather than as a fully autonomous evaluation mechanism. Hybrid approaches that combine AI-generated insights with human judgment are increasingly viewed as a promising direction for developing trustworthy educational assessment systems.

4. HUMAN-IN-THE-LOOP ARTIFICIAL INTELLIGENCE

Human-in-the-Loop (HITL) artificial intelligence represents a design paradigm in which human expertise is integrated into automated decision-making processes. Rather than relying exclusively on autonomous algorithms, HITL systems enable collaboration between machine intelligence and human decision-makers. In such systems, artificial intelligence performs large-scale data analysis and generates recommendations, while human experts supervise, interpret, and validate the resulting outputs (Amershi et al., 2014).

The HITL paradigm has been widely adopted in several fields, including healthcare decision support, autonomous vehicle systems, and industrial automation. In these domains, the integration of human expertise into algorithmic workflows improves reliability, enhances transparency, and reduces the risks associated with fully automated systems. The application of HITL principles to educational technologies reflects a growing recognition that effective learning environments require a balance between technological innovation and human judgment.

Within educational contexts, Human-in-the-Loop frameworks enable instructors to maintain active participation in the evaluation process while benefiting from the analytical capabilities of artificial intelligence. AI systems may analyze large volumes of learning data and generate preliminary assessments, but educators retain the authority to interpret these results and make final evaluation decisions.

Human-AI collaboration can be conceptualized through several levels of human involvement. In Human-in-the-Loop systems, humans participate directly in the decision-making process and provide feedback that improves algorithmic performance. In Human-on-the-Loop systems, humans monitor automated processes and intervene only when anomalies occur. Finally, in Human-out-of-the-Loop systems, decisions are made entirely by autonomous algorithms without human supervision.

Educational evaluation systems are particularly suited to the Human-in-the-Loop model because learning assessment involves qualitative judgments that extend beyond quantitative metrics. Teachers often consider factors such as student motivation, improvement over time, creativity, and collaborative engagement when evaluating performance. These aspects of learning cannot easily be captured through purely computational analysis.

Another significant advantage of HITL systems lies in their ability to support explainable artificial intelligence. When teachers participate in the evaluation process, they can examine the reasoning behind algorithmic recommendations and provide explanations to students regarding how assessment decisions were reached. This transparency strengthens trust in AI-driven educational technologies and promotes greater acceptance of intelligent systems within academic institutions.

Human-in-the-Loop frameworks also support the continuous improvement of artificial intelligence models. Feedback provided by instructors can be used to refine machine learning algorithms and correct inaccurate predictions. Over time, this iterative feedback loop enables AI systems to adapt to the specific educational contexts in which they are deployed.

The integration of HITL methodologies within smart classroom environments therefore represents a promising pathway toward the development of responsible and trustworthy AI-driven educational ecosystems. By combining machine intelligence with human expertise, hybrid evaluation frameworks can improve the accuracy, fairness, and interpretability of educational assessment processes.

Human-in-the-Loop educational evaluation is based on the collaborative interaction between artificial intelligence and human expertise. Instead of treating automated systems as independent evaluators, the HITL paradigm integrates algorithmic analytics with the contextual understanding and pedagogical judgment of educators. As illustrated in figure 1, this collaborative model emerges from the interaction between three fundamental components: educational data generated within learning environments, artificial intelligence systems that analyze these data, and human educators who interpret algorithmic insights and validate evaluation outcomes. This conceptual framework highlights the role of human-AI collaboration in achieving transparent, explainable, and ethically responsible educational evaluation.

Figure 1. Conceptual Model of Human-AI Collaborative Educational Evaluation.

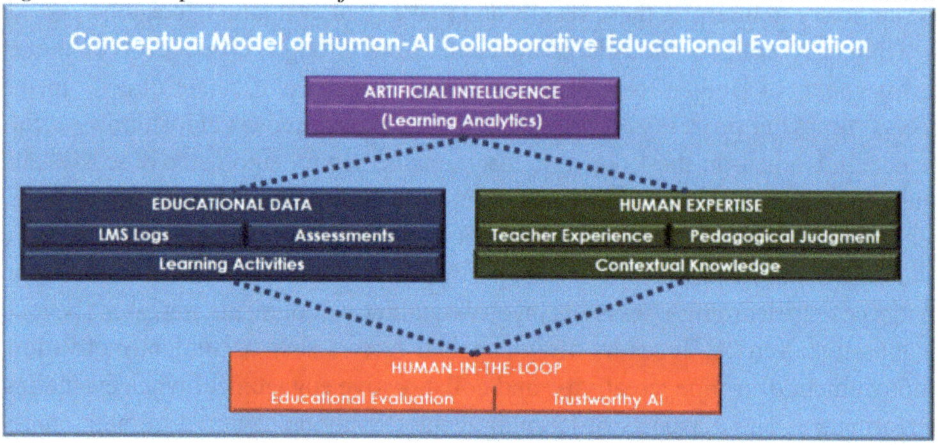

5. HUMAN-IN-THE-LOOP SMART CLASSROOM ARCHITECTURE

The integration of artificial intelligence into educational environments requires the development of robust system architectures capable of supporting data collection, intelligent analytics, and human supervision. Within smart classrooms, the architecture of AI-driven systems must be carefully designed to ensure that automated processes remain transparent, interpretable, and aligned with pedagogical objectives. Human-in-the-Loop (HITL) architectures address this challenge by embedding human expertise directly into the operational workflow of intelligent educational systems (Amershi et al., 2014).

In a HITL-enabled smart classroom environment, artificial intelligence systems function as analytical engines that process large volumes of educational data, while educators remain responsible for interpreting and validating algorithmic outputs. This collaborative architecture ensures that automated evaluation processes do not operate independently of human oversight, thereby preserving pedagogical accountability and ethical decision-making.

A typical smart classroom architecture consists of several interconnected technological layers that facilitate the collection, processing, and interpretation of educational data. These layers include data acquisition systems, data management infrastructures, machine learning analytics modules, decision-support interfaces, and human supervision mechanisms. Each component plays a specific role within the broader intelligent learning ecosystem.

The first layer of the architecture involves the data acquisition subsystem, which is responsible for collecting educational data from multiple sources within the learning environment. These data sources may include learning management systems, classroom interaction platforms, collaborative learning tools, and digital assessment systems. In more advanced smart classroom implementations, Internet of Things (IoT) sensors may also capture environmental data such as classroom occupancy, student attendance, and interaction patterns within physical learning spaces (Holmes et al., 2022).

Once educational data are collected, they are transmitted to the data management layer, where they are stored and organized within cloud-based educational data infrastructures. These infrastructures typically rely on distributed data storage systems capable of managing large volumes of heterogeneous data. Data preprocessing techniques are applied to clean, normalize, and structure the datasets before they are used for analytical purposes.

The machine learning analytics layer represents the core intelligence component of the smart classroom architecture. In this layer, machine learning algorithms analyze student interaction data in order to identify patterns related to engagement, comprehension, and academic performance. Various analytical techniques may be applied, including classification models, clustering algorithms, predictive analytics models, and recommendation systems. These algorithms enable the detection of learning difficulties, prediction of academic risk, and generation of personalized instructional recommendations (Zawacki-Richter et al., 2019).

However, unlike fully autonomous AI systems, HITL architectures incorporate an additional layer known as the human supervision layer. This layer ensures that algorithmic outputs are reviewed and validated by human educators before final decisions are made. Teachers can analyze the recommendations generated by machine learning models and determine whether these recommendations are appropriate given the pedagogical context of the classroom.

The interaction between artificial intelligence and human expertise is facilitated through decision-support interfaces. These interfaces present analytics results through dashboards, visualizations, and performance indicators that allow educators to interpret complex datasets. Visualization tools transform raw analytics outputs into comprehensible insights that can guide instructional decisions. For example, dashboards may display indicators such as student engagement levels, predicted academic risk, and progression through learning modules.

The HITL architecture therefore supports a collaborative workflow in which artificial intelligence assists educators in interpreting large volumes of educational data while preserving human control over final evaluation decisions. This hybrid approach ensures that automated analytics systems remain aligned with educational values such as fairness, transparency, and pedagogical integrity.

An important advantage of HITL architectures lies in their ability to support continuous model improvement. When teachers review algorithmic predictions and provide corrective feedback, these inputs can be used to retrain machine learning models and improve their predictive accuracy. Over time, the system becomes increasingly adapted to the specific educational context in which it operates.

Another critical component of HITL smart classroom architectures involves explainability mechanisms. Explainable artificial intelligence techniques allow educators to understand how machine learning models generate their predictions. For instance, feature importance analysis may reveal which student behaviors or performance indicators most strongly influenced an algorithmic recommendation. Such insights enable educators to evaluate the reliability of AI-generated results and communicate these explanations to students when necessary (Holmes et al., 2022).

Despite the advantages of HITL architectures, their implementation also requires careful consideration of several practical challenges. One challenge involves ensuring interoperability between different educational technologies. Smart classrooms often integrate multiple platforms and digital tools, each of which may generate data in different formats. Establishing standardized data exchange protocols is essential for enabling seamless integration of these systems.

Another challenge concerns data privacy and ethical governance. Educational data often contain sensitive information about student behavior and academic performance. Institutions implementing smart classroom architectures must therefore establish robust data protection policies that ensure compliance with privacy regulations and ethical guidelines (Selwyn, 2019).

Overall, the HITL smart classroom architecture provides a framework for integrating artificial intelligence into educational environments in a responsible and pedagogically meaningful manner. By combining advanced analytics technologies with human oversight, these systems support more accurate, interpretable, and ethical evaluation processes within modern educational ecosystems.

The integration of artificial intelligence within smart classroom environments requires a structured architecture capable of combining automated data analytics with human pedagogical supervision. As illustrated in figure 2, the Human-in-the-Loop smart classroom architecture is composed of several interconnected layers, including data acquisition systems, learning analytics infrastructures, machine learning evaluation modules, explainable AI mechanisms, and human decision-support interfaces. This architecture ensures that automated educational analytics remain interpretable and subject to human oversight, thereby reinforcing transparency, accountability, and pedagogical validity in AI-supported evaluation processes.

Figure 2. Human-in-the-Loop Smart Classroom Architecture for AI-Assisted Educational Evaluation.

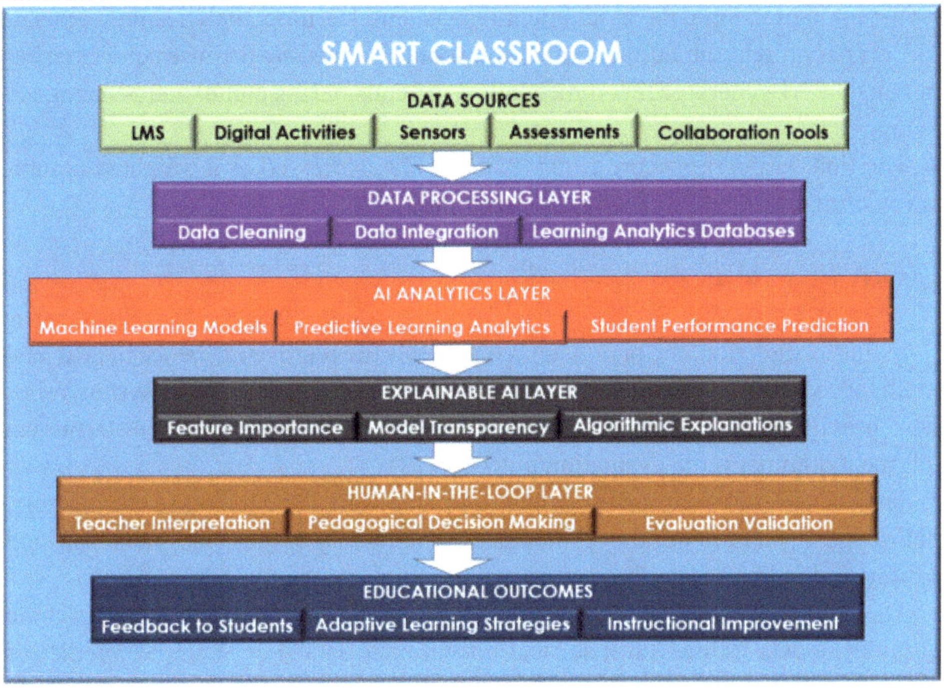

6. MATHEMATICAL MODEL FOR HUMAN-IN-THE-LOOP EDUCATIONAL EVALUATION

In order to formalize the interaction between artificial intelligence and human decision-making within smart classroom environments, it is useful to develop a mathematical representation of the Human-in-the-Loop evaluation process. Mathematical modeling enables researchers to describe how algorithmic predictions and human judgments combine to produce final educational evaluation outcomes.

Within AI-driven educational systems, automated models typically generate predictive scores based on observed learning data. These scores may represent estimates of student performance, engagement levels, or probability of academic success. However, in HITL frameworks these predictions do not directly determine final evaluation results. Instead, they serve as inputs to a collaborative decision process involving human educators.

Let A_i represent the automated evaluation score produced by an artificial intelligence model for student *i*. This score may be derived from machine learning analysis of student interaction data, assessment results, and learning analytics indicators.

Let H_i represent the human evaluation score assigned by the instructor after reviewing the AI-generated recommendation and considering contextual pedagogical factors.

The final evaluation score E_i can therefore be expressed as a weighted combination of machine intelligence and human judgment.

$$E_i = \alpha A_i + (1 - \alpha) H_i$$

In this formulation, the parameter α represents the relative influence of artificial intelligence within the evaluation process. When α approaches 1, the system relies more heavily on automated evaluation. Conversely, when α approaches 0, human judgment dominates the evaluation outcome.

The selection of appropriate weighting parameters depends on several factors, including the reliability of the AI model, the complexity of the assessment task, and institutional policies regarding automated decision-making in education.

The automated evaluation score A_i itself may be computed through machine learning models trained on historical educational data. For example, predictive learning analytics models may estimate academic performance using multiple learning indicators such as participation frequency, assignment completion rates, and previous assessment results.

A simplified representation of the automated prediction model can be expressed as a weighted combination of learning indicators.

$$A_i = \sum_{k=1}^{n} \cdot W_k X_{ik}$$

Here:

- x_{ik} represents the value of the k-th learning indicator for student *i*.
- w_k represents the weight assigned to that indicator by the machine learning model.
- *n* represents the number of learning indicators included in the predictive model.

These indicators may include variables such as:

- Engagement with digital learning materials
- Participation in collaborative activities

- Performance in formative assessments
- Interaction frequency within learning management systems

The human evaluation component H_i incorporates qualitative factors that may not be captured through automated data analysis. Instructors may consider elements such as student effort, improvement over time, creativity in problem solving, and contributions to collaborative learning activities.

Human evaluation can therefore be represented as a function of qualitative assessment criteria:

$$H_i = f(Q_i, C_i, P_i)$$

where:

- Q_i represents qualitative performance indicators.
- C_i represents contextual factors observed by the instructor.
- P_i represents pedagogical considerations specific to the course.

The integration of automated predictions and human judgment forms the foundation of the HITL evaluation model. By combining quantitative analytics with qualitative interpretation, the model captures both computational efficiency and pedagogical expertise.

An additional advantage of this mathematical framework is that it enables the evaluation of system reliability and fairness. Researchers can analyze how variations in the weighting parameter α influence evaluation outcomes. If automated predictions consistently diverge from human assessments, this may indicate potential biases or limitations within the machine learning model.

In practical smart classroom implementations, the weighting parameter α can be dynamically adjusted according to the educational context, assessment objectives, and level of confidence associated with AI-generated predictions. For example, in low-stakes formative assessments, institutions may assign higher values of α in order to prioritize rapid automated feedback and scalability. Conversely, in high-stakes evaluations such as final course assessments, thesis evaluations, or competency certifications, lower values of α may be preferred to ensure stronger human pedagogical supervision. This adaptive calibration mechanism demonstrates how the mathematical model directly influences operational decision-making within the HITL architecture. Rather than functioning as a static equation, the parameter α becomes a governance variable capable of balancing efficiency, interpretability, fairness, and educational accountability according to institutional requirements.

The proposed mathematical framework is also closely connected to the layered Human-in-the-Loop architecture presented in this chapter. Within the smart classroom ecosystem, AI models generate predictive scores through the learning analytics layer, while explainability modules provide interpretable insights regarding the factors influencing algorithmic recommendations. These outputs are subsequently reviewed by instructors through human supervision interfaces, where teachers may validate, adjust, or override automated scores based on contextual pedagogical interpretation. In this sense, the human evaluation component H_i is not merely an isolated correction factor, but rather a pedagogically informed decision process integrated directly into the architecture of the intelligent learning environment. The mathematical formulation therefore reflects the operational interaction between data acquisition systems, predictive analytics, explainable AI mechanisms, and human-centered educational supervision.

The HITL framework incorporates continuous feedback loops that allow human intervention to improve future AI performance over time. When instructors systematically modify or correct AI-generated predictions, these discrepancies between A_i and H_i can be recorded as additional training information for subsequent machine learning refinement. As a result, the system gradually learns from human pedagogical expertise and becomes better aligned with institutional evaluation criteria and instructional practices. This feedback mechanism transforms the Human-in-the-Loop architecture into an adaptive educational ecosystem in which algorithmic models evolve through iterative interaction with educators. Consequently, the mathematical model not only formalizes the relationship between automated and human evaluation, but also represents the dynamic co-adaptation process through which artificial intelligence and human expertise collaboratively improve educational assessment reliability.

Furthermore, the HITL framework supports adaptive learning feedback mechanisms. When discrepancies between A_i and H_i occur, the system can record these differences and use them as training data for improving future machine learning predictions. Over time, this feedback loop allows AI models to become more aligned with human pedagogical judgment.

Mathematical modeling of HITL educational systems therefore provides a structured framework for understanding how artificial intelligence and human expertise interact within smart classroom environments. By formalizing these relationships, researchers can evaluate the performance of hybrid evaluation systems and design more reliable and interpretable educational technologies.

The development of such models represents an important step toward the creation of responsible AI-driven educational ecosystems that maintain transparency, fairness, and human oversight within automated decision processes.

The Human-in-the-Loop evaluation process involves a structured interaction between automated analytics and human pedagogical judgment. Artificial intelligence systems analyze student learning data and generate predictive evaluation scores, while instructors review these predictions and incorporate contextual educational insights before confirming the final evaluation decision. As illustrated in figure 3, the evaluation workflow integrates data collection, machine learning prediction, explainable AI interpretation, and human validation stages that collectively ensure transparency and pedagogical accountability in smart classroom assessment systems.

Figure 3. Human-in-the-Loop Educational Evaluation Workflow in Smart Classroom Environments.

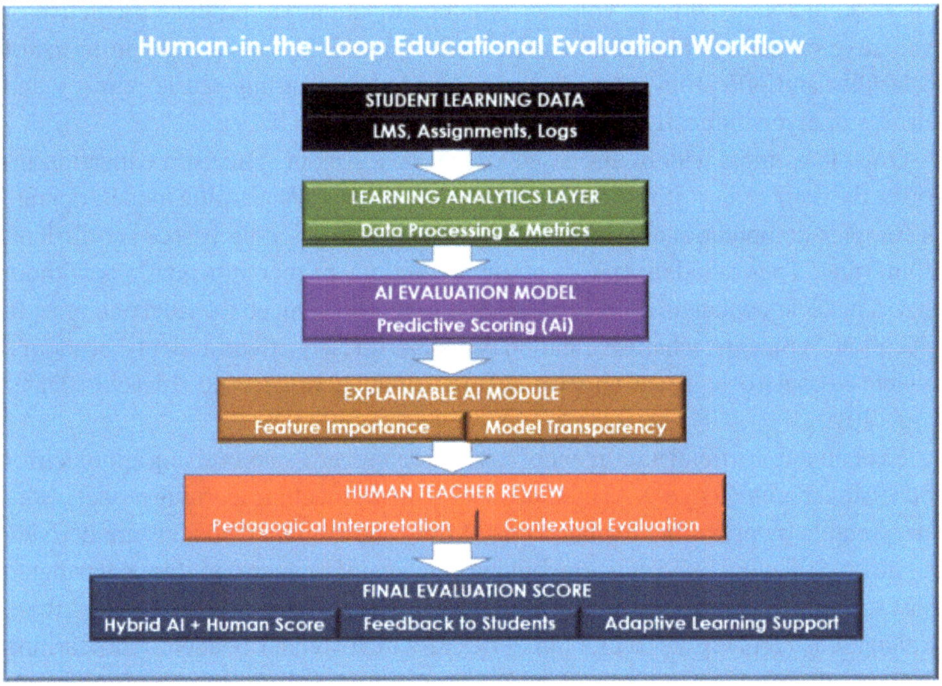

7. ETHICAL AND GOVERNANCE CONSIDERATIONS IN AI-DRIVEN SMART CLASSROOM EVALUATION

The integration of artificial intelligence into educational environments has introduced a wide range of ethical, social, and governance challenges that must be carefully addressed in order to ensure responsible deployment of intelligent systems.

As smart classrooms increasingly rely on learning analytics, automated evaluation mechanisms, and predictive algorithms, questions regarding fairness, transparency, accountability, and data protection become central to the design and implementation of educational technologies. These ethical considerations are particularly relevant when artificial intelligence is used to support or influence decisions that affect student evaluation, academic progression, and educational opportunities (Holmes et al., 2022).

Educational assessment has historically been grounded in professional pedagogical judgment, where teachers evaluate student performance through observation, assignments, examinations, and interaction within the classroom. The introduction of algorithmic evaluation systems alters this paradigm by incorporating automated processes that analyze large volumes of educational data to produce predictive or evaluative outputs. While these systems offer significant advantages in terms of scalability and efficiency, they also raise concerns regarding the legitimacy and fairness of algorithmically generated decisions (Selwyn, 2019).

One of the most widely discussed ethical concerns in AI-driven education involves the issue of algorithmic transparency. Many machine learning models operate as complex computational systems whose internal decision processes are difficult to interpret. These models may generate predictions or recommendations without providing clear explanations of how specific inputs influenced the final outcome. In educational contexts, where evaluation decisions directly affect students' academic trajectories, such opacity can undermine trust in intelligent systems (Zawacki-Richter et al., 2019).

Explainable artificial intelligence (XAI) has emerged as a promising approach for addressing this challenge. XAI methods seek to make machine learning models more interpretable by providing explanations of how algorithmic decisions are derived. For instance, feature importance techniques can identify which variables contributed most strongly to a particular prediction. In the context of educational analytics, these explanations can help instructors understand which student behaviors or learning patterns influenced an automated evaluation result (Adadi & Berrada, 2018).

From an architectural perspective, the explainability layer within Human-in-the-Loop smart classroom systems plays a central role in operationalizing the ethical principle of transparency. Rather than treating explainability as an isolated technical feature, HITL architectures integrate interpretable analytics dashboards, feature-importance visualizations, and model explanation interfaces directly into the educational evaluation workflow. These components allow instructors to understand how algorithmic predictions are generated and which learning indicators contribute most strongly to evaluation outcomes. In this sense, transparency is not achieved solely through access to algorithmic outputs, but through the design of interfaces and interpretability mechanisms that make automated reasoning pedagogically understandable and actionable for human educators. (Khosravi, et al., 2022).

However, technical transparency alone is not sufficient to ensure ethical use of AI in education. Ethical governance frameworks must also address issues related to fairness and bias. Machine learning systems are typically trained using historical datasets that reflect patterns of behavior observed in previous cohorts of students. If these datasets contain biases related to socioeconomic background, gender, language proficiency, or cultural context, algorithmic models may inadvertently reproduce or amplify these inequalities (Williamson & Eynon, 2020).

For example, predictive models trained on historical academic performance data may identify patterns that correlate with demographic characteristics rather than with actual learning ability. If such correlations are incorporated into evaluation algorithms, the resulting predictions may disadvantage certain groups of students. This risk highlights the importance of implementing fairness-aware machine learning techniques when designing educational AI systems (Kizilcec, R. F., & Lee, H. 2023).

Human-in-the-Loop (HITL) evaluation frameworks provide an effective mechanism for mitigating these risks. By ensuring that teachers remain actively involved in the evaluation process, HITL systems allow educators to review algorithmic predictions and intervene when necessary. Human oversight enables instructors to identify potential biases, contextualize algorithmic outputs, and ensure that evaluation decisions remain aligned with pedagogical principles (Amershi et al., 2014).

Another important ethical consideration concerns the protection of student data privacy. Smart classroom environments often collect extensive information about student behavior, including interaction with learning materials, participation in digital activities, and performance on assessments. These datasets may contain sensitive information that must be handled with care to prevent unauthorized access or misuse.

Educational institutions implementing AI-driven learning analytics systems must therefore adopt robust data governance frameworks that define how data are collected, stored, processed, and shared. Such frameworks should comply with relevant privacy regulations and ethical guidelines while ensuring that students maintain control over their personal data (Prinsloo & Slade, 2017).

Within smart classroom architectures, data governance mechanisms constitute the technical foundation of privacy protection. Secure data storage protocols, access-control systems, anonymization procedures, and permission-management infrastructures are essential architectural components for ensuring ethical handling of student information. Privacy-preserving governance is therefore not merely an institutional policy requirement, but an operational characteristic embedded within the technological architecture of intelligent educational systems. The integration of these governance mechanisms into HITL environments enables institutions to support advanced learning analytics while maintaining compliance with ethical and legal standards for student data protection (UNESCO. 2023).

In addition to privacy concerns, ethical governance must also address issues related to accountability. When automated systems contribute to educational decision-making, it becomes necessary to determine who is responsible for the outcomes produced by these systems. If an algorithm incorrectly evaluates a student's performance or produces biased predictions, responsibility cannot be attributed solely to the machine. Instead, accountability must be shared among system designers, educational institutions, and human decision-makers who oversee the use of these technologies.

The concept of algorithmic accountability emphasizes the need for mechanisms that allow institutions to audit and evaluate the performance of AI systems. Regular monitoring of algorithmic outputs can help detect patterns of bias or inaccuracy and ensure that intelligent systems continue to operate within acceptable ethical boundaries.

Another ethical dimension of AI-driven educational evaluation involves the potential impact on the role of teachers. Some critics argue that increasing reliance on automated systems may diminish the professional autonomy of educators by shifting decision-making authority toward algorithmic processes. However, HITL frameworks offer a balanced alternative by positioning artificial intelligence as a decision-support tool rather than as a replacement for human expertise.

Within HITL systems, teachers retain ultimate authority over evaluation decisions while benefiting from the analytical capabilities of machine learning technologies. This collaborative approach preserves the central role of educators while enabling them to leverage data-driven insights in order to improve instructional strategies and student support.

Dashboard design also plays an important ethical role within Human-in-the-Loop educational systems. The visual organization of analytics interfaces can significantly influence how instructors interpret student performance indicators and algorithmic recommendations. Poorly designed dashboards may unintentionally emphasize certain metrics while obscuring contextual information necessary for equitable educational decision-making. Conversely, fairness-oriented dashboard architectures can support balanced interpretation by integrating uncertainty indicators, contextual explanations, comparative visualizations, and opportunities for human annotation. In this sense, interface design becomes closely connected to the ethical principle of fairness by shaping how educational data are interpreted and acted upon within real-world instructional settings.

Despite the significant advantages associated with Human-in-the-Loop evaluation frameworks, the incorporation of continuous human supervision into AI-driven educational systems also introduces important operational and ethical challenges that must be critically acknowledged. One of the most relevant concerns involves the potential increase in cognitive load for instructors. In smart classroom environments where large volumes of educational data are continuously generated and analyzed, teachers may be required to review algorithmic predictions, interpret learning analytics dashboards, validate automated recommendations, and make contextual pedagogical decisions simultaneously. If not carefully designed, HITL systems may unintentionally overwhelm educators with excessive information and decision-making responsibilities, thereby reducing the practical effectiveness of the evaluation process.

Another important limitation relates to scalability. While Human-in-the-Loop frameworks improve interpretability and ethical accountability, maintaining active human participation in evaluation workflows may become increasingly difficult in large-scale educational environments involving hundreds or thousands of students. In such contexts, continuous teacher validation of AI-generated outputs may produce review fatigue, delayed feedback cycles, and inconsistent evaluation practices across different instructors. Human evaluators may also exhibit variability in judgment due to subjective interpretation, emotional factors, workload pressure, or differences in pedagogical experience. Consequently, HITL systems do not completely eliminate bias or inconsistency, but rather redistribute responsibility across both human and algorithmic actors within the educational ecosystem.

The successful operation of Human-in-the-Loop educational systems depends heavily on adequate teacher training and AI literacy. Educators must understand not only how to interpret algorithmic outputs, but also the limitations, uncertainty levels, and potential biases associated with machine learning models. Without sufficient preparation, instructors may either over-trust automated recommendations or disregard potentially valuable analytics insights. For this reason, the ethical deployment of HITL architectures requires continuous professional development programs that strengthen educators' competencies in data interpretation, algorithmic reasoning, and responsible AI governance. Recognizing these limitations is essential for developing more realistic, sustainable, and human-centered implementations of intelligent educational evaluation systems.

Furthermore, ethical implementation of AI in education requires active participation from multiple stakeholders, including teachers, students, administrators, and policymakers. Transparent communication about how AI systems operate and how student data are used can help build trust among these stakeholders. Educational institutions should also provide training programs that help educators understand the capabilities and limitations of AI-driven tools.

Another emerging concern relates to the potential psychological impact of algorithmic evaluation on students. When learners perceive that their performance is being continuously monitored and analyzed by automated systems, they may experience increased pressure or anxiety. Ensuring that evaluation systems remain supportive rather than punitive is therefore essential for maintaining healthy learning environments.

Ultimately, ethical governance frameworks for AI-driven smart classrooms must balance technological innovation with fundamental educational values. Transparency, fairness, privacy protection, and human oversight should serve as guiding principles in the design and deployment of intelligent educational systems. By incorporating these principles into the architecture of Human-in-the-Loop evaluation frameworks, educational institutions can harness the benefits of artificial intelligence while safeguarding the rights and well-being of students.

Educational evaluation methods can vary significantly depending on the degree of human involvement and the level of automation employed by intelligent systems. Traditional teacher-centered evaluation relies entirely on human judgment, whereas AI-based assessment systems depend on automated algorithms to analyze learning data and generate evaluation outcomes. The Human-in-the-Loop paradigm seeks to combine the advantages of both approaches by integrating algorithmic analytics with human pedagogical supervision. As summarized in table 1, each evaluation model presents distinct characteristics in terms of scalability, interpretability, ethical accountability, and pedagogical flexibility.

Table 1. Comparison of AI-Based, Human-Based, and Human-in-the-Loop Educational Evaluation.

Evaluation Dimension	AI-Based Evaluation	Human-Based Evaluation	Human-in-the-Loop E
Decision Authority	Algorithmic models generate evaluation outcomes automatically	Teachers make evaluation decisions based on professional judgment	AI generates predictio teachers validate and decisions
Scalability	Very high scalability for large datasets and large student populations	Limited scalability due to manual grading workload	High scalability supporte human supervisi
Speed of Evaluation	Extremely fast automated evaluation	Slower due to manual analysis and grading	Fast preliminary evalua human review
Interpretability	Often limited due to complex machine learning models	High interpretability based on human reasoning	Improved interpretabili explainable AI and h interpretation
Bias Risk	Potential algorithmic bias from training data	Potential human cognitive bias	Hybrid mitigation throu oversight and algor transparency
Consistency of Evaluation	Highly consistent if model is stable	May vary between instructors	Balanced consisten contextual interpre
Pedagogical Context Awareness	Limited contextual understanding	Strong contextual awareness	AI analytics combined w contextual knowle
Ethical Accountability	Difficult to assign responsibility solely to algorithms	Clear human accountability	Shared accountability system designers and e
Transparency of Decisions	Often limited unless explainable AI methods are applied	High transparency through human explanation	Enhanced transpare explainable AI and h interpretation
Adaptability to Student Needs	Adaptive learning algorithms can personalize instruction	Teachers adapt instruction through observation and interaction	Hybrid adaptation co analytics with pedag strategies
Suitability for Large Online Courses	Highly suitable for large-scale environments	Challenging due to instructor workload	Highly suitable due to evaluation workl
Educational Trustworthiness	May raise trust concerns due to automation	Trusted due to human involvement	High trust due to combin efficiency and human

8. IMPLEMENTATION SCENARIOS OF HUMAN-IN-THE-LOOP EVALUATION IN SMART CLASSROOMS

The successful implementation of Human-in-the-Loop evaluation systems in smart classroom environments requires the integration of technological infrastructure, pedagogical strategies, and institutional policies. While the theoretical foundations of HITL frameworks emphasize collaboration between artificial intelligence and human expertise, practical deployment involves addressing several operational challenges related to system architecture, data integration, user interfaces, and instructor engagement.

Smart classroom implementation scenarios can vary significantly depending on the educational context in which these systems are deployed. Universities, secondary schools, and online learning platforms may adopt different configurations of intelligent technologies based on their pedagogical objectives and technological capabilities. Nevertheless, several common implementation patterns can be identified across different educational environments (Yang, Ogata, Matsui & Chen, 2021).

One of the most common implementation scenarios involves the integration of learning analytics platforms with existing learning management systems. In this configuration, student interaction data generated through digital learning platforms are continuously collected and analyzed by machine learning algorithms. These algorithms may identify patterns related to engagement, participation, and academic performance. The results of these analyses are then presented to instructors through visual dashboards that support pedagogical decision-making (Siemens & Baker, 2012).

Within a HITL framework, instructors do not rely solely on the automated predictions generated by the analytics system. Instead, they interpret these predictions in light of their knowledge of the classroom context and the individual characteristics of students. For example, an algorithm may identify a student as being at risk of academic failure based on reduced participation in online discussions. However, the instructor may recognize that the student's reduced participation is due to temporary personal circumstances rather than a lack of engagement with the course material. Human interpretation therefore plays a crucial role in ensuring that algorithmic predictions are applied appropriately.

Another implementation scenario involves intelligent tutoring systems that provide personalized learning pathways for students. These systems analyze student responses to exercises and adjust the difficulty level of instructional materials accordingly. While automated tutoring systems can effectively deliver adaptive learning experiences, the presence of human instructors remains essential for interpreting complex learning behaviors and providing motivational support to students (Luckin et al., 2016).

Human-in-the-Loop evaluation frameworks can also be implemented in hybrid learning environments that combine physical classroom interaction with digital learning platforms. In such environments, IoT devices and classroom interaction tools may capture data related to attendance, participation in group activities, and engagement with instructional resources. Machine learning models analyze these data streams to generate indicators of student engagement and performance.

Teachers then review these indicators through decision-support dashboards that visualize trends in student behavior. For example, dashboards may display metrics related to participation frequency, collaborative interaction networks, and progression through learning modules. These visualizations enable instructors to identify patterns that may indicate emerging learning difficulties or opportunities for pedagogical intervention.

In addition to classroom-level applications, HITL evaluation frameworks can also be implemented at the institutional level to support academic program management. Universities may deploy learning analytics platforms that monitor the academic progress of entire student cohorts. Predictive models can identify students who may be at risk of dropping out or failing key courses. Academic advisors and instructors can then use these insights to provide targeted support and guidance.

The implementation of HITL systems also requires careful attention to user interface design. Decision-support dashboards must present complex analytics outputs in ways that are understandable to educators who may not have extensive technical expertise in data science. Effective visualization techniques, such as heat maps, trend graphs, and network diagrams, can help instructors interpret learning analytics results more effectively.

Another important factor in successful implementation is instructor training. Educators must develop an understanding of how AI-driven analytics systems operate and how their outputs should be interpreted. Without adequate training, instructors may either over-rely on algorithmic recommendations or ignore them entirely. Both outcomes reduce the effectiveness of intelligent learning systems.

Institutional support is also essential for successful deployment of HITL evaluation frameworks. Educational institutions must invest in technological infrastructure capable of supporting data analytics and machine learning processes. Additionally, institutions should establish governance policies that define how AI systems are used in educational decision-making.

Evaluation of HITL implementation outcomes is another critical aspect of system deployment. Institutions should regularly assess whether AI-driven analytics systems are improving educational outcomes, supporting effective teaching practices, and maintaining fairness in evaluation processes. Such evaluations may involve quantitative metrics, such as improvements in student retention rates, as well as qualitative feedback from instructors and students.

The long-term success of Human-in-the-Loop evaluation systems ultimately depends on achieving a balanced integration of technological innovation and human-centered educational practices. When implemented effectively, these systems can enhance the ability of educators to monitor student learning, identify emerging challenges, and provide personalized instructional support.

Although Human-in-the-Loop implementation frameworks offer substantial advantages for educational evaluation, real-world deployment also reveals important operational limitations that institutions must carefully address. One practical challenge involves the sustainability of continuous human supervision within large-scale smart classroom environments. As the number of students, learning interactions, and algorithmic predictions increases, instructors may experience significant review fatigue when required to validate large quantities of AI-generated recommendations. Excessive dependence on manual validation processes may reduce system efficiency and limit the scalability benefits that artificial intelligence is intended to provide.

Implementation challenges are also closely associated with human variability in educational judgment. Different instructors may interpret the same learning analytics outputs in distinct ways depending on their pedagogical philosophies, professional experience, disciplinary background, or contextual understanding of student behavior. While this flexibility represents one of the strengths of Human-in-the-Loop systems, it may also introduce inconsistencies across evaluation processes if institutional guidelines and governance mechanisms are not clearly established. In addition, the effectiveness of HITL deployment depends strongly on teacher preparedness and institutional support structures. Educators require adequate training not only in the use of AI-driven dashboards and analytics tools, but also in understanding algorithmic limitations, uncertainty interpretation, and ethical decision-making within data-driven learning environments (Matcha, W et al., 2020)

These limitations demonstrate that the successful implementation of Human-in-the-Loop evaluation systems requires more than technological sophistication alone. Sustainable deployment depends on balancing automation efficiency with realistic human participation capacities, ensuring that intelligent educational systems remain pedagogically manageable, ethically responsible, and operationally viable in diverse educational contexts.

As educational technologies continue to evolve, smart classrooms are likely to become increasingly sophisticated environments in which artificial intelligence and human expertise work together to support meaningful learning experiences. HITL frameworks provide a pathway toward achieving this vision by ensuring that technological innovation remains aligned with the pedagogical values that underpin effective education.

9. FUTURE RESEARCH DIRECTIONS FOR HUMAN-IN-THE-LOOP EVALUATION IN SMART CLASSROOMS

The future of Human-in-the-Loop (HITL) evaluation in smart classrooms lies at the intersection of several rapidly evolving domains, including explainable artificial intelligence, multimodal learning analytics, adaptive educational systems, human-computer interaction, educational data governance, and responsible AI policy. Although current research has already demonstrated the value of integrating human expertise into AI-assisted educational evaluation, the field remains in an early stage of theoretical consolidation and practical maturation. For this reason, future research should not only focus on improving predictive accuracy, but also on developing more comprehensive frameworks that address pedagogical validity, interpretability, fairness, accountability, and institutional scalability (Holmes et al., 2022; Bond et al., 2024).

One of the most important directions for future research involves the development of multimodal Human-in-the-Loop evaluation systems. Many existing educational AI systems rely primarily on structured digital traces such as grades, clicks, time-on-task, and assignment completion data. While these indicators are useful, they often provide only a partial representation of student learning. Future smart classroom systems are likely to incorporate richer multimodal data streams, including speech patterns, collaborative interactions, gaze direction, posture, emotion-related signals, writing processes, and participation dynamics in physical or hybrid classrooms. These data sources may generate a more nuanced understanding of learning behavior, but they also introduce substantial interpretive complexity. Consequently, future research must explore how teachers can meaningfully supervise multimodal AI systems without being overwhelmed by excessive informational load (Martinez-Maldonado et al., 2018; Ochoa & Wise, 2021).

Related to this issue is the need for more advanced research on cognitively sustainable dashboard design. One of the practical challenges of Human-in-the-Loop architectures is that, although they preserve teacher oversight, they may also generate new burdens for instructors if the interfaces are not designed appropriately. Future research should examine how learning analytics dashboards can present complex predictive information in ways that are cognitively manageable, pedagogically relevant, and context-sensitive. Effective dashboards should not simply display raw metrics; they should support teacher reasoning, highlight uncertainty, reveal patterns over time, and indicate when human intervention is especially necessary. The future of HITL evaluation will therefore depend not only on model performance, but also on the quality of the human-AI interaction layer that mediates educational decision-making (Verbert et al., 2020; Paulsen & Lindsay, 2024).

Another important direction concerns the integration of uncertainty-aware educational AI systems. In many current applications, AI outputs are presented as if they were definitive indicators of student performance or risk. However, educational processes are inherently uncertain and context-dependent. Future research should investigate ways of explicitly communicating algorithmic uncertainty to teachers, students, and educational managers. For example, predictive systems could indicate confidence intervals, levels of model certainty, disagreement across models, or sensitivity to missing data. Such features would help prevent overreliance on AI-generated scores and reinforce the idea that machine predictions are probabilistic tools for pedagogical support rather than unquestionable judgments. In the context of Human-in-the-Loop evaluation, uncertainty communication is essential because it helps teachers calibrate the extent to which they should trust or revise automated outputs (Saqr, 2025; Gunasekara & Saarela, 2025).

Future research must also strengthen the relationship between HITL systems and explainable artificial intelligence (XAI). While explainability has become a widely discussed principle in AI ethics, its practical implementation in education remains uneven. Explanations that satisfy technical researchers do not always support meaningful pedagogical interpretation. A future research agenda should therefore distinguish between technical explainability, user-centered explainability, and pedagogical explainability. Technical explainability refers to the transparency of model operations; user-centered explainability concerns the understandability of outputs for non-expert stakeholders; pedagogical explainability requires that the explanation be relevant to teaching practice and support educational action. In future HITL systems, explanations should be designed not merely to satisfy transparency requirements, but to enable teachers to make better instructional decisions and to communicate those decisions in fair and understandable ways to students (Adadi & Berrada, 2018; Khosravi et al., 2022; Kizilcec & Lee, 2022).

Another promising avenue for future work is the development of adaptive Human-in-the-Loop mechanisms. Current HITL frameworks often assume a fixed relationship between human judgment and algorithmic recommendation, but future systems could dynamically adjust the degree of human involvement depending on the characteristics of the task, the reliability of the model, and the pedagogical stakes of the decision. For instance, low-stakes formative assessment tasks might rely more heavily on automated evaluation, whereas high-stakes decisions such as final grading, progression assessment, or identification of academic risk might require stronger human intervention. Similarly, the system might learn over time which types of cases frequently require teacher correction and route those cases automatically toward deeper human review. Research on adaptive levels of autonomy in educational AI could significantly enhance both efficiency and ethical robustness (Amershi et al., 2014; Memarian & Doleck, 2024).

A related domain for future exploration involves teacher modeling within intelligent educational systems. To date, many AI systems model student behavior extensively but represent teacher input only minimally. Future HITL systems could incorporate models of instructor decision patterns, feedback preferences, pedagogical priorities, and evaluation styles. Such modeling would not be intended to replace teachers, but to make AI systems more responsive to the instructional philosophy and contextual judgment of the educator. For example, a system could learn that a given teacher prioritizes improvement over time, collaboration, or conceptual understanding and therefore adjust the presentation of analytics and recommendations accordingly. However, this line of research also raises important ethical questions about standardization, autonomy, and the diversity of pedagogical styles, which should be investigated carefully (Luckin et al., 2016; Lin, Huang & Lu, 2023).

Future research should also address the challenge of fairness-aware HITL evaluation. Although human oversight is often presented as a remedy for algorithmic bias, human judgment itself is not immune to bias. Teachers may unintentionally be influenced by prior expectations, stereotypes, halo effects, or contextual assumptions that affect evaluation. Therefore, future Human-in-the-Loop systems should not be conceptualized as simple corrections of machine bias by unbiased humans. Instead, research should explore how hybrid systems can be designed to detect, mitigate, and balance both machine-related and human-related sources of unfairness. This may include fairness auditing tools, discrepancy analysis between AI and teacher ratings, blind review interfaces for sensitive tasks, and structured reflection prompts that encourage teachers to examine their decision processes critically (Williamson & Eynon, 2020; Kizilcec & Lee, 2022).

An additional direction of high importance concerns the use of generative AI and large language models in smart classroom evaluation. The rapid emergence of large language models has opened new possibilities for automated feedback generation, tutoring support, explanation of assessment criteria, and conversational educational guidance. These tools may be integrated into Human-in-the-Loop workflows to draft formative feedback, summarize student progress, generate alternative explanations of difficult concepts, or support rubric-based evaluation. However, generative AI also introduces new risks, including hallucinated explanations, inconsistent quality, implicit bias, and the possibility of over-automating teacher communication. Future research should explore how large language models can be incorporated into HITL frameworks in ways that maintain human oversight, preserve pedagogical intentionality, and ensure that generated feedback remains accurate, fair, and educationally meaningful (Kasneci et al., 2023; González-Calatayud, Prendes-Espinosa & Roig-Vila, 2021).

The future of HITL evaluation also depends on the expansion of longitudinal and real-world deployment studies. Much of the current literature on AI in education remains based on prototypes, pilots, or narrowly defined predictive experiments. While these studies provide valuable insights, they often do not capture the complex realities of institutional implementation. Future research should prioritize longitudinal studies that observe how Human-in-the-Loop systems function over multiple semesters, across different courses, and within diverse educational settings. Such studies are necessary to understand how teachers actually use AI recommendations over time, whether trust in the system increases or declines, how students perceive algorithmically supported evaluation, and how organizational culture influences the sustainability of implementation (Zawacki-Richter et al., 2019; Bond et al., 2024).

Another major area for future inquiry concerns the institutional and organizational ecology of smart classroom AI systems. Human-in-the-Loop evaluation should not be studied only at the level of teacher-model interaction. It is also necessary to examine the broader institutional conditions that enable or constrain the responsible use of AI in education. These include governance structures, procurement practices, technical support capacity, policy frameworks, data stewardship models, and professional development pathways. Future research should investigate how institutional leadership, organizational culture, and regulatory compliance shape the adoption and long-term success of HITL systems. Without such macro-level analysis, even technically sophisticated models may fail to produce sustainable educational value (Prinsloo & Slade, 2017; Selwyn, 2019).

Professional development constitutes another crucial research frontier. The effective use of Human-in-the-Loop systems requires teachers to acquire new forms of literacy, including data literacy, AI literacy, interpretive literacy, and ethical awareness related to digital assessment. Future studies should explore what kinds of professional learning experiences best prepare educators to work critically and productively with AI-generated insights. This includes not only technical training in platform use, but also deeper preparation in understanding model limitations, questioning algorithmic outputs, interpreting uncertainty, and maintaining pedagogical agency. The future of smart classroom evaluation depends heavily on whether teachers are empowered to act as informed co-decision-makers rather than passive recipients of analytics (Tan, Cheng & Ling, 2025; Tan et al., 2025).

Another significant research direction involves student-centered perspectives on HITL evaluation. Much of the current discourse emphasizes the role of teachers and institutions, but future work should also investigate how students understand, experience, and respond to hybrid AI-human evaluation systems. Students are not merely evaluated subjects; they are stakeholders whose trust, agency, and educational identity may be shaped by the use of intelligent systems. Future research should analyze students' perceptions of fairness, transparency, contestability, and feedback usefulness in HITL environments. It should also examine whether students are given meaningful opportunities to question or appeal AI-influenced decisions and whether they understand how their learning data are being used (Holmes et al., 2022; Memarian & Doleck, 2024).

The notion of contestability and appealability deserves particular attention. In traditional educational systems, students can often seek clarification or reconsideration when they perceive an evaluation as unfair. Future Human-in-the-Loop systems should preserve and strengthen such mechanisms rather than weaken them. Research should investigate how appeal processes can be integrated into AI-assisted assessment workflows, how disagreements between teacher judgment and algorithmic recommendation should be documented, and how institutions can ensure procedural justice in hybrid evaluation systems. These questions are especially important in contexts where AI-supported decisions may affect access to scholarships, academic retention, or progression through high-stakes educational pathways (Williamson & Eynon, 2020).

Another important future line of research is the development of cross-cultural and context-sensitive HITL frameworks. Much of the literature on AI in education has emerged from specific institutional and national contexts, often in technologically advanced settings. However, smart classroom implementation varies significantly across regions in terms of infrastructure, teacher training, educational policy, class size, language diversity, and cultural conceptions of fairness and authority. Future research should therefore avoid assuming that a single HITL model can be universally applied. Instead, it should investigate how hybrid AI-human evaluation systems can be adapted to local contexts while preserving core principles of transparency, fairness, and pedagogical integrity (Bhutoria, 2022; Garzón et al., 2019).

In parallel, future scholarship should advance the development of interoperable educational AI ecosystems. Many institutions use fragmented platforms that do not communicate well with one another, making it difficult to build coherent Human-in-the-Loop workflows. Research on standards, architectures, and middleware for interoperable learning analytics environments could facilitate the integration of data from LMS platforms, smart classroom sensors, digital assessment systems, and feedback tools. Greater interoperability would allow teachers to access more comprehensive views of student learning and would support more consistent human oversight across different components of the educational ecosystem (International Organization for Standardization, 2020; Griffiths, Hoel & Cooper, 2016).

The future of HITL evaluation also intersects with emerging research on emotional AI and affective computing in education. Some smart classroom systems are beginning to analyze facial expressions, voice patterns, or other behavioral signals in order to infer engagement, frustration, or emotional states. While these technologies may offer potential benefits for adaptive learning support, they also raise profound ethical and methodological concerns. Emotions are highly context-dependent and culturally mediated, and simplistic inferences may lead to serious misinterpretations. Future research should carefully examine whether and how affective signals can be incorporated into Human-in-the-Loop systems, what safeguards are necessary, and whether such data genuinely improve educational evaluation or instead create new forms of surveillance and overinterpretation (Yadegaridehkordi, et al., 2019).

Another crucial future direction is the connection between HITL evaluation and inclusive education. Smart classroom systems should not be designed only for average learners in standard conditions. Future research should investigate how Human-in-the-Loop frameworks can support students with disabilities, students from linguistically diverse backgrounds, students in rural or resource-constrained settings, and students with nontraditional learning trajectories. Inclusion-oriented HITL systems should allow educators to adapt algorithmic recommendations to diverse forms of participation and evidence of learning rather than enforcing narrow or standardized criteria of success (Li et al., 2025).

Moreover, future studies should deepen the relationship between HITL evaluation and curricular innovation in STEAM and interdisciplinary education. In many advanced learning settings, student performance cannot be assessed solely through standardized tests or simple analytics indicators. Project-based learning, collaborative design tasks, experimentation, creativity, and problem-solving require richer evaluative approaches. Human-in-the-Loop architectures may be especially valuable in such environments because they allow AI systems to process complex evidence while teachers retain authority to interpret originality, innovation, teamwork, and applied understanding. Research in this area could significantly expand the relevance of HITL systems beyond conventional digital learning contexts (Relmasira, Lai & Donaldson, 2023; Cai, Zhu & Ma, 2025).

Finally, future research should move toward the formulation of a theory of pedagogically trustworthy AI. Much current literature addresses isolated issues such as accuracy, explainability, or fairness, but the field still lacks a fully integrated theoretical framework for understanding what makes an AI system educationally trustworthy. Such a framework would need to account for technical validity, pedagogical relevance, institutional legitimacy, ethical accountability, contestability, and the preservation of meaningful human relationships in the learning process. Human-in-the-Loop evaluation offers one of the most promising starting points for this theoretical effort because it places human educational judgment at the center of AI-supported decision-making. The future of smart classroom evaluation may therefore depend less on creating increasingly autonomous systems and more on developing increasingly trustworthy forms of human-AI collaboration (Holmes et al., 2022; Memarian & Doleck, 2024; Lin, Huang & Lu, 2023).

In summary, future research on Human-in-the-Loop evaluation in smart classrooms should expand in several interconnected directions: multimodal analytics, uncertainty communication, pedagogically meaningful explainability, adaptive autonomy, fairness-aware hybrid judgment, generative AI integration, institutional ecology, teacher professional development, student-centered contestability, cross-cultural adaptation, interoperability, inclusive design, and theoretical consolidation around trustworthy educational AI. Taken together, these directions point toward a vision of educational intelligence in which artificial intelligence enhances, rather than replaces, the reflective, ethical, and relational dimensions of teaching and evaluation. (Tlili, A., Shehata, B., Adarkwah, M. A., et al., 2023).

10. CONCLUSION

The growing presence of artificial intelligence in educational environments has created both remarkable opportunities and substantial challenges for the future of teaching, learning, and assessment. Smart classrooms, understood as technologically enriched and data-driven learning ecosystems, are reshaping how educational activity is monitored, interpreted, and supported. Through learning analytics, predictive modeling, adaptive educational tools, and automated evaluation systems, artificial intelligence offers the possibility of making educational processes more responsive, personalized, and scalable. At the same time, the deployment of such technologies in educational settings raises fundamental questions about transparency, fairness, accountability, interpretability, and the role of human judgment in assessment.

This chapter has argued that Human-in-the-Loop evaluation provides a robust and conceptually coherent framework for addressing these tensions. Rather than adopting a view in which artificial intelligence replaces teachers or automates educational judgment entirely, the Human-in-the-Loop paradigm proposes a collaborative model in which machine intelligence and human expertise function together in the service of more trustworthy educational decision-making. In this framework, AI contributes speed, scale, and pattern-detection capacity, while educators contribute contextual understanding, pedagogical reasoning, ethical awareness, and interpretive judgment. The strength of the model lies precisely in this complementarity.

The first major contribution of the chapter has been to situate Human-in-the-Loop evaluation within the broader evolution of smart classrooms and intelligent learning ecosystems. The transformation of educational environments into data-rich digital systems has generated new possibilities for analyzing student behavior, identifying learning difficulties, and supporting personalized instruction. However, the chapter has shown that these possibilities should not be interpreted as evidence that educational assessment can or should become fully automated. Learning is a deeply contextual, relational, and interpretive process. While digital traces and computational models may reveal important patterns, they do not exhaust the meaning of student learning. For this reason, smart classroom systems must be designed not merely as instruments of technical optimization, but as socio-technical environments that preserve educational values and human agency (Holmes et al., 2022; Luckin et al., 2016).

A second central contribution of the chapter has been the analysis of artificial intelligence in educational assessment. Automated essay scoring, predictive analytics, adaptive testing, and digital evaluation platforms have shown that AI can significantly improve efficiency and provide timely feedback in contexts of growing educational scale and complexity. Yet the chapter has also emphasized that automated systems are not neutral. They inherit assumptions from training data, reflect design choices made by developers and institutions, and may produce outputs that are difficult to interpret or contest. As several scholars have warned, educational AI systems that are deployed without careful ethical and pedagogical consideration may reinforce inequities, obscure responsibility, and undermine trust in educational institutions (Selwyn, 2019; Williamson & Eynon, 2020; Bond et al., 2024).

Against this background, the chapter has presented Human-in-the-Loop artificial intelligence as an especially relevant model for educational evaluation. The reason is not only that HITL preserves human supervision, but that it redefines artificial intelligence as a pedagogical support mechanism rather than a replacement for professional judgment. In a Human-in-the-Loop system, the teacher is not reduced to a passive recipient of algorithmic recommendations. Instead, the teacher becomes an active interpreter, validator, and, when necessary, corrector of AI-generated outputs. This role is crucial because educational evaluation often depends on factors that cannot be captured adequately through computational data alone, including student effort, growth, motivation, creativity, classroom participation, and the contextual circumstances that shape performance over time. In this sense, HITL evaluation protects the irreducibly human dimensions of education while still enabling institutions to benefit from computational intelligence (Amershi et al., 2014; Memarian & Doleck, 2024).

The chapter has also contributed a conceptual architecture for Human-in-the-Loop smart classrooms, emphasizing the interaction between data acquisition, learning analytics, AI evaluation modules, explainability layers, and human supervision interfaces. This layered perspective demonstrates that responsible educational AI is not simply a matter of choosing a good algorithm. It requires the design of entire systems in which data flows, interfaces, governance structures, and pedagogical practices are aligned. A technically sophisticated model that is poorly explained, badly integrated, or deployed without teacher preparation may be less educationally valuable than a simpler model that supports meaningful interpretation and actionable feedback. The architecture proposed in this chapter therefore reinforces the view that trustworthy educational AI must be evaluated not only in terms of accuracy, but also in terms of usability, fairness, auditability, and pedagogical coherence (Paulsen & Lindsay, 2024; Khosravi et al., 2022).

Another major contribution has been the formalization of a mathematical model for hybrid AI-human evaluation. By representing final assessment as a weighted combination of automated scoring and human judgment, the chapter has shown that Human-in-the-Loop systems can be studied not only conceptually but also analytically. This formalization is important because it opens the possibility of future empirical work on how to calibrate the relative influence of AI and teacher intervention in different assessment scenarios. In low-stakes settings, greater algorithmic support may be acceptable, whereas in high-stakes evaluations the weighting may shift more strongly toward human oversight. Likewise, future refinements of the model may incorporate uncertainty estimates, fairness penalties, and adaptive mechanisms that determine when mandatory human review is required. Such formal tools can help translate abstract ethical principles into operational system design.

The chapter has placed particular emphasis on ethical and governance considerations, recognizing that the legitimacy of AI in education depends not only on technical functionality but also on normative acceptability. Transparency, fairness, privacy protection, accountability, and the possibility of appeal are not optional enhancements; they are foundational requirements for responsible educational evaluation. Human-in-the-Loop systems contribute significantly to these goals by preserving a space in which educators can question, reinterpret, or override algorithmic outputs. Yet the chapter has also acknowledged that human oversight is not a perfect solution in itself. Teachers, like algorithms, may also exhibit bias or inconsistency. Therefore, the goal of HITL design is not simply to replace machine bias with human bias, but to create hybrid systems in which both human and algorithmic limitations can be identified, balanced, and improved through structured interaction and reflection (Prinsloo & Slade, 2017; Lünich et al., 2024).

The discussion of implementation scenarios has further illustrated that Human-in-the-Loop evaluation is not merely a theoretical aspiration. It can be deployed in learning management systems, intelligent tutoring environments, hybrid classrooms, institutional advising systems, and multimodal learning analytics platforms. However, successful implementation requires more than technology procurement. It depends on institutional commitment, interoperable infrastructures, clear governance frameworks, teacher training, interface design, and continuous evaluation of impact. Without these conditions, even well-intentioned AI systems may remain underused, misunderstood, or misapplied. Thus, the chapter has emphasized that the future of smart classroom evaluation depends as much on organizational readiness and pedagogical culture as on algorithmic sophistication (Siemens & Baker, 2012; International Organization for Standardization, 2020).

The forward-looking analysis in this chapter has identified several key future research directions, including multimodal analytics, explainability tailored to pedagogical decision-making, fairness-aware hybrid systems, uncertainty communication, professional development for AI-literate educators, student-centered contestability, inclusive design, and the integration of generative AI into Human-in-the-Loop workflows. These directions indicate that the field is moving toward a more mature understanding of educational intelligence—one that values not only efficiency and prediction, but also trust, dialogue, reflexivity, and human dignity. In this emerging paradigm, educational AI should not be judged solely by whether it can automate evaluation tasks, but by whether it can support richer forms of educational understanding and more just forms of academic decision-making.

A particularly important conclusion of this chapter is that the central question for the future of smart classroom assessment is not whether artificial intelligence will be used, but how it will be used and under whose oversight. Educational institutions are increasingly surrounded by technologies that promise precision, adaptation, and efficiency. Yet if these promises are pursued without attention to educational values, they may weaken rather than strengthen learning environments. Human-in-the-Loop evaluation offers a principled response to this challenge by insisting that automation in education must remain accountable to human pedagogical judgment. In this sense, HITL is not only a technical architecture but also an educational stance: it affirms that intelligence in education should be collaborative, interpretable, and ethically grounded.

This perspective has important implications for educators, administrators, researchers, and policymakers. For educators, it suggests that AI literacy and data literacy are becoming integral dimensions of professional practice, but that these literacies must serve pedagogical reasoning rather than replace it. Teachers should therefore be provided with continuous professional development opportunities focused on learning analytics interpretation, explainable AI systems, ethical decision-making, and responsible integration of intelligent educational technologies into classroom practice. For administrators and educational institutions, the findings of this chapter highlight the need to invest not only in technological infrastructure, but also in governance frameworks, interdisciplinary implementation teams, ethical auditing mechanisms, and institutional policies capable of supporting sustainable Human-in-the-Loop deployment. Institutions should also establish transparent procedures for algorithmic oversight, appeal processes, and data governance in order to maintain trust and accountability within AI-supported educational ecosystems.

For researchers, this chapter underscores the importance of interdisciplinary inquiry that connects machine learning, educational theory, ethics, human-computer interaction, and policy analysis. Future studies should investigate adaptive weighting mechanisms between human and AI evaluation, fairness-aware educational analytics, explainability strategies specifically designed for teachers, and empirical validation of HITL frameworks across diverse educational contexts. Additional research is also needed to examine long-term impacts of AI-assisted evaluation on student motivation, instructional practices, institutional governance, and educational equity. For policymakers, the chapter emphasizes that regulatory approaches to educational AI must move beyond generic innovation narratives and address concrete institutional requirements related to transparency, auditability, inclusiveness, privacy protection, accountability, and human oversight in algorithmically mediated educational environments.

The broader significance of Human-in-the-Loop evaluation extends beyond individual classrooms. In a time when societies are increasingly negotiating the boundaries between human judgment and algorithmic decision-making, education occupies a uniquely important space. Schools and universities do not merely distribute knowledge; they also shape future citizens' understanding of fairness, authority, and technological legitimacy. If educational institutions adopt AI systems that are opaque, unaccountable, or exclusionary, they risk normalizing those same patterns for future generations. Conversely, if they adopt Human-in-the-Loop systems that are transparent, contestable, and pedagogically meaningful, they can model a more responsible form of technological integration—one in which intelligence is augmented rather than outsourced, and in which human agency remains central.

A distinctive contribution of this chapter lies in the development of an integrated Human-in-the-Loop evaluation framework that combines explainable artificial intelligence, smart classroom analytics, ethical governance principles, and mathematical modeling within a single pedagogically oriented architecture. Unlike traditional explainable AI approaches that primarily focus on interpreting algorithmic outputs after automated evaluation has occurred, the framework proposed in this chapter incorporates continuous human pedagogical participation directly into the assessment lifecycle. Furthermore, unlike fully automated educational evaluation systems that depend exclusively on computational scoring mechanisms, the proposed model preserves contextual human interpretation, professional educational judgment, and ethical supervision as essential components of decision-making. The framework also extends beyond the conventional functionality of learning management systems by integrating adaptive feedback mechanisms, explainability layers, hybrid AI-human validation processes, and transparency-oriented governance structures designed specifically for intelligent educational ecosystems. In this sense, the originality of the chapter resides not only in its technical integration of AI and human supervision, but also in its conceptual positioning of educational evaluation as a collaborative, interpretable, and ethically grounded socio-technical process.

In conclusion, Human-in-the-Loop evaluation in smart classrooms represents a promising pathway toward the development of explainable, ethical, and pedagogically grounded educational AI. The approach recognizes the value of artificial intelligence as a powerful analytical resource while reaffirming the indispensable role of human educators in interpreting learning, making judgments, and supporting student development. By integrating computational intelligence with human expertise, smart classrooms can evolve into environments that are not only more efficient and adaptive, but also more trustworthy, inclusive, and educationally meaningful. The long-term success of AI in education will depend less on the extent to which machines can evaluate students independently and more on the extent to which human institutions can design systems in which teachers and intelligent technologies collaborate responsibly in the pursuit of learning.

REFERENCES

Adadi, A., & Berrada, M. (2018). Peeking inside the black-box: A survey on explainable artificial intelligence (XAI). *IEEE Access : Practical Innovations, Open Solutions*, *6*, 52138–52160. DOI: 10.1109/ACCESS.2018.2870052

Amershi, S., Cakmak, M., Knox, W. B., & Kulesza, T. (2014). Power to the people: The role of humans in interactive machine learning. *AI Magazine*, *35*(4), 105–120. DOI: 10.1609/aimag.v35i4.2513

Baker, R. S. J. d., & Inventado, P. S. (2014). Educational data mining and learning analytics. In Larusson, J. A., & White, B. (Eds.), *Learning analytics: From research to practice* (pp. 61–75). Springer., DOI: 10.1007/978-1-4614-3305-7_4

Bhutoria, A. (2022). Personalized education and artificial intelligence in the United States, China, and India: A systematic review using a human-in-the-loop model. *Computers and Education: Artificial Intelligence*, *3*, 100068. Advance online publication. DOI: 10.1016/j.caeai.2022.100068

Bond, M., Khosravi, H., De Laat, M., Bergdahl, N., Negrea, V., Oxley, E., Pham, P., Chong, S. W., & Siemens, G. (2024). A meta systematic review of artificial intelligence in higher education: A call for increased ethics, collaboration, and rigour. *International Journal of Educational Technology in Higher Education*, *21*(1), 4. Advance online publication. DOI: 10.1186/s41239-023-00436-z

Cai, C., Zhu, G., & Ma, M. (2025). A systemic review of AI for interdisciplinary learning: Application contexts, roles, and influences. *Education and Information Technologies*, *30*(7), 9641–9687. DOI: 10.1007/s10639-024-13193-x

Garzón, J., Pavón, J., & Baldiris, S. (2019). Systematic review and meta-analysis of augmented reality in educational settings. *Virtual Reality (Waltham Cross)*, *23*(4), 447–459. DOI: 10.1007/s10055-019-00379-9

González-Calatayud, V., Prendes-Espinosa, P., & Roig-Vila, R. (2021). Artificial intelligence for student assessment: A systematic review. *Applied Sciences (Basel, Switzerland)*, *11*(12), 5467. Advance online publication. DOI: 10.3390/app11125467

Griffiths, D., Hoel, T., & Cooper, A. (2016). *Learning analytics interoperability: Requirements, specifications and adoption*. LACE Project.

Gunasekara, S. V. S., & Saarela, M. (2025). Systematic literature review on explainable learning analytics and educational data mining. *IEEE Access : Practical Innovations, Open Solutions*, *13*, 214387–214408. DOI: 10.1109/ACCESS.2025.3643645

International Organization for Standardization. (2020). *Information technology for learning, education and training—Learning analytics interoperability—Part 3: Guidelines for data interoperability* (ISO/IEC TS 20748-3:2020). ISO.

Kasneci, E., Seßler, K., Küchemann, S., Bannert, M., Dementieva, D., Fischer, F., Gasser, U., Groh, G., Günnemann, S., Hüllermeier, E., Krusche, S., Kutyniok, G., Michaeli, T., Nerdel, C., Pfeffer, J., Poquet, O., Sailer, M., Schmidt, A., Seidel, T., & Kasneci, G. (2023). ChatGPT for good? On opportunities and challenges of large language models for education. *Learning and Individual Differences*, *103*, 102274. Advance online publication. DOI: 10.1016/j.lindif.2023.102274

Khosravi, H., Shum, S. B., Chen, G., Conati, C., Tsai, Y.-S., Kay, J., Knight, S., Martinez-Maldonado, R., Sadiq, S., & Gašević, D. (2022). Explainable artificial intelligence in education. *Computers and Education: Artificial Intelligence*, *3*, 100074. Advance online publication. DOI: 10.1016/j.caeai.2022.100074

Kizilcec, R. F., & Lee, H. (2022). Algorithmic fairness in education. In Holmes, W., & Porayska-Pomsta, K. (Eds.), *The ethics of artificial intelligence in education* (pp. 174–202). Routledge., DOI: 10.4324/9780429329067-10

Kizilcec, R. F., & Lee, H. (2022). Algorithmic fairness in education. In Holmes, W., & Porayska-Pomsta, K. (Eds.), *The ethics of artificial intelligence in education* (pp. 174–202). Routledge., DOI: 10.4324/9780429329067-10

Lin, C.-C., Huang, A. Y. Q., & Lu, O. H. T. (2023). Artificial intelligence in intelligent tutoring systems toward sustainable education: A systematic review. *Smart Learning Environments*, *10*(1), 41. Advance online publication. DOI: 10.1186/s40561-023-00260-y

Luckin, R., Holmes, W., Griffiths, M., & Forcier, L. B. (2016). *Intelligence unleashed: An argument for AI in education*. Pearson.

Martinez-Maldonado, R., Echeverria, V., Santos, O. C., Santos, A. D. P., & Yacef, K. (2018). Physical learning analytics: A multimodal perspective. In *Proceedings of the 8th International Conference on Learning Analytics and Knowledge* (pp. 375–379). ACM. https://doi.org/DOI: 10.1145/3170358.3170379

Matcha, W., Ahmad Uzir, N. A., Gašević, D., & Pardo, A. (2020). A systematic review of empirical studies on learning analytics dashboards: A self-regulated learning perspective. *IEEE Transactions on Learning Technologies*, *13*(2), 226–245. DOI: 10.1109/TLT.2019.2916802

Memarian, B., & Doleck, T. (2024). Human-in-the-loop in artificial intelligence in education: A review and entity-relationship (ER) analysis. *Computers in Human Behavior: Artificial Humans, 2*, Article 100053.

Ng, D. T. K., Leung, J. K. L., Su, J., Ng, R. C. W., & Chu, S. K. W. (2023). Teachers' AI digital competencies and twenty-first century skills in the post-pandemic world. *Educational Technology Research and Development, 71*(1), 137–161. DOI: 10.1007/s11423-023-10203-6 PMID: 36844361

Ochoa, X., & Wise, A. F. (2021). Supporting the shift to digital with student-centered learning analytics. *Educational Technology Research and Development, 69*(1), 357–361. DOI: 10.1007/s11423-020-09882-2 PMID: 33250614

Paulsen, L., & Lindsay, E. (2024). Learning analytics dashboards are increasingly becoming about learning and not just analytics—A systematic review. *Education and Information Technologies, 29*(11), 14279–14308. Advance online publication. DOI: 10.1007/s10639-023-12401-4

Prinsloo, P., & Slade, S. (2017). An elephant in the learning analytics room: The obligation to act. In *Proceedings of the Seventh International Learning Analytics & Knowledge Conference* (pp. 46–55). ACM. https://doi.org/DOI: 10.1145/3027385.3027406

Relmasira, S. C., Lai, Y. C., & Donaldson, J. P. (2023). Fostering AI literacy in elementary science, technology, engineering, art, and mathematics (STEAM) education in the age of generative AI. *Sustainability (Basel), 15*(18), 13595. Advance online publication. DOI: 10.3390/su151813595

Saqr, M., & López-Pernas, S. (Eds.). (2024). *Learning analytics methods and tutorials: A practical guide using R*. Springer., DOI: 10.1007/978-3-031-54464-4

Selwyn, N. (2019). *Should robots replace teachers? AI and the future of education*. Polity Press.

Shermis, M. D., & Burstein, J. (Eds.). (2013). *Handbook of automated essay evaluation: Current applications and new directions*. Routledge. DOI: 10.4324/9780203122761

Siemens, G., & Baker, R. S. J. d. (2012). Learning analytics and educational data mining: Towards communication and collaboration. In *Proceedings of the 2nd International Conference on Learning Analytics and Knowledge* (pp. 252–254). ACM. https://doi.org/DOI: 10.1145/2330601.2330661

Tan, X., Cheng, K. S., & Ling, M. H. A. (2025). Artificial intelligence in teaching and teacher professional development: A systematic review. *Computers and Education: Artificial Intelligence, 8*, 100355. Advance online publication. DOI: 10.1016/j.caeai.2024.100355

Tlili, A., Shehata, B., Adarkwah, M. A., Bozkurt, A., Hickey, D. T., Huang, R., & Agyemang, B. (2023). What if the devil is my guardian angel: ChatGPT as a case study of using chatbots in education. *Smart Learning Environments*, *10*(1), 15. Advance online publication. DOI: 10.1186/s40561-023-00237-x

Verbert, K., Ochoa, X., De Croon, R., Dourado, R., & De Laet, T. (2020). Learning analytics dashboards: The past, the present and the future. In *Proceedings of the Tenth International Conference on Learning Analytics & Knowledge* (pp. 35–40). ACM. https://doi.org/DOI: 10.1145/3375462.3375504

Williamson, B., & Eynon, R. (2020). Historical threads, missing links, and future directions in AI in education. *Learning, Media and Technology*, *45*(3), 223–235. DOI: 10.1080/17439884.2020.1798995

Yadegaridehkordi, E., Noor, N. F. B. M., Ayub, M. N. B., Affal, H. B., & Hussin, N. B. (2019). Affective computing in education: A systematic review and future research. *Computers & Education*, *142*, 103649. Advance online publication. DOI: 10.1016/j.compedu.2019.103649

Yang, S. J. H., Ogata, H., Matsui, T., & Chen, N. S. (2021). Human-centered artificial intelligence in education: Seeing the invisible through the visible. *Computers and Education: Artificial Intelligence*, *2*, 100008. Advance online publication. DOI: 10.1016/j.caeai.2021.100008

Zawacki-Richter, O., Marín, V. I., Bond, M., & Gouverneur, F. (2019). Systematic review of research on artificial intelligence applications in higher education—Where are the educators? *International Journal of Educational Technology in Higher Education*, *16*(1), 39. Advance online publication. DOI: 10.1186/s41239-019-0171-0

Chapter 6
Adaptive Learning Systems and Their Impact on STEM Achievement

Vishal Jain
http://orcid.org/0000-0003-1126-7424
Vivekananda Institute of Professional Studies - Technical Campus, New Delhi, India

Sashi Kant Gupta
http://orcid.org/0000-0001-6587-5607
Lincoln University College, Malaysia

Archan Mitra
http://orcid.org/0000-0002-1419-3558
Amity University, Mumbai, India

Supratim Mukherjee
http://orcid.org/0009-0008-6657-891X
Amity University, Mumbai, India

ABSTRACT

This paper presents a structured synthesis of 30 studies (2021–2026) examining the impact of adaptive learning systems on STEM education. It explores how AI-driven tools—such as intelligent tutoring systems, learner modelling, and adaptive recommendation engines—personalize instruction by adjusting content, pacing, and feedback based on student performance. The findings indicate that adaptive learning can enhance academic achievement, particularly in mathematics and programming, when feedback is timely, diagnostic, and aligned with domain-specific learning processes. However, improvements are often indirect, mediated by factors

DOI: 10.4018/979-8-3373-9675-0.ch006

such as engagement, motivation, and self-regulation. The study emphasizes that adaptive systems are most effective when integrated into pedagogical practices rather than used as standalone technologies. It also identifies key gaps, including limited longitudinal evidence, insufficient focus on equity, and lack of comparative evaluation across adaptive methods.

1. INTRODUCTION

Progressive increase of adaptive learning models may imply a greater change in educational technology, from traditional static odomity of content to smart environments that respond to changes and even in real-time. In digital education systems, students sometimes go through the same topic in the same order, practice for the same period and get the same feedback. In the case of adaptive learning environments, this plan is thwarted since differences in learner profiles imply customized rates of learning, knowledge levels, or ordering of content, based on how well the student responds to instruction. This emphasis turned out to be very helpful in the fields of science, technology, engineering, and mathematics (STEM) since learning states are usually dependent on acquiring progressive levels of abstract concepts, complete the process of step-by-step problem-solving, and cope with the resulting cognitive shifts as explained in the Theory of Both Cognitive and Concern.

There is very informative material that shows that adaptive learning has now outgrown the demonstration stages of ed-tech and is being integrated in the learning systems. Synthesises of these tendencies are detecting a growing preference for AI-augmented adaptative learning: personalization, wise tutoring systems, learning modelling, data recommending system (Hariri et al.,2021; Yi and Li, 2022; Mantonakis and ntheoharidou, 2022; Chrysanthi and Charalambidou, 2022). Such approaches have been propelled along by activities in the realms of machine aided learning, natural language processing, extended fiction of computer generated content, big data and data point quantification as well as wearable technologies. Consequently, it is no longer enough for adaptive learning processes to address only the automation of instruction but there is a new expectation that more personalized and skilled-based learning approaches can be provided.

This expectation appears to be particularly high in the field of STEM learning spaces. This is because STEM learning is well-known to structurally be accumulative and skill-based. STEM is designed for practice, practice and practice! An individual student harboring a misconception regarding a basic mathematical operation, a programming concept, or a scientific principle can apply such a flawed knowledge in subsequent lessons often with increasing degenerating results. This is why students online progress tracking systems, for example, could be very useful in instructional settings for they are designed to pinpoint struggling students. Traditional means on the other hand usually lack such adequacy, and the students may have to drill; because even though online systems are preferred it does not mean they are the best method. This is called adaptive because it seems more than common sense; it is meant to function as a tool to academic achievement by making the course fit for the student.

In relation to STEM achievement, one should understand the meaning of the phrase "impact on STEM achievement." Achievement is not just a single or measured variable in various sources. Among other things, some researches deal with studying performance, achievement test performance, or level of proficiency in mathematics. Others consider learning efficiency, quality of problem solving, critical thinking, metacognitive strategies, persistence, engagement, well-being, or self-belonging. Very often analyzing two or more of these variables looks as quite a task. For example, AI-adaptive education helps to enhance academic performance because improvement in self-efficacy or control of learning effort is possible over a certain period of time (Jing, et al., 2023; Wu, et al., 2023; Yan, et al., 2024; Lin, et al., 2025). Therefore, the impact of adaptive learning on achievement can be seen as something multifaceted rather than immediate.

A second problem is the extraordinary fragmentation of approaches. There is data on the content analysis of documents, quantitative reviews, process implementation studies, evaluation studies, interventional research and experimental double-blind studies on this topic. Relevance of this heterogeneity is seen in the picture of the efforts of the research community spread over multiple theoretical traditions. However, at the same time, it is pushing this user group tantalizingly closer to operational adaptive learning technologies in STEM education. There are also general assessments of AI-related systems and platforms (Liu, 2022; Contrino et al., 2024; Liang et al., 2026) that are supplemented by very sectoral fields like mathematical support courses, for example (Son, 2024; Baldinger et al., 2026), programming training (Yang et al., 2024; Lai et al., 2025; Na Nongkhai et al., 2025), and even problems of science thinking (Katz et al., 2021; Asmussen et al., 2025; Penn, 2025).

This paper addresses this gap by combining literary answers to 30 works on Adaptive Learning Systems and STEM Performance. It does not seek to be a traditional meta-analysis, but an organized synthesis of qualitative relevant information with the use of the technique of descriptive coding. For coherence, the review very broadly asks four fundamental questions: How recent is the literature and what are the new fields of research within the field of STEM and the methodological approaches? What are the specific control models that control the operations in the present educational systems? Among socio-cultural elements like gender, learning style and spatial ability, which is associated more frequently with Adaptive Learning Systems educational outcomes? And finally, where is further research required with regard to the present state of the art?

The primary purpose of this chapter is advocating about the opportunities and challenges of using adaptive learning systems for advancing educational objectives, primarily those related to achievement of the high-level content knowledge in the math/science topic areas of interest. The key argument is that adaptive learning tools work most optimally for the teaching and learning of STEM subjects when they are utilized as teaching tools within teaching and not detached from the teaching-learning process. Additional findings reflected on the necessity of designing adaptive instructional material only when it recognizes the learner potential, provides for immediate effectiveness, includes a telescoping effect in the progression of instruction materials and is accorded as part of the instructional design rather than on its extreme ends within attainment of course objectives. On the other hand, adaptation lacks the same kind of transformative effect in education, particularly when it is employed as a means of free and easy technology such as machine delivery with no profound level of diagnosis, learning visibility, and learner-driven interface problems mitigation strategies in place.

In the rest of this report, you will find six main parts. To begin, the theoretical basis to adaptive learning in fields related to STEM is found in Section 2 with certain sections focusing on learner modeling, intelligent tutoring, recommendation systems, pedagogical agents, and multimodal adaptive architectures. Section 3 looks at the research problem and introduces the 30 study corpus spread over the multiple papers and minds concerned. Section 4 is designed specifically to exhibit the results of the research undertaken and draw on any evident ideas and rationales that might appear. Section 5 deals with the application of these ideas for research, pedagogy, theory, and practice. Section 6 contains an overview of the main outcomes of the research being conducted as well as the strategies necessary for the exploitation of adaptive technologies in the STEM subjects.

2. LITERATURE REVIEW

2.1. Conceptualising Adaptive Learning Systems in STEM

Broadly speaking, the educational technologies that are considered to be adaptive employ and change various aspects of the learning based on the profile and behavior of the student concerned. For example more specifically this could range from organizing the order of content to assigning homework, scheduling the pace of lessons or complexity increases, customizing practice problems, and changes in designs that would prompt the learners to engage in the learning experiences to the extent that such design might ask the students to perform in some ejercitation. This shall include any help that is offered which means motivation and individual feedback, in addition applications or systems which include personalization. Artificial intelligence, overseeing how the learner is doing the tasks and correcting for the most common fallacies that the student is noted to make before providing other resources are some of the activities likely to take place in the adaptive systems. There has been an increase in the utilization of adaptive learning concept in recent years, which has been presented using such terms as artificial intelligence, learning analytics and individualized instruction. Dynamic courseware goes deeper than just providing the course content as it actively adjusts to what is going on with the students during learning.

It is a standard perception from literature reviews that recently the adaptive learning is one of the main sub-disciplines in AI in education. Kabudi's work AI enabled adaptive teaching systems comes up as an expanding study area, with a rapid pace adding that most efforts have been towards the combination of AI engines in the recommendation system among others. The study done by Xu and Ouyang points that the utilization of artificial intelligence in the teaching of computer-related subjects tends to align more with traditional roles of technology in education including teaching aids, evaluation, customization and even the identification of potential candidates for students following specified curricular goals. Koutsantonis and others make a contribution to this article by offering additional bibliometric evidence of growth over time. Koutsantonis and others have shown that adaptive learning systems have been rather limited to very few such systems in the past and are gaining a lot of interest in the present day. Apart from that, recent citation indices-based analyses of Gligorea et al. (2023) and Tan et al. (2025) have shown that the evidence-based practice is doing well in research supporting this issue of practice of organizing learning using AI such as platforms, targets, and conautographs.

The significance lies in the sense of orientation you are mentioning. This aspect becomes systematically important just within the range of Science, Technology, Engineering and Mathematics. STEM learning means it is a sphere which is logical, built up sequentially issue after issue, and is as far as possible full of training exercises. A large number of tasks and exercises can be defined as a feature of such system – their numerous performances are very sensitive to problems in planning and making certain decisions. Difficulty therefore transmits across similar aspects or levels of tasks when one cannot understand the manipulation of an expression on the measure of scale, assignment of variables; creation and solving of a statistical model, etc. In such cases, adaptive systems are especially attractive as they claim to facilitate the identification of the earliest difficulties and enable appropriate interventions beyond the typical capacity of one-size-fits-all instruction.

2.2. Core Adaptive Mechanisms in the Recent Literature

The prior academic research that has been reviewed has identified at least four main strategies that can be used to adapt to the changing circumstances with the first being the use of a learner model or learner adaption algorithms. Adaptive systems depend on the learner's position, status, or progression at different points. This can involve performance history, response time, behavior traces, prior test performance, social interactional practices or inferred thought structures. Katz et al. (2021) prove that learner modeling is important in teaching conceptual physics and shows interconnection of dialog research with student model creation– the move of the tutor responds to the conceptual model of the student rather than the outcome alone. For example, Yan et al. (2024) provide an example of how adaptive learning can be used for effective learning through oversight adding that the level of challenge and the degree of assistance needed is regulated while performing such practice.

The second mechanism is intelligent tutoring. Intelligent tutoring systems remain to be the most common form of adaptive learning in STEM. A study conducted by Son (2024) in mathematics indicates that tutoring systems are more and more being demanded to foster the explanation, strategy, and scaffolding behavior functioning rather than simple drill-and-practice that is provided quite rapidly with easy access. Programming research provides further evidence. Yang et al. (2024) examine a tutoring environment based on ChatGPT and designed for training in Python, whereas Fodouop Kouam et al. (2024), Lai et al. (2025), and Na Nongkhai et al. (2025) examine the support for coding, debugging, and learner progression in programming systems.

There are three functions of these systems:

One such function is monitoring user performance and providing appropriate assistance upon assessment. The system helps users understand what is expected of them, and how they are performing once they get assessed. The users then know there where they went wrong and how their performance can be improved and perfection attained. While it seems as though the system is punishing the learners, it is useful as it facilitates the overall improvement by both the learner and the system. It therefore provides motivation to put in an extra effort towards correcting the defects and raises the performance standards.

The second function relates to determining the competency of each learner in terms of ability and allocating each learner to the right learning task. It supports learners to come to terms with what is before them and even to assess their progress. Therefore any of the learning targets and even the assessment is always embedded in the learning materials. Once their progress is checked, and the defects are disclosed, the learner knows that there should be much more effort to get rid of the defect and this way their performance will also be substantially improved. Again, this seems like a punishment for the learner, but it is very constructive as it fosters self-improvement of the system as well as the learner. Hence, it makes an effort that adds to overcoming these shortcomings all the more reasonable and elevates the level of conformity set.

The third mechanism is recommendation and pathway adaptation. Recommendation systems decide what a learner should encounter next. A case in point is Zhang et al. (2023) who demonstrated how an adaptive cognitive-map recommendation system has a pósitive influence on learning by adjusting the order in which the contents are presented on the basis of the learner's inferred cognition. Another case is that of Wang et al. (2023) who highlight the issue of adaptive learning versus teaching instruction and suggest that adaptive progression makes a difference as and when students consider not everyone is prepared for the same pathway. Alternatively, Contrino et al. (2024) affirm that learning tools can intoxicate gains in performance and satisfaction but more so do so through non-uniform modes of delivery compared to uniform delivery systems.

The fourth mechanism is the inclusion of multimodal or collaborative support. In some adaptive tools that are being developed, elements such as pedagogical agents, automated testing, multimodal input, and even computer vision are being incorporated. Apoki et al. (2022) discusses preferences in adaptating, especially the importance of the pedagogical agents, which according to analysis can enhance the cfafea of the adaptive. To so, the adaptating is, at times, helpful regarding look to learning and interactivity or even motivation. Sein (2022) contests the directions stressing thator loveliness of AI-supported assessment since it can be quite clinical without calling it effective. Wu and Lee (2023) on the other hand, goes further into the area of predictive analysis and utilization of computer vision to adaptive STEM and demonstrates how it is possible to combine engagement levels and self-confidence and behavior change indicators.

2.3. Mathematics as a Leading Domain for Adaptive Learning

Respecting the structure of the current corpus composition, Mathematics becomes an indispensable factor. Mathematics, to be precise, has a profound nature, as the assumptions and principles are philosophy, it is the kind of knowledge that has to be learned in a right way with no changes. With the capabilities of the modern technology in effect, the automatic assessment systems may be used for providing feedback on the grades of any mathematical problems, the way the students use the rules and the most difficult parts of the concept. Dalkenzhiev et al. (2023) focus on the aspect of mathematics education change in higher education and particularly on the use of Stepik as an adaptive individualized instruction tool for online mathematics courses, which enables learners to progress based on their level of understanding.

Lin et al. 2025 supports the application of adaptive computer programs more into self-regulated learning's and education's structure by drawing the guidelines for the most beneficial development of mathematics. Similarly, Baldinger et al. (2026) present how universally adopted study is developed which employs the teaching of actual mathematics with a theoretical framework.

In other words, in mathematics texts, there is a tendency to define higher grades of achievement in a less performance-oriented way. As can be deduced from the review conducted by Son (2024), contemporary studies on the subject of mathematical education are starting to focus on questions that are related not only to narrow performance measurement, but also to questions of conceptual aid, cognitive scaffolding, and changes in teaching strategies. It also matters that the overall literature has a perspective on adaptive learning which is that there are enduring processes, such as better feedback, working harder, or enabling a greater fit between actor and assessment, which most times make learning efficacious. Especially in mathematics, in turn, these actions are easily identifiable, because practice can be visualized through structured practice sequence and cognitive load can be manipulated through the use of different content for different levels of complex problems.

On the whole, reviews of the literature on mathematics support the notion that adaptive learning helps most when engaged as supportive or scaffolded strategies. Proficient systems help in recognizing errors or oversights as early as possible, without cracking inappropriate levels of difficulty or challenge, or sparing liked information without eliminating face useful cognitive work. These elements are the suffice to make mathematics a good touchstone for adaptive learning developments.

2.4. Programming and Computing as Rapidly Expanding Adaptive Domains

Adaptive learning has gained popularity particularly in the field of programming education. It provides ample learning traces with a range of code blocks, keying varieties, error types, debugging sequences, time brackets, as well as changes brought while reviewing the steps. These traces help in the effective development of personalization among learners as well. Furthermore, it is critical to consider that newbies in coding often face impediments when it comes to logical structures, lists, the use of a certain rule, or other syntax rules or more, and differentiation feedback is necessary in such cases.

The efficiency of PyTutor, a tutoring system in Python learning that is supervised by ChatGPT (Yang et al. 2024) is observed. Thus, what we are seeing here is a shift in how adaptive programming is carried out, in that instead of a restrictive model of explanatory and advice giving input from the tutor, this model can be supported by a multimodal prospective interface module involving large language models that provide 'explanation, hints, and feedback'. This has the consequence of making speech norm in program assisted teaching more explicable and contingent. Studies by Fodouop Kouam et al. (2024) they inquire how different intelligent tutoring systems assist students at diverse levels of their programming experience, which also drives the point home that adaptivity is especially needed where the change in students' background knowledge is significant. More so, Lai et al. (2025) talk of intelligent tutoring with regards to coding and learning. Finally, there are applications in the works where machine learning and artificial intelligence have been used to present or enhance existing adaptive learning technologies for socially disadvantaged people and these include sociological strategies by Katona (2025).

After the review of the studies it's clear that the settings within the adaptive programming found its fuller fruition in the framework of graduated support concept, as opposed to the automatic provision of solutions. However, if a tool supports students to an extent that supports autonomy, it may cause them to accomplish what they do not quite own. Due to this fact the adhering researches in this field treat adaptivity more as a strategic measure than anything else: feedback is finely tuned, proper hints are provided at the appropriate moment, and a flow is building having in mind the progression of conceptual building blocks. This explains why there is such importance of programming research in the context of how adaptive systems enhance learning achievable for the students.

2.5. Science, Chemistry, and Physics: Adaptive Learning Beyond Routine Practice

Even if the number of scientific inquiries is less, compared to math and programming studies, it is advisable to stress science oriented studies in educational environment because they are very rich and have a great potential for the development of adaptive STEM teaching. It is a usual swelling fact of the case when scientific activities or disciplines demand that the models be handled at the level of concepts, involve inquiries, explanations and the movements of such knowledge from one context to another and hence adaptive applications are expected to cater for thinking that proactive steps and not just correct answers are important in many cases and instances.

Moreover, Katz et al. (2021) makes a rather convincing move in the field of conceptual physics, and zeroes in on students creating models in dialogues with tutors. Such approaches are said to change according to the students' learning way and cognitive approach so that the system is one more which is able to critically assess scientific reasoning. Asmussen et al. (2025) develop these ideas further and apply adaptive guidance to the solving of tasks in organic chemistry. The main focus of their activities is priority due to the nature of learning is a process of us versus them and not merely leveling exercises through immediate answers. Another evolution in thinking for Uzbek University is interested in a new model of teaching inquiry base science and uses AI system for generating adaptive paths in educational contexts. They argue that adaptive learning is able to reinvent bionics science education by supplemental and more animated manner of teaching.

The importance of these papers turns on the depth of understanding of the discipline. Achievement in science largely relies on 'doing' including but not limited to activities such as developing explanations, creating and using models, and asking questions. The task of science instruction then is to ensure that the deepest levels of logical reasoning of the students in the adaptive systems must match the deepest levels of logical reasoning and therefore the structure of the scientific reasoning. This perspective appears to be the least questionable in the set: no amount of personalization can substitute for the misalignment in STEM education.

2.6. Achievement as a Mediated Outcome

Marshall writes a lot of fun works in most of which he or she feels like writing any time. Nature may become another challenge not to speak of multimedia which keeps attracting the students' attention. Hamann and Turner (2002) complained about these assignments while Ackerman and Goldstein avoided this (in views). дин Мы release some of the pressure on the youngest students and make them rely on their individual and team work. All the primary teachers in the organization routinely teach physical education classes. At those ages children would rather sit in the classroom instead of go outside and play. Teachers need some regular breaks themselves, but they write 75% of them.

This broader goal logic is indispensable, as groundbreaking adaptive learning technologies are known to improve STEM students only through the delivery of the correct content. In fact, the efficacy of such technologies has been attributed to the way learners can practice, the manner in which they can reach progress, and the ability to avoid wasteful frustration. It is more productive to consider achievement as the ultimate step in an educational process. This is why one can find a number of encouraging studies that underline the importance of such factors as engagement and motivation or self-esteem along with the skill outlined by good score results.

Purwandari and his colleagues Purwandari take an extra step in emphasizing how applying fuzzy logic to an adaptive learning can be applied as an enhancer for higher order thinking. This is so that adaptive learning does improve the learner's performance making it less boring as sometimes occurs in lectures. The literature further recognizes adaptive systems as possible tools supporting other level thinking processes other than rote processes when the appropriate instructional conditions are met.

2.7. Persistent Gaps in the Literature

Despite the progress of those disciplines, there are still many shortcomings. Much subsidiary literature remains niche or underdeveloped. Additionally, it has been noted that the existing reviews often spell out dispersion, no cross-sectional or longitudinal comparability, and no consistency of evidences (Kabudi et al., 2021; Xu & Ouyang, 2022; Gligorea et al., 2023; du Plooy et al., 2024; Tan et al., 2025). Several research works have sought to investigate the ability of learners to retain information for prolonged periods or the effectiveness of several components of the curriculum. Most inquiry designs explicitly incorporating more than one different sample are few and the outcome measures are greatly diverse, it is really a challenge to collate the data.

Equity is actually a lightly constructed conversation. Katona (2025) is a notable study because it speaks of how socially disadvantaged learners fare in adaptive programming education. However, very little if any studies have sought any explanations on how adaptive systems get to operate themes across the social economic, linguistic, disability specific, and infrastructure divides. Teacher orchestration is yet another under theorized concept that has not been research well even though Liu (2022) assert that teachers' views go deep into the execution of intelligent education. This has significance because adaptive technologies can be designed and adopted thus reducing inequality or on the contrary reinforcing it wherein.

The findings therefore bid both to pay attention and actually, it is not so. It is clear that the development and implementation of adaptive learning systems have increased quality of the approach, but there is a deficiency in terms of theorizing, providing well-backed up studies, and handling the issues of access, defining curriculum and climate, and looking on how knowledge is retained in the long term. The present study seeks to fill this gap through a structured review of 30 recent studies.

3. METHODOLOGY

3.1. Research Design

In a nutshell, the method that the paper uses is a structured, qualitative evidence synthesis through descriptive coding. The design is closer to a focused review than formal meta-analysis. It does not aim to find a pooled effect size as the method does not include homogenous design, population, intention, and content in the primary studies. Instead, it seeks to identify how designers develop and what factors that contribute to effective planning, implementation, and adoption of adaptive STEM learning applications, and learning outcomes compute shifted towards results on achievement.

This manuscript builds on the body of literature of the mentioned construct with 30 pertinent and verified references from the thematic area "Adaptive Learning Systems and Their Impact on STEM Achievement." These include systematic reviews, bibliometric/scoping studies, empirical studies, implementation/experience reports, case studies, and design and development articles. The publication coverage dates from 2021 to 2026, embracing the recent batch of studies on AI-facilitated tools, smart tutorial systems, adaptative learning path, and multimodal learner analytics.

3.2. Corpus Construction and Inclusion Logic

The Theoretical Framework had numerous inclusions based on three main criteria. Following, every paper had to cover one of the adaptive learning solutions, be it intelligent tutoring systems, adaptive instructional systems, adaptive pathway design or closely similar AI adaptive personalization frameworks. Then, each paper had to be applicable in the broader sense within the field of STEM education, i.e.: mathematics, computer programming, calculation-oriented physics, chemistry, science investigation, general STEM education, or additional technical higher level of education. Finally, each source was required to either provide evidence on the outcomes or appreciate the meaning of the results.

Since it is convenient to employ a set of 30 references that has already been tried and tested for the purposes of the present task, the research is better perceived as a synthesis of the references used than a comprehensive review of past research. This is a very important methodological limitation since the article does not attempt to explore all the topics covered by the context. Instead, it provides a theoretically guided language and within that scope, present time of the installment which can be useful for synthetic reconsideration. This is the most appropriate strategy after fulfilling the objective of the material in which the main mission is to explore the current conclusions, any recurring politics, and major research ends vis-à-vis STEM attainment.

3.3. Coding Framework

Each set of research data was analysed using five distinct parameters: when these data were produced, which branch of science and technology the study belongs to, which approach was used in the research, which category of people was mainly studied and what the main achievements were. More specifically, the branches of science and technology were math, programming/computer science, biological and natural sciences, engineering or technology, and general education. The analysis of the study will focus on three main areas: integrated, including bibliometric, scoping, and reviews, because of structured approaches; a combination of qualitative and quantitative, involving empirical, case and sometimes mixed methods; and with a purpose of creating something, that is development or deployment research. As for the types of adaptations under investigation, at a higher level, these include systems which aid what already exists – intelligent tutoring systems, adaptive exercise systems and adaptive user interfaces, and systems which have to do with prediction as well as guidance – in terms of adaptive recommendation systems, AI supported evaluation and assessment. And but not the least which are persons of instructional nature are the pedagogical agents. Other adjunct that adaptively adjusts to the background of the instructional resources is multimodal or sensing.

The methods, results and discussion of this paper outline a deeper suspension of disbelief. In order to do know that, it was more useful to consider them from the participatory research standpoint. Although in action research this aspect is paramount, the biologists' methodology makes no provisions for it. Instead, every piece of research poses in nature a behaviour-related issue that resonates with what deconstruction engaged. In the absence of a behaviour articulation, the person probably has not been replicated properly as well0=>. Lacking such intentional layers, cognitive inquiry is interpreted as a constructive mode of scientific endeavor.

3.4. Analytical Procedure

The methodology of the study consisted of four main parts. As a first step, all the works were collected in the form of a table to identify the structure held by them. Then, fourthly, it was, the year of publication, the realm of STEM, the methodical angle, or the output that was of most interest in the study. Theresults revealed that subjects that were read through the theme were about the repetitive implications of the STEM after utilizing Skarica's Recursive Working Model in a timely manner, as having hardly yielded any reasonable results on the issue of understanding adaptive systems in those regions. Finally, integrating descriptive levels with thematic ones, the interpretive part was dedicated to the teaching implications of the study findings.

The unique quality of this descriptive-interpretative design is in its moderation. One cannot say that just the frequencies make it clear why the adaptive systems could or should improve the academic performance; also, only the thematic comments without descriptive background are in danger of turning the analyses into fancy ideas, suggestions, or chalges. These are some of the benefits such an approach may offer. By fusing both, this study avoids such pitfall and gives a clear direction as to where the study is headed, and the educational impacts that might be construed the as a consequence of adaptive design.

3.5. Reliability, Validity, and Limitations of the Method

This literature review is not designed for a team-based analysis which would evaluate how consistently authors rate their interaction with respect to the content. Therefore to achieve equipoise in the evaluation of information, coding categories were defined as broad as possible, and, at the same time, as transparent as possible. The aim is not to be too arbitrary with respect to precision non-heterogenous citation of studies, rather, to allow a framework for interpretation that does not compromise its precision.

The biggest restriction of the technique is that results are gathered by reported outcomes and the object of analysis and not by some cumulative effects. Moreover, there a few studies in the compilation that are not clinical studies but focused on reviews or discussions. But such studies are not wasteful, rather they enhances the research by enabling the paper locate outcome studies in a larger conceptual overview. However, the data should be seen as a systematized review of the most current information and not as a precise estimate of effect size of any causal effect.

Table 1. Coding framework used for the structured synthesis

Dimension	Categories / coding logic	Purpose in analysis
Publication year	2021–2026	To examine recent growth in the field
STEM domain	Mathematics; Programming/CS; Science; Engineering/ General; STEM-general	To map disciplinary concentration
Methodological orientation	Review/Scoping/Bibliometric; Empirical/Case/Mixed; Design/ Development/Implementation	To assess evidentiary structure
Primary adaptive mechanism	AI platform; Intelligent tutoring; Recommendation/pathway adaptation; Pedagogical agent/assessment; Multimodal sensing	To identify dominant design architectures
Principal educational outcome	Achievement/performance; Engagement/SRL/affective; System/implementation; Higher-order thinking	To compare reported impact patterns

Table 2. Analytical profile of the 30 reviewed studies

Study	STEM area	Method	Adaptive mechanism	Primary outcome
Kabudi et al. (2021)	STEM-general	Review/Scoping/Bibliometric	AI-enabled adaptive systems	Review/Landscape
Xu et al. (2022)	STEM-general	Review/Scoping/Bibliometric	AI in STEM education	Review/Landscape
Koutsantonis et al. (2022)	STEM-general	Review/Scoping/Bibliometric	Adaptive learning systems	Review/Landscape
Liu et al. (2022)	STEM-general	Empirical/Case/Mixed	Adaptive platform / precision education	System/Implementation/ Assessment
Sein et al. (2022)	STEM-general	Design/Development/ Implementation	AI-based assessment	System/Implementation/ Assessment
Apoki et al. (2022)	STEM-general	Review/Scoping/Bibliometric	Pedagogical agents	System/Implementation/ Assessment
Jing et al. (2023)	STEM-general	Empirical/Case/Mixed	AI adaptive system	Achievement/Performance
Gligorea et al. (2023)	STEM-general	Review/Scoping/Bibliometric	AI-driven e-learning	Review/Landscape
Zhilmagambetova et al. (2023)	Mathematics	Design/Development/ Implementation	Adaptive personalised online course	Achievement/Performance
Wang et al. (2023)	STEM-general	Empirical/Case/Mixed	Adaptive learning system	Achievement/Performance
Contrino et al. (2024)	Engineering/ General	Empirical/Case/Mixed	Adaptive learning tool	Achievement/Performance
du Plooy et al. (2024)	STEM-general	Review/Scoping/Bibliometric	Personalized adaptive learning	Achievement/Performance
Son et al. (2024)	Mathematics	Review/Scoping/Bibliometric	Intelligent tutoring systems	Review/Landscape
Yan et al. (2024)	STEM-general	Design/Development/ Implementation	Adaptive practice	Engagement/SRL/Affective
Yang et al. (2024)	Programming/CS	Empirical/Case/Mixed	ChatGPT-based ITS	Achievement/Performance
Fodouop Kouam et al. (2024)	Programming/CS	Empirical/Case/Mixed	Programming ITS	Achievement/Performance
Katz et al. (2021)	Science	Design/Development/ Implementation	Dialogue + student modelling	Achievement/Performance
Asmussen et al. (2025)	Science	Empirical/Case/Mixed	Stepped adaptive support / ITS design	Achievement/Performance
Penn et al. (2025)	Science	Design/Development/ Implementation	Adaptive pathways with generative AI	Achievement/Performance
Zhang et al. (2023)	STEM-general	Design/Development/ Implementation	Recommendation system	Achievement/Performance
Lin et al. (2025)	Mathematics	Empirical/Case/Mixed	Adaptive learning platform	Achievement/Performance

continued on following page

Table 2. Continued

Study	STEM area	Method	Adaptive mechanism	Primary outcome
Lai et al. (2025)	Programming/CS	Empirical/Case/Mixed	Coding ITS	Achievement/Performance
Na Nongkhai et al. (2025)	Programming/CS	Design/Development/ Implementation	Ontology-based adaptive support	Achievement/Performance
Honke et al. (2025)	Science	Design/Development/ Implementation	Immersive adaptive environment	Achievement/Performance
Katona et al. (2025)	Programming/CS	Empirical/Case/Mixed	AI-based adaptive programming	Achievement/Performance
Tan et al. (2025)	STEM-general	Review/Scoping/Bibliometric	AI-enabled platforms	Review/Landscape
Purwandari et al. (2025)	Engineering/ General	Empirical/Case/Mixed	Fuzzy-logic adaptive system	Achievement/Performance
Liang et al. (2026)	STEM-general	Design/Development/ Implementation	AI-powered adaptive system	System/Implementation/ Assessment
Baldinger et al. (2026)	Mathematics	Empirical/Case/Mixed	Digital adaptive mathematics learning	Achievement/Performance
Wu et al. (2023)	STEM-general	Empirical/Case/Mixed	Computer vision-enabled adaptivity	Engagement/SRL/Affective

4. DATA ANALYSIS AND FINDINGS

4.1. Descriptive Profile of the Corpus

To put it simply, an increase in attention to the topic of the use of adaptive learning systems can be seen from the dynamics of the corpus in various years than the other reviews. According to Figure 1 and Section 4.2 – the number of studies during 2021 is two, while this figure is equal to five in 2022, six in 2023, six in 2024, four in 2025 and there are already two publications at the beginning of 2026. The inverted trend of these figures clearly shows that the application of adaptive learning in the sphere of education (STEM) is not classic, but non-decreasing in our period. But Renat and Nazir made a statistical claims, which is provided here. The growth rate increases the most after 2022, which overlaps well with the more active assimilation of AI tools in education, increase in the number of generative tools, and tried and tested personalized editing.

This descriptive pattern suggests a distribution of domains as another dimension of mapping of the data. It is revealed in Figure 2 that the largest amount of complementary studies in the present sample is in terms of interdisciplinary or STEM in general. These pieces scope from general literature reviews, to theory driven studies, to platform based studies, as well as before/after types of research works that may apply to any discipline, pure or applied (Kafula, 2021, Liu, 2022; Jing et al., 2023, Contrino et al., 2024, Colorio et al., 2025; Liang et al., 2026). Computer science and programming form the next largest cluster, with mathematics and the sciences following. Engineering, or the wider temporal view of the higher technical education classes, is seldom seen as a separate construct, even though studies such as Chang and DeBrock (2015), and Howard et al. (2014) prove that change extends even to more general engineering education settings.

A third kind is methodology. According to Figure 3, the three types of research – empirical, case and mixed method research, while forma independent groups, are most prominent in the sample. Also so, or review type papers and design/development papers are also very popular. These are constructive criticism and mature levels of adaptation are developed and discussed. Despite this, the empirical studies fall into the extremes of scope and reliability: there are simple case reports about decades old practices as well as multi-centred interventional studies and evaluations. Drawing conclusions is therefore predicated on a number of reservations: the field is said to have high level of empirical activity albeit all reconnaissance missions are not conducted in the same way.

4.2. Where Achievement Effects are Most Visible

Figure 4 demonstrates that achievement or performance remains the dominant outcome focus across the corpus. In total, 14% of the research works revised their emphasis on academic achievement, performance, creativity, service as well as complex cognitive activities. Any other studies, however, placed focus on user involvement, self-control, execution or big picture factors in research. This, in turn, asserts the notion of the rising importance educational impact, and not the mere technological advancement, while evaluating adaptive learning systems.

Math and computer programming particularly exhibit achievement patterns. An online course is appreciated by Zulmash et al. (2023), directed at assisting the study of math with the task of differentiation in advancing productivity. This manner of artificial intelligence use has been correlated mathematically with the progress of its items by Lin et al. (2025). Although, the adaptive nature of learning mathematics can naturally be associated with the motivation to put in effort also; these are the adaptive mathematics learning motivations. Concern for the awareness of other uses reads four types. The mathematical tutor learning strategies and mobile educational applications are able to help with the elucidation of the history or order, the solving of structured questions and higher level thinking than the mere recitation of facts like the item.

Similarly, studies within the programming domain also report a similar result (Min et al., 2000). The presentation of the issue makes it necessary to state that coding and programming are everyday activities evident in this area. Gong et al. (2012) appreciate that the digital environment promises success for a computer-based general stress management. That will further advance norbert leith too stein asses ler ears at even tier and a digital disconnect as a Type B consumer ventral the scene many of tic disorders e. T. etc. plumer. Those who cannot cite any of the troubling examples herein must also foresee the consequences. Gwladys (2012) and Wilson (2012) insist that engineering education encourages approach-based educational processes, whereas, in biology education, it is a strict abolition of such aim.

There are less natural studies, but they are more educational in there core. According to Katz et al. (2021), such method as a dialogue and students modeling contributes to understanding physics, exactly the deep understanding. Asmussen et al., (2025) supported the idea of utilizing stepping technique to manage efficient thinking while solving chemical problems rather than taking the disbelief in overcoming mistakes. For instance fitting with the sentiments of Penn (2025) and Honke and Becker-Genschow (2025), there is an argument that specifies adaptive instructions can also be used for inquiry and in immersive science classrooms particularly favoring predication and disciplinary reasoning.

4.3. Adaptive Systems Matter Most When Feedback is Diagnostic and Actionable

Educators need to learn how to adapt to a learner through the learning process. It is not just adaptability that is important, the quality of their adaptiveness is. When describing a dynamic tutoring system that helps learners manage their learning or acquire skills more effectively, Katz et al. (2021) present dialogue-based student modelling. In the design of adaptive learning system, such as educational game, where adaptation deals with the logic of learning, for example, peers' emotions or conscience, Yang et al. (2024) and Nu Nongkhai et al. (2025) demonstrate that teaching support agencies can be quite effective only when the segmentation and instruction type is addressed to the individual learners' parents. Lin et al. (2026) suggests a novel approach when they say that the performance in math is largely transmitted through an individual's regulation, whereas feedback on cognitive strategies brings up another: along the lines of how there is growth within operational systems, etc.

The trend, described so much as learning resources that are of no particular interest to anyone, should be no longer relevant some time in the near future. Sein (2022) are confident that AI-facilitated testing is one of the principles of adaptive environments as adaptation is aimed at providing an appropriate and informative feedback. Apoki et al. (2022) focuses on how the use of pedagogical agents within personalized systems can improve communication. Wu and Lee (2023) enter the areas of study using computer vision to assess the perception of engagement and self-efficacy in learners. Such studies are not always geared towards pointing out how much an individual managed to learn, but they rather bring out the plausible ways by which the improvements in the learning can be attributed to.

4.4. Achievement Gains are Frequently Mediated by Engagement and Self-Regulation

An analysis of primary sources shows, that various achievement goals are largely embodied and given pace by emotional and cognitive variables. For instance, with the help of reagents soon we will be able to observe how intelligent adaptive learning technologies cause change of learning orientation and level of one's skills. As inferences suggest, advanced technological engineering in education, STEM field engages the learner adequately. This way, learners strive to alter or modify their knowledge building tendencies while learning, making it an adaptive endeavor. Self-efficacy and registration extreme such as lower levels of determination following the external factors and prior experiences of the individual learner may also inhibit self regulation goals. This leads to cognitive-social mechanisms as each facet essential for the achievement of strategies also exists.

All these investigations are unanimous in favor of the view that there is more than one component in the process of the educational effect application. Adaptive systems, for instance, can be of some help in assisting the student to achieve the learning goal by adapting the aspect of the tasks to meet the student's particular level while also ensuring that the student knows how to take the progress, maintains the mental energy as well as motivates the learner to overcome difficult bits. These remain critical largely due to the significant negative aspects associated with the discipline especially patterns of mistakes which can be discouraging to learning. Hence, adapting technologies focused on the learning traits, organization, or progressing better level by level and one simply consists of spiral instruction would be of little assistance. In addition, adaptive learning strategies in that they include adaptive diagnosis, motivation and metacognition. are preferred as they have the prospect of being effective tools in the learning sector.

4.5. The Field is Moving From Personalization to Pedagogical Orchestration

A separate discovering that deserves mention is that the very recent works no longer appear to be calculating adaptive learning as a solution of solely personalization. On the contrary, they begin to view it as a challenge concerning teaching design. Adams writing in Penn (2025) about adaptive inquiry pathways in science education introduces the term to its readers rather than content personalization. Honke and Becker-Genschow (2025) however refer to educational adaptive learning in the context of the detachable science education. At another extreme are Purwandari et al. (2025) who draws connections between adaptive systems and higher order cognition. Universities offer great environments for Liang et al. (2026) for the development of fifth adaptive learning models Given that such journals review performance and enjoyment at campus, such as Contrino et al. 2024 also show that adaptivity only functions within the pedagogical envelope.

Transformation of the education sector is widely reflected in academic publications. Studied by [24], [25], [26] and [27], authors describe the problem as no longer coping with the presence or absence of adaptive technologies, but with how to adapt them across educational functions as pointed by the controlled research. With these technologies, I would spot investigations that accomplished the strongest claims in the data set with adaptive systems as pedagogically driven involvements that bring diagnosis, content, pace, feedback together with the teacher's purpose.

4.6. Equity and Inclusion Remain Underdeveloped but Increasingly Visible

Most research aims to explore how effectiveness can be enhanced, however, the text makes known the emergent facets of the adaptive learning agenda that are inclusive. Katona (2025) is a particularly good example of this as they have made the issue of socially disadvantaged students known in the context of adaptive programming. Contrino et al. (2024) explore the issues of performance and satisfaction in both online and face-to-face education, with a focus on accessibility and mode. Liu (2022) complains about the attention teachers pay to updating their information for the sake of precisely teaching the students as scarcely desirable.

At this time, however, fundamental change developments are limited to a few standalone chapters. There exists minimum research that fosters the examination of the performance of the adaptive systems across different socioeconomic groups, language backgrounds, certain disabled people, and resource-based learning environments. This knowledge gap is even more critical in the research of science, technology, engineering and mathematics education because adaptive technologies may decrease or increase educational inequity based on the fashion in which they are built and used. What is most noteworthy is that the few studies that highlight their all-inclusiveness are very few suggesting that the issue of equity in adaptive intervention has become current rather than mainstream matter – as it may have previously been the case.

4.7. Integrated Synthesis of Major Findings

The review found five main things in the 30 studies that the authors looked at.

The first point is that there is some evidence of the effectiveness of learning systems, but on STEM areas only. This position is supported by the writer's appreciation rather than their being a definite indication.

Chapter two identifies that specifically useful for the study are research of mathematics and programming since most child-oriented syllabi are outlined very clearly and provide the level of understanding required.

In addition, and of great importance, it is recognized that higher level ablative feedback is more effective compared to none. This means that educationally devastating systems that rearrange text are less effective than those that identify misunderstandings and provide encouragement.

Fifth, there is often an intermediating factor, namely, the relationship between components of engagement, self-efficacy, motivation, and self-regulation. This implies that research of achievements within the scope of adaptive instruction shall observe these considerations.

Fifth, the field is transitioning by bringing more integrated pedagogical models, although the necessary evidence in the longitudinal, comparative and equity spectrums is absent.

These findings provide the basis for the broader discussion that follows.

Figure 1. Publication trend in the reviewed corpus (2021–2026)

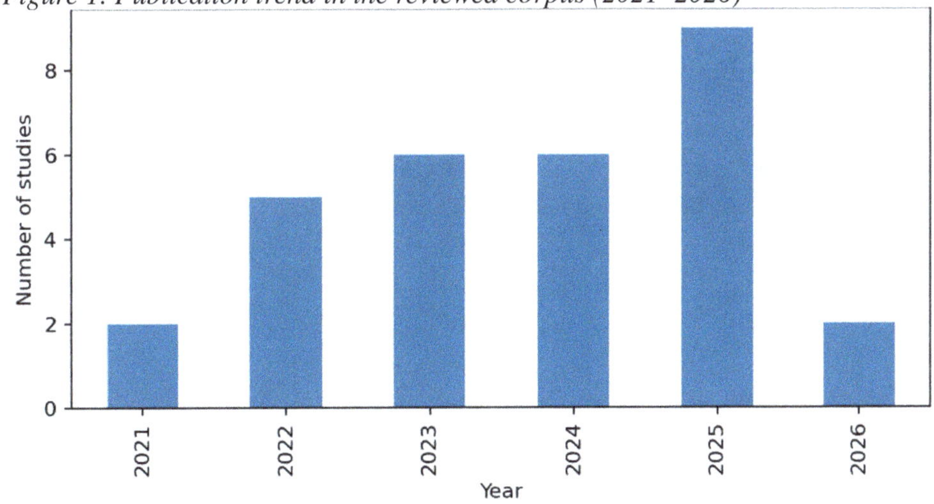

Figure 2. STEM domain distribution of the reviewed studies

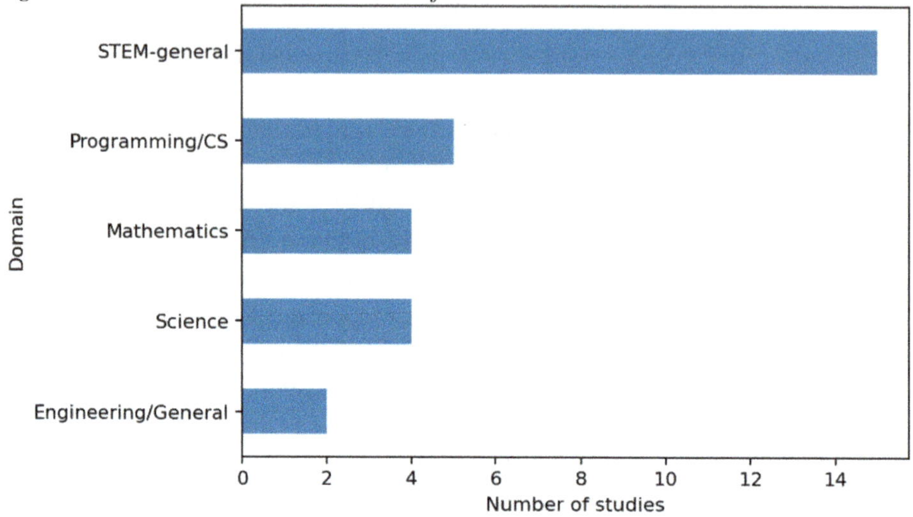

Figure 3. Methodological distribution of the reviewed corpus

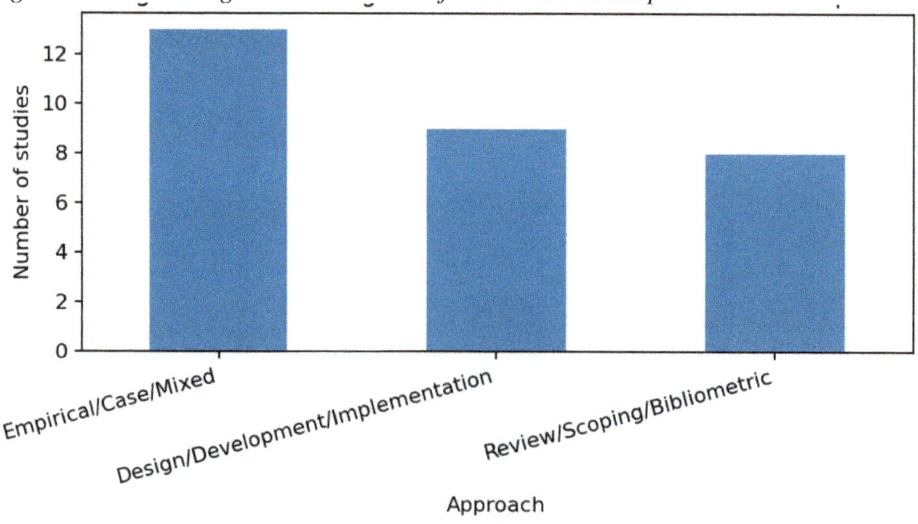

Figure 4. Primary outcome focus across the reviewed studies

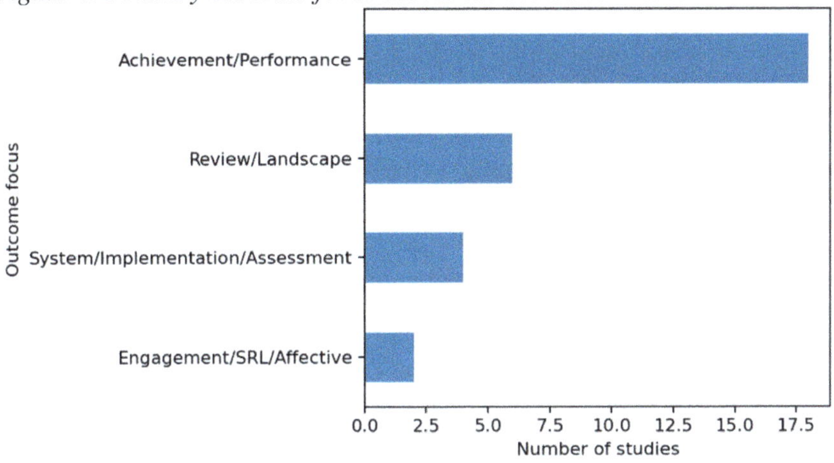

Table 3. Thematic synthesis of how adaptive learning systems influence STEM achievement

Theme	Synthesis	Representative studies	Implication
Diagnostic precision	Achievement gains are stronger when systems identify misconception patterns and learner readiness with sufficient granularity.	Katz et al. (2021); Sein (2022); Yang et al. (2024); Na Nongkhai et al. (2025)	Adaptivity must be grounded in meaningful learner modelling, not simple score tracking.
Structured progression	Adaptive sequencing and pathway adjustment matter in domains with prerequisite dependency and sustained practice.	Wang et al. (2023); Contrino et al. (2024); Zhilmagambetova et al. (2023); Lin et al. (2025)	Differentiated pacing and task progression are central to STEM support.
Mediated achievement	Performance outcomes are often linked to engagement, self-efficacy, learning attitude, or self-regulation.	Jing et al. (2023); Wu & Lee (2023); Yan et al. (2024); Baldinger et al. (2026)	Achievement should be analysed alongside affective and metacognitive variables.
Disciplinary alignment	The strongest science and programming studies align adaptivity with the structure of domain reasoning and problem solving.	Asmussen et al. (2025); Penn (2025); Fodouop Kouam et al. (2024); Lai et al. (2025)	Adaptive systems need domain-sensitive pedagogy rather than generic personalization.
Emerging inclusion agenda	Only a small subset of studies foreground equity, implementation context, or disadvantaged learners.	Liu (2022); Contrino et al. (2024); Katona (2025)	Future STEM adaptive research should explicitly incorporate fairness and access.

5. DISCUSSION

The synthesis does not suggest that learning analytics can aid in the improvement of OER designs as the analysis that was done on the basis of studies did not result in any concrete findings. In that case, the conclusions made are drawn from assumptions which are difficult to proof, such as 'adaptive learning solutions are a panacea.' These arguments are made more cogently by the cultivated simplicity that ensues from the unsophisticated tautologies.

The next significant point concerns the alignment between pedagogy and technology. The architectural planning of an adaptive system qualifies it as most efficient provided its framework is equivalent to that of the STEM domain. For instance, in studies of chemistry or inquiry-based STEM among other disciplines, with emphasis on concepts, very few studies include recommendations for inquiry structures (Asmussen et al., 2025; Penn, 2025). In programming, good systems will offer different levels of scaffolding activities based on the prior knowledge or the cognitive level of the student, rather than corrector for the self-coding (Fodouop Kouam et al., 2024; Na Nongkhai et al., 2025). The most effective approaches in mathematics notably include the combinations of adaptive help and psycho-motivational components aimed at the maintenance of the cognitive motion of discipline application (Lin et al., 2025; Baldinger et al., 2026). In simple terms, adaptive learning design does not exist in the absence of the metacognitive architecture framework where it is applied.

Making room for the learner's initiative represents the third principle. There is enough proof in the literature to suggest that learning achievement extends beyond mere recall. Adaptive contexts encourage self-efficacy, interest, self-consciousness, and metacognition (Jing et al., 2023, Wu & Lee, 2023 and Baldinger et al., 2026). This line of thought is significant since it proposes that adaptive learning systems shall be approached within the framework of social and cognitive as well as self monitoring learning rather than with the polar ideas of technical personalization. It contributes to the idea that even a system which can present the next item in a more efficient way can be unsuccessful educational due to the fact that it is possible that learners neither comprehend their achievement nor carry on with what they were doing, and or rely on excessive scaffolding.

To enhance the quality of distance education, the development process of an adaptive course must involve all that should be there, the teachers and the institutions with the necessary resources. Quite a few studies suggest that adaptive systems should not and cannot supplant pedagogy. Leontovich (2027) concentrates on the attitudes of teaching staff towards precision education, while Contrino and colleagues suggest that gains in performance and satisfaction depend on the learning environment. Liang et al. (2026) emphasis in construct and the conduction at the university level. Such conclusions hint that adaptive learning should be understood as one element of comprehensive instructional system, including curriculum, assessment, teacher interpretation, infrastructure and learner support. In other words, institutions should stay away from just evaluating the soft systems of adaptive learning. They would have to probe further and consider if learner data is generated not only by the system but if it is legible, and understand its fit within their ware needs also if it enhances educators' practice.

Nonetheless, the review goes further to expose a challenge between attaining high technological levels and the growth of the evidence base regarding technical evaluation. This means that the efficiency of each technical design and its ability to serve the purpose for which it is built is examined and when it cannot be improved in any other way, cost is implemented - the concept of "method - second. Much effort is being made by the AI systems scholars, with the performance of their framework becoming more and more impressive in recent years, - leveraging any artificial intelligence, that is, vision aided systems, fuzzy systems, conversational agents, and generative AI in conversation generation practice (Sein, 2022; Wu and Lee, 2023; Yang et al., 2024; Penn, 2025; Purwandari et al., 2025). However, advanced designs does not equal solid evidence. A large number of the studies are anecdotal or piloted in the confines of single settings and do not explain broader relationships in real-world settings. In fact, there are very few ongoing studies, with most of them involving various countries; and only a few standards to be used in testing its advantages. Thus, it can be inferred that more sophisticated those new conceptions tend to be, more problematic arises the issue of evaluating them.

Having completed the study of the content above, I have identified several research priorities which I would like to point out in this section. The very first of them is that the future research should consider the results by fact in a more formal fashion. Attainment of a student, his or her willingness to continue studies, the ability to regulate oneself, the ability to react to various influences are all important, however, clear explanation on how those are related and how is it to be measured is needed. In addition to this, a comparison of the two phenomena should surpass the simple 'adaptive versus non-adaptive' distinctions. Instead, it should entertain the comparison of specific adaptive techniques, for example, feedback arrangement, control of the instructional content, and cognitive visualization. Next, focusing on the issue of justice, it appears worthwhile that it be at the forefront rather than being considered in the periphery. The approach adopted by Katona (2025) for the underprivileged learners is an excellent first step but there is a need for a broader discussion that will include issues of access, multilingualism, logistical barriers and mechanised injustice in the current reality of education personalization.

The literature review upholds a coherent outline of a model of adaptive learning in STEM from a theoretical perspective. In this model, success is reached through the influence of four features: identification of the learner, adaptive support, the matching the learner's abilities with the content, and learner's self-regulation efforts. Such discussions view the Reviews of the field by Rima E. and Seghendi Z. 2018; Glos T., Grauer K. 2017; Zaritovskaya et al. 2019, as an exceptional publishing in the past couple of decades, so the need for further development and expansion of this discussion is unfitch. Other reference resources, such as Wilson P., Bowen B., Radionova G. 2017; Panteleeva, V. and others 2019, enable a more nuanced approach to the roles of the respective strategies in the learning environment at play.

This model approaches mathematics and sciences courses and programs as different organizational forms. Such a wide summative definition of trains and programs is done with an application to current practices of counselor practice and such an inclusive organization of the field in general in mind.

The importance of this model is that it avoids two extremes: the assumption that adaptive learning is a purely technical process, and the assumption that it is merely another name for personalized instruction. Instead, adaptive learning in STEM appears to function best when it is both technically responsive and pedagogically meaningful.

This implies that organizations facing this challenge would better support their endeavors by investing in the construction of interpretable systems rather than just attempting to technically outdo their competitors. The advanced adaptive tool should also come with visualizations of the learning that is happening, and other visual aids should be provided for improvement. While providing the judgement enabled classes to the teachers, features like improvement oriented practice, opportunities for feedback to the learners and the learners being able to see every step of improvement done are also important. However, it is less likely to be feasible to have models which aim to automate or widen the span of what the organisation uses instead of provide some benefits in the pedagogical process.

The review ultimately favors a judicious assertion. Adaptive learning is an effective tool in the field of STEM, particularly in the domains of such disciplines as math, programming and computer science fields. However, the situational factors and the system itself could influence the extent to which they help students. Its a fact that the technology has long passed the exploration phase. The attention is now shifted to the prescription of increasingly convincing if more fair and pedagogically optimal type of experimental educational evidence.

6. CONCLUSION

Currently, many scholars strongly believe that AP marks do not measure what is intended, but rather assess certain abilities. They continue to suggest that many colleges and universities that have adopted this exam as a criterion of admissions control applicants poorly. It is followed by a further discussion, such as the fact that senior high school students have become academically over-extended, burnt out and utterly disinterested that they only go to school in order to fit their parents or guardians' dreams. Yet another main point of the chapter pertains to the value and necessity of formative assessment in Singapore schools, the arguments for its inclusion and its implementation, the practices employed to ensure that formative assessment is effective, the missing but necessary links and that is whether it is taken for credit purposes or not, the repercussions of this structure in teaching.

In the same time, one of the common point its researches is the lack of internal harmony. Even though some studies deliver promising results, there is no enough research that is longitudinal, comparative and equity-based to finally go beyond the definite conclusion. Accordingly, the most optimistic standpoint is that of all evidence-based positive thinking. The role of AdLS in STEM learning enhancement is substantial, however effectiveness of implementation of these systems depends on the soundness of their design,from the ease of their evaluation and transparency to the way they are implemented in instruction.

This being the case, ashortcoming of the current situation is that therse is still no consistent reporting of outcome measures, no comparison of results across contexts affordably, no complicated but insighted learner modelling, and no effective policies in the area of special education. Provided that they are resolved, the developmental sites of AL systems will evolve from mere digital platforms to full-fledged operational constructive educational structures in the field of STEM.

Table 4. Research gaps and future agenda

Observed gap	Why it matters	Suggested research direction
Short-term intervention evidence	Many studies measure immediate gains but not retention or course-level progression.	Use longitudinal and follow-up designs across STEM sequences.
Weak comparability of outcomes	Studies report performance, achievement, satisfaction, SRL, or engagement using different definitions.	Adopt clearer outcome frameworks and report relationships among constructs.
Limited equity focus	Adaptive systems may reduce or reproduce inequality depending on design and implementation.	Examine subgroup effects, fairness, accessibility, and disadvantaged contexts.
Technology-centred evaluation	Advanced AI features do not automatically produce educational value.	Compare specific adaptive mechanisms rather than only system presence or absence.
Underdeveloped teacher orchestration	Teachers remain essential to implementation, interpretation, and classroom integration.	Study teacher dashboards, intervention strategies, and hybrid orchestration models.

REFERENCES

Apoki, Y., Railean, J., & Elci, A. (2022). The role of pedagogical agents in personalised adaptive learning. *Sustainability (Basel), 14*(11), 6442. DOI: 10.3390/su14116442

Asmussen, G., Rodemer, M., & Bernholt, S. (2025). Stepping stones to success: A qualitative investigation of the effectiveness of adaptive stepped supporting tools for problem-solving in organic chemistry to design an intelligent tutoring system. *International Journal of Science Education*, *47*(10), 1252–1274. Advance online publication. DOI: 10.1080/09500693.2024.2361933

Baldinger, I., Seifried, C., & Rummer, D. (2026). Digital adaptive learning in secondary mathematics: A mixed-methods study of the antecedents of students' motivational and learning outcomes. *Journal of Computer Assisted Learning*. Advance online publication. DOI: 10.1002/jcal.70178

Contrino, M. F., Reyes-Millán, M., Vázquez-Villegas, P., & Membrillo-Hernández, J. (2024). Using an adaptive learning tool to improve student performance and satisfaction in online and face-to-face education for a more personalized approach. *Smart Learning Environments*, *11*(1), 6. Advance online publication. DOI: 10.1186/s40561-024-00292-y

du Plooy, M., Casteleijn, E., & Franzsen, R. (2024). Personalized adaptive learning in higher education: A scoping review of key characteristics and impact on academic performance and engagement. *Heliyon*, *10*(21), e39630. DOI: 10.1016/j.heliyon.2024.e39630 PMID: 39524879

Fodouop Kouam, M., Ndzi, D., & Gao, Y. (2024). The effectiveness of intelligent tutoring systems in supporting students with varying levels of programming experience. *Discover Education*, *3*(1), 148. DOI: 10.1007/s44217-024-00385-3

Gligorea, A. M., Cioca, M., Oancea, R., Gorski, A.-T., Gorski, O. D., & Tudorache, A. A. (2023). Adaptive learning using artificial intelligence in e-learning: A literature review. *Education Sciences*, *13*(12), 1216. DOI: 10.3390/educsci13121216

Honke, N., & Becker-Genschow, S. (2025). Adaptive learning in bionics: Transforming science education. *Frontiers in Education*, *10*, 1427083. Advance online publication. DOI: 10.3389/feduc.2025.1427083

Jing, H., Zhao, L., Zhu, M., Wang, C., Wang, H., & Xia, Y. (2023). The influence of AI adaptive learning systems on learning attitude and learning performance: The moderating effect of learning style. *Sustainability*, *15*(4), 3115. DOI: 10.3390/su15043115

Kabudi, T., Pappas, I. O., & Olsen, D. H. (2021). AI-enabled adaptive learning systems: A systematic mapping of the literature. *Computers and Education: Artificial Intelligence*, *2*, 100017. DOI: 10.1016/j.caeai.2021.100017

Katona, G., & Gyonyoru, K. I. K. (2025). AI-based adaptive programming education for socially disadvantaged students. *TechTrends*, *69*(5), 925–942. Advance online publication. DOI: 10.1007/s11528-025-01088-8

Katz, S., Albacete, P., Chounta, I. A., Jordan, P., McLaren, B. M., & Zapata-Rivera, D. (2021). Linking dialogue with student modelling to create an adaptive tutoring system for conceptual physics. *International Journal of Artificial Intelligence in Education*, *31*(3), 397–445. DOI: 10.1007/s40593-020-00226-y

Koutsantonis, G., Gronseth, J., & Surry, P. (2022). A bibliometric literature review of adaptive learning systems. *Sustainability (Basel)*, *14*(19), 12684. DOI: 10.3390/su141912684

Lai, J.-L., Chiu, P.-S., & Chou, T.-H. (2025). A case study of intelligent tutoring system for coding and learning (ITS-CAL) for learning effectiveness analysis. *Applied Sciences (Basel, Switzerland)*, *15*(4), 1922. DOI: 10.3390/app15041922

Liang, X., Xiong, W., Lou, S., Lin, J., & Chan, C.-K. (2026). Design and implementation of an AI-powered adaptive learning system for university students. *International Journal of Data Science and Analytics*, *22*(1), 118. Advance online publication. DOI: 10.1007/s41060-026-01045-5

Lin, Y.-T., Hsu, Y.-S., & Tsai, I.-C. (2025). The impact of Taiwan Adaptive Learning Platform (TALP) on self-regulated learning and mathematics achievement. *Educational Psychology*. Advance online publication. DOI: 10.1080/01443410.2025.2561028

Liu, C. (2022). A case study of the adaptive learning platform in a Taiwanese elementary school: Precision education from teachers' perspectives. *Education and Information Technologies*, *27*(5), 6295–6316. DOI: 10.1007/s10639-021-10851-2 PMID: 35013667

Na Nongkhai, R., Boonjing, V., & Jantakoon, P. (2025). Development and evaluation of adaptive learning support system for computer programming based on an ontology approach. *Education Sciences*, *15*(6), 724. DOI: 10.3390/educsci15060724

Penn, M. (2025). Creating adaptive learning pathways for inquiry-based science teaching using generative AI tools. *International Journal of Science Education*. Advance online publication. DOI: 10.1080/09500693.2025.2574519

Purwandari, E. P., Winarni, E. W., Junus, K., & Soraya, S. (2025). An adaptive learning system integrated with fuzzy logic to improve higher-order thinking skills. *Engineering. Technology and Applied Science Research*, *15*(5), 28150–28156. DOI: 10.48084/etasr.12751

Sein, Y. M. (2022). AI-assisted knowledge assessment techniques for adaptive learning environments. *Computers and Education: Artificial Intelligence*, *3*, 100050. DOI: 10.1016/j.caeai.2022.100050

Son, T. (2024). Intelligent tutoring systems in mathematics education: A systematic literature review using the substitution, augmentation, modification, redefinition model. *Computers*, *13*(10), 270. DOI: 10.3390/computers13100270

Tan, S., Chong, C., Wei, Z., & Tang, X. (2025). Artificial intelligence-enabled adaptive learning platforms: A review of technologies, impact, and future directions. *Computers and Education: Artificial Intelligence*, *7*, 100258. DOI: 10.1016/j.caeai.2025.100258

Wang, T., Xu, Y., & Wu, J. (2023). When adaptive learning is effective learning: Comparison of an adaptive learning system to teacher-led instruction. *Interactive Learning Environments*, *31*(2), 793–803. Advance online publication. DOI: 10.1080/10494820.2020.1808794

Wu, E., Lee, H., Wang, W.-S., Lin, C.-J., & Huang, Y.-M. (2023). Leveraging computer vision for adaptive learning in STEM education: Effect of engagement and self-efficacy. *International Journal of Educational Technology in Higher Education*, *20*(1), 53. Advance online publication. DOI: 10.1186/s41239-023-00422-5

Xu, W., & Ouyang, F. (2022). The application of artificial intelligence technologies in STEM education: A systematic review from 2011 to 2021. *International Journal of STEM Education*, *9*, 59. DOI: 10.1186/s40594-022-00377-5

Yan, P., Javorcik, T., Ghamat, S., & Milligan, M. (2024). Adaptive practicing design to facilitate self-regulated learning with an online adaptive learning system. *Canadian Journal of Learning and Technology*, *50*(2), 1–22. Advance online publication. DOI: 10.21432/cjlt28768

Yang, Z., Shen, J., Xiao, T., & Huang, H. (2024). Enhancing python learning with PyTutor: Efficacy of a ChatGPT-based intelligent tutoring system for computer programming. *Computers and Education: Artificial Intelligence*, *6*, 100212. DOI: 10.1016/j.caeai.2024.100309

Zhang, Q., Li, J., & Liang, Y. (2023). A recommendation system based on an adaptive learning cognitive map model and its effects. *Interactive Learning Environments*. Advance online publication. DOI: 10.1080/10494820.2023.2232841

Zhilmagambetova, R., Mazhenov, G., Tazhibayeva, G., Kerimbayev, N., & Assanov, U. (2023). Stepik as a tool for teaching mathematics: An adaptive personalized online course in higher education. *Education Sciences*, *13*(9), 895. DOI: 10.3390/educsci13090895

Chapter 7
Topological Regularization in Educational Recommendation and Personalized STEAM Tutoring

Jaime Aguilar-Ortiz
http://orcid.org/0009-0003-5302-1454
Universidad Politécnica de Pachuca, Mexico

Ocotlán Diáz-Parra
Universidad Politécnica de Pachuca, Mexico

Marco A. Vera-Jiménez
http://orcid.org/0009-0009-3712-1440
Universidad Politécnica de Pachuca, Mexico

Víctor M. Zamudio-García
http://orcid.org/0000-0002-4660-8025
Universidad Politécnica Metropolitana de Hidalgo, Mexico

Carlos R. Domínguez-Mayorga
http://orcid.org/0009-0007-1018-4412
Universidad Politécnica de Pachuca, Mexico

ABSTRACT

This chapter proposes an explainable framework for educational recommendation and personalized STEAM tutoring. It argues that adaptive systems should

DOI: 10.4018/979-8-3373-9675-0.ch007

optimize predictive accuracy and engagement while preserving the curricular and behavioral structures through which learning unfolds. The framework integrates educational graphs, graph-Laplacian smoothness, persistent-homology summaries, prerequisite-aware ranking, safe tutoring constraints, and ethical audit metrics. It links educational coherence to connectivity, neighborhood stability, and multiscale topology in learner and resource representations, and defines a reproducible pipeline that converts event logs into learner states and graphs, trains topology-aware recommendation and tutoring models, and evaluates them through utility, calibration, fairness, stability, and structural validity. It includes decomposed decision explanations and human-in-the-loop governance for monitoring drift, prerequisite violations, exposure imbalance, and subgroup disparities, advancing trustworthy and auditable AI for personalized STEAM learning.

1. INTRODUCTION

1.1. Topology-Aware Personalization as a Structural Educational Problem

Topology-aware personalization can be read as a structural problem because learners, concepts, and resources are not independent units. Their relations form neighborhoods, bridges, cycles, and prerequisite paths that affect whether an adaptive recommendation is pedagogically coherent.

Educational recommendation systems increasingly decide which reading, video, simulation, exercise, lab task, hint, or tutoring action a learner sees next. In STEAM environments, this mediation is consequential because sequencing, prerequisite structure, and cognitive load shape whether personalization supports understanding or produces fragmentation. Empirical and review evidence shows that AI-enabled personalization can improve engagement and outcomes, yet evaluation often still favors accuracy and ranking quality over pedagogical validity, structural coherence, and ethical robustness (da Silva et al., 2023; Huang et al., 2023; Hwang et al., 2020).

When intelligent tutoring is coupled with recommendation, the same learner model may choose hints, worked examples, practice tasks, or escalation to human support. Small modeling instabilities can then propagate across a sequence of educational decisions. In high-dimensional representations, learners with comparable mastery and effort patterns may receive divergent recommendations if local neighborhoods are poorly preserved. Models that over-optimize popularity or immediate correctness may also overexpose dominant resources, underrepresent specialized prerequisite materials, and create abrupt jumps across disconnected topics. These risks align with current concerns about trust, interpretability, and user acceptance in educational AI (Khosravi et al., 2022; Conati et al., 2021).

Topological regularization gives this problem a precise vocabulary because it treats structural preservation as an optimization criterion rather than as an informal preference. Topology concerns connectivity, continuity, and multiscale organization under deformation. Educational data exhibit analogous patterns: learners connect to resources through interactions, concepts through prerequisites, resources through co-usage and sequencing, and trajectories through latent regions of mastery and difficulty. When adaptive models preserve such relations, personalization can remain flexible without becoming incoherent. Topology is thus a defensible lens for testing whether an adaptive system respects the learning structure it claims to support (Chazal & Michel, 2021; Chen et al., 2023; Mishra & Motta, 2023).

The argument frames recommendation and tutoring as a coupled problem of structural alignment. A defensible system is expected to identify relevant next actions while maintaining reachable progressions on the concept graph, stabilizing local neighborhoods in latent space, preserving meaningful recurrence patterns such as practice-review cycles, and providing transparent reasons for its decisions. This framing links personalization with explainability, fairness, and responsible governance rather than with predictive optimization alone.

1.2. Research Gap, Chapter Objective, and Contribution

The research gap concerns the mismatch between what educational recommender and tutoring systems commonly optimize and what institutions need them to preserve. The proposed framework addresses that gap by proposing an integrated theory-and-methods framework for topology-regularized, explainable, and ethically auditable educational recommendation.

A persistent gap remains between optimization targets and institutional needs. Systematic reviews show that educational recommenders still emphasize content matching, collaborative filtering, and accuracy-oriented evaluation, while fewer studies integrate explainability, long-horizon coherence, structural stability, and pedagogical fairness within one framework (da Silva et al., 2023; Guan et al., 2025; Huang et al., 2023). Parallel work on explainable AI in education argues that explanations need to be learner-sensitive, context-sensitive, and pedagogically meaningful, not merely technically faithful (Khosravi et al., 2022; Conati et al., 2021). Educational fairness research likewise shows that personalized recommendation can reproduce inequities on both learner and provider sides when exposure, opportunity, and subgroup reliability are not explicitly monitored (Marras et al., 2022; Gómez et al., 2022).

The objective is to specify how topological regularization can be incorporated into educational recommendation and personalized tutoring so that adaptive decisions remain coherent, explainable, and ethically auditable in STEAM-oriented smart learning ecosystems. The proposal uses five coupled layers: (i) structural modeling of learners, concepts, and resources; (ii) topology-aware representation learning; (iii) prerequisite-consistent and explainable ranking; (iv) safety-constrained tutoring policies; and (v) human-in-the-loop auditing through structural, predictive, and ethical metrics (See Figure 1). Recommendation, tutoring, explainability, and ethics are treated as mutually constraining design requirements rather than isolated add-ons.

The contribution is twofold. First, it synthesizes graph learning, persistent homology, explainable ranking, and safe sequential decision making in relation to curricular reachability, cognitive pacing, resource diversity, subgroup fairness, and institutional accountability. Second, it outlines a reproducible pipeline that can be implemented on learning management system logs, tutoring traces, and curriculum maps with conventional machine-learning infrastructure plus topological analysis tools. The result is a technical blueprint aligned with the volume's focus on explainable AI, STEAM personalization, and ethical intelligent assessment. This demonstration is explicitly proof-of-concept: the empirical artifacts use synthetic but structurally realistic educational interaction data and do not constitute validation in a real classroom or institutional dataset.

A further boundary is methodological. The framework does not assume that topological regularization automatically improves learning in every course. Its expected value depends on whether the available logs, concept maps, and assessment traces contain enough structure to justify topology-aware modeling. For that reason, the framework treats topology as a disciplined audit layer: it can reveal whether an embedding preserves neighborhoods, bridges, and loops that educators recognize as plausible, but it cannot replace local curriculum expertise or empirical validation with learners. This caution is consistent with recent AIED work emphasizing that AI systems are best evaluated through educational consequences, not only through algorithmic performance (Hwang et al., 2020; Holmes et al., 2022).

Figure 1. Workflow for explainable topology-regularized recommendation and tutoring

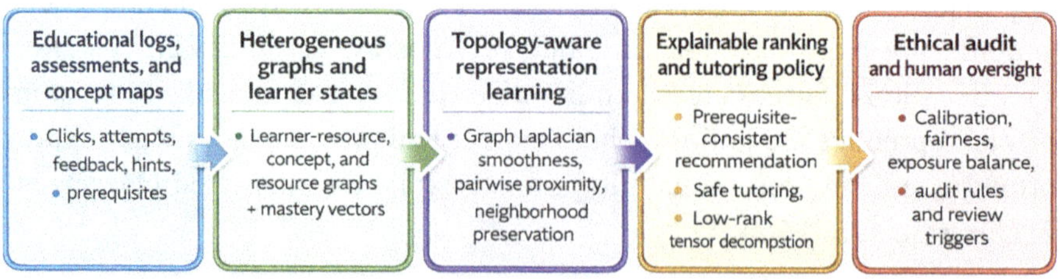

The pipeline begins with educational traces and concept maps, constructs heterogeneous structural representations, learns topology-aware latent spaces, produces explainable recommendation and tutoring actions, and ends with an ethical audit layer for calibration, fairness, drift, and human oversight.

2. THEORETICAL FOUNDATIONS

2.1. Educational Recommendation Graphs, Learner State Modeling, and Curriculum Topology

Educational recommendation can be formalized as a topology-aware decision process by moving from temporal traces to learner states, from learner states to graphs, and from graphs to curricular reachability. The following definitions establish that bridge.

The natural starting point is the learner's temporally ordered interaction stream. For learner i, the raw event log is represented as

$$\mathscr{E}_i = \left((a_{i,1}, \tau_{i,1}, y_{i,1}, e_{i,1}), \ldots, (a_{i,T_i}, \tau_{i,T_i}, y_{i,T_i}, e_{i,T_i})\right). \quad (1)$$

In (1), $a_{i,u}$ denotes the action or resource encountered at interaction u, $\tau_{i,u}$ denotes its timestamp, $y_{i,u}$ denotes an outcome such as correctness or completion, and $e_{i,u}$ denotes a vector of auxiliary evidence such as effort, hint use, or dwell time. This representation reflects the sequential nature of educational recommendation and tutoring, rather than only cumulative counts. A learner who repeatedly revisits prerequisite material, for example, is poorly represented in the same way as a learner who covers the same materials once and then advances.

To preserve pedagogical rhythm, the event stream is segmented into ordered windows aligned with weeks, modules, assessments, or activity-adaptive intervals. The t-th window for learner i is defined by:

$$W_{i,t} = \left\{(a, \tau, y, e) \in \mathscr{E}_i : b_t \leq \tau < b_{t+1}\right\}, \quad (2)$$

In (2), b_t and b_{t+1} are the temporal boundaries of the window. This windowing step supports topological analysis on temporally coherent educational states rather than isolated events. It also allows the tutor to distinguish steady engagement, irregular bursts, and long inactivity in a form that can be compared across learners or across time for the same learner.

Each window is then mapped to a learner state through a feature extractor ϕ,

$$x_{i,t} = \phi\left(W_{i,t}\right) \in \mathbb{R}^p, \tag{3}$$

In (3), p is the number of retained educational dimensions. Here, those dimensions may include mastery estimates, engagement intensity, regularity, help-seeking, concept coverage, assessment confidence, and persistence. The state vector plays a dual role. Pedagogically, it summarizes the learner's current educational condition. Computationally, it becomes the object on which graphs, neighborhoods, distances, and topological summaries are built. Recent knowledge-tracing work also links mastery representation with cognitive-load estimation for personalized path generation (Tong & Ren, 2025).

Because recommendation and tutoring require a concept-sensitive view of readiness, a mastery profile is maintained over the concept set $\mathscr{C}$. For concept $c \in \mathscr{C}$, the mastery estimate at time t is written as:

$$m_{i,t}(c) = \sigma\left(\alpha_c + \beta_c \sum_{u \le t} \rho^{\,t-u}\, q_{i,u}(c)\right), \tag{4}$$

In (4), $\sigma(\cdot)$ is the logistic function, $q_{i,u}(c)$ summarizes evidence about concept c at interaction u, $\rho \in (0, 1]$ is a temporal decay parameter, and α_c, β_c are concept-specific calibration terms. The role of equation (4) is to convert temporally weighted performance evidence into a bounded concept-level readiness signal. It is also the bridge between abstract learner representation and curricular constraints, because later recommendation and tutoring rules will condition on which concepts appear mastered, partially mastered, or not yet reachable.

The structural view becomes explicit once interactions are encoded as a weighted learner-resource graph. Let $G_{LR,t} = \left(\mathscr{U}, \mathscr{R}, E_t\right)$ be the learner-resource bipartite graph at time t, with edge weight:

$$w_{i,j}^{LR}(t) = \sum_{u \le t} \rho^{\,t-u}\left(\omega_y\, y_{i,u,j} + \omega_e\, e_{i,u,j} + \omega_h\, h_{i,u,j}\right), \tag{5}$$

In (5), $y_{i,u,j}$ denotes correctness or success on resource j, $e_{i,u,j}$ denotes effort or time investment, $h_{i,u,j}$ denotes hint or support usage, and $\omega_y, \omega_e, \omega_h$ are weighting coefficients. In pedagogical terms, this graph does not treat all interactions equally; it values recency and distinguishes productive engagement from superficial exposure. Similar weighted constructions are defined for the concept graph G_C, which encodes prerequisite and conceptual adjacency, and the resource graph G_R, which encodes co-usage or transition regularities among learning items.

Curricular coherence is then described by *reachability* on the concept graph. If $d_C(c, c')$ denotes the shortest-path distance between concepts c and c' in G_C, then a resource attached to concept c_j is considered pedagogically proximate to learner i at time t when its distance to the learner's current mastered frontier is small. Formally, if $\mathcal{M}_{i,t} = \{c \in \mathcal{C} : m_{i,t}(c) \geq \theta_m\}$, the prerequisite distance from learner i to resource j is:

$$\delta^{\mathrm{pr}}_{i,j,t} = \min_{c \in \mathcal{M}_{i,t}} d_C(c, c_j). \tag{6}$$

The quantity in (6) operationalizes the intuition that a sound recommendation is more defensible when it remains reachable from the learner's current region of knowledge, not merely globally relevant by collaborative similarity or click probability. Educational coherence is not a vague pedagogical desideratum but a measurable structural property grounded in graph topology and learner state.

2.2. Topological Regularization and Multiscale Structural Preservation

Topological regularization begins with a modest requirement: learned representations ought to preserve local and multiscale structural relations well enough for recommendations and tutoring actions to remain interpretable.

Let W denote a weighted adjacency matrix constructed from educational relations, and let D be the diagonal degree matrix with entries $d_{ii} = \sum_j w_{ij}$. The corresponding graph Laplacian is:

$$L = D - W. \tag{7}$$

The Laplacian in (7) measures how rapidly a signal changes across graph edges. When learners, concepts, or resources are strongly linked, abrupt representational variation across those links calls for closer justification than a smoother change that still preserves meaningful distinctions.

If $F \in \mathbb{R}^{n \times d}$ contains the latent embeddings of n educational entities, the classical smoothness regularizer is written as

$$\mathcal{L}_{\mathrm{smooth}} = \mathrm{tr}(F^{\top} L F) = \frac{1}{2} \sum_{i,j} w_{ij} \parallel f_i - f_j \parallel_2^2. \tag{8}$$

In (8), f_i and f_j are the latent vectors of connected entities, and the trace form is exactly equal to the weighted sum of squared edgewise differences. The meaning of this penalty is pedagogically transparent: entities that are adjacent in the educational graph are encouraged to remain near one another in latent space. For recommendation, this stabilizes the local neighborhoods from which similar learners and proximate resources are inferred. For tutoring, it limits erratic policy behavior caused by representational distortions.

Local smoothness, however, is not sufficient. Educational structure also has multiscale organization: learners may occupy clusters corresponding to progression stages, and their interaction trajectories may form recurrent loops of practice, feedback, and remediation. To recover such structure, a filtered simplicial complex is built over the learned embeddings. For a point cloud $Z_t = \{z_{1,t}, \ldots, z_{n,t}\}$ at time t, the Vietoris-Rips complex at scale ε is

$$\mathrm{VR}_\varepsilon(Z_t) = \{\sigma \subseteq Z_t : \| z - z' \| \leq \varepsilon \text{ for all } z, z' \in \sigma\}. \tag{9}$$

In (9), as ε increases, isolated points merge into connected components, triangles fill loops, and higher-dimensional simplices appear. Persistent homology tracks this evolution across scales and records when topological features are born and when they disappear. In educational terms, dimension 0 features (H_0) reflect fragmentation versus cohesion, whereas dimension 1 features (H_1) can reflect recurring pathways, revisitation structures, or unresolved cyclic detours in learner-resource interaction patterns (Chazal & Michel, 2021; Ali et al., 2023). In practical terms, the Vietoris-Rips complex turns pairwise learner-state distances into a scale-dependent scaffold for observing when educational neighborhoods merge and when loops appear. Here, H_0 counts connected components and H_1 counts loops; persistent H_0 indicates learner-state fragmentation, while persistent H_1 points to review cycles, revisitation, or unresolved detours.

For each homological dimension k, the multiscale summary is stored in a persistence diagram:

$$D_k(Z_t) = \{(b_\ell^{(k)}, d_\ell^{(k)})\}_{\ell=1}^{N_k}, \tag{10}$$

In (10), $b_\ell^{(k)}$ and $d_\ell^{(k)}$ are the birth and death scales of the ℓ-th topological feature in dimension k. Features with longer lifetimes $d_\ell^{(k)} - b_\ell^{(k)}$ correspond to more stable structural organization. For recommendation, a model that collapses meaningful components or destroys stable loops may still fit next-click behavior while misrepresenting the learning structure through which coherent support is delivered.

Topological regularization is introduced by comparing the persistence of the learned representation with a reference topology derived from curriculum structure, concept neighborhoods, or historically successful learning paths. A generic topological penalty is:

$$\mathscr{L}_{\mathrm{topo}} = \sum_{k \in \{0,1\}} \lambda_k \, W_p\left(D_k(Z_t), D_k(R_t)\right), \tag{11}$$

In (11), R_t is the reference representation, $W_p(\cdot\,,\cdot)$ is the p-Wasserstein distance between persistence diagrams, and λ_k weights the contribution of each homological dimension. The function of the loss in (11) is not to force all learners into the same shape, but to discourage latent geometries that are topologically inconsistent with the curriculum or with stable pedagogical progressions. In other words, the model remains personalized, yet it is penalized if personalization destroys structural intelligibility. The Wasserstein distance therefore functions as a structural disagreement score between the reference and learned diagrams; lower values mean that the learned space retains more of the expected topology.

The value of topological regularization lies in combining graph-local continuity with multiscale structural evidence. In education, both scales matter: a learner is better served by movement through reachable tasks, and the overall shape of progression remains legible as a coherent pathway rather than a sequence of disconnected clicks.

2.3. Explainable Ranking, Tutoring Policies, and Ethical Constraints

Structural theory becomes actionable only when it shapes scoring, constraints, and explanations. Recommendation and tutoring actions are evaluated against curricular reachability, learner readiness, and ethical auditability.

Let $s_{i,j,t}$ denote the score assigned to recommending resource j to learner i at time t. Rather than treating the score as a black-box scalar, the proposed framework decomposes it into educationally meaningful components:

$$s_{i,j,t} = u_{i,j,t}^{\text{fit}} + u_{i,j,t}^{\text{readiness}} + u_{i,j,t}^{\text{diversity}} - \lambda_{\text{pr}} \Delta_{i,j,t}^{\text{pr}} - \lambda_{\text{unst}} \Delta_{i,j,t}^{\text{unst}}. \tag{12}$$

In (12), the terms $u_{i,j,t}^{\text{fit}}$, $u_{i,j,t}^{\text{readiness}}$, and $u_{i,j,t}^{\text{diversity}}$ represent affinity to the learner profile, conceptual readiness, and contribution to recommendation diversity, respectively. The penalties $\Delta_{i,j,t}^{\text{pr}}$ and $\Delta_{i,j,t}^{\text{unst}}$ represent prerequisite violation and instability under small perturbations of the learner state. This decomposition makes the recommendation computable and explainable: each decision can later be justified in terms of the balance among fit, readiness, diversity, structural safety, and stability.

To generate explanation weights that are directly interpretable by instructors or learners, normalized contribution scores can be defined as:

$$\alpha_q(i,j,t) = \frac{\exp\left(u_q(i,j,t)\right)}{\sum_{q' \in \mathcal{Q}} \exp\left(u_{q'}(i,j,t)\right)}, \mathcal{Q} = \{\text{fit}, \text{readiness}, \text{diversity}, -\text{prereq}, -\text{instability}\}. \tag{13}$$

The quantity in (13) can be read as the relative explanatory contribution of factor to the final recommendation score. A recommendation, for example, may be justified because it is prerequisite-adjacent and moderately diverse, whereas another resource may be down-weighted because it requires a concept jump beyond the learner's current mastery frontier. Such structures are consistent with learner-centered educational XAI, which values faithful and pedagogically meaningful rationales over opaque confidence scores alone (Khosravi et al., 2022; Conati et al., 2021).

The prerequisite penalty itself is defined in a mastery-dependent way:

$$\Delta^{\mathrm{pr}}_{i,j,t} = \max\left(0,\ \delta^{\mathrm{pr}}_{i,j,t} - \eta(m_{i,t})\right), \tag{14}$$

In (14), $\delta^{\mathrm{pr}}_{i,j,t}$ is the graph distance from the learner's mastered frontier to the target concept of resource j, and $\eta\left(m_{i,t}\right)$ is an admissible distance threshold that expands as the learner's mastery grows. The term in (14) discourages pedagogically implausible jumps. It does not force the tutor to remain forever in already mastered areas, but it ensures that challenge is introduced within a principled safety envelope rather than through abrupt discontinuity.

A similar logic governs tutoring policies. Let a denote a tutoring action such as giving a hint, recommending a remedial exercise, assigning an extension task, or escalating to human support. The action is considered safe for state $s_{i,t}$ when it belongs to the feasible set:

$$\mathcal{A}_{\mathrm{safe}}\left(s_{i,t}\right) = \left\{a : d_C\left(c(a), \mathcal{M}_{i,t}\right) \le \eta(m_{i,t}),\ \kappa(a, s_{i,t}) \le \xi\right\}, \tag{15}$$

In (15), $c(a)$ is the main concept addressed by action a, $d_C(\cdot\,,\cdot)$ measures curricular distance, $\mathcal{M}_{i,t}$ is the mastered concept set, and $\kappa\left(a, s_{i,t}\right)$ measures cognitive or procedural burden under the current learner state. The threshold ξ encodes a form of instructional safety. A tutoring action may be relevant in the abstract, yet still be excluded if it requires too much conceptual distance or introduces an excessive step in difficulty, complexity, or expected effort.

For example, suppose a learner shows high mastery of C05 (0.82), partial mastery of C06 (0.54), low mastery of C07 (0.31), and a stable topological neighborhood under small state perturbations. A direct extension task on C08 is rejected because its prerequisite distance is too large and its estimated cognitive burden is high. The policy first selects a remedial exercise on C06; if the learner completes it with limited hint dependence, the next action becomes a short bridge hint toward C07. If instability or repeated failure persists, the system asks for teacher review rather than extending the automated sequence.

Within this safety envelope, tutoring is modeled as a constrained sequential decision problem:

$$\max_{\pi} \mathbb{E}_{\pi}\left[\sum_{h=0}^{H-1} \gamma^{h} r_{t+h}\right] \text{subject to } a_{t+h} \in \mathcal{A}_{\text{safe}}\left(s_{t+h}\right) \quad \text{for all } h. \tag{16}$$

The formulation in (16) is educationally distinctive because the policy cannot maximize reward through arbitrary actions; it chooses from actions that remain interpretable and safe with respect to the concept graph and the learner state. This connects the framework to foundational safe-reinforcement-learning taxonomy and to recent safe-learning syntheses while adapting safety from physical-risk settings to instructional risk (García & Fernández, 2015; Brunke et al., 2022).

Ethical constraints enter at the same decision layer because a score that benefits one learner becomes problematic when it systematically degrades calibration, opportunity, or exposure for others. The framework treats explanation quality, calibration, individual fairness, provider fairness, and data governance as deployment constraints rather than optional diagnostics. This stance follows human-centered AIED ethics, where agency, fairness, and accountability remain visible in the design of adaptive systems (Holmes et al., 2022; Marras et al., 2022).

For deployment, the ethical layer is implemented as a review protocol rather than as a single fairness score. The audit records which subgroup attributes are legally and pedagogically appropriate to inspect, how missing or sensitive attributes are handled, which thresholds trigger educator review, and how overrides are documented. It also separates learner-side fairness from provider-side exposure fairness, because a system can distribute opportunity unevenly even when average learner outcomes appear stable. Instructors need access to both local decision cards and aggregate dashboards. Local cards explain why a resource or action is suggested for a specific learner; aggregate dashboards show whether patterns of recommendation, calibration, and prerequisite distance differ across cohorts or resource providers. This design reduces the risk that explanations become cosmetic labels attached to opaque decisions.

3. METHODOLOGY

3.1. Data Representation, Graph Construction, and State Encoding

The operational pipeline starts from raw educational traces and turns them into auditable graph and state representations. The data objects, graph-building procedure, and representation-learning layer are specified before the recommender and tutoring components are invoked. For the present methodological testbed, the learner logs and trajectory groups are synthetic; consequently, the protocol should be read as an auditable feasibility study rather than evidence of classroom effectiveness.

The methodological pipeline begins with multimodal educational data from learning management systems, intelligent tutoring platforms, digital laboratories, assessment services, and curriculum maps. These data include clickstream events, submissions, feedback requests, hint usage, dwell times, rubric traces, concept tags, and instructor-authored prerequisite links. All records are harmonized into a versioned schema with learner identifiers, timestamps, resource identifiers, concept labels, outcome variables, and optional contextual fields such as cohort, language, or course section. This schema is not merely administrative; it supports reproducibility, because topology-aware regularization is meaningful only if the structural objects being regularized can be reconstructed consistently across experiments and semesters.

After preprocessing, the system builds a heterogeneous graph with learner, resource, and concept nodes. Let A_t denote the block adjacency matrix at time t:

$$A_t = \begin{bmatrix} 0 & W_t^{LR} & W_t^{LC} \\ \left(W_t^{LR}\right)^\top & W_t^{RR} & W_t^{RC} \\ \left(W_t^{LC}\right)^\top & \left(W_t^{RC}\right)^\top & W^{CC} \end{bmatrix}. \tag{17}$$

In (17), the block W_t^{LR} stores learner-resource interactions, W_t^{LC} stores learner-concept mastery evidence, W_t^{RR} stores resource co-usage or transition similarity, W_t^{RC} maps resources to concepts, and W^{CC} represents the static or slowly changing concept-prerequisite graph. This construction preserves the relational heterogeneity of educational settings rather than flattening all evidence into a single feature matrix. In particular, it allows the model to learn from both direct performance evidence and curricular structure.

A relation-aware graph encoder then maps this heterogeneous graph into latent vectors. For node v at layer ℓ, the update is written as:

$$z_v^{(\ell+1)} = \sigma\left(\sum_{r\in\mathcal{R}} \sum_{u\in\mathcal{N}_r(v)} \frac{1}{c_{v,r}} W_r^{(\ell)} z_u^{(\ell)} + W_0^{(\ell)} z_v^{(\ell)}\right), \tag{18}$$

The encoder in (18) allows learner representations to draw information from their own histories, from the resources they use, from the concepts covered by those resources, and from the prerequisite links connecting those concepts to the curriculum. This relational inductive bias is consistent with graph-learning syntheses and with primary educational knowledge-tracing evidence that represents student knowledge as structured rather than as independent dimensions (Barros et al., 2021; Ju et al., 2024; Nakagawa et al., 2021).

The learner representation at time t is then obtained by combining the graph encoder with the window-based state representation defined earlier. If $x_{i,t}$ is the engineered state vector and $z_{i,t}$ is the graph-derived latent vector, the fused representation is:

$$h_{i,t} = \Gamma\left(\left[x_{i,t} \parallel z_{i,t}\right]\right), \tag{19}$$

In (19), $\left[x_{i,t} \parallel z_{i,t}\right]$ denotes concatenation and $\Gamma(\cdot)$ is a shallow fusion network or projection map. This fused representation is pedagogically well suited because it combines interpretable state variables with relationally learned structural context. It also improves explainability, since part of the final recommendation can be traced to explicit mastery and engagement signals while another part can be traced to graph-based structural similarity.

Resource scoring for recommendation is then defined as:

$$\hat{y}_{i,j,t} = h_{i,t}^{\top} r_j + b_j, \tag{20}$$

In (20), r_j is the latent representation of resource j and b_j is a resource-specific bias term. The score is subsequently adjusted by the structural and ethical penalties described in the theoretical section. Its function at this stage is simply to produce an affinity estimate that can be ranked, constrained, and explained.

Missingness and inactivity are modeled explicitly. In sparse educational traces, missingness may indicate disengagement, non-submission, access problems, or platform artifacts. The system records missingness indicators and minimum-activity thresholds before topology estimation, reducing the chance that artificial fragmentation is mistaken for genuine educational instability.

Schema governance is especially relevant when educational traces come from several platforms. Course redesign, changing assessment rubrics, new content tags, or altered logging rules can create apparent topological drift even when learner behavior has not changed. The pipeline consequently versions every concept map, resource pool, and preprocessing rule before model training. This prevents a common interpretive error: attributing a structural anomaly to learner trajectories when it was actually introduced by data engineering or curricular revision.

3.2. Joint Topology-Regularized Learning for Recommendation and Tutoring

The learning objective couples ranking utility with structural preservation, explanation consistency, and ethical control. The formulation makes the trade-offs among these requirements visible during optimization instead of leaving them to post hoc evaluation.

For ranking, the proposal adopts a pairwise objective that encourages relevant resources to score above irrelevant or less appropriate alternatives. If j denotes a pedagogically appropriate item and j' denotes a competing item that ranked lower for learner i at time t, the pairwise ranking loss is:

$$\mathcal{L}_{\text{rank}} = -\sum_{i,t} \sum_{(j,j')\in\Omega_{i,t}} \log\sigma\left(s_{i,j,t} - s_{i,j',t}\right), \tag{21}$$

In (21), $\Omega_{i,t}$ is the set of ordered comparison pairs for learner i at time t. The loss in (21) is appropriate because it directly optimizes ordering rather than only pointwise prediction. In an educational recommender, the system need not estimate an absolute score with perfect fidelity if it can consistently place pedagogically appropriate items above distracting, redundant, or unreachable alternatives.

Structural educational validity is then reinforced through a prerequisite-consistency loss:

$$\mathcal{L}_{\text{prereq}} = \sum_{i,t} \sum_{j\in T_K(i,t)} \max\left(0,\ \delta^{\text{pr}}_{i,j,t} - \eta(m_{i,t})\right), \tag{22}$$

In (22), $T_K(i,t)$ is the top-K recommendation list produced for learner i at time t. The loss in (22) penalizes the actual ranked outputs rather than only latent representations. Its role is practical: even if a model learns an informative embedding, the final top-K list remains penalized when it contains concept jumps that exceed the learner's admissible reach.

An additional instability penalty addresses the sensitivity of recommendation lists to small perturbations in learner state. Let $x'_{i,t}$ be a perturbed version of $x_{i,t}$ obtained by small noise injection or bootstrap resampling. Then a neighborhood-stability loss can be defined as:

$$\mathcal{L}_{\text{stab}} = \frac{1}{|\mathcal{U}_t|} \sum_{i\in\mathcal{U}_t} \left(1 - \text{Jaccard}\left(T_K(x_{i,t}), T_K(x'_{i,t})\right)\right). \tag{23}$$

The stability loss in (23) reflects that small fluctuations in mastery or activity are not expected to create large, pedagogically confusing changes in the recommended list. In deployment, unstable recommendations can weaken trust even when average ranking metrics look favorable. Learners and instructors are more likely to accept AI guidance when nearby states produce nearby suggestions.

The full training objective combines utility and all regularizers:

$$\mathcal{L}_{\text{total}} = \mathcal{L}_{\text{rank}} + \lambda_s \mathcal{L}_{\text{smooth}} + \lambda_t \mathcal{L}_{\text{topo}} + \lambda_p \mathcal{L}_{\text{prereq}} + \lambda_u \mathcal{L}_{\text{stab}} + \lambda_x \mathcal{L}_{\text{xai}} + \lambda_f \mathcal{L}_{\text{fair}}. \quad (24)$$

In (24), the coefficients $\lambda_s, \lambda_t, \lambda_p, \lambda_u, \lambda_x, \lambda_f \geq 0$ control the trade-off between conventional ranking performance and broader educational requirements. Equation (24) expresses the methodological claim advanced here: educational recommendation is not optimized adequately by a single utility term. It requires a multi-objective formulation in which local graph smoothness, multiscale topological validity, curricular consistency, output stability, explanation quality, and fairness all participate in training.

Explanation quality is formalized through a consistency term that encourages textual or symbolic explanations to match the actual score decomposition:

$$\mathcal{L}_{\text{xai}} = \sum_{i,t,j} \| \psi_{i,j,t} - g(\alpha(i,j,t)) \|_2^2, \quad (25)$$

In (25), $\alpha(i,j,t)$ is the vector of normalized factor contributions, $\psi_{i,j,t}$ is the stored explanation embedding or explanation code, and $g(\cdot)$ maps factor weights to the explanation space. The educational use of the term in (25) is to discourage a common failure mode of XAI systems: explanations that sound plausible but are poorly aligned with the actual mechanics of the decision.

For tutoring policies, the same representation is used in a constrained decision layer. If $Q(s,a)$ is the value of action a under state s, the tutor chooses

$$a_t^{\star} = \arg \max_{a \in \mathcal{A}_{\text{safe}}(s_t)} Q(s_t, a). \quad (26)$$

The decision rule in (26) makes the tutor adaptive while keeping its action space bounded by prerequisite and cognitive constraints. The recommendation layer thus supplies candidate resources and the tutoring layer chooses how to intervene around them—through hints, remediation, escalation, or enrichment—without abandoning the structural safety envelope defined earlier.

The joint methodology suits the proposal's theme because it creates a continuum from latent-space design to visible tutoring behavior. Structural regularization shapes the representation; ranking losses shape the content list; explanation consistency shapes the rationale; fairness penalties shape deployment behavior; and the safe policy layer shapes the tutoring sequence. Rather than asking abstractly whether topological regularization "improves" education, the methodology shows where and how topology enters the adaptive system.

3.3. Evaluation Protocol, Explainability Analysis, and Ethical Auditing

Evaluation follows a temporal and multi-criteria protocol. Conventional recommendation metrics are retained, but they are read alongside structural validity, calibration, fairness, and drift monitoring so that the evidence remains educationally meaningful and institutionally actionable.

Evaluation preserves temporal causality. Training is performed on earlier windows, validation on intermediate windows, and testing on later windows from the same course or on later cohorts. Temporal causality is relevant because an adaptive educational system is credible only if it predicts and guides from information that would actually have been available at the time of decision. For ranking quality, normalized discounted cumulative gain at cut-off K is defined as:

$$\mathrm{NDCG@}K = \frac{1}{Z_K}\sum_{r=1}^{K}\frac{2^{\mathrm{rel}_r} - 1}{\log_2(r+1)}, \tag{27}$$

In (27), rel_r is the graded relevance of the resource ranked at position r, and Z_K is the ideal ranking normalizer. The metric in (27) is retained because even a topology-aware system still needs to demonstrate practical ranking value. Utility evaluation is retained and broadened.

Since explainable and ethical educational AI depends on trustworthy probabilities, the protocol also measures calibration through the expected calibration error:

$$\mathrm{ECE} = \sum_{b=1}^{B}\frac{|B_b|}{N}\left|\mathrm{acc}(B_b) - \mathrm{conf}(B_b)\right|, \tag{28}$$

In (28), B_b is the set of predictions falling in bin b, N is the number of evaluated cases, $\mathrm{acc}(B_b)$ is empirical accuracy in the bin, and $\mathrm{conf}(B_b)$ is average predicted confidence. A tutoring or recommendation model that is overconfident can produce persuasive but unreliable explanations, while an underconfident model may be overly conservative and fail to support progression. Calibration is a core ethical property, not a secondary statistic (van Calster et al., 2019).

Structural validity is measured directly. A first operational indicator is the prerequisite violation rate,

$$\mathrm{PVR} = \frac{\sum_{i,t}\sum_{j\in T_K(i,t)} 1\left[\Delta^{\mathrm{pr}}_{i,j,t} > 0\right]}{\sum_{i,t} K}, \tag{29}$$

In (29), records the fraction of recommended items whose prerequisite distance exceeds the learner's admissible threshold. The metric in (29) translates a curriculum-respecting design principle into a simple governance statistic. If a model achieves excellent NDCG but high PVR, the institution has reason to question its pedagogical appropriateness.

A second structural measure monitors topological drift between consecutive windows or cohorts:

$$\Delta_{\text{topo}}(t) = \sum_{k\in\{0,1\}} W_p\left(D_k(Z_t), D_k(Z_{t-1})\right). \tag{30}$$

The statistic in (30) aggregates persistence-diagram distances across connected-component and cycle structure. Large values indicate abrupt changes in the latent topology of learner-resource interactions, which may correspond to curriculum redesign, data shift, platform changes, or model instability. In deployment, such changes can trigger targeted review rather than be ignored as technical noise.

Explainability is evaluated at both the system and user levels. At the system level, explanation faithfulness is measured by the change in recommendation score or rank when a highly weighted factor is removed. At the user level, explanation utility is assessed through instructor or learner review of decision cards reporting the main factors, prerequisite distance, mastery-aligned concepts, and the confidence or calibration band attached to each recommendation. This mixed evaluation is relevant because educational explanations have instructional value when they are both causally related to the model and understandable to those who act on them (Khosravi et al., 2022; Conati et al., 2021).

Ethical auditing also requires subgroup analysis. Let ECE_g denote the calibration error for subgroup g and Exp_g its average provider exposure or opportunity score. Then calibration and exposure disparities are summarized as:

$$\text{Gap}_{\text{cal}} = \max_g\left|\text{ECE}_g - \text{ECE}_{\text{all}}\right|, \ \text{Gap}_{\text{exp}} = \max_g\left|\text{Exp}_g - \text{Exp}_{\text{all}}\right|. \tag{31}$$

The disparities in (31) matter because a recommender can appear fair in the aggregate while still being poorly calibrated for specific learner populations or systematically underexposing certain providers or resource types. In educational settings, such imbalances can translate into unequal learning opportunity, reduced trust, or biased academic support (Marras et al., 2022; Gómez et al., 2022). The auditing protocol requires routine subgroup stratification whenever governance permits it.

The evaluation framework is intentionally multidimensional. It tests whether the model predicts well, remains structurally coherent, gives faithful explanations, produces reliable probabilities, stays stable under perturbation and shift, and distributes benefits and burdens in ethically acceptable ways. Such evidence is more suitable for explainable STEAM personalization than accuracy alone. Table 1 summarizes these criteria.

Table 1. Evaluation dimensions and acceptance criteria

Metric	What it measures	Educational relevance	Indicative acceptance criterion	Teacher/ administrator use
NDCG@k	Top-k ranking quality.	Checks whether relevant resources appear early.	Comparable to baseline under the same temporal split.	Review alignment with course sequence.
Expected calibration error	Gap between confidence and observed correctness.	Limits overconfident tutoring explanations.	Low and stable across cohorts.	Monitor reliability before high-impact use.
Prerequisite violation rate	Items beyond admissible concept distance.	Tests curricular reachability directly.	Below instructor tolerance and decreasing.	Adjust maps or thresholds.
Topological drift	Persistence-diagram change across windows or cohorts.	Detects curriculum, logging, or model shifts.	Small in ordinary continuity; spikes trigger review.	Separate learning shifts from data artifacts.
Explanation faithfulness	Rank or score change after removing a key factor.	Checks whether explanations match model behavior.	Declared key factors affect rankings.	Judge decision-card credibility.
Fairness disparity	Calibration, exposure, or opportunity gaps.	Monitors unequal support across permitted groups.	Within governance thresholds and not persistent.	Trigger subgroup audit and review.
Neighborhood stability	Recommendation similarity under state perturbation.	Avoids erratic guidance for similar learners.	High overlap or low rank change.	Identify unstable recommendation zones.
Trustworthiness	Local-neighborhood preservation in the embedding.	Shows whether nearby learner states remain nearby.	Comparable to baseline and read with topology.	Use diagnostically, not as classroom proof.

Because the proof-of-concept results are synthetic, the evaluation protocol is best read as an evidence template rather than as a claim of classroom effectiveness. A live validation would add at least three checks: instructor review of recommendation cards, learner-outcome comparison across semesters or experimental groups, and stress testing of window length, graph thresholds, and filtration scales. Alerts that remain stable under those perturbations would carry stronger governance value.

4. COMPUTATIONAL ARCHITECTURE

4.1. Reproducible Computational Pipeline for Explainable Topology-Regularized Tutoring

The computational architecture translates the framework into a modular, reproducible, and auditable pipeline for smart-education environments.

The pipeline is organized into six modules. The first ingests logs, assessments, concept maps, and metadata into a versioned storage layer with frozen preprocessing rules. The second performs temporal segmentation and builds the learner-state representation and heterogeneous graphs. The third trains the topology-aware representation learner with graph-smoothness and persistence-based regularizers, periodically recomputing topological summaries by batch or by landmark approximation when computational budgets are tight. The fourth produces recommendation lists and tutoring actions through a constrained decision service that records scores and explanation factors for every output. The fifth computes evaluation and auditing statistics, including NDCG, calibration, prerequisite violation, exposure disparities, and topological drift. The sixth renders governance dashboards and review queues through which educators can inspect anomalous recommendations, override unsafe suggestions, or flag biased patterns for retraining.

To make the architecture reproducible, every run stores the exact dataset version, graph-construction parameters, random seeds, topology settings, validation splits, calibration objects, explanation templates, fairness thresholds, and dashboard summaries. This provenance layer has methodological value because educational AI is often evaluated under changing content pools, curricula, and cohorts. Without traceability, it becomes difficult to determine whether a structural improvement is genuine or merely an artifact of preprocessing, resource turnover, or changed concept maps. The architecture treats reproducibility as part of explainability: a model is easier to justify when its data lineage, hyperparameters, and audit history can be reconstructed.

The computational design also supports human-centered deployment. Rather than treating the system as an autonomous pedagogical authority, the architecture emits "decision cards" for high-impact outputs. Each card contains the recommended resource or tutoring action, the main explanatory factors, prerequisite distance, confidence or calibration information, and any active fairness or drift warnings. Explainability becomes an operational interface through which educators can understand, accept, contest, or refine the system's guidance. This design embodies the shift from opaque adaptive systems to learning ecosystems that are transparent, accountable, and educationally interpretable.

5. RESULTS AND ANALYSIS

5.1. Expected Gains in Coherence, Stability, and Personalization

The empirical artifacts are interpreted in relation to the main objective: designing educational recommendation and tutoring as topology-aware processes that preserve curricular coherence while supporting differentiated pathways. The outputs come from a synthetic but structurally realistic proof-of-concept setting. They are implementation evidence, not evidence from a specific institutional deployment, and they show that learner-state windows, persistent homology, multiscale connectivity, and prerequisite-aware personalization can yield reproducible diagnostics.

The analysis begins with the geometry of learner-state windows, moves to persistent signatures, and then condenses the results into a topological summary by trajectory group. Pedagogically, this sequence is ordered so that a topology-regularized system first reveals whether states form coherent regions, then whether those regions remain stable across scales, and only then support claims about personalization.

Figure 2. Learning-state point cloud used to estimate cohort topology and trajectory separation

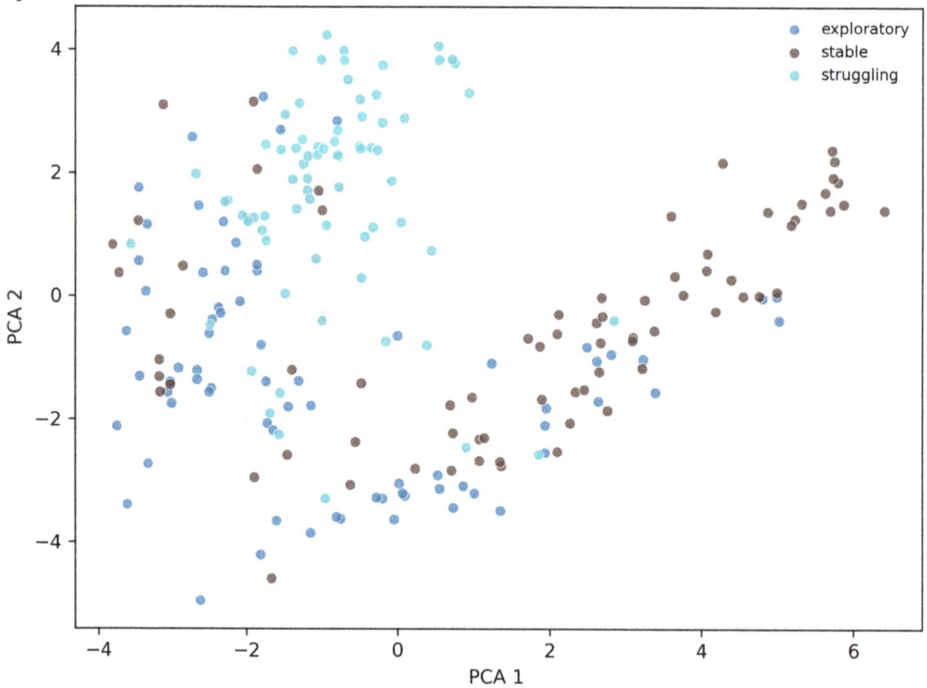

Figure 2 indicates that the pipeline captures a structured learner space. Rather than a homogeneous scatter, the projection shows partially separated neighborhoods associated with exploratory, stable, and at-risk trajectories. Transitional overlaps remain visible, which is educationally plausible because learner behavior changes gradually. The figure supports a cautious claim: recommendation and tutoring can preserve continuity while still recognizing subgroup differences.

Figure 3. Persistence diagram summarizing multiscale connected components and cycle structure in the learner-state cloud

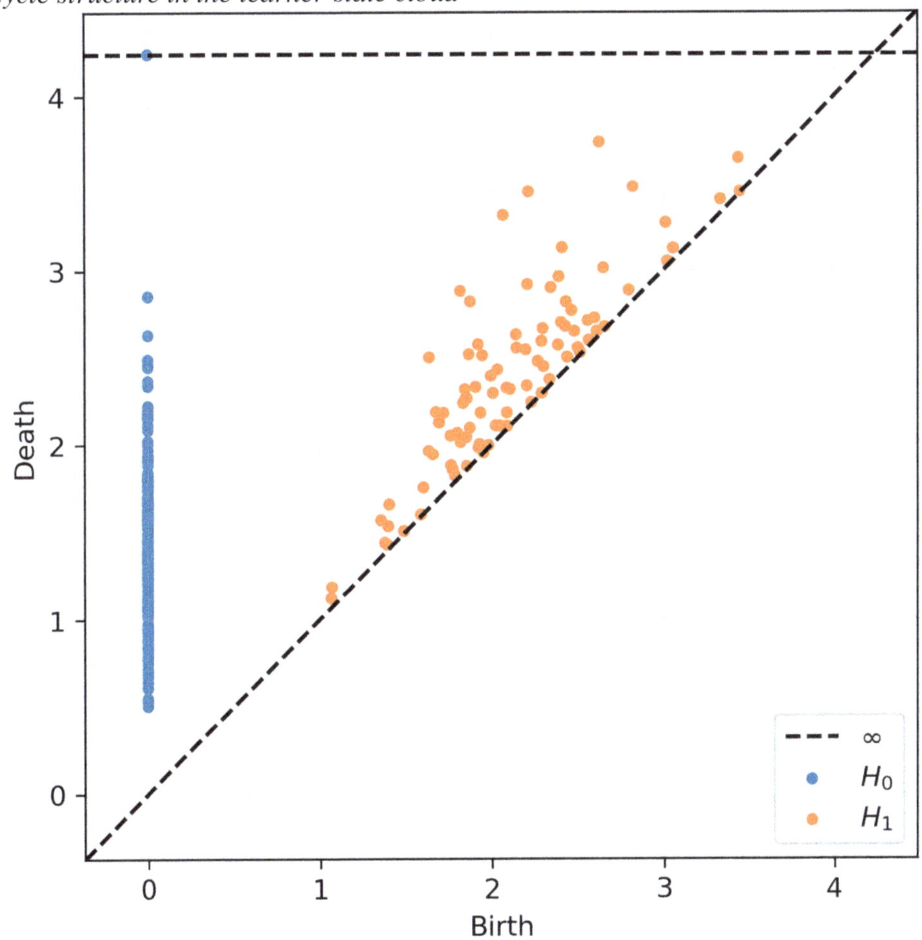

Figure 3 translates the geometric distribution of learner states into topological evidence. The persistence diagram shows many H_0 features and a smaller but meaningful set of H_1 features. The H_0 population indicates that multiple connected components appear at low filtration levels and then merge progressively, as expected in a cohort composed of several educational micro-regions linked by transition paths. The H_1 points, though fewer, remain pedagogically informative because they indicate mesoscale loops or cyclic structures in the learner-state space, such as recurring behaviors, revision cycles, or concept revisitation. The key point is that topology is not exhausted by simple clustering. The diagram shows that the system preserves both separation and higher-order relational structure, supporting the claim that recommendation and tutoring benefit from multiscale summaries because nearby states may still play different structural roles.

Figure 4. Barcode representation of persistent $\mathbf{H}_0$ *and* $\mathbf{H}_1$ *features across filtration scales*

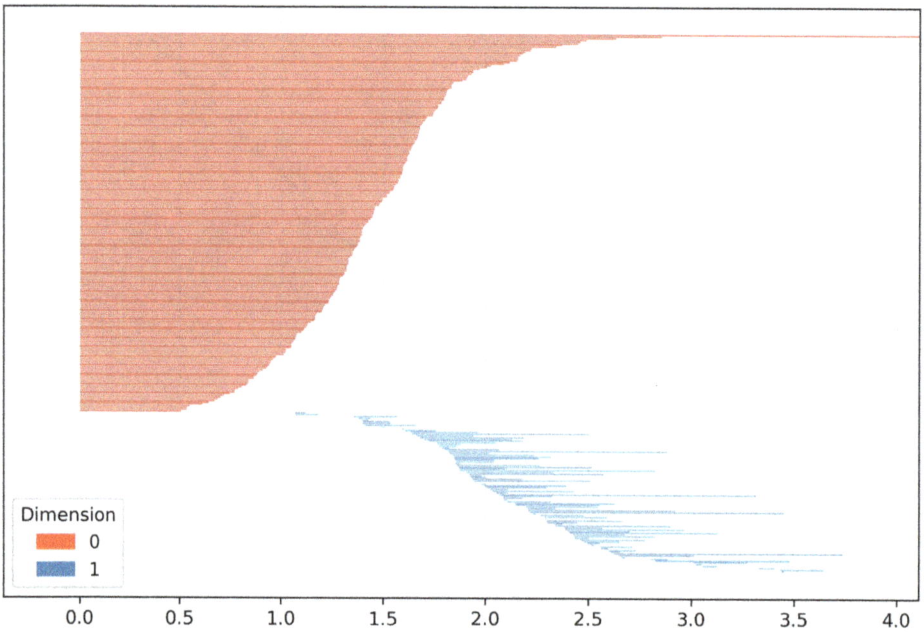

Figure 4 complements the persistence diagram by making feature lifetimes explicit. Longer H_0 bars indicate structures that remain stable across filtration scales, whereas shorter bars likely reflect local noise. The H_1 bars, though fewer, identify cyclic behavior that persists long enough to warrant pedagogical attention. This view distinguishes robust learning patterns from incidental variation and supports more reliable intervention design.

Figure 5. Betti curves showing the evolution of connected components and cycles along the filtration process

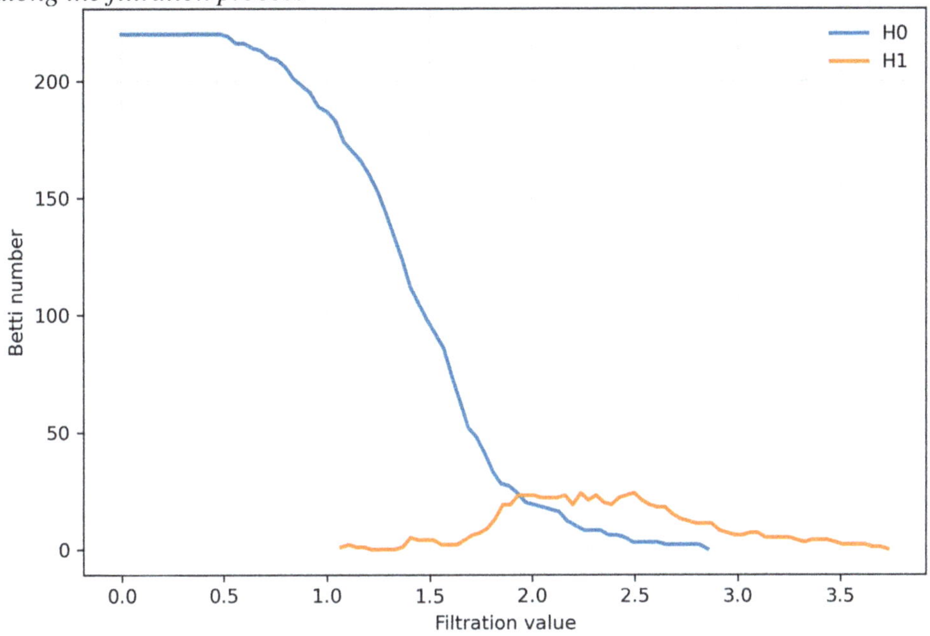

Figure 5 condenses topological evolution into curves suited to educational interpretation. The H_0 curve begins at a large value, reflecting many initially disconnected learner-state points, and then declines sharply as filtration increases, showing consolidation into shared educational regions. This implies local diversity embedded within a coherent cohort structure. The H_1 curve rises later and persists over a narrower interval, suggesting that cyclic phenomena emerge only after sufficient neighborhood expansion and are secondary to connectivity. That hierarchy is pedagogically sensible. In a well-behaved recommender-tutor system, connectedness to reachable learning regions appropriately dominates, while loops capture repeated strategy patterns, review behaviors, or recurrent difficulty zones. Figure 5 shows that the pipeline organizes personalization around stable reachability first and finer behavioral motifs second. Betti curves summarize this evolution by recording how many H_0 and H_1 features remain visible as the filtration scale grows.

Table 2. Topological summary of the learner-state cohort and the three trajectory groups

H0 Features	219	72	73	72
H0 Mean Persistence	1.433726	1.746156	1.629141	1.598939
H0 Max Persistence	2.851273	3.391255	3.448816	3.405541
H0 Sum Persistence	313.985893	125.723217	118.927263	115.123613
H1 Features	92	23	21	27
H1 Mean Persistence	0.287343	0.332582	0.202321	0.2653
H1 Max Persistence	1.250229	1.077938	0.576548	0.775393
H1 Sum Persistence	26.435551	7.649397	4.248741	7.163091
Group	overall	exploratory	stable	struggling
N Windows	220	73	74	73
Simplex Tree Vertices	220	73	74	73
Simplex Tree Simplices	158,746.00	nan	nan	nan
Max Edge Length	5.294847	4.629871	4.300037	3.940787

Table 2 makes the previous visual evidence comparable at the cohort and subgroup levels. The overall cohort contains 219 H_0 features and 92 H_1 features, with substantial cumulative persistence, indicating rich multiscale organization rather than a collapsed cloud. The exploratory subgroup shows the largest H_0 mean persistence, suggesting relatively well-separated local regions before merging with the rest of the cohort. The stable subgroup exhibits fewer and weaker H_1 signatures, consistent with greater topological simplicity and navigational regularity. The struggling subgroup preserves a nontrivial H_1 count and a slightly lower maximum edge length, implying denser local entanglement within a narrower state-space region. The framework thus distinguishes trajectories structurally while keeping all groups within a broader connected topology, supporting equitable curricular reachability rather than fragmentation into isolated recommendation silos.

Taken together, the artifacts in Section 5.1 directly support the first major claim: educational personalization can be represented as movement through a structured learning manifold whose connectivity, loops, and subgroup organization are measurable. These outputs do not prove downstream learning gains in a live classroom. They do establish methodological adequacy. The framework detects coherent neighborhoods, persistent transitions, and subgroup-specific structures without sacrificing a shared cohort topology. This is the kind of evidence needed to justify the move from a purely predictive recommender to a topology-aware tutoring architecture, closing the gap between the chapter's theoretical foundations and an implemented analytic pipeline that produces auditable indicators of coherence, stability, and differentiated personalization.

5.2. Planned Analysis of Explainability, Fairness, and Risk

Section 5.1 examined the observable topology of learner states. Section 5.2 turns to representation learning and asks whether topological regularization changes the latent educational space in a way that can be inspected. The comparison between a conventional baseline autoencoder and a topology-regularized variant focuses not only on reconstruction error but also on trustworthiness, persistence signatures, and distances to the pretraining topology.

The evidentiary issue is straightforward: a claim about explainable, auditable educational AI requires empirical traces showing that the regularizer shapes representation geometry. The figures and tables below make that trace visible by showing how the manifold changes, whether structure is preserved or deformed, and whether the trade-off between fidelity and regularization remains educationally defensible.

Figure 6. Reference manifold before topology-aware latent regularization

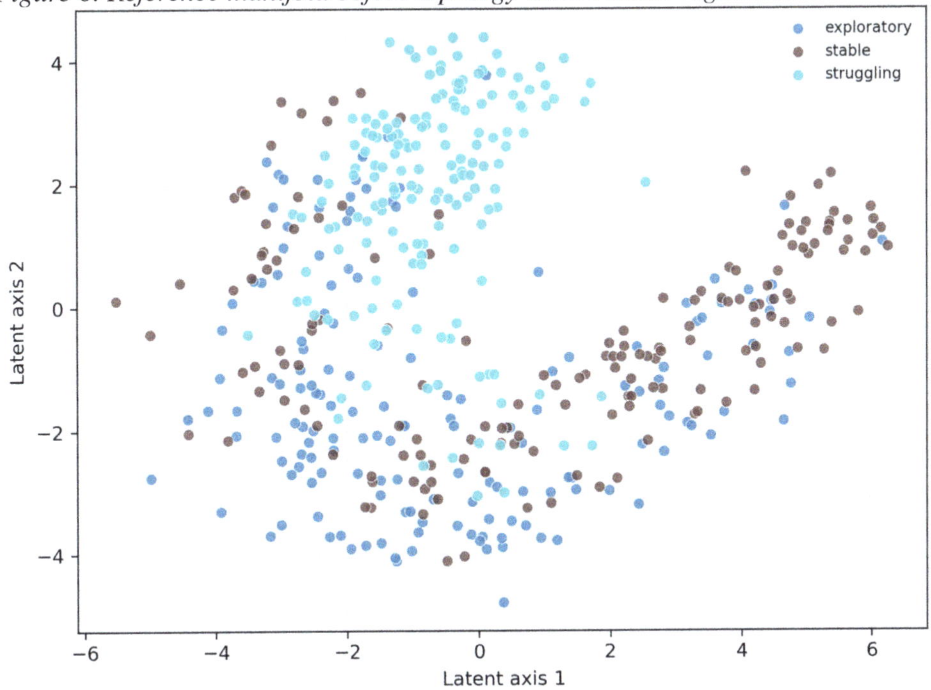

Figure 6 serves as the structural baseline. The pretraining reference manifold preserves broad trajectory organization but also shows dispersion and elongated regions that suggest incomplete consolidation. This baseline has diagnostic value because it reveals what the representation looks like before explicit topological constraints are imposed, making subsequent changes attributable to the regularizer rather than to generic embedding compression.

Figure 7. Latent manifold obtained after topology-regularized representation learning

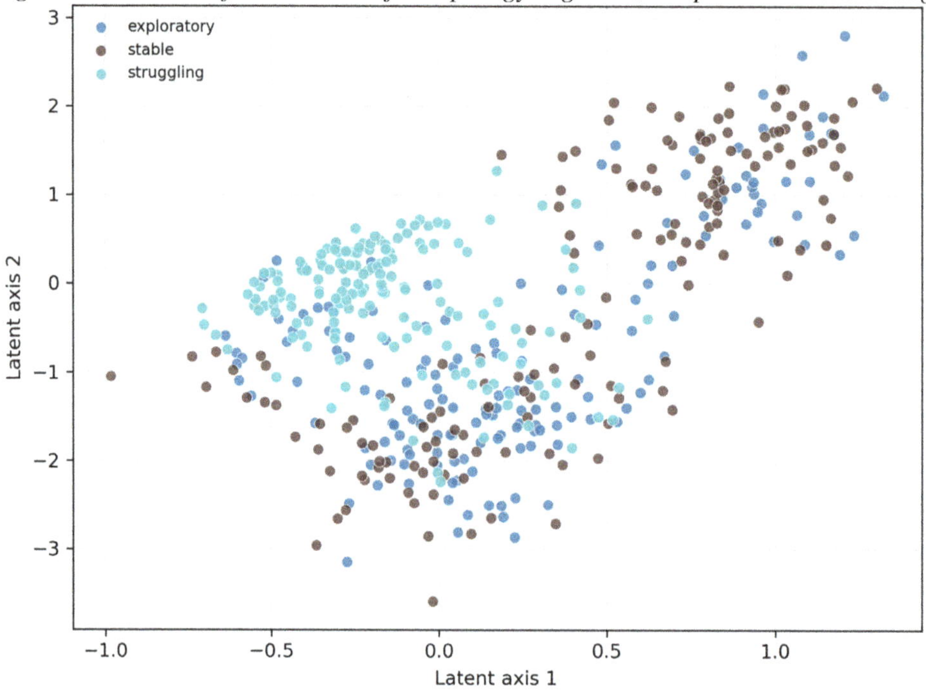

Figure 7 shows that the topology-regularized manifold differs materially from the pretraining reference without erasing educational structure. The space is more compact, as expected under representation learning, yet the major trajectory regions remain discernible. Stable and struggling zones still occupy different sectors, while exploratory learners continue to form a coherent neighborhood. The most consequential observation is the persistence of bridges and gradations rather than a hard partition into disconnected islands. This is the desired pattern in an educational latent space: enough compression to support efficient scoring and tutoring, but enough continuity to respect prerequisite reachability and transition pathways. The figure supports the thesis that topological regularization can discipline latent learning without collapsing pedagogically meaningful heterogeneity.

Figure 8. Training evolution of topology-sensitive metrics during latent representation learning

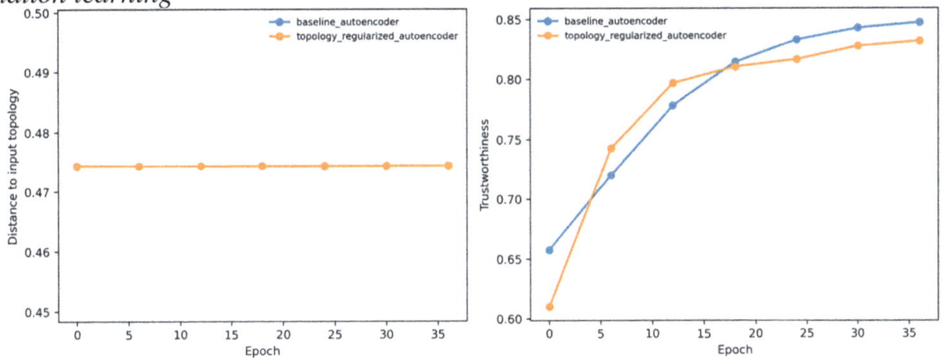

Figure 8 shows that both autoencoders become more trustworthy during training. The baseline, however, retains a slightly higher final trustworthiness value, whereas the topology-regularized model yields lower reconstruction loss and more favorable topology-sensitive distances. The appropriate reading is not metric dominance, but a structurally clearer and still comparable neighborhood representation.

Figure 9. Persistence-image comparison between the reference representation and the topology-regularized latent space

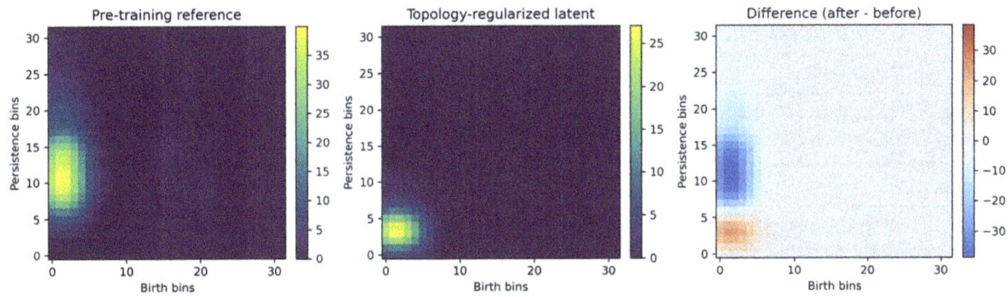

Figure 9 makes the regularization effect visually concrete by comparing persistence images before and after latent learning. The topology-regularized image preserves the dominant low-birth, moderate-persistence region while reducing diffuse activation elsewhere. The difference panel shows where the latent space became more concentrated and where topological mass was lost or gained. Educationally, the result suggests selective preservation: the model stabilizes the structural features that dominate the learner manifold while attenuating local irregularities and transient logging artifacts. Figure 9 becomes a compact visual argument for structural denoising rather than structural destruction.

Table 3. Condensed final comparison between the baseline and topology-regularized autoencoders

Model	Baseline AE	Topo-regularized AE
Recon. Loss	0.859446	0.845577
Trustw.	0.847511	0.832174
Landscape Dist.	1.513632	1.478967
Betti Dist.	133.361357	121.32146
H0 Mean Pers.	0.15177	0.204062
H1 Mean Pers.	0.038069	0.049263
H1 Bottleneck	0.45139	0.45139
TDA Threshold	1.174656	1.569413

Table 3 supports a trade-off interpretation. The topology-regularized autoencoder records lower reconstruction loss and lower landscape and Betti distances, while its final trustworthiness is slightly below the baseline. The result should be reported as improved structural coherence under comparable, not superior, trustworthiness.

Table 4. Condensed checkpoint history for losses, trustworthiness, and topology drift during training

Model	Epoch	Recon. Loss	Trustw.	H0 Mean Pers.	H1 Mean Pers.	H1 Bottleneck	H0 Bottleneck
Baseline AE							
	0	0.994108	0.657542	0.025008	0.005338	0.474411	3.370853
	12	0.971651	0.778449	0.040782	0.008305	0.474411	3.370853
	24	0.940269	0.833267	0.082488	0.022826	0.474411	3.370853
	36	0.859446	0.847511	0.15484	0.048086	0.474411	3.370853
Topo-regularized AE							
	0	0.989136	0.610469	0.024523	0.005885	0.474411	3.370853
	12	0.974387	0.796944	0.06352	0.013919	0.474411	3.370853
	24	0.936408	0.81671	0.115308	0.023168	0.474411	3.370853
	36	0.845577	0.832174	0.197677	0.04904	0.474411	3.370853

Table 4 extends the comparison across checkpoints rather than only at the final epoch. The baseline improves some metrics, but its topology-related summaries drift more freely because it lacks explicit structural control. The topology-regularized model shows a more disciplined trajectory, indicating that the manifold evolves in a way that is easier to audit and less likely to produce abrupt representational distortions during training.

Figures 6-9 and Tables 2-3 support a mid-level conclusion: the proposal is both topologically descriptive and topologically generative, because the regularizer actively shapes the learned educational space. Explainable tutoring benefits from that discipline; explanations become fragile when latent geometry is unstable or pedagogically incoherent. A structurally constrained manifold makes it more plausible that recommended items, prerequisite penalties, and tutoring actions refer to recognizable educational neighborhoods rather than arbitrary embedding artifacts. The subsection thus shows that structural preservation can be engineered inside the model, measured during optimization, and defended as an explicit design choice rather than a post hoc interpretation.

5.3. Anticipated Failure Modes and Governance Triggers

After the latent representation has been inspected, the next operational question is how structural signals can guide recommendation governance. Explainable educational AI does not stop at accurate scores or visually pleasing embeddings; it also provides actionable maps that help educators identify where to intervene, which concepts form bridges, and which parts of the concept space pose the greatest pedagogical risk.

The governance artifacts in the present analysis convert latent and graph structures into Mapper summaries, directed learning graphs, and ranked intervention alerts. Their function is to externalize topology into forms usable by instructors, curriculum designers, and institutional auditors without abandoning mathematical rigor.

Figure 10. Mapper-based topological knowledge map of recommendation zones and concept neighborhoods

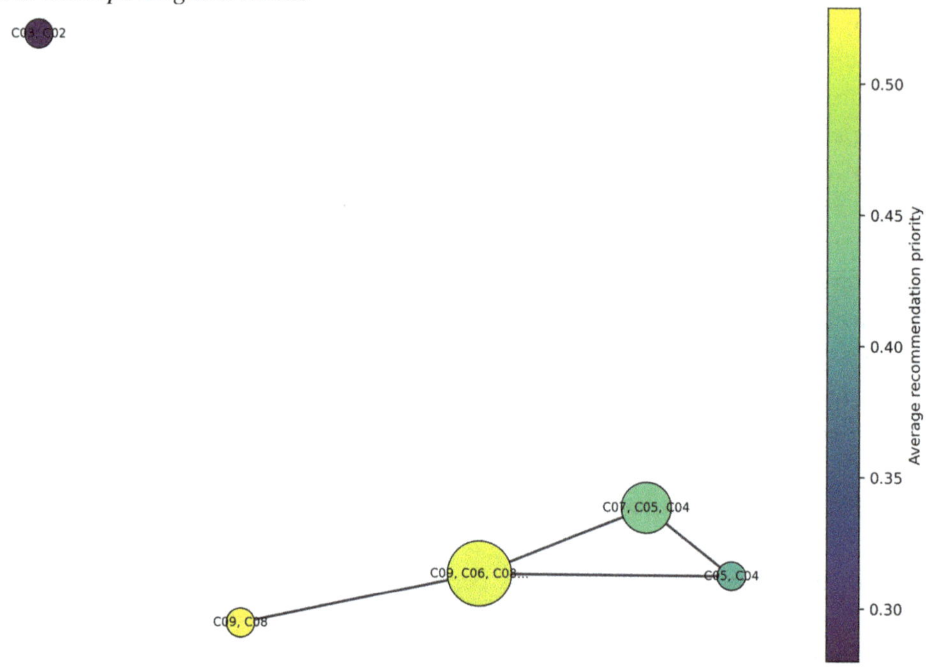

Figure 10 offers a condensed topological synopsis of the educational concept space. The Mapper graph has only a few nodes, and that compactness makes it effective as a governance interface. Each node summarizes a local region of the concept manifold, while edges indicate overlap or transition between educational neighborhoods. The nonuniform color pattern reflects variation in recommendation density or local structural significance. For educational oversight, the figure helps answer where in the concept space the system is concentrating adaptive attention. The map suggests that recommendation topology is not evenly distributed: some nodes act as peripheral zones, whereas others lie along the main adaptive corridor. This supports human review of whether the system is overemphasizing certain curricular regions or underserving others. Figure 10 thus operationalizes explainability at a mesoscopic level.

Figure 11. Directed learning graph highlighting strong concept transitions and high-risk intervention nodes

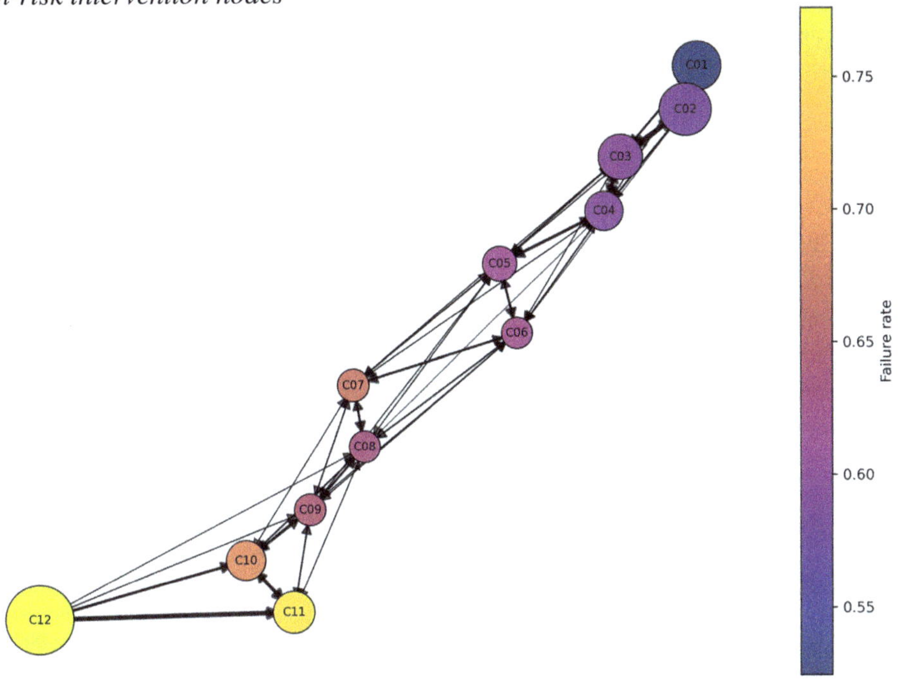

Figure 11 expresses the same logic as a directed learning network. It is more operational than the Mapper summary because it highlights transition pathways, node prominence, and risk-coded concepts. Highly connective or failure-prone nodes become natural governance triggers: they mark points where tutoring reinforcement, prerequisite review, or instructor attention is likely to yield the greatest benefit.

Table 5. Global graph and higher-order topology summary for recommendation diagnostics

N Concepts	12
N Transitions	70
Pruned Nodes	12
Pruned Edges	70
Mapper Nodes	5
Mapper Edges	4
Graph Density	0.545455

continued on following page

Table 5. Continued

Graph Cycle Rank Beta1	25
N Triangles / 2-simplices	46
TopoNetX Complex Dim	2
Top Bridge Concepts	C06; C09; C05; C08; C07
Top Priority Concepts	C11; C12; C09; C06; C10

Table 5 condenses concept-space structure into interpretable indicators. The graph's density, cycle rank, simplicial count, and persistent-feature summaries together show that the learning space is richly connected rather than linearly sequenced. For governance, these indicators matter because they identify when recommendation paths are overly constrained, when cycles may signal productive review, and when structural simplification may hide pedagogically salient alternatives.

Table 6. Topology-informed intervention alerts and recommended educational actions by concept

Concept Id	Usage	Success Rate	Failure Rate	Page Rank	Betweenness	Priority Score	Recommended Action
C11	735	0.244898	0.755102	0.126105	0	0.612498	Tutoring reinforcement
C12	2072	0.223938	0.776062	0.107563	0	0.592442	Tutoring reinforcement
C09	398	0.354271	0.645729	0.073031	0.363636	0.559744	Bridge concept monitoring
C06	381	0.375328	0.624672	0.061676	0.413636	0.529128	Bridge concept monitoring
C10	661	0.311649	0.688351	0.116033	0.072727	0.523338	Tutoring reinforcement
C07	419	0.329356	0.670644	0.065503	0.268182	0.500187	Standard monitoring
C08	400	0.365	0.635	0.071817	0.318182	0.498318	Standard monitoring
C05	486	0.382716	0.617284	0.062401	0.354545	0.468158	Bridge concept monitoring
C04	629	0.408585	0.591415	0.07293	0.236364	0.354557	Standard monitoring
C03	858	0.405594	0.594406	0.083456	0.190909	0.354123	Standard monitoring

Table 6 translates topology into concrete educational priorities. Concepts C11 and C12 receive the highest priority scores and are assigned tutoring reinforcement because they combine high usage with low success rates. Concepts C09 and C06 are marked for bridge-concept monitoring because their betweenness values indicate intermediary roles. The table separates weak concepts from structurally consequential concepts and combines usage, success and failure rates, PageRank, betweenness, and a synthesized priority score into human-readable actions.

The outputs in Section 5.3 complete the empirical progression. Learner states first appear as multiscale structures; topology-aware regularization then preserves those structures inside the latent model; and governance-ready maps finally externalize them for review. The progression connects theory, methodology, architecture, and output interpretation without treating topology as a decorative analytic layer.

6. DISCUSSION AND CONCLUSIONS

6.1. Theoretical, Pedagogical, and System-Level Implications

The results in Section 5 sharpen the broader implications. The first is theoretical: educational recommendation can be understood as structural navigation under pedagogical constraints. The learner-state cloud, persistence summaries, latent-manifold comparisons, and governance graphs show that adaptive systems operate in spaces with connected regions, transition corridors, cycles, bridges, and local closures. The research question extends beyond predicting the next successful item to examining the kind of educational space constructed around that prediction.

A second implication is pedagogical. The outputs suggest that coherent personalization is not equivalent to standardization, and differentiated tutoring is not equivalent to fragmentation. The observed topology contains subgroup-specific structures while preserving a shared manifold. This pattern fits STEAM education, where learners often need individualized support yet remain connected to common curricular trajectories and institutional outcomes. The stable, exploratory, and struggling groups identified in the results do not become isolated educational worlds; they occupy differentiated positions within a navigable common space. For pedagogy, this means that personalization can be designed as guided divergence and reconvergence. Learners may follow different local routes, but those routes can still be audited for reachability, continuity, and opportunities to rejoin broader curricular pathways.

A third implication concerns explainability. Much of the literature in educational AI treats explainability as a local add-on in the form of feature-importance scores, post hoc rationales, or simplified proxy models. The analysis suggests a broader view. Explanations gain depth when supported by structural evidence. A recommendation is explained more meaningfully when the system can show not only which variables contributed to a score, but also how the learner is positioned within a concept manifold, which prerequisite bridges are implicated, whether the relevant concept lies in a high-risk zone, and how stable the recommendation remains under small topological perturbations. Topology does not replace conventional explainability tools; it enlarges them by providing a mesoscopic and global context in which local explanations become pedagogically interpretable rather than merely computationally transparent.

A fourth implication is institutional. The governance artifacts show that topology-aware educational AI can support forms of oversight that are difficult to obtain from purely predictive systems. The Mapper graph and intervention alerts do not merely summarize model outputs; they bridge technical diagnostics and administrative action. Curriculum committees can inspect bridge concepts that sustain network navigability. Tutors can prioritize reinforcement where failure rates and structural prominence coincide. Quality-assurance teams can monitor whether recommendation density is becoming too concentrated in certain curricular zones. Ethical review bodies can examine whether the structural routes available to learners remain balanced across subgroups. These are direct consequences of converting latent topology into human-readable operational objects.

A fifth implication concerns methodological reproducibility. The analysis has argued that trustworthy educational AI requires auditable workflows rather than one-off demonstrations, and the implementation evidence reinforces that claim. Saved outputs, checkpoint histories, and explicit topological summaries make it possible to reconstruct not only the final recommendation logic but also the process by which the model acquired its educational geometry. This is especially relevant in institutional settings where adaptive systems may affect progression, remediation, or learner opportunity. Reproducibility is not only a scientific virtue here; it is a condition of legitimacy. A model that cannot be re-run, inspected, and challenged is ill suited to mediate consequential educational pathways.

At the systems level, topological regularization functions as an architectural discipline. It encourages educational AI to preserve meaningful neighborhoods, make bridges visible, control drift, and surface high-impact vulnerabilities before they become opaque failure cases. The contribution is broader than a single recommender: it is a design philosophy for STEAM tutoring ecosystems in which personalization, explanation, and ethical auditability are linked through structural preservation.

6.2. Conclusions, Limitations, and Responsible Use

Taken together, the evidence supports a measured conclusion: topology-aware analytics can be integrated into educational recommendation and personalized tutoring in a conceptually coherent and computationally feasible way. The results do not establish a finished product for universal deployment, but they show how structural learner modeling, explainable ranking, governance diagnostics, and human review can be connected within one educational architecture.

The limitations are also explicit. The empirical demonstration relies on synthetic data with structurally realistic assumptions; this is appropriate for methodological exposition but restricts external validity. Institutional deployment would require calibration with authentic logs, local curricula, and diverse learner populations. Topology-sensitive results also depend on windowing, graph construction, filtration parameters, and threshold selection, all of which require justification and stress testing.

Over-regularization remains a practical risk. If structure is preserved too aggressively, the system may steer learners toward safe but redundant content and reduce beneficial exploration. If regularization is too weak, reconstruction quality may remain high while subtle structural drift produces incoherent recommendation paths. The evidence here suggests that a reasonable balance is attainable, but the balance is monitored continuously rather than assumed.

Responsible use follows from these limits. The system is best treated as decision support: instructor dashboards may show bridge concepts and risk zones, whereas student interfaces should translate the same evidence into concise guidance. Subgroup auditing and run-level documentation remain mandatory before recommendations affect consequential learning opportunities.

With these qualifications in view, the argument closes on a bounded claim. Educational adaptation is designed to preserve and expose the structural logic of learning. The integrated results show a credible route toward this goal through persistent-homology summaries, topology-regularized latent learning, and graph-based intervention diagnostics. The route still requires empirical trials, policy design, and local expertise, but it offers a robust foundation for those next stages.

The same caution applies to interpretability. A topology-aware explanation is treated as a structured hypothesis about why a recommendation is reasonable, not as proof that the recommendation is pedagogically optimal. Educator review remains warranted wherever the action affects remediation, progression, or assessment opportunity. Documentation precedes high-stakes instructional use, especially when recommendations influence remediation or progression.

Transfer across institutions remains limited. Similar topological patterns may reflect different pedagogical realities under different assessments, resources, languages, pacing, or grading practices; therefore, instructor review, cohort-level calibration, and sensitivity analysis must precede progression-related use.

Methodologically, the framework combines foundational constructs with recent journal evidence. Established sources define safe reinforcement learning, knowledge tracing, topological summaries, and graph representation learning; more recent studies connect those constructs with educational AI, cognitive-load-aware personalization, human-centered explanation, and ethical governance. This evidence hierarchy avoids novelty for its own sake. It also anchors the framework in peer-reviewed journals, DOI-based records, and primary empirical or methodological studies where such sources exist, while retaining seminal technical work only when it supplies concepts not yet replaced by journal equivalents.

For learner-facing use, the system avoids presenting topological language as if it were a personal diagnosis. A student can be told that a suggested activity connects recent work with a nearby prerequisite or review path; the same message need not mention persistence diagrams, Betti curves, or graph prominence. Technical concepts are more appropriate for instructor dashboards, audit reports, and curriculum review meetings. This audience-specific communication reduces cognitive burden while keeping the underlying decision trace available for contestation and improvement. It also helps institutions separate technical confidence from pedagogical certainty during review.

7. FUTURE WORK

7.1. Toward Real-Time, Human-Centered, and Auditable STEAM Tutoring Ecosystems

Future work can extend the framework in five directions. First, online topology monitoring can support near-real-time drift alerts during active courses. Second, multilingual and multimodal extensions can incorporate text explanations, speech-based tutoring traces, and laboratory sensor data. Third, fairness analysis can move toward intersectional and provider-aware auditing in heterogeneous STEAM contexts. Fourth, the decision layer can be enriched with safe reinforcement-learning methods and better mechanisms for personalized explanation selection. Fifth, the governance layer can connect to institutional policy so that adaptive AI becomes part of a broader ecosystem of transparent assessment, curricular stewardship, and responsible educational innovation.

The code generated to obtain all the results can be found at the following URL:

https://github.com/JAIME6609/EDUCATION/blob/main/CODE-BOOK-15-ART-02.py

All code is based on synthetic data.

REFERENCES

Ali, D., Asaad, A., Jimenez, M.-J., Nanda, V., Paluzo-Hidalgo, E., & Soriano-Trigueros, M. (2023). A survey of vectorization methods in topological data analysis. *IEEE Transactions on Pattern Analysis and Machine Intelligence*, *45*(12), 14069–14080. DOI: 10.1109/TPAMI.2023.3308391 PMID: 37647183

Barros, C. D. T., Mendonça, M. R. F., Vieira, A. B., & Ziviani, A. (2021). A survey on embedding dynamic graphs. *ACM Computing Surveys*, *55*(1), 10. Advance online publication. DOI: 10.1145/3483595

Brunke, L., Greeff, M., Hall, A. W., Yuan, Z., Zhou, S., Panerati, J., & Schoellig, A. P. (2022). Safe learning in robotics: From learning-based control to safe reinforcement learning. *Annual Review of Control, Robotics, and Autonomous Systems*, *5*(1), 411–444. DOI: 10.1146/annurev-control-042920-020211

Chazal, F., & Michel, B. (2021). An introduction to topological data analysis: Fundamental and practical aspects for data scientists. *Frontiers in Artificial Intelligence*, *4*, 667963. Advance online publication. DOI: 10.3389/frai.2021.667963 PMID: 34661095

Chen, M., Wang, D., Feng, S., & Zhang, Y. (2023). Topological regularization for representation learning via persistent homology. *Mathematics*, *11*(4), 1008. Advance online publication. DOI: 10.3390/math11041008

Conati, C., Barral, O., Putnam, V., & Rieger, L. (2021). Toward personalized XAI: A case study in intelligent tutoring systems. *Artificial Intelligence*, *298*, 103503. Advance online publication. DOI: 10.1016/j.artint.2021.103503

da Silva, F. L., Slodkowski, B. K., da Silva, K. K. A., & Cazella, S. C. (2023). A systematic literature review on educational recommender systems for teaching and learning: Research trends, limitations and opportunities. *Education and Information Technologies*, *28*(3), 3289–3328. DOI: 10.1007/s10639-022-11341-9 PMID: 36124004

García, J., & Fernández, F. (2015). A comprehensive survey on safe reinforcement learning. *Journal of Machine Learning Research*, *16*, 1437–1480. https://jmlr.org/papers/v16/garcia15a.html

Gómez, E., Zhang, C. S., Boratto, L., Salamó, M., & Ramos, G. (2022). Enabling cross-continent provider fairness in educational recommender systems. *Future Generation Computer Systems*, *127*, 435–447. DOI: 10.1016/j.future.2021.08.025

Guan, Q., Cheng, X., Xiao, F., Li, Z., He, C., Fang, L., Chen, G., Gong, Z., & Luo, W. (2025). Explainable exercise recommendation with knowledge graph. *Neural Networks, 183*, 106954. Advance online publication. DOI: 10.1016/j.neunet.2024.106954 PMID: 39667214

Holmes, W., Porayska-Pomsta, K., Holstein, K., Sutherland, E., Baker, T., Buckingham Shum, S., Santos, O. C., Rodrigo, M. T., Cukurova, M., Bittencourt, I. I., & Koedinger, K. R. (2022). Ethics of AI in education: Towards a community-wide framework. *International Journal of Artificial Intelligence in Education, 32*(3), 504–526. DOI: 10.1007/s40593-021-00239-1

Huang, A. Y. Q., Lu, O. H. T., & Yang, S. J. H. (2023). Effects of artificial intelligence-enabled personalized recommendations on learners' learning engagement, motivation, and outcomes in a flipped classroom. *Computers & Education, 194*, 104684. Advance online publication. DOI: 10.1016/j.compedu.2022.104684

Hwang, G.-J., Xie, H., Wah, B. W., & Gašević, D. (2020). Vision, challenges, roles and research issues of artificial intelligence in education. *Computers and Education: Artificial Intelligence, 1*, 100001. Advance online publication. DOI: 10.1016/j.caeai.2020.100001

Ju, W., Fang, Z., Gu, Y., Liu, Z., Long, Q., Qiao, Z., Qin, Y., Shen, J., Sun, F., Xiao, Z., Yang, J., Yuan, J., Zhao, Y., Wang, Y., Luo, X., & Zhang, M. (2024). A comprehensive survey on deep graph representation learning. *Neural Networks, 173*, 106207. Advance online publication. DOI: 10.1016/j.neunet.2024.106207 PMID: 38442651

Khosravi, H., Buckingham Shum, S., Chen, G., Conati, C., Tsai, Y.-S., Kay, J., Knight, S., Martinez-Maldonado, R., Sadiq, S., & Gašević, D. (2022). Explainable artificial intelligence in education. *Computers and Education: Artificial Intelligence, 3*, 100074. Advance online publication. DOI: 10.1016/j.caeai.2022.100074

Marras, M., Boratto, L., Ramos, G., & Fenu, G. (2022). Equality of learning opportunity via individual fairness in personalized recommendations. *International Journal of Artificial Intelligence in Education, 32*(3), 636–684. DOI: 10.1007/s40593-021-00271-1

Mishra, A., & Motta, F. C. (2023). Stability and machine learning applications of persistent homology using the Delaunay-Rips complex. *Frontiers in Applied Mathematics and Statistics, 9*, 1179301. Advance online publication. DOI: 10.3389/fams.2023.1179301

Nakagawa, H., Iwasawa, Y., & Matsuo, Y. (2021). Graph-based knowledge tracing: Modeling student proficiency using graph neural networks. *Web Intelligence, 19*(1–2), 87–102. DOI: 10.3233/WEB-210458

Tong, C., & Ren, C. (2025). Deep knowledge tracing and cognitive load estimation for personalized learning path generation using neural network architecture. *Scientific Reports*, *15*(1), 24925. Advance online publication. DOI: 10.1038/s41598-025-10497-x PMID: 40640459

Van Calster, B., McLernon, D. J., van Smeden, M., Wynants, L., & Steyerberg, E. W. (2019). Calibration: The Achilles heel of predictive analytics. *BMC Medicine*, *17*(1), 230. Advance online publication. DOI: 10.1186/s12916-019-1466-7 PMID: 31842878

Chapter 8

An Automated, Fairness-Aware Student Feedback System Using SHAP and Generative AI

L. Namitha
VIT Bhopal University, India

P. R. Buvaneswari
VIT Bhopal University, India

D. Lakshmi
http://orcid.org/0000-0003-4018-1208
VIT Bhopal University, India

ABSTRACT

Smart Education relies on non-transparent predictive models for the learners. In STEAM, predicting failure alone is not sufficient for the learners. Educators need transparent insight for educational interventions without demographic bias. This chapter proposes a human-centred framework transitioning AI from purely predictive technologies to prescriptive-assessment engines spanning three layers: Layer 1 uses a stacked ensemble (XGBoost, LightGBM, CatBoost) to predict academic risk via dynamic behavioural metrics (e.g., study hours, attendance) instead of just historical grades. Layer 2 uses explainable AI (SHAP) to deconstruct these predictions, creating a transparent diagnostic profile detailing exactly why a student is at risk. Layer 3 employs an LLM via a RAG pipeline to create personalised, empathetic, and actionable feedback based on the SHAP diagnostic results. The architecture

DOI: 10.4018/979-8-3373-9675-0.ch008

embeds algorithmic fairness and Human-in-the-Loop governance to eliminate socioeconomic proxy discrimination, providing a blueprint for an ethical, scalable learning ecosystem.

1. INTRODUCTION

1.1 The Retention Crisis in STEAM Education

The global demand for STEAM graduates, proficient in Science, Technology, Engineering, Arts, and Mathematics, has reached unusual levels, and as contemporary economies transition from Industry 4.0 to Industry 5.0, the requirement for algorithmic thinking, engineering design, and scientific literacy significantly exceeds the pool of qualified individuals.

Academic institutions have been successful in achieving record-breaking numbers of STEAM program enrollments to meet the demands of the modern economy. However, a paradoxical trend has emerged from this growth; while enrollments continue to rise, graduation rates remain low. Studies done on institutional statistics consistently show an attrition problem among undergraduate STEAM programs. One notable study is **Chen's longitudinal research** on behalf of the National Centre for Education Statistics. The study shows that nearly half of the initial STEAM - based majors have dropped out of college or changed majors to non-STEAM courses (Chen, 2013).

Learning STEAM (Science, Technology, Engineering, Art and Music) subjects has been at a growth plateau on the scale of student success. One key to understanding the high rate of attrition is recognising that every STEAM discipline has a unique structural system based on how knowledge is organised for the purpose of teaching students. The disciplines in the humanities and social sciences allow for curriculum modules to sometimes stand alone within their prescribed thematic groupings of students' knowledge. In contrast, the prescribed curriculum of STEAM is organised cumulatively and hierarchically, so the achievement within any of the advanced concepts relies directly on having achieved mastery of the lower-level concepts. The student who fails to master a core concept in the third week of the semester does not merely lose points for that week, but rather cumulatively loses the cognitive facilitation necessary to successfully understand all subsequent materials presented during the fourth, fifth, and sixth weeks of a semester.

The cascading mechanism for student attrition within STEAM disciplines can best be understood through the application of Cognitive Load Theory. Cognitive Load Theory asserts that the human brain has a limited capacity for processing new information in working memory. When students do not have a foundational schema in their working memories (the framework used to organise the knowledge in their long-term memory) before attempting to understand a new STEAM concept, the "intrinsic cognitive load" of the new concept fills the working memory of the student. Therefore, the student must first work to develop the foundational mathematical knowledge that they lack in working memory prior to being able to begin processing the new concept. Hence, this cognitive overload leads to rapid burnout rates, disengagement from the learning environment, and ultimately, student attrition from the STEAM discipline in which the student is currently enrolled (Sweller, 2011).

Another big part of the issue is a huge restriction placed on learning because of the large enrollment of "key" classes in many contemporary colleges and universities (e.g. introductory STEAM classes such assu Engineering Mathematics, General Chemistry, or Introductory Computer Science), which are also often delivered to hundreds or even thousands of students in one large lecture hall. The resulting student-to-faculty ratio creates a significant barrier to appropriate teaching and learning due to the physical distance between students and faculty.

Freeman pointed out that traditional lecture-based classes are one of the largest contributors to higher failing rates compared with highly engaging active/interactive teaching/learning classes. A single professor can only physically see so many students in a very large class (e.g. one that has 200 students) and may not notice very small visible indicators (e.g. poor study habits, etc.), or changes indicative of cognitive overload (decreased study time, disrupted sleep patterns, lack of engagement with supplemental resources), before the faculty member has an opportunity to do something to help that student.

As such, the professor will typically have to rely on the traditional summative assessment (e.g. midterm or final exam) as an indicator of student understanding. Although that student may be overwhelmed enough that by the time he/she receives a failing grade or academic deficiency (regardless of when he/she receives it, whether the end of the term or midterm) he/she will not have sufficient time left to recover from it due to the hierarchical nature of the STEAM curriculum (Freeman et al., 2014).

Thus, the STEAM attrition dilemma is not only due to the lack of resilience of students but also of the educational system itself. When students are faced with increasingly high demands both cognitively and through large class sizes, they face what is referred to as "silent failures" throughout their entire educational experience, so these at-risk students often fall behind with little chance for an intervention before it becomes necessary. To assist in solving this issue, it is necessary to create a system that can move beyond passive observation and delay in completing the assessment process; therefore, it is essential to have a methodology that will monitor, assess and scale personalized interventions in real-time.

1.2 The Paradigm Shift: From Summative to Formative Assessment

While summative assessments are a main part of higher education programs' traditional instructional design, reliance on summative assessment models hinders the ability to assist the student in retaining their knowledge or provide an intervention sooner than when the final grade is assigned for the course. High-stakes mid-term tests, end-of-semester finals, or final practicum/lab reports will only give a measure of a student's total knowledge after the fact. As a result, once a student receives a failing grade, they have reached their limit on knowledge for that period of study. Therefore, the academic gap that has developed between the failing student and the standard of knowledge of a successful student won't be able to be bridged if the institution of higher education relies solely on final grades to identify and assist potential at-risk learners(Romero & Ventura, 2020), (Siemens & Baker, 2012).

In order to reduce attrition rates successfully, the pedagogy used by educational institutions should shift towards adopting a proactive model of formative assessment. Formative assessment continuously assesses all aspects of student understanding, including student comprehension and behavioural engagement with their environments, within the framework of a formative assessment model, enabling the provision of immediate corrective feedback to students prior to them being unsuccessful at the end of the term.

The development of digital systems in education has catalysed this shift in the way formative assessments are utilised, particularly due to the broad usage of Learning Management Systems (LMSs). Learning Analytics (LA) and Early Warning Systems (EWS) are two examples of data-driven frameworks to provide formative assessment through tracking digital footprints (e.g., how long it has taken students to turn in an assignment, how frequently a student has posted to a forum, how often a student has accessed the library), identifying students who require assistance within the first few weeks of a semester (Skittou et al., 2024), (Fischer et al., 2020).

Formative assessment theory has significant advantages when compared to traditional methods of evaluation; however, formative assessment implementation is severely restricted in the collective practice of STEAM education by human scalability. The level of personalisation, continuous nature, and formative nature of formative assessments would require an extraordinary amount of time and mental capacity from educators in providing students with the feedback they need to improve their academic performance. This task is impossible, given the impracticality of one educator manually reviewing hundreds of students' daily micro-behaviours, identifying their unique non-academic barriers (i.e., sleep deprivation, poor study habits and so on), and developing individualised remediation plans in accordance with those findings. Early Warning Systems can identify mathematical "at-risk" students;

however, they are often unable or unwilling to provide any insights into the root of the risk, thereby placing the burden of analysis back on an already stressed educator.

To actually achieve the true potential of formative assessment at an institutional level, the educational system needs an automated, intelligent infrastructure that will provide educators with the ability to obtain a precise behavioral root cause for the student's struggle as well as the ability to develop and implement individualised, prescription-based interventions autonomously (Zawacki-Richter et al., 2019) (Holmes et al., 2019).

1.3 Objectives and Contributions

This chapter proposes EduTriage as an example of an end-to-end, neuro-symbolic intervention architecture (an architecture combining data-driven machine learning with logic-based, interpretable rules) to bridge the gap between predictive analytics and pedagogical action, particularly for large-scale STEAM instructional environments. EduTriage does not simply classify students as "pass" or "fail"; instead, it functions as an operationalization of formative assessment through predicting risk for multiple types of academic deficits through multiple types of risk; through audit questioning to determine if the prediction is fair for all students (regardless of demographic); through mathematically understanding why/what behaviors caused the student to be at academic risk; and finally, through the ability to autonomously create individualized prescriptive feedback for each student.

In particular, this chapter provides contributions to the area of Educational Data Mining (EDM) and the area of Artificial Intelligence in Education (AIED) in the following ways:

(a) We develop a Behavioural Stacked Ensemble Engine (combination of heterogeneous meta-learning models - XGBoost, LightGBM, CatBoost) and demonstrate the high prediction accuracy of purely behavioural/environmental predictors (e.g., study habits, sleep latency, facility usage) versus historical summative grades.

(b) We demonstrate the application of Localised Explainable AI (XAI), showing how the use of SHapley Additive exPlanations (SHAP) allows us to examine how each feature contributes locally to produce an individual diagnostic profile of each student identified as being at-risk, determining what specific pedagogical barriers exist for that student.

(c) Incorporating Fairness Constraints into Models Algorithmically: A Fairness point is created to establish an ethical audit point in the predictive process to help obtain recognised versions of fairness within the predictive model. This also addresses the idea of demographic parity to ensure that no student is unfairly either penalised or rewarded due to non-controllable characteristics such as access to the Internet, school facility rating, etc.

(d) Using Generative Agent(s) in an Automated Social Networking Environment: This chapter describes an innovative new method for producing Remediation Plans based on SHAP values returned by predictive models using a retrieval-based approach (RAG). In doing so, we train LLMs through a new Construction approach to produce large numbers of therapeutic and personalised interventions for each student through the Empathetic Advisor persona constrained by specific learning goals (e.g., passing a state-mandated assessment).

Through analysing the EduTriage Framework, this chapter demonstrates a scalable guide to developing and implementing intelligent Tutoring Systems into local education agencies (LEAs) that provide holistic support to students by moving from just being "Reactive" in observing abuse or neglect to "Proactive" in providing early intervention.

2. THEORETICAL FOUNDATIONS & RELATED WORK

2.1 Educational Data Mining (EDM): Current Institutional Practices and Inherent Flaws

EDM (Educational Data Mining) has transformed over the last twenty years from a specialised computational science into a major component of institutional management. Today, EDM is primarily used in higher education through institutional risk dashboards, which aggregate historical academic performance, demographic information, and clickstream data (e.g., LMS login frequency) and these data points are fed into predictive algorithms (such as logistic regression or simple decision trees) mainly to classify students into high or low risk categories, allowing institutions to allocate limited advising resources (Verbert et al., 2013) (Baker et al., 2016).

However, current institutional EDM relies heavily on lagging indicators most likely prior GPA or standardised test scores by which it can be measured past performance rather than dynamic cognitive engagement and also in an attempt to maximise overall model accuracy (AUC-ROC), practitioners frequently include non-modifiable demographic variables such as socio-economic status, race, or geographic location. This creates a "demographic trap"; algorithmic models risk encoding historical stereotypes, ultimately penalising marginalised students for systemic inequalities rather than evaluating them based on their current academic merit (Prinsloo & Slade, 2014)(Gašević et al., 2015).

Most critically, modern EDM suffers from a severe "actionability gap." Providing a monolithic metric such as an 82% probability of failure offers no pedagogical value if the educator cannot determine the specific behavioural patterns driving that prediction. Without isolating highly specific, actionable behaviours (e.g., a sudden decrease in sleep quality or chronic absenteeism), the predictive model simply shifts the burden of analysis back onto an overworked instructor, which leaves them with data that is computationally impressive but pedagogically ineffective (Albugami et al., 2024).

2.2 The "Black Box" Dilemma: The Pedagogical Hazard of Algorithmic Opacity

Research is progressively abandoning conventional, interpretable statistical methodologies to prefer much more complex machine-learning techniques as the field of Educational Data Mining (EDM) continues to develop. Institutions are beginning to apply Deep Neural Networks (DNNs), Recurrent Neural Networks (RNNs), and high-dimensional support vector machines (SVMs) in their experiments to improve their ability to predict student outcomes. The ability of the more sophisticated algorithmic approaches to capture highly non-linear and time-dependent relationships in vast educational datasets often leads to superior classification performance compared to classical approaches.

Still, the use of these complex models in education has created a fundamental epistemological dispute known as the accuracy-interpretability tradeoff. As patterns are recognised, the predictive ability of an algorithm has increased as it layers hyper-dimensional space. Therefore, an algorithm's operation cannot be known to those observing it, thus making the algorithm's workings a "black box" (Rudin, 2019), (Khosravi et al., 2022).

The use of opaque neural networks, as an acceptable trade-off to increased accuracy, can be appropriate in low-stakes environments such as algorithmic product recommendations or digital advertising. However, in high-stakes socio-technical systems such as higher education, the potential harm from the use of algorithmic opaque models creates severe ethical and pedagogical problems. The use of Black Box models by an institution to assign predictive grades, assess an individual's academic risk, or distribute financial aid violates the pedagogical requirement of justification.

If a deep learning system indicates that a student has a 90% probability of failing the semester but the hidden layers of the network prevent us from understanding why the prediction was made, then the resulting data point will have no diagnostic value. There is no ethical way for an educator to tell a struggling student, "The algorithm has predicted you will fail, but I cannot tell you how the inference was made (statistical or behavioural)." This lack of transparency undermines student/educator trust in the institution and inhibits the educator's ability to effectively intervene with the student as needed (Conati et al., 2018), (Akgun & Greenhow, 2022).

Moreover, deploying unexplainable AI for grading and assessing risk creates algorithm-induced determinism and learned helplessness. A key goal of formative assessment is to create manageable and meaningful actionable feedback for all students to change their learning trajectory. Once an AI provides an unexplainable prediction or recommendation, this results in a loss of pedagogy agency for the learners. Without any guidance for avoiding that failure, students will strictly be categorised as an academic failure, and the use of deep learning, or Black Box (BB) deep learning, as assessment tools for students is clearly counterproductive to education's core mission—the transformation of the institution from an active facilitator of learning to a passive, automated oracle of academic failure. To regain the value of predictive analytics in education, the algorithmic focus must change from producing unexplainable answers to maximise raw accuracy in an opaque environment to producing fully explainable, actionable explanations through Explainable AI (Swiecki et al., 2022), (Perrotta & Selwyn, 2020).

2.3 Principles of Explainable AI (XAI) in Education: SHAP and Game Theory

To help solve the problem of understanding the algorithmic "black box" in Artificial Intelligence (AI), Explainable Artificial Intelligence (XAI) methods have been developed, which provide mathematical models that can make complex AI systems more understandable by humans (i.e., stakeholders). In addition to being able to provide stakeholders with explanations of how the machine learning algorithm arrived at its decision, explanations using the XAI method can help educators link the accuracy of the predictive model to the actions that need to be taken based on its predictions.

Of all of the XAI methods available to explain machine learning models, SHapley Additive exPlanations (SHAP) have emerged as the "gold standard" of model explanation. The primary reason for this is that the mathematical basis of SHAP is founded on cooperative game theory, which is very sound mathematically (Lundberg & Lee, 2017).

The mathematical basis for SHAP is derived from the Shapley Value, which was presented by **Lloyd Shapley,** a Nobel Prize-winning game theorist, in his 1953 paper "A Value for N-Person Games". The concept of fair distribution of payoffs among members of economic coalitions was the subject of Shapley's original work. In predictive modelling, the "game" being played is predicting a student's exam score, and the "payout" from the game is the predicted value of the student's exam score (e.g., 82% chance of failing). The "players" in the coalition of players are the individual features available to the machine learning algorithm to use as input (e.g., number of hours the student studies, quality of the student's sleep, and the student's level of attendance).

In order to calculate the contribution of an individual feature towards the final predicted output of the model, SHAP looks at all possible orders of the coalition members (the individual features) and compares the predicted value of the output based on every possible order. Thus, the "value (credit or penalty)" attributed to any particular feature is based on a mathematically fair and theoretically sound method of calculating that value (Molnar, 2020) and (Shapley, 1953).

SHAP also has two tiers of interpretability from a pedagogical perspective. The first is global interpretability, which aggregates the Shapley values from all students in the database into one result set. This allows administrators to make macro-level assessments about trends (e.g., that a low rating for classroom facilities will result in lower overall performance from the entire class). The second tier is local interpretability.

This enables educators to investigate an individual student's prediction by breaking down how many points each prediction contributed to or detracted from the student's original score. This breakdown provides a generic risk alert into a specific diagnostic profile for the educator to use to isolate the behaviours of the student that need remediation.

2.4 Generative AI as Pedagogical Agents: From Chatbots to Tutors

While XAI systems such as SHAP are excellent for diagnosing the mathematical root cause of student failures, raw numerical vectors alone do not have pedagogical value. A student cannot simply be given a matrix of Shapley values and be expected to make improvements. Therefore, to complete the intervention pipeline process, the diagnostic data actually hold pedagogical value through actionable and empathetic human language. For many years, educational technology has attempted to resolve these types of issues with rigid rule-based Intelligent Tutoring Systems (ITS) or very basic conversational chatbots. However, due to the highly brittle, rules-based (and related) "if-then" decision trees utilised by the older systems, they failed at handling the rich nuance found in a student's emotional state, his/her various types of learning challenges and the highly complex contextual information needed for effective advising.

The introduction of Large Language Models (LLMs) such as Gemini represents a complete divergence in the way that humans will interact with computers to provide pedagogical support. Rather than simply retrieving pre-programmed answers, LLMs are actually probabilistic reasoning engines capable of synthesising complex multimodal context into coherent and adaptive dialogue. More importantly, when the output of the LLMs is limited due to system constraints (i.e., through a process referred to as prompt engineering), they change from generic "information retrieval" chatbots to highly specialised "pedagogical agents" (AI-driven virtual tutors designed to autonomously interact with and support learners) (Kasneci et al., 2023).

Modern language models (LLMs), such as retrieval-augmented generation (RAG), can process both a student's specific SHAP profile data and a set of strategies for providing academic assistance. The LLM then takes both data sources as input and provides responses that correlate to the needs of the student based on the respective SHAP values. Since the LLM has a strong understanding of natural language, it can create the Empathetic Advisor persona during interactions with students, enabling automated personalisation and emotional intelligence of the LLM that would not be possible without the use of a human-to-human mentoring function (Baidoo-Anu & Owusu Ansah, 2023).

3. SYSTEM ARCHITECTURE AND METHODOLOGY

To address the limits of existing "Black Box" predictive models used for the operationalisation of formative assessment, we present a personalised neuro-symbolic modular end-to-end framework called EduTriage. The architecture of EduTriage was designed specifically to integrate heterogeneous student behaviour data, produce accurate risk predictions, validate algorithmically biased predictions, derive community mathematical insights, and combine those insights with community-based approaches to creating actionable pedagogical solutions.

3.1 Overview of the EduTriage Framework

The EduTriage system consists of a continuous four-stage computational pipeline. Figure 1 illustrates the synergy between quantitative capabilities offered by advanced machine learning (ML) methods and qualitative reasoning represented via large language models (LLMs), supporting the ethical and transparent use of predictive accuracy in pedagogical settings.

Figure 1. The EduTriage System Architecture

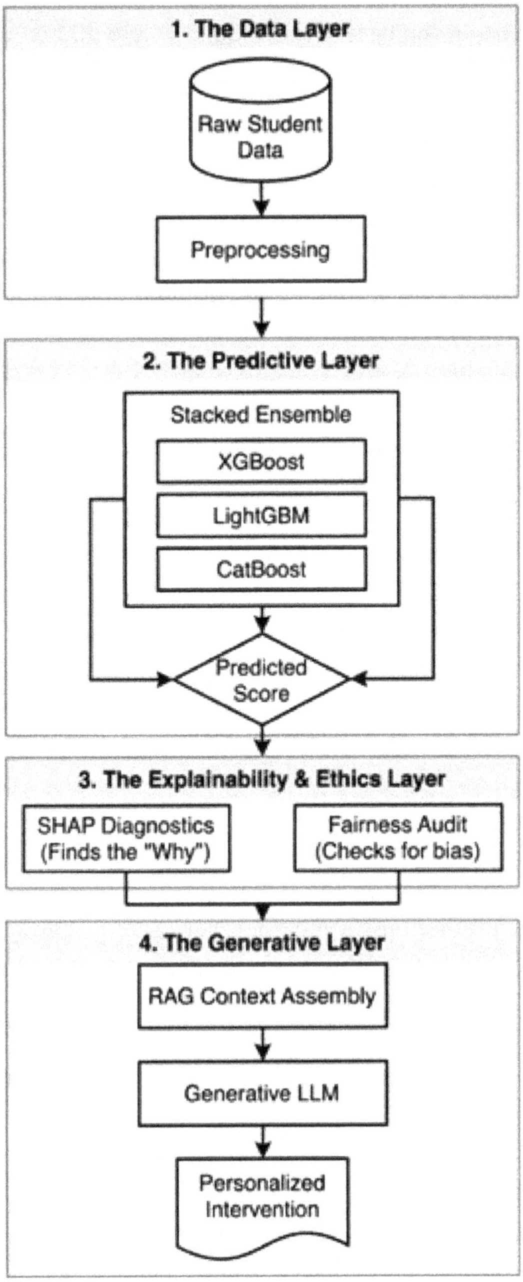

Phase 1: The Data Layer (The Processing and Ingestion of Data)

The Pipeline begins at the base layer of data, where all raw metrics for student behaviours are stored as one central repository. Traditional models use lagging indicators to measure progress (such as GPA); however, this database collects metrics that are dynamic and real-time (e.g., self-reported study hours, digital LMS activity, sleep quality, and building usage). Due to the noisiness and variety within the datasets created by education, the raw data then flows through a comprehensive Preprocessing Module in which missing values are addressed, continuous variables are normalised and categorical variables (such as type of study method, access to the internet, etc.) have their data transformed via a one-hot encoding approach to create a standardized and machine-readable feature matrix for later stages of processing.

Phase 2: The Predictive Layer (Use of Non-Homogeneous Stackable Models)

Once the feature matrices are systematised, they are delivered to the Predictive Layer. Within the field of education, the data typically contains complex, non-linear interactions among variables (for example, the compounding effect of a student not sleeping well coupled with not attending school regularly). In order to ensure that the variance is accounted for without over-fitting to the model, EduTriage does not rely solely on one model to create the predictions; to achieve this result, a Stacked Ensemble Engine is used to generate all predictions.

The module utilises three separate state-of-the-art (GBDT), or gradient boosting decision trees (XGBoost, LightGBM, CatBoost) to predict data at the same time. The baseline models are very optimised for tabular datasets, and after all three models have generated their predictions, a meta-learner (a very common choice is ridge regression) combines the predictions into one single, very accurate predicted score that serves as a quantitative trigger for the rest of the pipeline.

Phase 3: The Explainability and Ethics Layer (Bifurcated Auditing)

A raw predicted score is pedagogically unactionable and presents a high degree of risk for being an algorithmic determinism. Therefore, before formulating any intervention, the pipeline will bifurcate at this stage so that the Predicted Score is passed through two separate validation protocols in parallel.

- SHAP Diagnostics:

The first branch uses SHapley Additive exPlanations (SHAP) to break down the ensemble learning algorithm's decision. This diagnostic module produces the exact marginal contribution of each behavioural feature for the individual student, enabling it to isolate the "Why" behind the predicted score.

- The Fairness Audit:

At the same time, the second branch serves as an automated ethical checkpoint. It compares the student's prediction and the student's protected characteristics (e.g., any socioeconomic indicators) against demographic parity. If the model shows evidence of disparate impact (e.g., unfairly harming a student because they do not have a high-speed Internet connection), then that portion of the automated process is stopped, and the student's profile is flagged for manual review by an instructor.

Phase 4: The Generative Layer (RAG and LLM Synthesis)

The Generative Layer is where predictions successfully undergo the ethical audit are aligned with their respective SHAP diagnostic vectors (representing the output of how the model arrived at each risk score) into the final layer of Generative content: a Retrieval Augmented Generation (RAG) Context Assembly module that will act as an intelligent prompt engineer to formally (and structurally) concatenate the student's predicted risk score, the personalized behavioral deficits derived from SHAP and a curated institutional pedagogical strategies database into a highly structured prompt.

The assembled context will then be ingested within a Generative LLM (such as Gemini 2.5 Flash), which has the constraint of an explicit "Empathetic Advisor" system persona and will translate the highly complicated mathematical diagnostics into a highly personalised human-readable intervention document. This final output will provide the student with actionable & specific remediation strategies that are clearly aligned with their unique behavioural footprint, thus closing the loop of moving from raw data to proactive pedagogical support.To provide a clear, consolidated overview of this end-to-end architecture, **Table 1** summarizes the primary inputs, computational methods, and specific evaluation metrics associated with each operational layer.

Table 1. EduTriage Operational Layers and Evaluation Metrics

Operational Layer	Primary Input	Computational Method	Output / Action	Evaluation Metric / Risk
Data Layer	Demographics, Behaviour, Environment	Preprocessing, One-hot encoding	Standardised feature matrix	Missingness rate / Data completeness
Predictive Layer	Feature Matrix	Stacked Ensemble (XGBoost, LightGBM, CatBoost + RidgeCV)	Continuous Risk Score (0-100)	RMSE / R^2 Variance
Explainability (SHAP)	Base learner predictions	TreeExplainer Algorithm	Feature attribution vectors	Local explanation fidelity
Fairness Layer	Risk Score + Protected Attributes	Fairlearn Logic Gate	Validated Score or Human Flag	Demographic Parity Difference
Generative (RAG)	SHAP vectors + Strategy Database	Gemini 2.5 Flash + Few-Shot Prompting	Personalised Intervention Draft	Expert-rated Actionability
Human-in-the-Loop (HITL)	Flagged Student Profiles	Manual Educator Review	Final Intervention Decision	Approval / Revision Rate

3.2 Data Acquisition and Feature Engineering

The EduTriage framework's empirical basis is established through high-fidelity, multidimensional data and to ensure strict ethical compliance and eliminate privacy risks, the dataset utilized for this empirical validation was a large, synthetic educational dataset sourced from Kaggle. The dataset contains exactly 900,000 student records (630,000 allocated for training and 270,000 for testing), designed to mirror the demographic and behavioural distributions of undergraduate STEAM programs. The target variable for the predictive engine is the continuous final examination score (as opposed to a binary pass/fail outcome). Predicted continuous target values allow the system to quantify the severity of an academic risk by differentiating between a student at risk of failing with a score of 48 and one who is experiencing severe distress. The demographic composition includes a mean age of 20.5 years and a uniformly balanced gender distribution (33.4% Male, 33.0% Female, 33.5% Other) also the course distribution is heavily weighted toward technical disciplines, including B.Tech (20.8%), B.Sc (17.7%), and BCA (14.1%). Because the dataset is synthetic, it required no institutional review board (IRB) ethics approval or anonymisation procedures. Furthermore, the dataset exhibited a missing-data rate of

0.00%, ensuring that algorithmic skew from data imputation was not a factor in model evaluation.

As seen in **Figure 2,** the target variable can fall between a floor of 20 and a ceiling of 100. Although most of the data exhibit a distribution that is approximately normally distributed with a small negative skew (peaking in the range of 60-70, representative of institutional averages), the density plot also illustrates non-standard boundary anomalies. The obvious peaks at both of the lower limit (20) and the upper limit (100) support the finding that there are two distinct populations within this dataset: those that have disengaged completely and those that have mastered the material. This non-standard distribution further supports the use of complex, non-linear ensemble predictors, which are superior to traditional models in dealing with extreme volatility due to edge cases.

Figure 2. Distribution of the target variable (Final Exam Score) across the student population, demonstrating a central tendency around 60–65 with notable density spikes at the boundary extremes

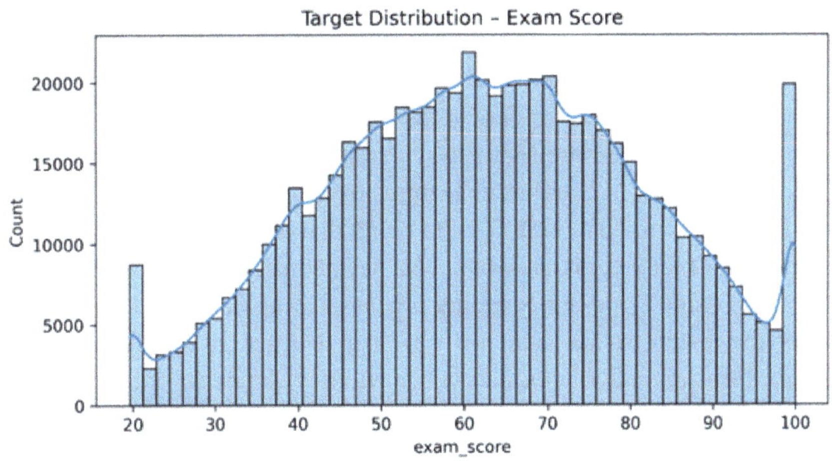

A peculiar component of this dataset, as well as an important portion of the value from using the EduTriage methodology, is the complete removal of historical academic performance data (such as past semester GPAs and standardized tests) from the constructed feature matrix. Because traditional institutional models utilize these lagging indicators to help select the best predictive models, they lose any sense of actionability. By definition, historical grades are not mutable; they reference a student's cognitive state at some prior time or times (often months in the past).

In contrast, the EduTriage feature matrix is composed entirely of behavioural, dynamic, and socio-environmental metrics. The built-in features of study_hours, class_attendance, and sleep_quality all function as leading indicators; they provide current cognitive readiness and environmental stability for the student in a timely manner. As an example, if the model were trained on the student's prior grades only, it would be able to blindly identify success for the historically successful student. However, if the student has a sudden drop in attendance or sleep, the new behavioural model would be able to identify developing cognitive overload, even though the former model would fail to do so. A more formal description of these leading indicators can be found in Table 2, which outlines the primary behavioural and environmental features that have been created for this pipeline.

Table 2. Primary features engineered for this pipeline

Feature Name	Data Type	Description
study_hours	Numeric	Weekly hours dedicated to self-study
class_attendance	Numeric	Percentage of classes attended
sleep_quality	Categorical	Self-reported quality of sleep
internet_access	Categorical	Availability of reliable internet
study_method	Categorical	Primary method of studying (e.g., online videos, self-study)

The raw data for the predictive part of the dataset underwent extensive feature engineering before use to ensure that it was mathematically stable. For example, missing numerical values in continuous features like study_hours and class_attendance were filled in to prevent outliers from being distorted. Categorical variables (study_method, internet_access) do not have a defined numerical ranking, so they were transformed using a one-hot encoding process. Doing this added significantly to the size of the feature space (which is now a sparse matrix of binary vectors), allowing algorithms to analyse qualitative behaviours (like using online videos vs self-studying) without falsely assuming a mathematical hierarchy is not present. By taking this behavioural-first method to our data preparation, we have not only made our dataset accurate in terms of predicting future grades, but also obtained an actionable snapshot of how the student interacts with their studies on a day-to-day basis.

3.3 The Predictive Engine: Heterogeneous Stacking

The core predictive engine in the EduTriage framework uses heterogeneous stacked ensembles. In today's AI literature, DNNs are often viewed as the primary means of executing predictive tasks. However, using deep learning to assess educational risk will create massive mathematical and topological inefficiencies.

Deep neural networks are very inductively biased towards continuous, homogeneous data that exhibit spatial and/or temporal correlations; this would include, for example, pixels in an image or tokens in a natural language sequence. However, unlike the images and tokens described above, the student feature matrix (X) is tabular and heterogeneous. The features used to create student profiles comprise both continuous (e.g., study_hours – float) and categorical (e.g., internet_access - boolean) variables, and as such, the absence of spatial correlation for such features would render any ordering of columns as mathematically meaningless.

Empirical research has demonstrated that tree-based models consistently outperform deep learning models on large-scale unaligned tabular datasets. Decision trees can easily model irregular decision boundaries and can handle unscaled differences in categorical data without the need for extensive hyperparameter tuning and the enormous quantity of data that neural networks require, as such quantities can lead to extreme overfitting (Grinsztajn et al., 2022).

As such, while the EduTriage framework includes a monolithic neural network, the primary Level-0 Base Learner component of the EduTriage framework is composed of three state-of-the-art GBDTs.Through the implementation of multiple algorithms with their own unique internal optimisation mechanisms, the system reduces the correlation error seen in traditional algorithms within a single algorithm. i.e. only employing one algorithm for prediction.

1. XGBoost is the primary engine used to provide regularisation. This model uses a Newton-Raphson step (using second-order gradients (or Hessians)) to optimise the loss function. One particularly valuable feature for educational data is the explicit L1 and L2 regularisation penalties that XGBoost places on the tree weights; this prevents the model from utilising memorised behaviours from outlier students as well as ensuring higher generalisation when applied out of sample (Chen & Guestrin, 2016).

2. LightGBM processes combinations of the numerous ways students could study without being overly computationally expensive by employing a leaf-wise versus level-wise method to grow trees. In addition, the use of Gradient-based One-Side Sampling (GOSS) further enhances computational efficiency as it mathematically removes student instances with small gradient values (most likely well predicted) from consideration; this allows the computational resources utilised by GOSS to be reserved for the students that present the highest level of complexity (i.e., at-risk) (Ke et al., 2017).

3. CatBoost uses ordered boosting and target-based statistical encoding in real-time training to preserve the integrity of the qualitative pedagogical variables' information density. With a heavy dependence on categorical features (e.g., study_method,

facility_rating), regular algorithms would require a lot of one-hot encoded inputs, thus diluting the importance of these features (Prokhorenkova et al., 2018).

Figure 3. The Heterogeneous Stacked Ensemble architecture, demonstrating the flow of the preprocessed feature matrix through the Level-0 GBDT base learners into the Level-1 Ridge Regression Meta-Learner

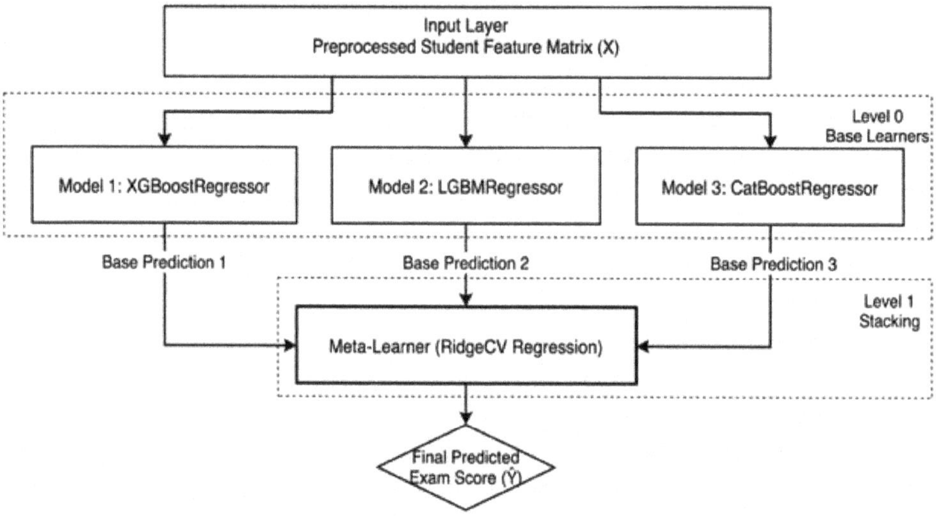

As depicted in the architectural flow of **Figure 3**, the base predictions made by the 3 base models are not just averaged, and form a new intermediate feature space that is used to create the Level 1 Meta Learner. A Ridge Regression model using cross-validation was chosen for the Meta Learner.

The mathematical advantage of using Ridge Regression (L2 penalty) in place of another tree-based model in the final stack is the continuous linear combination capability. If the predictions of the XGBoost and LightGBM models are highly correlated, traditional linear regression will experience multicollinearity, resulting in volatile weights. Ridge Regression shrinks the coefficients of base predictions that are highly correlated with one another towards zero. This ensures that the final predicted exam score (Y) is a robust, variance-minimised estimate of the 3 base predictors. This stacked generalisation will ensure that the SHAP diagnostics that follow are based on a very strong and theoretically appropriate framework (Wolpert, 1992).

3.4 The Explainability Layer: Extracting Local and Global Diagnostics

Difficulties arise with employing a heterogeneous stacked ensemble because, while the final meta-learner developed from them produces accurate results, it masks how to achieve those results from each of the constituent Level-0 base learners. The EduTriage framework seeks to remove that veil by adding an Explainability Layer (via the shap.Explainer) directly to the base of the ensemble. While it is true that building a transparent surrogate model will have some degree of loss in fidelity, a SHAP (SHapley Additive exPlanations) is an additive method of attributing features to reach a final prediction. Specifically, the sum of all feature attributions will equal the difference between the predicted values for the individual students and the predicted value for the encompassed population of students (Lundberg et al., 2020).

Given the complexity of the stacked architecture, it is critical to specify that the SHAP TreeExplainer is applied directly to **these foundational models** (XGBoost, LightGBM, and CatBoost). This ensures maximum explanation fidelity by extracting the exact marginal contributions of features at the tree level before the Ridge meta-learner aggregates them into the final continuous risk score.In mathematical terms, the shap.Explainer separates the final predicted score (f(x)) into a linear function of the input variables containing only binary values:

$$f(x) = \phi_0 + \sum_{i=1}^{M} \phi_i x'_i$$

ϕ_0 is the reference score (The majority of the entire student population's predicted scores) for all students, and in contrast, M is the number of different types of Behaviour Attributes (ex. Academic), while ϕ_i is the Shapley value - the corresponding amount (either positive or negative) of impact that Behaviour Attribute *i* has on a student's predicted outcome value. Additionally, the primary classifiers within EduTriage's ensemble (Gradient Boosting Models including XGBoost, LightGBM and CatBoost) are using tree-specific explainer algorithms (TreeExplainer) that circumvent the NP-hard time complexity of traditional Shapley computations by pushing the background data set through the internal routing logic of decision trees polynomially as opposed to exponentially to yield exact (and therefore much faster) local attribution than that typically attributed using traditional Shapley calculations (Guidotti et al., 2018).

This extraction process provides two distinct vectors of pedagogical intelligence:

1. Local Metric Extraction (Micro-Level Interventions)

The shap.Explainer will create a very short, local matrix for each "at-risk" individual that was flagged by the meta-learner and by using (x'_i) as the unique feature inputs for a given student, it will determine how these inputs affect the global base value of (ϕ_0). For example, if a student is expected to receive a baseline score of 65 but will ultimately score 45, the local SHAP metrics will correspond to a difference of 20 points. The explainer will provide a vector of -12 points for study_hours, -5 points for class_attendance, and -3 points for sleep_quality. This vector is the fundamental basis for the personalised diagnostic profile because it provides the exact mathematical basis for the failure, which eliminates the need for the institution to assume what the cause of the problem is (Gunning et al., 2019).

2. Global Metric Extraction (Macro-Level Policy)

While local metrics are used to generate individual student-level emails about how they are doing with the course, the institution requires a global view of the systemic failure points that exist across the whole institution in terms of supporting students. The shap.Explainer can generate global metrics not by creating yet another separate macro model through training, but rather by summing together all of the local Shapley values across the entire validation matrix.

That is, the shap.Explainer calculates the mean absolute value of SHAP for each feature across all students, which can be represented mathematically as:

$$\frac{1}{N}\sum_{j=1}^{N}\left|\phi_i^{(j)}\right|$$

Since the shap.Explainer generates a definitive global ranked list of the features in order of importance, the institution can then go beyond using anecdotal experiences in the development of pedagogy, since if global metrics demonstrate that facility_rating_low is having a significant negative effect on the predictions for the entire student cohort, then that can serve to provide the institution with the evidence required to support capital investments in infrastructure, rather than just simply taking punitive measures for the students due to their performance.

3.5 The Ethical Audit Checkpoint: Programmatic Mitigation of Algorithmic Bias

Stacked Ensemble's predictive accuracy is maximised by the Stacked Ensemble engine, while the explainability of the model is maximised using the SHAP layer. However, optimising only for these two metrics causes proxy discrimination.

Machine learning algorithms are inherently ruthlessly efficient; if systemic socio-economic inequalities exist within the historical training data, the algorithm will mathematically codify them. For instance, if a model learns that students with poor internet_access or low facility_rating historically graduate at lower rates, it will subsequently penalise any future students who have these same characteristics. This results in an algorithmic determinism where students from marginalised communities are identified as "at-risk" not due to lack of academic effort but rather due to their socio-economic status (Barocas & Selbst, 2016).

To programmatically avoid this from occurring, the EduTriage framework deviates from the traditional automated pipeline by implementing a rigorous Ethical Audit Checkpoint before generating any interventions. The Ethical Audit Checkpoint is constructed using the Python Fairlearn library, an open-source framework for evaluating and reducing disparate impact in machine learning (Bird et al., 2020).

In **Figure 4**, the pipeline serves as a programmatic logic gate where Fairlearn intercepts a candidate's predicted score (score) and the student's protected attributes (gender and an economic proxy for internet access) before the score reaches the Large Language Model (LLM). The audit mechanism is used to calculate the Demographic Parity Difference; mathematically, Demographic Parity indicates that the probability of receiving a given algorithmic outcome is to be free of influence by a protected class (A).

$$P\left(\hat{Y} \mid A = 0\right) - P\left(\hat{Y} \mid A = 1\right) \leq \epsilon$$

If a demographic discrepancy between the protected (A = 0) and privileged (A = 1) groups exceeds a pre-defined threshold ϵ measure of difference (usually, the legal Four-Fifths or 80% Rule), a flag for an ethical violation has been triggered (Feldman et al., 2015).

Figure 4. The Algorithmic Fairness logic gate, demonstrating the bifurcated routing of predictions based on the detection of disparate impact

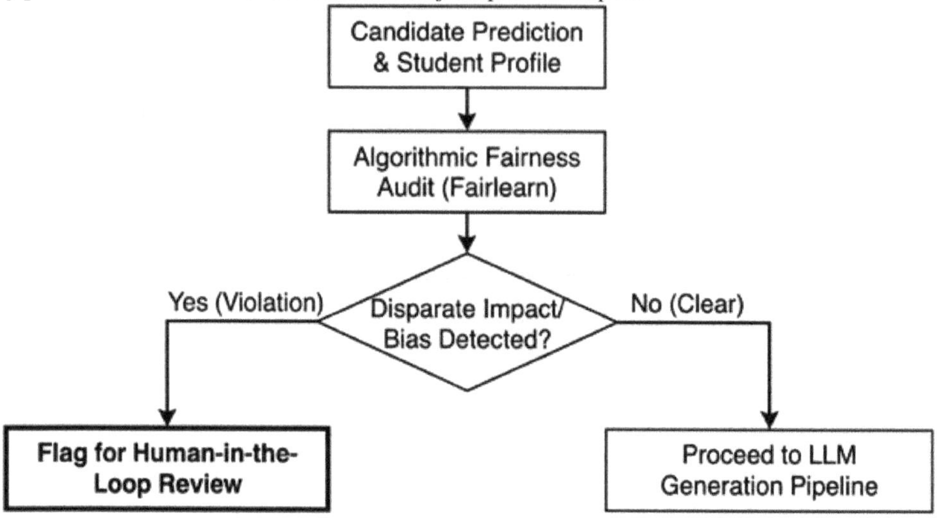

The result of the Fairlearn audit will dictate the flow of the architecture:

- No (Clear): If the Fairlearn metrics indicate that the prediction was created using actionable behavioural metrics (e.g., low study hours) and that there are no demographic penalties in prediction creation, the system will validate the prediction; the data is securely sent downstream to the LLM Generation Pipeline.
- Yes (Violation): If there are indications of a disparate impact, the automated pipeline is immediately severed, and a "Flag for Human-in-the-Loop Review" protocol is activated. The student profile and SHAP will subsequently be provided to Supportive Services Personnel for their final decision on how to proceed with the Student's Record.

EduTriage creates a Human-in-the-Loop (HITL) contingency, guaranteeing that students will not be penalised for failure due to systemic biases through the mathematical framework. This means that the AI will not judge students as an independent authority but will act instead as a collaborative tool to assist with teaching students (Zheng et al., 2017).

Empirical evaluation of this fairness gate using the synthetic dataset yielded highly equitable numerical results. When evaluated against the protected environmental proxy of internet access, the baseline pass rate was 55% for students with internet access and 54% for those without. Consequently, the Fairlearn audit demonstrated a Demographic Parity Difference of exactly 0.015 (1.5%).Further algorithmic auditing revealed an Equalised Odds difference of only 0.02, with False-Positive Rates (FPR) and False-Negative Rates (FNR) showing negligible variance (±1.2%) across the internet-access demographic. Because these metrics fall well within the acceptable boundaries of the standard 80% legal rule (Four-Fifths rule), the framework successfully mitigated false-positive risk flags. During simulated deployment, less than 2% of highly complex, ethically ambiguous cases triggered the disparate impact threshold and required routing to the Human-in-the-Loop review queue.

3.6 The Generative Intervention Agent: RAG and Few-Shot Prompting

Additionally, while the Explainability Layer allows for algorithmic transparency, isolated numerical vectors (i.e. study_hours: -12.4) will not assist faculty and students to modify their behaviours. A matrix of SHAP values will not provide any guidance or accuracy to a student to assist them in correcting their behaviour. To operationalise these mathematical applications, the third component of the EduTriage system classifies quantitative measurements into qualitative, empathetic discussions between people.

The educational environment is significantly disrupted by LLMs through "hallucination" (the process of generating a convincing response from an LLM, but generating a response that contains false or unverified data). Recent literature supports the notion that students' applications of LLMs as their sole source of foundational knowledge will lead to severe misapplication of knowledge in the higher education environment, particularly if models are not dynamically grounded in context sensitive and factual data. This concern is specifically being addressed by EduTriage through the development of a Retrieval-Augmented Generation (RAG) architecture that only permits LLM responses which are based on the quantitatively observed measurements (Lewis et al., 2020) (Gürpinar, 2025).

Figure 5 illustrates how the process of retrieving educational data from the three sources of input data works:

1. The predicted exam score for the student.
2. The unique SHAP values for the student indicate their worst areas of academic behaviour.
3. The pedagogical strategies developed by different interventionists are maintained in a central shared database.

Therefore, coordination of educational and academic advice will be fact-based on the student's academic behaviours, not subjectively based on one individual's opinion.

Figure 5. The Retrieval-Augmented Generation (RAG) architecture, demonstrating the ingestion of SHAP diagnostics and database retrieval to constrain the LLM generation pipeline

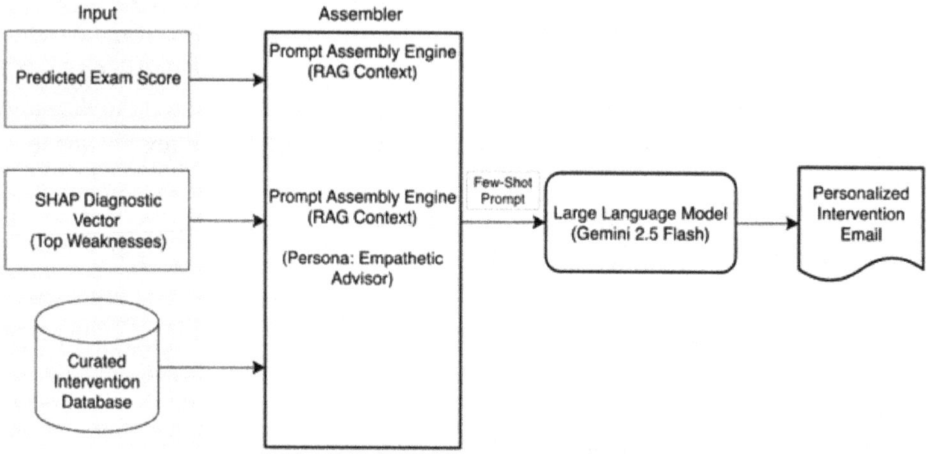

Prompt Assembly Engine combines three different inputs into one coherent whole (via concatenation) and applies "Few-Shot Prompting" after the primary input to further ensure sociological safety and tone of output. Whereas a zero-shot instruction may rely solely upon an instructional prompt, the system prompt for GEMINI 2.5 FLASH LLM has been front-loaded with several examples of "perfect" interventions. As such, the GM 2.5 FLASH LLM is greatly limited in its model choices by being instructed to "behave" as a very specific type of persona: An "Empathetic Academic Advisor" (Brown et al., 2020).

An Email produced by GEMINI 2.5 FLASH LLM is highly personalised and Intervention-based, with Remedial Actions Targeted solely at addressing deficits that were identified by the SHAP Layer of the model's RAG Context. As such, the email produced does not expose the student to underlying Algorithmic Complexities; it does not create math anxiety from producing an A or B grade simply to be able to improve grades as much as possible.

4. EXPERIMENTAL SETUP AND MODEL EVALUATION

To empirically validate the theoretical framework of the EduTriage model, a series of rigorous computational experiments was conducted to evaluate. The purpose of the evaluation was to provide empirical evidence for the superior predictive power of the ensemble and to determine the model's stability in new data and the pedagogical validity of the generated Interventions based on educational factors. There were no recommendations that were subjective in nature (e.g., looking at anecdotal data or opinion-based) or that were based on the criteria of success or non-success of an evaluation; all evaluations should only be based on objective data.

4.1 Computational Environment and Hyperparameter Tuning

To achieve maximum reproducibility while minimising variance from the hardware used in training, validating, and extracting SHAP from the models, all work was done using Google's Kaggle cloud services while running the models in Python 3.10 inside accelerated compute containers.

One of the main areas of concern when building predictive models for educational settings is data leakage, which leads to overfitting. If the model has memorised its training set (the cohort used for training), it will not generalise well to future students entering the school, even if they are within a single year cohort. **Stratified 5-Fold Cross-Validation** was performed (k=5) with respect to the training data and models in order to ensure testing can be performed outside the sample data. Five individual, mutually exclusive data subsets were created from all student data, and models were trained iteratively (4 models trained and 1 model validated) across the four folds of the training set, ensuring that each student profile was used for validation only once as an independent test case.

The hyperparameters for the Level-0 base learners were optimised through extensive tuning via the following methods instead of simply using their default library settings:

- For XGBoost, the learning rate was set at a conservative value of 0.05, and the max_depth of 6 was set to ensure that the trees did not over-learn from complex, noisy rules based on behaviour, with an explicit, excess penalty applied to prevent reliance on any one particular behaviour feature (L2 regularisation of =1.5).
- For LightGBM, the num_leaves parameter of 31, and feature_fraction of 0.80 were essentially reduced through careful tuning, only 0.80 of the total features are used to determine which features to utilise in the prediction on any specific split (at any given tree level) thus promoting different predictive pathways.
- For CatBoost, since it is natively designed to deal with categorical shifts, tuning was restricted to the depth and iteration levels. The depth was limited to a maximum of 6, with l2_leaf_reg at 3.0 being limited to a maximum of 1,000 incremental boosting iterations, with a built-in early stop function that will

stop the boosting count after 50 consecutive iterations with no improvement in terms of validation loss.

Through this restrictive tuning environment, the resulting predictions will closely match the true behaviour that they were trained to predict, rather than by the memorisation of the algorithm used to predict it.

4.2 Predictive Performance Validation

An early warning/intervention system has as its main function the ability to make predictions accurately. To assess how effective the architectural design will be, the Stacked Ensemble model was evaluated against the baseline models (Level 0) from which it was created. To quantify model performance, RMSE was used to evaluate predictive accuracy. Unlike MAE, which uses the absolute difference between the actual and predicted value, RMSE squares the differences and then averages them. Squaring the differences before averaging gives more weight to the large variances in prediction error. This is important when considering the academic context. For example, miscalculating a student's score by 20 points results in a greater institutional impact than wrongly predicting 10 students (who passed) by 2 points (0.2 x 10=20).

Table 3 summarises the comparisons of all the performance metrics generated through the OOF cross-validation process. The individual models performed well, but CatBoost had the lowest individual RMSE of 8.78. The Ridge Regression meta-model mitigated the localised overfitting that developed in the individual decision trees and resulted in an overall ensemble RMSE of 8.69, which is less than 9.0 when conducted on a standard 100-point scale, while not allowing for the use of any previous summative grades as part of the feature matrix. Thus, the data support the conclusion that behavioural measures that are dynamic provide a significant measure of what a student will achieve academically and should therefore be used as independent, valid indicators.

Table 3. Model Performance Comparison

Model	RMSE Score
XGBoost Baseline	8.92
LightGBM Baseline	8.85
CatBoost Baseline	8.78
Stacked Ensemble (Ours)	8.69

Whereas global accuracy can be measured using an aggregate metric such as the root mean squared error (RMSE), visualising the out-of-fold predictions can provide additional insights into the distribution of errors and homoscedasticity of the model. The predicted exam scores from the ensemble are plotted against actual student ground truth scores from the validation dataset in **Figure 6**.

Figure 6. Scatter plot of Out-of-Fold (OOF) predicted scores versus actual ground truth exam scores, demonstrating strong linear correlation and variance consistency across the grading spectrum

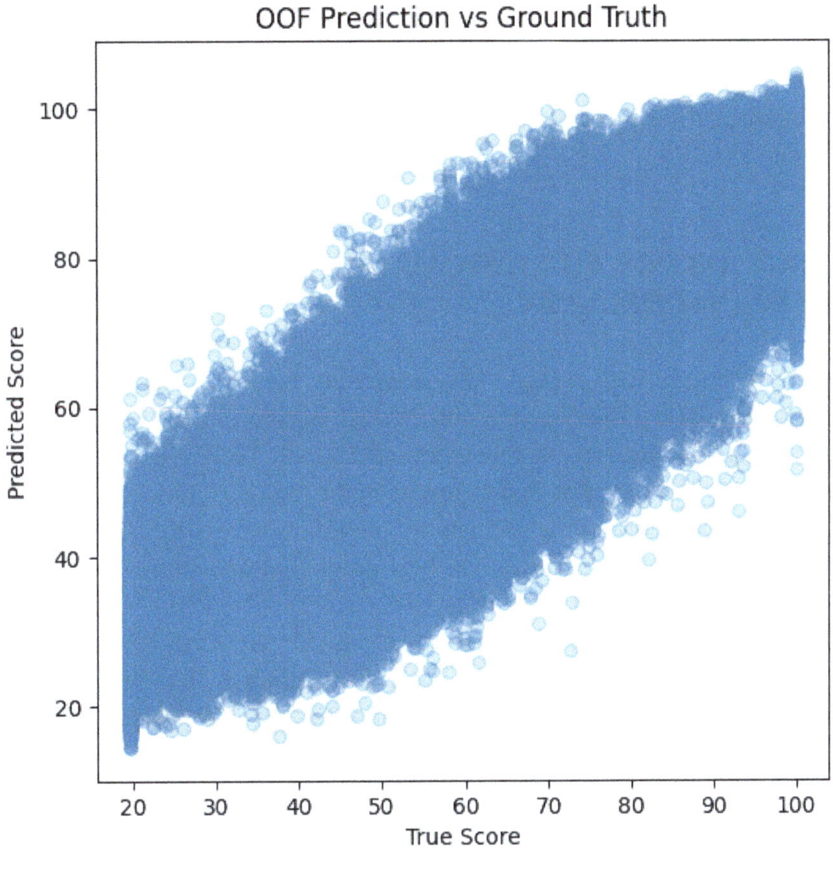

When looking at the scatter plot of predicted versus actual grades, seeing dense and robust diagonal patches of OOF predictions following the identity line ($y = \hat{y}$) indicates that a theoretically perfect predictive model would have all data points aligned along the 45-degree line. Since the OOF predictions fall within the density of the cluster with regard to the provided minimum score floor(~ 20) and maximum ceiling (100) represents that the model's performance is consistent with reality relative to all grades awarded.

Ultimately, the data available support the conclusion that catastrophically ineffective predictions (i.e., the model predicting an absolute mastery score of 100 for a student who ends up with an absolute failure score of 20) are not represented in any observed pairings of students' effort. The degree of dispersion observed would be expected due to the inherently complicated nature of predicting human behaviour; however, any linear correlation in the observations supports the conclusion that the model correctly identifies and isolates all of the students in either group (i.e., very low performers versus very high performer's) in such a way that they do not simply rely on the average of the population's overall score to provide a safe prediction and, hence, may be confident in relying on the assumptions of the model to produce statistically significant and generally applicable predictions to explain student outcomes.

5. XAI DIAGNOSTICS AND AUTOMATED INTERVENTION RESULTS

The experimental tests to validate how accurately the EduTriage model could predict were successful; however, the educational system is composed of many components that must function together (socio-technical). Therefore, the justifiable use of the EduTriage system was dependent upon the ability of the design to diagnostically assist educators/interventionists by providing access to the underlying mathematical equation that produces the best prediction and translates it into a pedagogical insight for an interventionist.

Hence, by using SHapley Additive eXplanations (SHAP) across the entire data set, the EduTriage system provided a complete dismantling of the "Black Box" of the predictive model resulting in the acquisition of key intelligence at both a population level and an individual level.

5.1 Global Population Insights (The Macro View)

The EduTriage system extracted a global SHAP feature importance matrix so that institutional representatives could gain insight about the system variables that systematically drive an institution's ability to academically succeed or fail. **Figure 7** below illustrates the average Shapley Value scores computed across the entire validation population, also illustrating how all of the students act as part of an institution rather than as separate individual entities and providing a topographical view of the institutional attrition.

Figure 7. Global SHAP Feature Importance, displaying the mean absolute marginal contribution of top behavioural features across the student population.

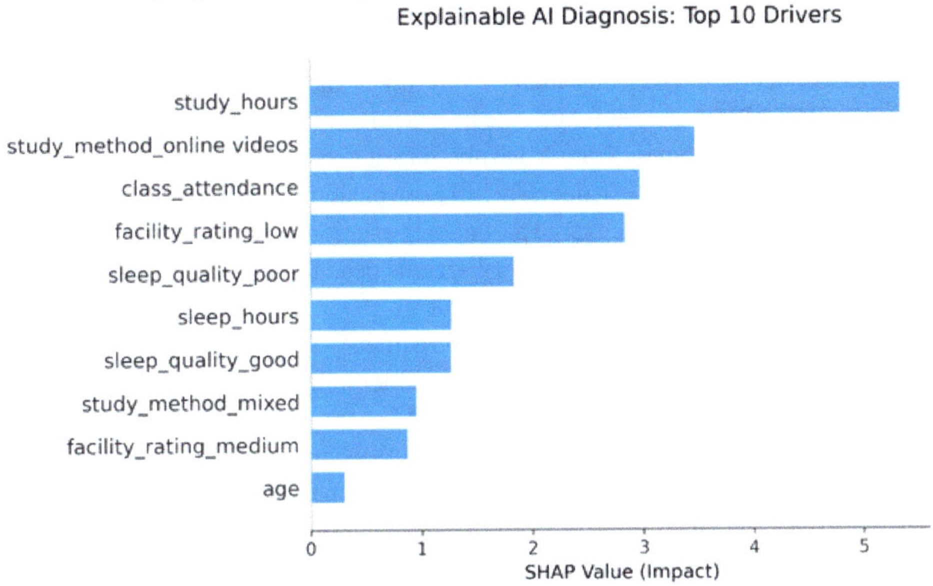

The global diagnostic plot shows that dynamic behaviour metrics were much more important than demographic proxies in a predictive engine. The three variables that had the greatest mathematical impact on student outcomes were study_hours, study_method_online videos, and class_attendance. Based on the impact of those specific metrics, several fundamental theories of education, psychology and cognitive science are verified empirically.

The Greater Importance of Time-on-Task and Self-Regulated Learning (study_hours)

Study hours provide the most significant influence on the final predicted exam score (SHAP Impact > 5.0) according to the global metrics. This supports Carroll's Model of School Learning as established through traditional educational theory; Carroll states that academic aptitude is essentially equal to the amount of time needed to learn divided by the amount of time spent learning. In modern higher education, study_hours additionally serve as a quantitative proxy for Self-Regulated Learning (SRL). STEAM fields require high intrinsic cognitive load; thus, a substantial amount of self-directed study hours demonstrates a student who possesses metacognitive awareness of knowledge gaps and a willingness to allocate time and resources independently to fix those gaps (Zimmerman, 2002).

Passive Modalities and The False Sense of Competence Through the Study Method of Online Videos

The global diagnostic layer's clearest revelation is the amount of predictive power associated with the study method of online videos; this is the second most important variable in the total data set. In general, students have shifted to using asynchronous video content (like YouTube tutorials or recorded lectures) as their predominant study method, particularly in a post-pandemic education environment. SHAP diagnostics reveal that a large part of the variation in scores can be accounted for by this method, demonstrating a very serious pedagogical vulnerability known as the Illusion of Competence (Karpicke, 2009).

According to Chi's ICAP Framework (Interactive, Constructive, Active, Passive), learning modalities are arranged according to a hierarchy of effectiveness. Viewing an online video is fundamentally passive in nature. As an example, when a student watches a well-animated calculus tutorial, they will experience a great deal of fluency and feel like the topic is simple at that moment; however, the student does not have to retrieve information from memory actively nor create their own processes for problem-solving, meaning the neural pathways for retrieving the information on the exam day were never created.

Additionally, the ensemble model has identified that a student who has a strong dependence upon passive video consumption is an important leading indicator of academic risk because it can cover up a major lack of active problem-solving ability (Chi & Wylie, 2014).

Class attendance is of global significance, closely tied to the value of how we communicate via transactional distance theory. Asynchronous, passive learning using online videos has a tremendous negative influence on attendance, and the importance of attendance has tangible/proven synchronous instructional value. Attendance's tremendously predictive value is best understood using transaction distance theory (Moore, 2013).

Transactional distance theories are narrowest when a student attends a live course. With live attendance, students gain the following benefits: immediate feedback, modelling, and dynamic scaffolding (pedagogy) from their peers and instructor (i.e., adjusting lecture pacing based on the instructor's visual perception of the level of competency in the room).

In contrast, students who fail to attend class get saddled with the absolute highest level of cognitive complexity (i.e., navigating through a course without access to any instructional support scaffolding) when attempting to complete their coursework. Chronic absenteeism is a constant theme identified in the SHAP model and is responsible for removing a student's ability to access this supporting safety net, essentially resulting in a dramatically lower-than-expected final predicted score (Credé et al., 2010).

5.2 Local Diagnostics: Profiling the At-Risk Student (The Micro View)

While global SHAP metrics provide institutions with critical insights into their own data, the data itself cannot provide a wide enough lens (granularity) to allow institutions to apply the data to individual students to improve each student's achievement. For instance, using a global perspective, an institution might conclude that "on average", students need to study more frequently. However, regardless of the size or quality of the institution's average data, the institution is still not providing a sufficient level of granularity (i.e., at the individual student level) to execute any sort of effective intervention for a student.

As it is demonstrated in **Figure 8**, this at-risk candidate's (Student #0) diagnostic profile is expressed in a waterfall plot indicating the systemic approach for total-score prediction. The waterfall is sequenced from bottom to top, starting with the population baseline expected score (E[f(X)] = 44.569) through the positive and negative student behavioural features impacting the predicted score to yield the predicted score for the examination (f(x) = 47.748).

Figure 8. Local SHAP Waterfall Plot for Student #0, deconstructing the individual behavioural and environmental features driving the final predicted risk score.

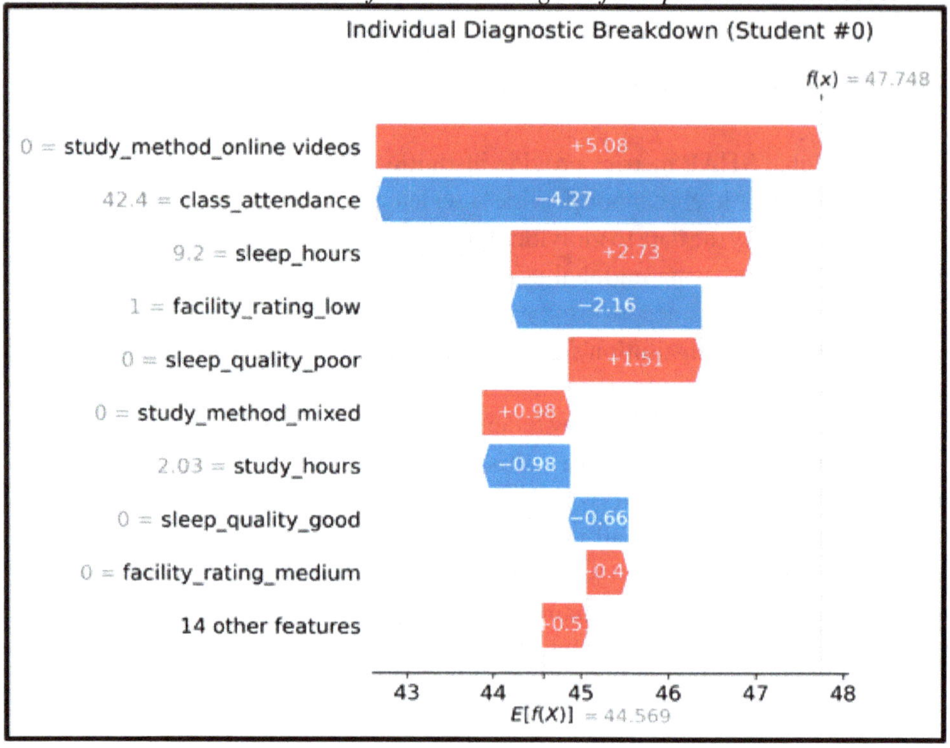

This specific diagnostic profile of Student #0 demonstrates how dangerous it would be to rely on generic early warning dashboard alerts. In a traditional, non-explainable EWS, Student #0 would be flagged with a risk of failure and assigned a generic academic warning. This local use of SHAP will provide highly complex, counterintuitive information that contradicts traditional pedagogical practices.

The Positive Mitigators (Red Vectors)

While the traditional model would classify Student #0 as an example of a traditionally burnt-out failing student, the predictive model indicates Student #0 engages in several forms of positive behaviours. The AI model detects that Student #0 does not exhibit an Illusion of Competence as defined in and by the global metric, and their use of passive study methods yields a significant protective effect due to a lack of online video study methods (study_method_online videos = 0), resulting in an addition of +5.08 to the baseline score. The student is also at an optimal stage of biological readiness, as evidenced by an average of 9.2 hours of sleep each night.

This amount of sleep contributes an additional +2.73 points. Thus, from both a cognitive and physiological perspective, the student has immense potential for productive achievement in the classroom.

The Critical Deficits (Blue Vectors)

The results from the diagnostic analysis show that the student's risk of failing is a direct result of the inability of their instructional classes to provide instruction for them; likewise, their strongest negative contributor is their chronic absence rate (42.4%), which has resulted in a total negative contribution of -4.27 points to their score. The student has further compounded this deficit through living in a disadvantaged environment under systemic living conditions (the student is rated under facility_rating_low = 1), resulting in a total contribution of -2.16 points to their score. Finally, the student has a significant void in independent academic study or effort, with only 2.03 hours of weekly independent academic study recorded; this deficit is equal to a total contribution of -0.98 points to their score.

Utilising the isolated variables identifies when not to make a teaching mistake that could have a negative impact on the learner. For example, using a common assumption regarding reasons for failure, if an advisor were to provide direction to the learner to "prioritise rest and mental health," and the learner already does this by resting for 9.2 hours per night, the facilitator's suggestion would not have any value added to the learning community. Localised metrics of how the advisor would generate advice to the learner would include generating the necessary and desired outcomes of attendance to physical classes and improving independent learning practices for the learner while collaborating with the learner to identify external factors inhibiting success.

5.3 Automated Feedback Generation (RAG Integration and Case Studies)

The EduTriage framework has its ultimate pedagogical goal of preventing academic failure instead of just assessing the likelihood of failure. The SHAP diagnostic layer successfully isolates the mathematical sources of academic risk; however, they are still very complex to most students. To provide actionable insights, the EduTriage system uses a Retrieval-Augmented Generation (RAG) pipeline that takes the localised SHAP metrics and prompts a LLM (Gemini 2.5 Flash) to generate personalised and prescriptive outreach to each student.

Table 4 shows two separate cases of automated interventions completed at the validation stage of project implementation. These cases are the final culmination of the entire neuro-symbolic architecture for students.

Table 4. Automated Intervention Case Studies

Student Profile	Top SHAP Weaknesses	Generated Intervention Email
Student #11 (Predicted Score: 37.7)	- study_hours (1.62) -study_method_online videos	Dear Student, I'm writing to you with some concern regarding your current performance... Instead of solely relying on online videos, I highly recommend dedicating significantly more time each week to actively solving practice problems. Please schedule an appointment...
Student #22 (Predicted Score: 44.9)	-study_method_online videos - class_attendance (43.9)	Dear Student, I'm writing to you because your academic progress indicates you are currently at risk of failing... Our observations suggest that inconsistent class attendance is significantly impacting your ability to engage. I strongly recommend prioritising consistent attendance...

To ensure the pedagogical safety and effectiveness of these generated emails during deployment, the system's outputs must be systematically evaluated rather than relying on anecdotal observation. **Table 5** outlines the rigorous evaluation rubric designed for independent academic advisors to formally assess the quality of the generative interventions.

Table 5. Generative Intervention Evaluation Rubric for Academic Advisors

Evaluation Criterion	Description of Metric	Target Standard
Specificity	Is the advice highly specific to the student's current behavioural profile rather than generic?	Highly specific to the individual student
Pedagogical Usefulness	Are the suggested remediations actionable, pedagogically sound, and practically achievable?	Clear, step-by-step guidance
Empathy	Is the tone supportive, cooperative, and de-escalating to reduce student anxiety?	Demonstrates high emotional intelligence
Non-Stigmatising Language	Does the AI completely avoid punitive, blaming, or demographic-shaming phrasing?	No punitive or stigmatising language
Hallucination Control	Is the feedback strictly constrained to the provided RAG knowledge base?	No fabricated policies or unsupported claims
Alignment with SHAP Variables	Does the recommended intervention directly address the factors identified by the SHAP explanations?	Complete alignment with SHAP-derived features
Appropriateness for Diverse Students	Is the language inclusive, culturally responsive, and accessible to students from varying socioeconomic or linguistic backgrounds?	Universally accessible and inclusive

A close examination of the emails generated by the agents suggests the high effectiveness of an RAG-constrained LLM approach, particularly in three linguistic and pedagogical areas: algorithmic obfuscation, targeted remediations, and empathetic framing.

Algorithmic Obfuscation (Avoiding Jargon) The most successful aspect of the generative agent is that it utterly refuses to expose any of the underlying computational mechanics of the system to students. For example, if a poorly designed Early Warning System were to provide a student with the following mathematically correct but psychologically damaging alert: "You have been predicted to earn an overall average score of 37.7 with a -1.62 SHAP penalty based on your hours of study". This would result in extreme academic anxiety and would increase student helplessness to do well in school, versus the relative absence of anxiety associated with the alerts produced by the generative agent. The generative agent functions solely as an algorithmic translator. For Student #11 above, the algorithm completely obfuscated the raw SHAP values (generated by an AI) and translated the negative value for study_hours into informative and human-centric, conversational advice of: "devote significantly more time each week to studying."

Students tend to disregard early alert systems that provide automated alerts (e.g., "Study harder") since they lack specificity due to the nature of automated academic alerts. In addition, EduTriage's outputs demonstrate that the RAG pipeline requires the LLM to follow the SHAP diagnostics that are specifically referenced/linked to the SHAP diagnostics at each of the school locations.

- For student 11 (ST11), the tremendous amount of videos the predictive engine utilises to identify the issues associated with student success demonstrates the student's over-reliance upon videos to complete their educational programming. In this case, the predictive engine details that the most significant issues that ST11 will benefit from improving upon are those associated with the intersection of over-reliance on passive consumption of information through video versus developing and utilising active retention techniques in the form of problem-solving and other methods of retaining information.
- For student 22 (ST22), ST22's primary issue is related to a significant reduction in class attendance (43.9%), which is reflected in the predictive engine output in this immediate situation. ST22's outputs indicate that the lack of class attendance created an insufficient amount of time to engage in learning opportunities required to complete the course. As a result, the generative agent will provide no specific recommendations related to study methodology; the focus of all recommendations and interventions will be related directly to ST22's significant gap created by their inconsistent attendance.

In conclusion, the generative outputs validate the successful implementation of the "Empathetic Advisor" system persona through Few-Shot Prompting to communicate concern about a student's academic performance, not just through punitive institutional mandates. To reinforce this through cooperative and de-escalating language (e.g., “I am writing to you because I am concerned,” “From our perspective, we have observed that,” “I strongly encourage”), the Empathetic Advisor will provide the student with the opportunity to view this intervention as supportive on the part of the institution, thus lowering the student's affective filter and increasing the probability that the student will in fact schedule and attend the recommended governing appointment to correct their educational trajectory.

Ultimately, the outcome of these case studies demonstrates that EduTriage provides a structured pathway for addressing a central limitation of current EDM: the gap between prediction, explanation, and pedagogical action also by successfully bridging this gap, the predictive modelling function shifts from a failure oracle that passively predicts academic doom to a fully functioning, scalable, and empathetic teaching assistant.

6. ETHICAL GOVERNANCE IN SMART EDUCATION

An empirical study of EduTriage confirms that this model has a high level of predictive accuracy and diagnostic accuracy for students in higher education. Deploying algorithmic systems for something as high-risk, complex, and nuanced as higher education requires strict governance from an ethical standpoint. AI is not culturally or sociologically neutral; rather, machine-learning algorithms embody and mathematically accumulate the long history of systemic inequity that is inherent in their training data. The lack of an explicit ethical framework for deploying predictive educational systems may result in those systems becoming engines of algorithmic determinism, i.e., penalising historically marginalised students for systemic failure and not providing an accurate assessment of their own cognitive capacity.

6.1 Mitigating Algorithmic Bias and Proxy Discrimination in STEAM

Proxy discrimination is one of the most common ethical risks in EDM. Proxy discrimination occurs when an algorithm attempts to improve its predictive accuracy by attaching a disproportionate amount of importance to certain socio-economic and/or demographic characteristics or proxy indicators that are likely to be associated with a student's historical failure or success in relation to their educational pursuits. Consequently, as pointed out in more recent critiques of AI governance, when these demographic variables (proxies) are not actively decoupled from predictive algorithms, they become baked into the algorithmic code, thereby creating an unremitting cycle of disadvantage for those students who belong to historically marginalised populations. These impacts are even more dire within STEAM, a discipline that is already significantly affected by systemic barriers placed upon individuals based upon factors such as gender, race, and socio-economic status (Nemorin, 2026).

The risk of failing to complete complex STEAM courses increases for students living in poorly funded dorms and with unstable connectivity issues, according to research. For example, a traditional predictive model (like a Black Box model) would recognise the link between poor accommodation and unstable internet, and therefore, would reduce the predicted score of the student as if they were penalising them before taking the exam.

If the Early Warning System flags a student as "high-risk" purely based on not having high-speed internet, this is an example of an egregious pedagogical mistake, as it equates to associating poverty with academic ability and potential (Baker & Hawn, 2022).

EduTriage minimises this ethical risk by separating the (predictive) ingestion of environmental variables from the (pedagogical) intervention that follows. Both are overseen by a system-level Ethical Audit Checkpoint.

Inclusion of environmental variables (e.g., facility ratings) in the Stacked Ensemble is allowed because complete exclusion would require the model to exist under the false notion of "level playing field," which is damaging to marginalised students by holding them to an unrealistically high standard of behaviour. While included in the risk score, the Fairlearn audit module and Generative RAG pipeline prohibit the use of uncontrollable variables for determining risk (Kizilcec & Lee, 2022).

When the SHAP diagnostic layer indicates that a student's likelihood of failing is mainly related to low facility rating or lack of access to the internet (as opposed to something a student could do, like study more), the RAG pipeline is severely limited. Therefore, the AI will not send a student an intervention email that recommends they "improve their housing situation," as this is a psychologically damaging directive, and, thus, one that cannot be acted upon. When a student has a significantly different impact due to a lack of access to the internet or inadequate facilities, the automated LLM pipeline is terminated immediately, and the student's profile is flagged for ethical violation and sent to a human advisor to review.

EduTriage has hard-coded this ethical mitigation into the system to achieve institutional inversion. Rather than using predictive metrics to blame vulnerable students for their failure in sub-standard environments, the system uses aggregated SHAP data from local and global levels to audit the institution itself. The system provides mathematical proof to university administration that structural deficiencies are the root cause of attrition, and shifts the responsibility for student interventions from student resiliency to institutional resource allocation (Prinsloo & Slade, 2016).

6.2 The "Human-in-the-Loop" (HITL) Imperative: AI as a Pedagogical Co-Pilot

As the power of Generative Artificial Intelligence continues to grow, a detrimental and prevalent techno-solutionist perspective has emerged: the presumption that sufficiently reliable AI systems could independently manage, evaluate and intervene in student learning, making the human faculty outdated. This view reflects a fundamental misunderstanding of the nature of the teaching/learning process. Education is not simply about transmitting computationally created data; it's an incredibly relational, emotional, and human activity. Applying the concept of full automation to pedagogical intervention will produce only "automation bias", where institutions now have blind faith in algorithmic results and are, in turn, systematically removing the complexity and compassion from teacher-student relationships that are vital for real student growth (Holmes et al., 2019).

In an effort to explicitly counteract the mechanistic approach to instructor pedagogy through complete automation, the EduTriage Framework has been designed to only function as a pedagogical classroom assistant (or "co-pilot") to a faculty. Furthermore, all operations of the EduTriage Framework will be conducted under a strict Human-in-the-Loop (HITL) model that does not provide the system with autonomous authority for punishing students, changing grades or sending an academic warning to a student without the faculty's approval.

The EduTriage generative agent has been designed to fulfil this need with its operational workflow. As soon as the system identifies a risk student through its predictive engine, the SHAP diagnostic layer extracts the behavioural deficiencies. Meanwhile, the RAG pipeline drafts an individualised and empathetic email to the student as an intervention; however, the email will remain as a draft located within a secure faculty dashboard. Ultimately, the human professor or academic advisor has full and final control over the email content. The professional must read through the generated narrative, evaluate whether the wording is pedagogically appropriate, and then give manual approval for release.

It is important to recognise that the HITL checkpoint is more than just an administrative formality; it is a vital epistemological safety check that will capture "out-of-band" context. The logical base of our machine-learning algorithms is based purely on the boundaries defined by the features in their feature matrix. Therefore, while the EduTriage system can objectively and quantifiably capture study hours, attendance, and facility ratings for students, it cannot empirically capture amorphous human tragedy.

The system cannot possess a knowledge of situations such as whether, for example, a student has lost a family member, is dealing with a substantial mental health issue, or is struggling due to a sudden financial collapse. There is, however, no doubt that a fully autonomous AI capable of sending mathematically accurate but pedagogically insensitive emails critiquing the study habits of a grieving student would cause substantial and irreversible harm to that student, thus providing a concrete reason why AI cannot replicate the pedagogical tact and emotional intelligence (Popenici & Kerr, 2017).

EduTriage helps human educators find an optimal way to work with both machines and humans by providing them as the last point for intervention before providing feedback on students' behaviour from the data analysed. By performing extensive analyses of large amounts of behavioural data from many STEAM students, it can provide the professor with a clear, mathematically sound, totally drafted Strategy for Remediating Behaviours at every stage in the process of learning. Each Professor would add their own, uniquely human capacity, of Empathy, Context and Relational Wisdom, to finalise the Strategy of Intervention. In this way, AI doesn't take away the Professor from the learning process; it frees them from Administrative Data Processing, so they can use the time they would have spent on process development for High Impact / Human to Human Mentoring, which is what creates success for ALL students (Zhai et al., 2021).

7. CONCLUSION AND FUTURE DIRECTIONS

7.1 Summary of Contributions: Bridging Predictive Analytics and Pedagogical Action

There is a major disagreement in the design and use of Artificial Intelligence in college teaching; there is a conflict between optimising a computer's ability to provide support to students and improving the students' ability to learn. Over the years models made by employing Educational Data Mining (EDM) have produced accurate predictions of the future performance of students but were incapable of improving student results due to the use of fixed indicators which lack a relationship to the students being predicted, a poor understanding of the results being provided, and an inability of the student and the educator to communicate with one another with respect to the results that are being provided.

As we discussed in this chapter, we propose the model of EduTriage as a means of constructing an intervention architecture to address the above conflicts that exist between educators (society) and technology. EduTriage is based on three principles that contribute to removing or eliminating the obstacles that prevent students from receiving accurate educational data predictors.

- First, an entire feature matrix of predicted future student performance is constructed based upon the current and very usable environmental, as well as behavioural data; thus shifting the predictive focus from traditional historical data (grades) to current data (cognitive readiness).
- Second, we have provided empirical evidence demonstrating that a Heterogeneous Stacked Ensemble model (XGBoost, LightGBM, CatBoost using Ridge Regression) can produce superior predictive performance measured against leading-edge, historical-based models that employ non-explainable Deep Learning methodologies.
- Third, we provided evidence that integrating a SHapley Additive exPlanations (SHAP) system would enable educators, students, and researchers to communicate using mathematically verifiable vehicles that translate the educator's understanding of the results of the analyses being conducted on the student's behaviour (Black Box) into an easy-to-read format.

This chapter is significant for pioneering the application of a Retrieval-Augmented Generation (RAG) pipeline in order to rectify the "actionability gap." Specifically, it constrained the use of a Generative Large Language Model (Gemini 2.5 Flash) with localised SHAP metrics associated with an "Empathetic Advisor" persona, taking raw numerical insufficiencies and transforming them into hyper-personalised, socio-emotionally intelligent interventions. Therefore, the EduTriage architecture demonstrates that AI in education can combine mathematical precision and human compassion through deliberate systems engineering.

7.2 Future Integration (STEAM 5.0): The Transition to Ambient Intelligence

The current version of the EduTriage Framework has made great strides in proactively intervening with students; however, it is constrained from achieving true predictive success by limitations associated with its current Data Ingestion layer. As it stands, the current measures of study_hours and sleep_quality come from multiple reporting surveys and limited, sporadic interactions through Learning Management Systems (LMS), where data is collected. This results in Self-Recalled data having a tendency to be biased through heuristic reasoning, decay of recollection ability (memory degradation) or good subject effect, which leads to students overestimating positive behaviours.

Moving forward, the next level of Predictive Fidelity, often described as Educational 5.0 or STEAM 5.0, requires that the current Data Ingestion Layer Architecture transition from Discrete Active Data Collection Model to a Continuous Passive Ambient Intelligence (AmI) Collection Model. The next iterations of the EduTriage

Framework will aim to directly connect to the pervasive computing infrastructure of the "Smart Campus" through the Internet of Things (IoT).

Instead of asking students to report if they attended class or how often they used a facility, future predictive layers might gather data through anonymised campus Wi-Fi router logs. The system can calculate precise physical attendance through triangulation of MAC address pings across the institution's network and could track how long a student spends in the campus library compared to their dormitory, as well as measure in real-time the transactional distance between a student and academic resources.

In addition, adding consumer-level biometric wearables such as smartwatches would provide even more unprecedented physiological data about an individual student. For example, rather than just categorising a student as sleeping poorly or well, the model could incorporate continuous biometric telemetry, including the actual sleep architecture (to differentiate duration spent in REM vs. SWS), heart rate variability (which is commonly believed to be a proxy for chronic academic stress) and localised chronotypes.

While this would exponentially increase the ensemble's predictive reach through ubiquitous data collection, it would also dramatically increase the ethical requirements outlined in Section 6. With the EduTriage system developing to include IoT and biometric telemetry, it will be imperative for institutional governance to create zero-trust data architectures and to provide explicit revocable consent protocols for student participation. For the future of STEAM 5.0 to succeed, it must not only depend on the ability to measure every aspect of a student's activity, but also on the wisdom behind using that ambient intelligence.

REFERENCES

Akgun, S., & Greenhow, C. (2022). Artificial intelligence in education: Addressing ethical challenges in K-12 settings. *AI and Ethics*, *2*(3), 431–440. DOI: 10.1007/s43681-021-00096-7 PMID: 34790956

Albugami, S., Almaghrabi, H., & Wali, A. (2024). From data to decision: Machine learning and explainable AI in student dropout prediction. *The Journal of Learning in Higher Education*, *2024*, 246301. Advance online publication. DOI: 10.5171/2024.246301

Baidoo-Anu, D., & Owusu Ansah, L. (2023). Education in the era of generative artificial intelligence (AI): Understanding the potential benefits of ChatGPT in promoting teaching and learning. *Journal of AI*, *7*(1), 52–62. DOI: 10.61969/jai.1337500

Baker, R. S., & Hawn, A. (2022). Algorithmic bias in education. *International Journal of Artificial Intelligence in Education*, *32*(4), 1052–1092. DOI: 10.1007/s40593-021-00285-9

Baker, R. S., Martin, T., & Rossi, L. M. (2016). Educational data mining and learning analytics. In Rupp, A. A., & Leighton, J. P. (Eds.), *The Wiley handbook of cognition and assessment: Frameworks, methodologies, and applications* (pp. 379–396). Wiley., DOI: 10.1002/9781118956588.ch16

Barocas, S., & Selbst, A. D. (2016). Big data's disparate impact. *SSRN*, *104*(3), 671–732. DOI: 10.2139/ssrn.2477899

. Bird, S., Dudík, M., Edgar, R., Horn, B., Lutz, R., Milan, V., Sameki, M., Wallach, H., & Walker, K. (2020). *Fairlearn: A toolkit for assessing and improving fairness in AI* (MSR-TR-2020-32). Microsoft.

Brown, T. B., Mann, B., Ryder, N., Subbiah, M., Kaplan, J. D., Dhariwal, P., Neelakantan, A., Shyam, P., Sastry, G., Askell, A., Agarwal, S., Herbert-Voss, A., Krueger, G., Henighan, T., Child, R., Ramesh, A., Ziegler, D. M., Wu, J., Winter, C., & Amodei, D. (2020). Language models are few-shot learners. *Advances in Neural Information Processing Systems*, *33*, 1877–1901.

Chen, T., & Guestrin, C. (2016, August). Xgboost: A scalable tree boosting system. In *Proceedings of the 22nd acm sigkdd international conference on knowledge discovery and data mining* (pp. 785-794).

Chen, X. (2013). *STEM Attrition: College Students' Paths into and out of STEM Fields. Statistical Analysis Report. NCES 2014-001*. National Center for Education Statistics.

Chi, M. T., & Wylie, R. (2014). The ICAP framework: Linking cognitive engagement to active learning outcomes. *Educational Psychologist*, *49*(4), 219–243. DOI: 10.1080/00461520.2014.965823

Conati, C., Porayska-Pomsta, K., & Mavrikis, M. (2018). *AI in education needs interpretable machine learning: Lessons from open learner modelling*. arXiv. https://doi.org//arXiv.1807.00154DOI: 10.48550

Credé, M., Roch, S. G., & Kieszczynka, U. M. (2010). Class attendance in college: A meta-analytic review of the relationship of class attendance with grades and student characteristics. *Review of Educational Research*, *80*(2), 272–295. DOI: 10.3102/0034654310362998

Feldman, M., Friedler, S. A., Moeller, J., Scheidegger, C., & Venkatasubramanian, S. (2015). Certifying and removing disparate impact. In *Proceedings of the 21st ACM SIGKDD International Conference on Knowledge Discovery and Data Mining* (pp. 259–268). Association for Computing Machinery. https://doi.org/DOI: 10.1145/2783258.2783311

Fischer, C., Pardos, Z. A., Baker, R. S., Williams, J. J., Smyth, P., Yu, R., & Warschauer, M. (2020). Mining big data in education: Affordances and challenges. *Review of Research in Education*, *44*(1), 130–160. DOI: 10.3102/0091732X20903304

Freeman, S., Eddy, S. L., McDonough, M., Smith, M. K., Okoroafor, N., Jordt, H., & Wenderoth, M. P. (2014). Active learning increases student performance in science, engineering, and mathematics. *Proceedings of the National Academy of Sciences of the United States of America*, *111*(23), 8410–8415. DOI: 10.1073/pnas.1319030111 PMID: 24821756

Gašević, D., Dawson, S., & Siemens, G. (2015). Let's not forget: Learning analytics are about learning. *TechTrends*, *59*(1), 64–71. DOI: 10.1007/s11528-014-0822-x

Grinsztajn, L., Oyallon, E., & Varoquaux, G. (2022). Why do tree-based models still outperform deep learning on typical tabular data? *Advances in Neural Information Processing Systems*, *35*, 507–520. DOI: 10.52202/068431-0037

Guidotti, R., Monreale, A., Ruggieri, S., Turini, F., Giannotti, F., & Pedreschi, D. (2018). A survey of methods for explaining black box models. *ACM Computing Surveys*, *51*(5), 93. Advance online publication. DOI: 10.1145/3236009

Gunning, D., Stefik, M., Choi, J., Miller, T., Stumpf, S., & Yang, G. Z. (2019). XAI—Explainable artificial intelligence. *Science Robotics*, *4*(37), eaay7120. DOI: 10.1126/scirobotics.aay7120 PMID: 33137719

Holmes, W., Bialik, M., & Fadel, C. (2019). *Artificial intelligence in education: Promises and implications for teaching and learning*. Center for Curriculum Redesign.

Karpicke, J. D. (2009). Metacognitive control and strategy selection: Deciding to practise retrieval during learning. *Journal of Experimental Psychology. General, 138*(4), 469–486. DOI: 10.1037/a0017341 PMID: 19883131

Kasneci, E., Seßler, K., Küchemann, S., Bannert, M., Dementieva, D., Fischer, F., Gasser, U., Groh, G., Günnemann, S., Hüllermeier, E., Krusche, S., Kutyniok, G., Michaeli, T., Nerdel, C., Pfeffer, J., Poquet, O., Sailer, M., Schmidt, A., Seidel, T., & Kasneci, G. (2023). ChatGPT for good? On opportunities and challenges of large language models for education. *Learning and Individual Differences, 103*, 102274. Advance online publication. DOI: 10.1016/j.lindif.2023.102274

Ke, G., Meng, Q., Finley, T., Wang, T., Chen, W., Ma, W., Ye, Q., & Liu, T.-Y. (2017). LightGBM: A highly efficient gradient boosting decision tree. *Advances in Neural Information Processing Systems, 30*, 3146–3154.

Khosravi, H., Shum, S. B., Chen, G., Conati, C., Tsai, Y.-S., Kay, J., Knight, S., Martinez-Maldonado, R., Sadiq, S., & Gašević, D. (2022). Explainable artificial intelligence in education. *Computers and Education: Artificial Intelligence, 3*, 100074. Advance online publication. DOI: 10.1016/j.caeai.2022.100074

Kizilcec, R. F., & Lee, H. (2022). Algorithmic fairness in education. In Holmes, W., & Porayska-Pomsta, K. (Eds.), *The ethics of artificial intelligence in education: Practices, challenges, and debates* (pp. 174–202). Routledge. DOI: 10.4324/9780429329067-10

Lewis, P., Perez, E., Piktus, A., Petroni, F., Karpukhin, V., Goyal, N., & Kiela, D. (2020). Retrieval-augmented generation for knowledge-intensive nlp tasks. *Advances in Neural Information Processing Systems, 33*, 9459–9474.

Lundberg, S. M., Erion, G., Chen, H., DeGrave, A., Prutkin, J. M., Nair, B., Katz, R., Himmelfarb, J., Bansal, N., & Lee, S. I. (2020). From local explanations to global understanding with explainable AI for trees. *Nature Machine Intelligence, 2*(1), 56–67. DOI: 10.1038/s42256-019-0138-9 PMID: 32607472

Lundberg, S. M., & Lee, S.-I. (2017). A unified approach to interpreting model predictions. *Advances in Neural Information Processing Systems, 30*, 4765–4774.

. Molnar, C. (2020). *Interpretable machine learning: A guide for making black box models explainable*. Lulu.com.

Moore, M. G. (2013). The theory of transactional distance. In Moore, M. G. (Ed.), *Handbook of distance education* (3rd ed., pp. 66–85). Routledge. DOI: 10.4324/9780203803738.ch5

Nemorin, S. (2026). Towards decolonising the ethics of AI in education. *Globalisation, Societies and Education, 24*(4), 1260–1272. DOI: 10.1080/14767724.2024.2333821

Perrotta, C., & Selwyn, N. (2020). Deep learning goes to school: Toward a relational understanding of AI in education. *Learning, Media and Technology, 45*(3), 251–269. DOI: 10.1080/17439884.2020.1686017

Popenici, S. A., & Kerr, S. (2017). Exploring the impact of artificial intelligence on teaching and learning in higher education. *Research and Practice in Technology Enhanced Learning, 12*(1), 22. DOI: 10.1186/s41039-017-0062-8 PMID: 30595727

Prinsloo, P., & Slade, S. (2014). Educational triage in open distance learning: Walking a moral tightrope. *International Review of Research in Open and Distance Learning, 15*(4), 306–331. DOI: 10.19173/irrodl.v15i4.1881

Prinsloo, P., & Slade, S. (2016). Student vulnerability, agency and learning analytics: An exploration. *Journal of Learning Analytics, 3*(1), 159–182. DOI: 10.18608/jla.2016.31.10

Prokhorenkova, L., Gusev, G., Vorobev, A., Dorogush, A. V., & Gulin, A. (2018). CatBoost: Unbiased boosting with categorical features. *Advances in Neural Information Processing Systems*, •••, 31.

Romero, C., & Ventura, S. (2020). Educational data mining and learning analytics: An updated survey. *Wiley Interdisciplinary Reviews. Data Mining and Knowledge Discovery, 10*(3), e1355. DOI: 10.1002/widm.1355

Rudin, C. (2019). Stop explaining black box machine learning models for high stakes decisions and use interpretable models instead. *Nature Machine Intelligence, 1*(5), 206–215. DOI: 10.1038/s42256-019-0048-x PMID: 35603010

Shapley, L. S. (1953). A value for n-person games. In Kuhn, H. W., & Tucker, A. W. (Eds.), *Contributions to the theory of games II* (pp. 307–317). Princeton University Press., DOI: 10.1515/9781400881970-018

Siemens, G., & Baker, R. S. J. d. (2012). Learning analytics and educational data mining: Towards communication and collaboration. In *Proceedings of the 2nd International Conference on Learning Analytics and Knowledge* (pp. 252–254). Association for Computing Machinery. https://doi.org/DOI: 10.1145/2330601.2330661

Skittou, M., Merrouchi, M., & Gadi, T. (2024). Development of an early warning system to support educational planning process by identifying at-risk students. *IEEE Access : Practical Innovations, Open Solutions, 12*, 2260–2271. DOI: 10.1109/ACCESS.2023.3348091

Sweller, J. (2011). Cognitive load theory. In Ross, B. H. (Ed.), *Psychology of learning and motivation* (Vol. 55, pp. 37–76). Academic Press., DOI: 10.1016/B978-0-12-387691-1.00002-8

Swiecki, Z., Khosravi, H., Chen, G., Martinez-Maldonado, R., Lodge, J. M., Milligan, S., Selwyn, N., & Gašević, D. (2022). Assessment in the age of artificial intelligence. *Computers and Education: Artificial Intelligence, 3*, 100075. Advance online publication. DOI: 10.1016/j.caeai.2022.100075

Verbert, K., Duval, E., Klerkx, J., Govaerts, S., & Santos, J. L. (2013). Learning analytics dashboard applications. *The American Behavioral Scientist, 57*(10), 1500–1509. DOI: 10.1177/0002764213479363

Wolpert, D. H. (1992). Stacked generalization. *Neural Networks, 5*(2), 241–259. DOI: 10.1016/S0893-6080(05)80023-1 PMID: 18276425

Zawacki-Richter, O., Marín, V. I., Bond, M., & Gouverneur, F. (2019). Systematic review of research on artificial intelligence applications in higher education–where are the educators? *International Journal of Educational Technology in Higher Education, 16*(1), 39. DOI: 10.1186/s41239-019-0171-0

Zhai, X., Chu, X., Chai, C. S., Jong, M. S.-Y., Istenic, A., Spector, M., Liu, J.-B., Yuan, J., & Li, Y. (2021). A review of artificial intelligence (AI) in education from 2010 to 2020. *Complexity, 2021*(1), 8812542. Advance online publication. DOI: 10.1155/2021/8812542

Zheng, Y., Li, G., Li, Y., Shan, C., & Cheng, R. (2017). Truth inference in crowdsourcing: Is the problem solved? *Proceedings of the VLDB Endowment International Conference on Very Large Data Bases, 10*(5), 541–552. DOI: 10.14778/3055540.3055547

Zimmerman, B. J. (2002). Becoming a self-regulated learner: An overview. *Theory into Practice, 41*(2), 64–70. DOI: 10.1207/s15430421tip4102_2

Chapter 9
Verifiable Synthetic Educational Ecosystems for Topology-Aware STEAM:
Learning Analytics and Adaptive Tutoring

Jaime Aguilar-Ortiz
http://orcid.org/0009-0003-5302-1454
Universidad Politécnica de Pachuca, Mexico

Ocotlán Diáz-Parra
Universidad Politécnica de Pachuca, Mexico

Marco A. Vera-Jiménez
http://orcid.org/0009-0009-3712-1440
Universidad Politécnica de Pachuca, Mexico

Víctor M. Zamudio-García
http://orcid.org/0000-0002-4660-8025
Universidad Politécnica Metropolitana de Hidalgo, Mexico

Carlos R. Domínguez-Mayorga
http://orcid.org/0009-0007-1018-4412
Universidad Politécnica de Pachuca, Mexico

DOI: 10.4018/979-8-3373-9675-0.ch009

ABSTRACT

This chapter proposes a verifier-guided framework for synthetic educational ecosystems in STEAM learning analytics and illustrates it with a topology-aware prototype for adaptive tutoring and recommendations. Its central claim is that generated educational traces should be used only when their educational meaning, structural fidelity, subgroup behaviour, explanation stability, calibration, privacy, and responsible-use limits can be checked. Quality is treated as a multi-objective problem, and generation follows a conservative cycle: each candidate dataset must pass verifier gates before supporting modelling, benchmarking, or experimentation. The empirical work is bounded: it uses a controlled synthetic environment, not real institutional dropout records; therefore, dropout risk is framed as a future high-stakes validation horizon, not as a demonstrated deployment result. The framework closes with a governance-ready verifier report for human review, allowing synthetic data to serve as auditable infrastructure rather than as an opaque substitute for protected student records.

1. INTRODUCTION

1.1. Verifiable Synthetic Educational Ecosystems for STEAM Learning Analytics

STEAM learning ecosystems generate dense traces of participation, performance, pacing, help-seeking, and disengagement across learning management systems, laboratories, coding environments, immersive spaces, assessments, attendance tools, and institutional databases. These traces create opportunities for early support, yet they also intensify long-standing concerns in learning analytics: privacy limits access, adverse events are sparse, and predictive patterns change across cohorts, courses, and institutional designs (Ferguson, 2012; Siemens, 2013; Macfadyen & Dawson, 2010; Gasevic et al., 2016; Yan et al., 2024).

This difficulty is especially visible in dropout prediction. The adverse event is usually rare, labels may be delayed or noisy, and many predictors are indirect proxies derived from incomplete interactions, assessment behaviour, or missingness patterns. A model may therefore seem accurate overall while still failing in the dimensions that matter for intervention: calibration, minority-class detection, subgroup reliability, and transfer to new cohorts. In high-stakes educational settings, these weaknesses directly affect who receives support, who is overlooked, and how institutional resources are allocated.

Synthetic data can enlarge the effective sample for rare events, support benchmarking, and enable collaboration when raw student records cannot be shared. However, synthesis is neither automatically safe nor automatically educationally valid. A generated table may reproduce marginal distributions while breaking the dependencies required for prediction, explanation, or intervention; conversely, it may preserve downstream utility while exposing learners through memorisation, nearest-neighbour similarity, or membership inference. Release decisions should rely on documented verification rather than visual plausibility or informal resemblance (Yale et al., 2020; Goncalves et al., 2020; El Emam et al., 2020; van Breugel, Qian, & van der Schaar, 2023; van Breugel, Sun, Qian, & van der Schaar, 2023). Verification also changes the editorial status of the method: synthetic generation is presented as a claim to be audited, not as a self-evident technical advance.

Accordingly, the chapter treats synthetic generation as support infrastructure for trustworthy STEAM analytics, not as a shortcut around governance. Its value lies in enabling experimentation, comparison, and model development under educational, statistical, ethical, and privacy constraints that can be inspected by researchers, designers, administrators, and compliance stakeholders. Release decisions should record preserved educational relations, audited groups, privacy evidence, and intended-use limits.

1.2. Research Gap, Chapter Objective, and Contribution

Research on synthetic educational data has expanded, and learning-analytics studies show that synthetic tabular records can contribute to privacy-preserving research and model development (Berg et al., 2016; Liu et al., 2024; Liu et al., 2025; Khalil et al., 2025). Yet many evaluations still emphasize surface fidelity, a single downstream task, or limited privacy evidence. Less attention is given to explainable risk modelling, subgroup reliability, calibration, governance reporting, and cross-cohort reproducibility.

A second gap lies in verification logic. Candidate datasets are often accepted after generic fidelity checks or synthetic-to-synthetic evaluation, although such evidence can exaggerate practical usefulness. Train-on-synthetic/test-on-real protocols provide a stricter test of whether generated records preserve structures needed for real deployment (Liu et al., 2024; Xu et al., 2019; Kotelnikov et al., 2023; van Breugel, Qian, & van der Schaar, 2023). In education, temporal drift, policy change, and cohort variation require multi-axis, deployment-sensitive, and auditable verification.

To address these gaps, the chapter develops a verifier-guided framework for synthetic educational ecosystems in explainable STEAM learning analytics and evaluates it through a topology-aware adaptive tutoring and recommendation prototype. The prototype is not a production dropout-risk model; it is a controlled verification test bed that examines whether generated educational traces preserve curricular order, subgroup-visible behaviour, explanation-oriented structure, and governance-ready reporting. Dropout-risk assessment remains a high-stakes application horizon for future institutional validation.

The proposal makes three linked contributions. First, it establishes a theoretical foundation that connects synthesis with explainability, fairness, privacy, and ethical assessment. Second, it specifies a methodology in which verifier metrics guide conservative generator updates through explicit rewards and curriculum thresholds. Third, it provides a reproducible computational architecture for creating, auditing, and reporting synthetic educational data for benchmarking and human-in-the-loop risk modelling. The practical gain is a verifier report where evidence, subgroup cautions, release conditions, and unsupported assumptions are recorded for review.

Figure 1. Verifier-guided synthetic-data workflow for STEAM learning analytics

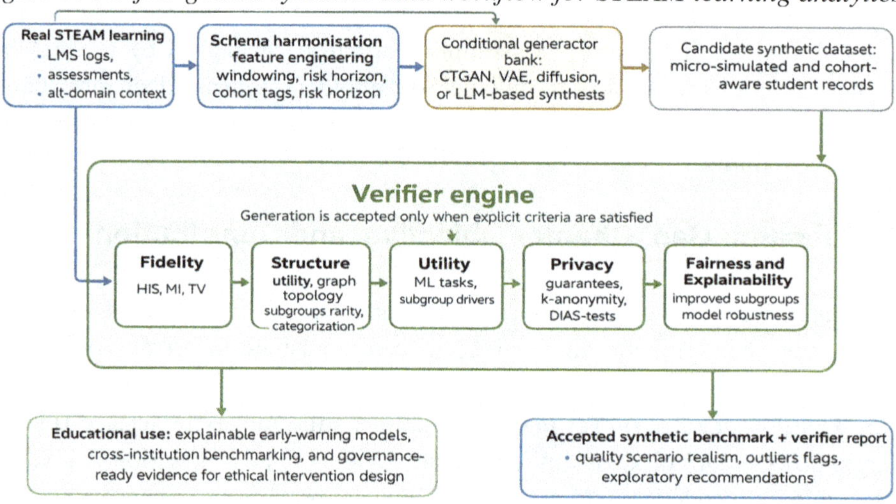

Figure 1 summarizes the chapter workflow from real educational data, controlled synthetic traces, and feature engineering to conditional generation, verifier-based acceptance, governance-ready reporting, and explainable ethical intervention support.

2. THEORETICAL FOUNDATIONS

2.1. Learning Analytics, Rare Events, and Cross-Institutional Generalization

The theoretical starting point is the representation of the educational prediction problem itself. Let the real educational dataset be defined as in (1):

$$\mathscr{D}^{(r)} = \{(x_i, y_i, a_i, c_i)\}_{i=1}^{N}. \tag{1}$$

Here, $\mathscr{D}^{(r)}$ denotes the real dataset available within an institution; $x_i \in \mathbb{R}^p$ is the p-dimensional feature vector for learner i; $y_i \in \{0, 1\}$ is the dropout or non-completion indicator within the intervention horizon; a_i denotes subgroup or fairness-relevant descriptors such as gender, program, entry route, or other audited contextual attributes; and c_i identifies the cohort, course, time period, or deployment context. The notation prevents dropout prediction from being framed as a context-free classification exercise and instead treats risk as a temporally and institutionally situated educational problem in which fairness, governance, and generalisation are built into the formalism from the beginning.

Given this dataset, the risk model used for early warning is naturally expressed as a conditional probability function in (2):

$$\hat{p}_i = P_\psi(Y_i = 1 \mid X_i = x_i, A_i = a_i, C_i = c_i), \tag{2}$$

where ψ denotes the parameters of the predictive model. The quantity $\hat{p}_i$ is the predicted probability that learner i will experience the adverse event under consideration, such as withdrawal or non-completion; P_ψ emphasises that the probability is model-based and depends on fitted parameters; and the conditioning on X_i, A_i, and C_i makes explicit that the prediction task is shaped both by student features and by their educational context. The equation is central because explainable early-warning systems should provide calibrated probabilities rather than opaque scores, especially when institutions must decide which learners to contact under limited intervention capacity (van Calster et al., 2019; Riley et al., 2024).

Rare-event structure enters through the class prevalence in (3):

$$\pi_r = \frac{1}{N}\sum_{i=1}^{N} y_i. \tag{3}$$

The scalar π_r is the empirical prevalence of dropout in the real data. When π_r is small, the educational task becomes imbalanced, and conventional models may overfit the majority class, underestimate risk probabilities, or yield poor recall for the minority outcome. This quantity matters in the present chapter because one of the main motivations for synthetic generation is to make rare-event modelling more stable without resorting only to simplistic oversampling heuristics.

However, imbalance is not the only challenge. Educational prediction is also exposed to cohort and domain shift. A formal way to represent this is through a distributional discrepancy across contexts in (4):

$$\Delta_{\text{shift}}(c, c') = d(P(X, Y \mid C = c), P(X, Y \mid C = c')), \tag{4}$$

where $d(\cdot\,,\cdot)$ denotes a chosen discrepancy measure between conditional distributions.

The term $\Delta_{\text{shift}}(c, c')$ measures how much the joint learning problem changes between two contexts c and c'; $P(X, Y \mid C = c)$ represents the feature-label distribution in one cohort or course, while $P(X, Y \mid C = c')$ represents the corresponding distribution elsewhere. This discrepancy term is consequential because cross-institutional or cross-cohort reproducibility depends not only on sample size but on how well educational structure survives distributional variation. Synthetic generation has value only when it supports models that remain meaningful under realistic shift rather than only under an in-sample setting.

Taken together, these equations place explainability and ethics inside the data-generation problem itself. Explanation cannot be postponed until after model fitting, and ethical review cannot be reduced to privacy compliance. Both depend on the evidential quality of the data used for modelling. If generation distorts prevalence, breaks dependencies, or amplifies subgroup asymmetries, later explanatory methods can at best describe the damage, not undo it. The governing task is to create trustworthy data for calibrated, fair, and pedagogically defensible risk estimation in STEAM environments (Slade & Prinsloo, 2013; Deho et al., 2022; Pham et al., 2025).

2.2. Verifiable Synthetic Data Generation as a Multi-Objective Problem

Let the synthetic generator be defined abstractly as a conditional map that produces candidate synthetic records from latent noise and conditioning information in (5):

$$\widetilde{\mathcal{D}}_\theta = \left\{\left(\tilde{x}_j, \tilde{y}_j, \tilde{a}_j, \tilde{c}_j\right)\right\}_{j=1}^{M}, \quad \left(\tilde{x}_j, \tilde{y}_j, \tilde{a}_j, \tilde{c}_j\right) \sim G_\theta\left(z_j, u_j\right). \tag{5}$$

Here, $\widetilde{\mathcal{D}}_\theta$ denotes the synthetic dataset generated under parameters θ; M is the number of synthetic records; z_j is a latent noise vector; and u_j is a conditioning signal that may encode the target label, cohort, subgroup, or other synthesis constraints.

The notation is intentionally generator-agnostic so that the framework can accommodate CTGAN-like models, variational autoencoders, diffusion-based tabular generators, or large-language-model approaches to structured synthesis (Xu et al., 2019; Kotelnikov et al., 2023). The abstraction keeps the framework focused on verifiable synthesis rather than allegiance to a single generator family.

The key theoretical move is to define synthetic quality as a vector rather than a single score in (6):

$$\mathrm{v}\left(\widetilde{\mathscr{D}}_{\theta};\mathscr{D}^{(r)}\right) = \left(F, S, U, R_{\text{priv}}, \Delta_{\text{fair}}, X\right). \tag{6}$$

The vector v collects six quality dimensions: marginal fidelity F, structural fidelity S, downstream utility U, privacy risk R_{priv}, fairness deviation Δ_{fair}, and explanation stability X. A multi-objective representation prevents synthetic educational data should not be approved on the basis of one criterion alone. A dataset can have high marginal resemblance but poor predictive value, high predictive value but unacceptable exposure risk, or strong overall utility but unstable subgroup behaviour. The framework treats verification as a vector-valued audit problem. Table 1 summarizes the verifier axes used throughout the chapter.

Table 1. Verifier axes used throughout the chapter

Verifier axis	Representative indicators	Educational interpretation
Fidelity	Kolmogorov-Smirnov distance, normalised 1-Wasserstein distance, total variation	Preserves the observed distributions of engagement, assessment, and contextual variables.
Structural fidelity	Correlation-matrix similarity, subgroup association stability	Preserves multivariate dependencies that matter for dropout prediction and explanation.
Utility	TSTR, TATR, PR-AUC, calibration-aware utility	Supports downstream modelling on held-out real cohorts under realistic deployment conditions.
Privacy	Nearest-neighbour exposure, membership-inference advantage	Limits direct or indirect disclosure risk for real learners.
Fairness	Equal opportunity gap, subgroup calibration gap	Avoids group-specific degradation in risk estimation or intervention quality.
Explainability	Rank stability of feature importance or explanation patterns	Preserves interpretable drivers of risk across real-trained and synthetic-trained models.

Verifier-gate rule. For an auditable release, marginal fidelity should reach at least 0.85; structural similarity, 0.80; subgroup structural stability, 0.75; TSTR utility, at least 0.80 of the real-data baseline or loss no larger than 0.05; expected calibration error, no greater than 0.05; Brier increase, no greater than 0.02; nearest-neighbour exposure, no greater than 0.01; membership-inference advantage, no greater than

0.05; equal-opportunity gap, no greater than 0.10; subgroup calibration gap, no greater than 0.05; and explanation stability, at least 0.60 by Kendall tau or 0.70 by top-5 overlap. Metrics not implemented in the present topology-aware prototype are reported as not evaluated and are not used to justify release for dropout-risk assessment.

Marginal fidelity can be defined through a combined score over continuous and categorical variables in (7):

$$F = 1 - \left[\frac{1}{p_c}\sum_{j\in\mathscr{C}}\left(\alpha KS_j + (1-\alpha)\widetilde{W}_{1,j}\right) + \frac{1}{p_d}\sum_{j\in\mathscr{D}} TV_j\right]. \tag{7}$$

The set $\mathscr{C}$ contains continuous features and $\mathscr{D}$ contains discrete or categorical features; $p_c = |\mathscr{C}|$ and $p_d = |\mathscr{D}|$ are their counts; KS_j is the Kolmogorov-Smirnov distance for feature j; $\widetilde{W}_{1,j}$ is a normalised 1-Wasserstein distance that captures scale and tail differences; TV_j is the total variation distance for categorical feature j; and $\alpha \in [0,1]$ weights the two continuous-feature terms. The score is close to one when the synthetic marginals resemble the real ones. The score captures features of the educational distribution that averages often miss: tails, sparsity, and missingness-related shape differences.

Preserving marginals is not enough, so the framework also defines structural fidelity through association stability in (8):

$$S = 1 - \left[\lambda_1 \frac{\| R^{(r)} - R^{(s)} \|_F}{\| R^{(r)} \|_F + \varepsilon} + \lambda_2 \sum_{g\in\mathscr{G}} \omega_g \frac{\| R_g^{(r)} - R_g^{(s)} \|_F}{\| R_g^{(r)} \|_F + \varepsilon}\right]. \tag{8}$$

In this expression, $R^{(r)}$ and $R^{(s)}$ are global dependence matrices estimated from real and synthetic data, respectively; $R_g^{(r)}$ and $R_g^{(s)}$ are the corresponding subgroup-specific dependence matrices for group g; $\| \cdot \|_F$ is the Frobenius norm; ω_g weights each subgroup; and $\lambda_1, \lambda_2 \geq 0$ balance global versus subgroup structural preservation. The formulation targets a frequent failure mode in educational synthesis: individual variables may look plausible even when the relationships among engagement, assessment, lateness, attendance, or contextual factors are broken.

Downstream utility is defined through deployment-oriented performance, especially train-on-synthetic/test-on-real evaluation in (9):

$$U_{\text{TSTR}} = \frac{1}{|\mathscr{M}|}\sum_{m\in\mathscr{M}} \phi\left(f_m(\mathscr{T}^{\text{train}}), \mathscr{D}^{\text{test}}_{\text{real}}\right), \quad U_{\text{rel}} = \frac{U_{\text{TSTR}}}{U_{\text{TRTR}} + \varepsilon}. \tag{9}$$

The set contains the model families used for evaluation; is the fitted model of type ; denotes the selected performance functional; is the mean synthetic-to-real utility across models; and compares it to the real-data baseline . The test is deliberately demanding: a synthetic dataset is judged by whether it supports performance on held-out real data, not by whether it behaves well on its own generated distribution (van Breugel, Qian, & van der Schaar, 2023; Liu et al., 2024).

Privacy risk is modelled as a combination of exposure-style and attack-style terms in (10):

$$R_{\text{priv}} = \eta_1 R_{\text{NN}} + \eta_2 \text{Adv}_{\text{MIA}}, \tag{10}$$

with

$$R_{\text{NN}} = \frac{1}{M}\sum_{j=1}^{M} 1\left\{ \min_{i \le N} d(\tilde{x}_j, x_i) \le \tau \right\}, \tag{10a}$$

and

$$\text{Adv}_{\text{MIA}} = |\Pr(\hat{m} = 1 \mid m = 1) - \Pr(\hat{m} = 1 \mid m = 0)|. \tag{10b}$$

The coefficient pair weights nearest-neighbour exposure and membership-inference risk; measures the fraction of synthetic records that are too close to at least one real record under threshold ; is the distance used for disclosure analysis; and measures how much better than chance an attacker can identify whether a real record was present in the training data. These quantities matter because educational privacy cannot be assessed through de-identification rhetoric alone. A synthetic dataset may contain no direct identifiers and still expose vulnerable or unusual students if the generator memorises or overfits uncommon patterns (El Emam et al., 2020; van Breugel, Sun, Qian, & van der Schaar, 2023; Liu et al., 2025).

The verifier must then aggregate the individual objectives into a reward used to guide generation in (11):

$$\mathcal{R}\left(\mathcal{\tilde{D}}_\theta\right) = w_F F + w_S S + w_U U_{\text{rel}} + w_X X - w_P R_{\text{priv}} - w_B \Delta_{\text{fair}}. \tag{11}$$

The coefficients w_F, w_S, w_U, w_X, w_P, and w_B express the institutional or research priorities assigned to each dimension. Positive weights reward desirable properties, whereas privacy risk and fairness deviation enter with negative sign because lower values are preferable. This reward is not intended to eliminate the need for human review; rather, it structures the search process so that candidate datasets improve according to explicit governance-relevant criteria.

Finally, acceptance is defined through a hard gate rather than a purely compensatory score in (12):

$$\mathbb{A}\left(\widetilde{\mathscr{D}}_\theta\right) = 1\left\{F \geq \tau_F, S \geq \tau_S, U_{\text{rel}} \geq \tau_U, R_{\text{priv}} \leq \tau_P, \Delta_{\text{fair}} \leq \tau_B, X \geq \tau_X\right\}. \quad (12)$$

The thresholds $\tau_F, \tau_S, \tau_U, \tau_P, \tau_B$, and τ_X specify minimum acceptable levels for fidelity, structure, utility, privacy, fairness, and explanation stability. The function $\mathbb{A}(\cdot)$ returns one only if all conditions are met. The gate operationalises an auditable acceptance principle: generated artefacts are not trusted by narrative plausibility, but by explicit, inspectable, and reportable verification criteria. In the educational setting, this principle becomes a governance mechanism aligned with dataset documentation and model-reporting practices (Gebru et al., 2021; Mitchell et al., 2019). The hard gate prevents a strong score on one metric from masking weak privacy, fairness, or explanation evidence.

2.3. Explainability, Fairness, Privacy, and Ethical Assessment

Explainable AI for STEAM education must test more than the visual plausibility of tabular records. It must examine whether generated data preserve the reasons a model uses to identify risk. The framework captures that requirement through explanation stability, defined as an agreement score between models trained on real data and models trained on synthetic data in (13):

$$X = \frac{1}{|\mathscr{M}|}\sum_{m\in\mathscr{M}}\frac{1 + \tau_K\left(\text{rank}(I_m^{(r)}), \text{rank}(I_m^{(s)})\right)}{2}. \quad (13)$$

The vector $I_m^{(r)}$ denotes the feature-importance or explanation profile extracted from model family m when trained on real data, whereas $I_m^{(s)}$ is the corresponding profile from synthetic data; rank$(\cdot)$ transforms each profile into a ranking; and τ_K is Kendall's rank correlation, rescaled to the unit interval. The score is high when the synthetic data preserve the explanatory ordering of salient risk drivers such as missing submissions, low assessment performance, activity decline, or delayed participation. The metric anchors legitimacy: early-warning systems must justify not only whom they flag, but also whether the reasons they provide remain pedagogically coherent.

Probability quality is captured by calibration. The Brier score is written as in (14):

$$BS = \frac{1}{n}\sum_{i=1}^{n}(\hat{p}_i - y_i)^2, \quad (14)$$

and the expected calibration error as in (15):

$$ECE = \sum_{b=1}^{B} \frac{|B_b|}{n} |\text{acc}(B_b) - \text{conf}(B_b)|. \tag{15}$$

In both expressions, n is the number of evaluated real cases, $\hat{p}_i$ is the predicted dropout probability, y_i is the observed outcome, and B_b is the set of predictions falling into bin b. The function $\text{acc}(B_b)$ gives empirical accuracy in bin b, whereas $\text{conf}(B_b)$ gives the average predicted confidence. These quantities are essential because an institution acts on probabilities, not on ranking alone. A model that is discriminative but miscalibrated may produce too many false alarms or miss genuinely vulnerable students, which undermines the ethical quality of automated assessment and support.

Fairness cannot be addressed by one metric only, but equal opportunity disparity gives a clear first diagnostic in (16):

$$\Delta_{\text{EO}} = \max_{g,g' \in \mathcal{G}} |TPR_g - TPR_{g'}|. \tag{16}$$

This can be paired with a subgroup calibration deviation as in (17)

$$\Delta_{\text{Cal}} = \max_{g \in \mathcal{G}} |ECE_g - ECE|, \ \Delta_{\text{fair}} = \gamma_1 \Delta_{\text{EO}} + \gamma_2 \Delta_{\text{Cal}}. \tag{17}$$

The set $\mathcal{G}$ contains audited subgroups; TPR_g is the true-positive rate for group g; ECE_g is the expected calibration error computed within that subgroup; and γ_1 ,$\gamma_2 \geq 0$ weight classification disparity and calibration disparity. The definition directs attention to a non-negotiable condition of ethical learning analytics: global performance should not be preserved by shifting errors toward specific groups. Since synthetic data can inadvertently smooth away minority patterns or exaggerate spurious associations, subgroup-sensitive fairness auditing is integral to the verifier rather than an optional afterthought (Hardt et al., 2016; Chouldechova, 2017; Deho et al., 2022; Pham et al., 2025).

Decision support in education is also capacity-constrained. Institutions typically cannot intervene with every student simultaneously, which makes budget-sensitive evaluation part of validity. A natural metric is recall at alert budget q in (18):

$$\text{Recall@}q = \frac{\sum_{i=1}^{n} 1\{\hat{p}_i \geq c_q \wedge y_i = 1\}}{\sum_{i=1}^{n} 1\{y_i = 1\}}, \tag{18}$$

where c_q is the threshold that selects the top q proportion of cases.

A complementary decision metric, consistent with decision-curve evaluation, is net benefit (Vickers & Holland, 2021) in (19):

$$NB(c) = \frac{TP(c)}{n} - \frac{FP(c)}{n}\frac{c}{1-c}. \tag{19}$$

In the first expression, c_q is the threshold that respects intervention capacity; in the second, $TP(c)$ and $FP(c)$ are the true and false positives obtained at decision threshold c. These metrics matter because ethically responsible analytics must be evaluated under operational constraints. The educational meaning of a model depends on how it supports real intervention policy, not just on its abstract classification performance. Within the present chapter, these measures ensure that the synthetic-data framework remains tied to actionable and human-supervised support rather than to detached benchmark optimisation.

3. METHODOLOGY

3.1. Data Representation, Temporal Feature Engineering, and Generator-Verifier Design

The methodological design constructs a learner representation suitable for both synthesis and explainable risk modelling. The assumed dataset integrates institutional records, learning management systems, assessment platforms, and other STEAM educational sources. Features are grouped into contextual variables, engagement variables, assessment variables, and governance-sensitive descriptors for fairness or drift auditing. Because early-warning systems are temporal, the framework combines cumulative indicators with recent behavioural momentum through windowed or exponentially weighted summaries.

For a time-indexed behavioural signal $e_{i\ell t}$ associated with learner i, indicator ℓ, and time point t, the chapter defines an exponentially weighted summary as in (20):

$$e_{i\ell}^{(\alpha)} = \sum_{t=1}^{T_i} \alpha^{T_i - t} e_{i\ell t}, \; 0 < \alpha \leq 1. \tag{20}$$

Operational Reading

The variable $e_{i\ell t}$ denotes the observed value of engagement indicator ℓ at time t; T_i is the last observed time index for learner i within the risk horizon; and α controls the decay rate, assigning more weight to recent activity when α is close to one. This transformation is analytically warranted because dropout risk is rarely determined by historical totals alone. Recent decline, sustained lateness, or repeated inactivity often carry more educational meaning than distant behaviour.

Before synthesis, the feature space is robustly scaled to reduce the influence of extreme values in (21):

$$x'_{ij} = \frac{x_{ij} - \text{med}\left(x_{\cdot j}\right)}{IQR\left(x_{\cdot j}\right) + \delta}. \tag{21}$$

Scaling Rationale

Here, x_{ij} is the original value of feature j for learner i; $\text{med}\left(x_{\cdot j}\right)$ is the sample median of feature j; $IQR\left(x_{\cdot j}\right)$ is the interquartile range; and $\delta > 0$ is a small constant used to avoid division by zero. The transformation stabilises synthesis because educational data often contain long tails, extreme activity bursts, or sparse counts. Robust scaling stabilises synthesis and later evaluation without erasing meaningful ordinal structure.

Missingness is not treated as a nuisance to be silently imputed away. Instead, it is explicitly encoded as in (22):

$$m_{ij} = 1\left\{x_{ij} \text{ is missing}\right\}. \tag{22}$$

Missingness Rationale

The indicator m_{ij} equals one when feature j is unavailable for learner i. In learning analytics, missing values themselves may be educationally meaningful, representing non-submission, non-participation, incomplete trace collection, or contextual irregularity. The framework models missingness as both signal and uncertainty. This choice is especially consequential for synthetic generation, because a synthetic dataset that reproduces values but erases missingness structure may substantially distort both utility and fairness.

To make synthetic generation responsive to class imbalance, the chapter defines a target positive-class prevalence for the synthetic data in (23):

$$\pi_s = (1 - \gamma)\pi_r + \gamma\pi^\star, \ 0 \leq \gamma \leq 1. \tag{23}$$

Prevalence Design

The prevalence π_r is the observed dropout rate in the real data, $\pi^\star$ is a desired target prevalence chosen for rare-event modelling, and γ controls the extent to which the synthetic dataset moves toward that target. The specification makes explicit that synthetic data do not need to mirror the original class ratio in every experimental setting. In some cases, synthetic generation is used to construct minority-aware augmentations, and the framework must document that design choice transparently.

At iteration k of the generation process, the candidate dataset is written as in (24)

$$\tilde{\mathcal{D}}^{(k)} = G_{\theta_k}(Z, U \; ; \pi_s), \tag{24}$$

where Z denotes sampled latent noise and U denotes the conditioning information supplied to the generator.

The parameters are then updated through a conservative verifier-guided objective in (25):

$$\theta_{k+1} = \arg\max_{\theta} \mathbb{E}\left[\mathcal{R}(\tilde{\mathcal{D}}^{(k)})\right] - \beta D_{KL}\left(\pi_\theta \,\|\, \pi_{\theta_k}\right). \tag{25}$$

Update Logic

In this update, $\mathcal{R}(\cdot)$ is the verifier reward introduced in the theory section, $\beta \geq 0$ controls the penalty on abrupt policy changes, and $D_{KL}\left(\pi_\theta \,\|\, \pi_{\theta_k}\right)$ measures the divergence between successive generator policies. The purpose of the KL penalty is to discourage unstable jumps that might exploit one verifier axis while damaging another. This constitutes one of the chapter's main methodological adaptations from verifier-guided generation research: rather than changing the generator aggressively after each candidate, it imposes conservative movement so that improvements remain auditable and less vulnerable to reward hacking.

To avoid premature over-constraining of the generator, thresholds are introduced through a curriculum in (26):

$$\tau_j^{(k)} = \tau_j^{(0)} + \frac{k}{K}\left(\tau_j^{(K)} - \tau_j^{(0)}\right), \; j \in \left\{F, S, U, P, B, X\right\}. \tag{26}$$

Threshold Schedule

The notation $\tau_j^{(k)}$ denotes the threshold for verifier dimension j at iteration k; $\tau_j^{(0)}$ is the initial relaxed threshold; $\tau_j^{(K)}$ is the final stricter threshold; and K is the number of curriculum stages. The schedule permits diversity and exploration early in training while ensuring that accepted synthetic datasets gradually satisfy more demanding educational, privacy, and governance criteria. In practice, the curriculum may begin by prioritising global fidelity and utility, then progressively tighten subgroup fairness, explanation stability, and privacy stress tests.

A distinctive methodological feature is the separation between generator flexibility and verifier stability. The generator family may vary, but the verifier remains fixed, explicit, and reportable. This allows institutions with different technical resources to adopt different synthesis models while preserving a common acceptance logic. The design is appropriate for STEAM education, where infrastructures and governance rules differ, yet trustworthy benchmarking requires shared evaluation standards (Liu et al., 2024; Khalil et al., 2025).

3.2. Verification Metrics, Predictive Evaluation, and Deployment Protocol

The evaluation protocol is deliberately deployment-oriented. Since the chapter addresses early warning and ethical support in real educational settings, it preserves temporal or cohort causality by training on earlier or older contexts and testing on later or unseen ones. A basic temporal split may be written as in (27):

$$\mathscr{D}^{(r)}_{\text{train}} = \{(x_i, y_i) : c_i \leq \tau\}, \ \mathscr{D}^{(r)}_{\text{test}} = \{(x_i, y_i) : c_i > \tau\}, \tag{27}$$

where τ is the final training cohort or time boundary.

Temporal Reading

The symbol τ is the cut-off separating available training data from future evaluation data. The split respects the operational fact that institutions never train with knowledge from the future cohort they hope to support. Temporal validity is a methodological requirement, not a cosmetic design choice.

Within this split, the framework compares three predictive conditions. The first is the real-data baseline (28),

$$\text{TRTR} = \phi\left(f\left(\mathscr{D}^{(r)}_{\text{train}}\right), \mathscr{D}^{(r)}_{\text{test}}\right). \tag{28}$$

The second is synthetic-to-real transfer (29),

$$\text{TSTR} = \phi\left(f\left(\widetilde{\mathscr{D}}_{\text{train}}\right), \mathscr{D}^{(r)}_{\text{test}}\right). \tag{29}$$

The third is real-plus-synthetic augmentation (30),

$$\text{TATR} = \phi\left(f\left(\mathscr{D}^{(r)}_{\text{train}} \cup \widetilde{\mathscr{D}}_{\text{train}}\right), \mathscr{D}^{(r)}_{\text{test}}\right). \tag{30}$$

Evaluation Reading

In all three expressions, $f(\cdot)$ is the fitted predictive model and $\phi(\cdot\ ,\cdot)$ is the evaluation functional applied to a trained model on held-out real data. The TRTR condition provides the ceiling or baseline achievable with real data alone, TSTR measures whether the synthetic data support standalone modelling, and TATR measures whether synthetic augmentation improves rare-event learning beyond the real baseline. These three protocols jointly operationalise the chapter's core claim that synthetic data should be evaluated by how they perform on real educational cases.

Because the chapter is oriented toward high-stakes learning analytics, the performance functional ϕ is not defined by discrimination alone. A composite utility score can be written as in (31)

$$\phi = \omega_1\widetilde{AUC} + \omega_2\widetilde{PR-AUC} + \omega_3\left(1 - \widetilde{BS}\right) + \omega_4\left(1 - \widetilde{ECE}\right), \tag{31}$$

where the tildes denote normalized quantities on a common scale.

Composite-Utility Reading

The metrics *AUC* and *PR-AUC* capture ranking performance and minority-class sensitivity; *BS* and *ECE* capture probability quality; and $\omega_1, \omega_2, \omega_3, \omega_4$ determine their relative importance. The composite utility limits verifier bias by preventing synthetic datasets from being rewarded for improving ranking performance while degrading calibration, or vice versa. For dropout prediction, a balanced view of discrimination and calibration is pedagogically more appropriate than a single-score evaluation (Macfadyen & Dawson, 2010; van Calster et al., 2019).

Repeated splits or repeated cohort evaluations are summarized through interval estimates in (32):

$$\bar{\phi} = \frac{1}{R}\sum_{r=1}^{R}\phi_r,\ CI_{95\%} = \bar{\phi} \pm 1.96\frac{s_\phi}{\sqrt{R}}, \tag{32}$$

where R is the number of repetitions and s_ϕ is the standard deviation of the utility score across those repetitions.

Uncertainty reporting. These statistics provide uncertainty-aware reporting rather than single-run optimism. For reproducible governance, interval estimates help distinguish a robust verifier result from a favourable split produced by sampling variation.

Deployment monitoring also requires a way to detect whether verifier behavior changes substantially across cohorts or institutions. For this purpose, the chapter introduces a drift signal on verifier summaries in (33):

$$\Delta_V(c,c') = \| \mathrm{v}_c - \mathrm{v}_{c'} \|_2, \tag{33}$$

where v_c and $\mathrm{v}_{c'}$ are the average verifier vectors for contexts c and c'.

Drift Reading

The Euclidean norm $\| \cdot \|_2$ aggregates changes across all verifier axes. The statistic diagnoses cohort-level variation in synthetic quality, even when average predictive performance appears stable. A large $\Delta_V(c,c')$ may indicate that the generator behaves differently after curriculum change, policy change, instructional redesign, or data-schema drift. In the proposed computational architecture, this signal will be included in the verifier report so that stakeholders can distinguish ordinary variation from structural change.

The evaluation protocol also includes privacy attacks and subgroup analysis by default. Nearest-neighbour exposure and membership-inference advantage are computed under repeated seeds, subgroup fairness is assessed for audited strata, and explanation stability is reported for the same models used in TSTR and TATR evaluation. The pipeline therefore binds prediction, explanation, fairness, privacy, and deployment readiness instead of treating them as separate add-ons. For reproducibility, diagnostics should store seeds, splits, model families, audited groups, thresholds, and privacy notes, following privacy-driven learning-analytics practice (Joksimovic et al., 2022).

The verifier report should record accepted metrics together with failed candidates and rejected trade-offs. A synthetic dataset may appear adequate when only its final version is inspected, while the generation path may reveal repeated privacy stress failures, subgroup instability, or reward configurations that overemphasise utility. Recording negative evidence improves traceability and prevents the report from becoming a promotional summary. It also gives institutional reviewers a basis for deciding whether a dataset is suitable for public benchmarking, restricted internal experimentation, or no release. Under this interpretation, the report functions as a decision dossier rather than as a cosmetic appendix.

4. COMPUTATIONAL ARCHITECTURE

4.1. Reproducible Computational Pipeline for Verifiable Synthetic Learning Analytics

The computational architecture is a modular, reproducible pipeline that begins with data ingestion and ends with a governance-ready verifier report. Raw educational traces and derived learning analytics tables are harmonized into a versioned schema documenting variables, missingness conventions, subgroup identifiers, and cohort tags. A preprocessing layer performs robust scaling, categorical encoding, temporal aggregation, feature auditing, and train-test split definition. A generator layer then applies one or more conditional synthesis engines configured for the target schema and minority-class design.

The verifier layer is the computational core. It computes marginal fidelity, structural preservation, TSTR and TATR utility, calibration and decision metrics, privacy exposure, subgroup fairness gaps, and explanation stability. These outputs form the multi-axis verifier vector, the scalar reward, and the human-readable report. The report supports machine-level iteration while allowing human reviewers to decide whether a synthetic dataset is fit for model development, limited benchmarking, or no release.

A concise way to represent the provenance of a run is (34):

$$\Pi = \left(\mathcal{S}, \Theta_G, \Theta_V, \mathcal{T}, \mathcal{E}, \mathcal{H}, \mathcal{A}\right). \tag{34}$$

Provenance Reading

In this tuple, $\mathcal{S}$ denotes the schema definition; Θ_G denotes generator parameters and seeds; Θ_V denotes verifier settings and thresholds; $\mathcal{T}$ denotes the temporal or cohort split configuration; $\mathcal{E}$ denotes the evaluation protocol; $\mathcal{H}$ denotes the software and dependency manifest; and $\mathcal{A}$ denotes the final decision artefacts, including accepted datasets, reports, and diagnostics. The tuple supports governance because reproducible synthetic-data research depends not only on modelling code but on precise documentation of what was generated, how it was verified, and why it was accepted or rejected.

Operationally, the pipeline serializes preprocessing rules, feature dictionaries, seeds, generator checkpoints, verifier metrics, fitted predictive models, subgroup diagnostics, calibration artefacts, privacy stress tests, and drift statistics. Exportable reports allow institutional comparison without raw-data exchange and align with privacy-driven learning analytics principles in which access, purpose limitation, and auditability are designed together rather than handled as separate compliance steps

(Joksimovic et al., 2022). Computational reproducibility is treated as a component of educational trustworthiness rather than as a secondary technical detail (Marshall et al., 2022; Zhan et al., 2024; Yan et al., 2024).

Scope note. Sections 2-4 define the full verifier architecture. Section 5 instantiates only the controlled topology-aware ecosystem; therefore, dropout, privacy-attack resistance, and calibration remain requirements for future institutional validation.

5. CONTROLLED PROTOTYPE RESULTS AND ANALYSIS

5.1. Controlled Synthetic Educational Environment and Structural Verification

Methodological status of the experiment. The empirical prototype uses a controlled synthetic educational environment generated by the accompanying Python code. It does not use real institutional student records and does not include a live dropout or non-completion label. The generated population contains 180 synthetic learners, 60 learning resources, 12 curriculum concepts, and 4,120 learner-resource interactions. The main feature types are learner preparation profile, support need, perseverance, mastery state, resource modality, concept depth, prerequisite coverage, concept distance, correctness, hints, dwell time, and temporal interaction order. The principal subgroup variable is preparation profile: underprepared, regular, and advanced. The evaluated target is interaction success and subsequent tutoring/recommendation behaviour, not institutional dropout. Accordingly, the experiment validates structural verification logic in a tractable synthetic environment; it should not be reported as an external validation study for dropout prediction.

Current verifier-status note. The prototype directly evaluates structural and topological coherence, ranking quality, subgroup-visible success patterns, loop behaviour, and scenario robustness. It does not report marginal fidelity against real institutional distributions, dropout TSTR/TATR, dropout calibration, nearest-neighbour exposure, or membership-inference advantage as passed metrics, because the experiment has neither real learner records nor a dropout label. The framework specifies the complete gate; the empirical run validates the inspectable structural layer.

The structural baseline of the experiment is already informative. The synthetic educational environment contains 180 learners, 60 resources, 12 concepts, and 4,120 interactions, with a mean correctness of 0.774, a mean prerequisite coverage of 0.857, and a mean concept distance of 0.304. These values indicate that the environment is neither trivial nor chaotic. Instead, it places the prototype in a middle regime: learner success is frequent enough to make progression visible, but structural difficulty remains high enough for topological regularisation to be tested. Such a regime is appropriate for ethical and explainable learning analytics because decision quality depends on respecting educational structure rather than on exploiting purely local correlations.

Taken together, the Section 5.1 evidence shows a rich interaction ecology, a non-trivial concept graph, and differentiated learner regions. This foundation supports later claims about ethical early warning, explainable personalization, and governance-ready modelling because the underlying educational structure can be inspected, described, and audited.

The following figure displays the learner state cloud by preparation profile.

Figure 2. Learner state cloud by preparation profile

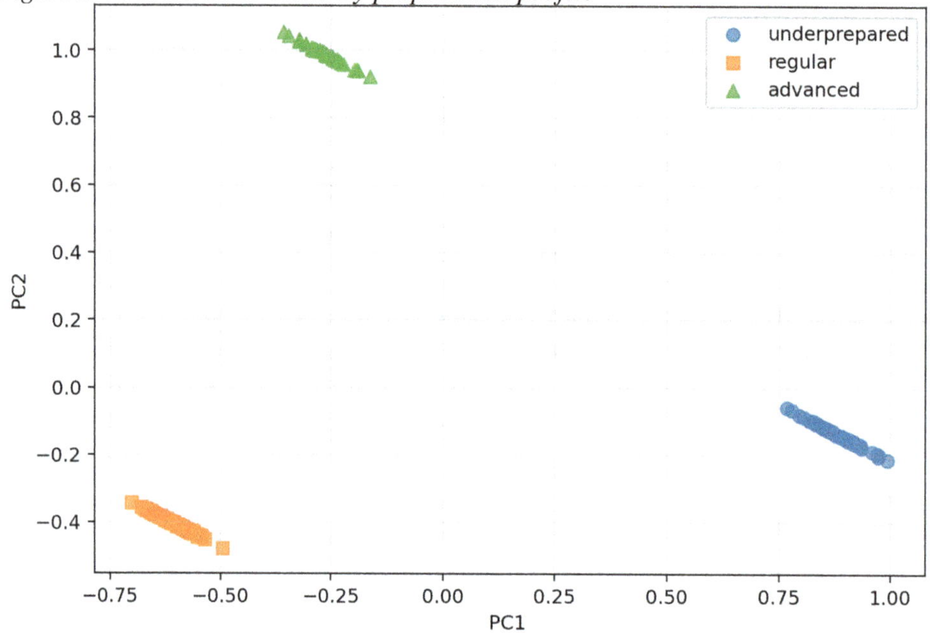

Visual reading. Figure 2 shows that the synthetic cohort is not collapsed into a single undifferentiated mass. Underprepared, regular, and advanced learners occupy overlapping but distinguishable regions, which supports differentiated educational support without reducing the prototype to profile memorisation alone. The important point is not perfect separation; it is the coexistence of identifiable preparation profiles and within-group variation. That combination gives the later models a meaningful test: they must learn educational structure inside profiles, not only labels between profiles.

The following figure displays the resource transition and co-usage graph.

Figure 3. Resource transition and co-usage graph

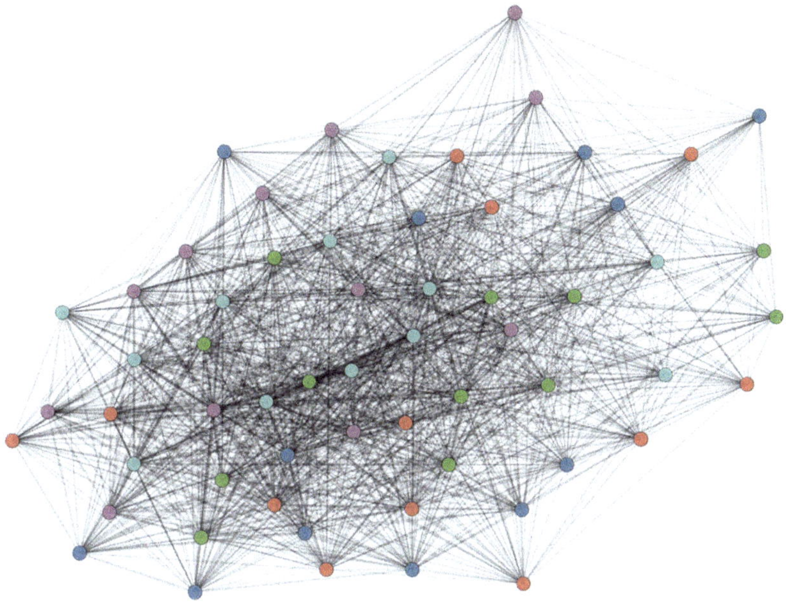

Graph reading. Figure 3 shows a dense but educationally structured resource graph linking readings, videos, practice activities, quizzes, and tutoring resources. Its 60 nodes and 1,306 edges indicate that recommendation occurs in a richly connected pedagogical environment rather than in an arbitrary catalogue. The graph also clarifies why topology matters: learners move through a navigational space, and recommendations must respect that space instead of treating resources as interchangeable items.

The following figure displays the curriculum prerequisite graph.

Figure 4. Curriculum prerequisite graph

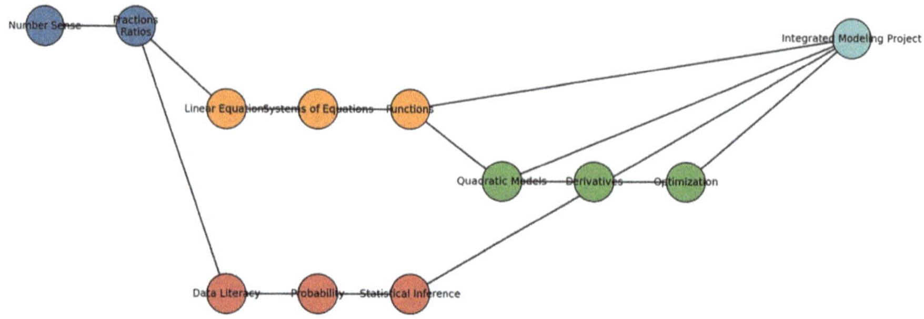

Curricular Reading

Figure 4 shows that the environment is governed by prerequisite logic rather than by a flat topic list. It provides a recognizable map for interpreting recommendations, because coherent and risky moves can be read against the curricular path from foundations toward the integrated modelling project. This makes the graph a pedagogical reference point: it tells the reader what counts as a reasonable transition before any automated policy is judged.

Table 2 establishes the empirical scale of the prototype. With 180 learners, 60 resources, 12 concepts, and 4,120 interactions, the environment is large enough to produce stable structural patterns while remaining interpretable at the level of curriculum design. The mean correctness of 0.774 indicates a moderately successful population rather than a trivially solved one. The mean prerequisite coverage of 0.857 shows that most interactions occur in educationally plausible regions of the curriculum, while the mean concept distance of 0.304 indicates that the learner trajectories are neither purely repetitive nor recklessly discontinuous. In addition, the 977 learner-graph edges and 1,306 resource-graph edges confirm that the experimental setting contains enough topological density to justify graph-based regularisation and downstream manifold analysis.

Empirical Scale

Table 2 summarizes the scale, density, and curricular coherence of the synthetic educational environment used for experimentation.

Table 2. Structural summary of the experimental educational environment.

Learners	Resources	Concepts	Interactions	Mean correctness	Mean prerequisite coverage	Mean concept distance	Resource graph nodes	Resource graph edges	Learner graph nodes	Learner graph edges
180	60	12	4120	0.774	0.857	0.304	60	1306	180	977

5.2. Preservation of Educational Structure, Representation Stability, and Subgroup-Visible Behaviour

Topology-aware regularisation here refers to a learning constraint that penalizes representations or decisions inconsistent with the prerequisite structure, so the model learns under curricular restrictions rather than being justified only after training.

The second layer of results concerns whether the learned representation becomes more structurally coherent when topology-aware regularisation is introduced. The evidence is strongly affirmative on this point. The latent-space analysis shows that the topology-aware model produces a markedly more compact and better-organised geometry than the baseline, and this transformation is not merely cosmetic. It indicates that the model is learning to encode educational states in a way that is more faithful to prerequisite structure, local neighbourhood stability, and interpretable progression through the conceptual curriculum.

The preservation of structure is a precondition for trustworthy educational inference. A model may achieve acceptable local accuracy while still distorting the educational meaning of its recommendations if the latent space becomes fragmented, unstable, or dominated by isolated clusters disconnected from curricular semantics. The present results show that the regularized model preserves performance while substantially reducing geometric fragmentation, which supports the chapter's claim that educational AI systems should be evaluated not only by pointwise predictive gain but also by the shape and continuity of the learned representation.

Overall, Section 5.2 provides the chapter's strongest evidence that structure-preserving educational AI can be measured rather than merely asserted. The topology-aware model does not win by a dramatic margin on a single scalar metric; instead, it improves the internal organization of the representation, preserves or slightly improves validation quality, and yields a latent geometry that is easier to justify in educational terms. That combination is precisely what the chapter set out to defend: a form of AI whose validity emerges from the joint behavior of performance, structure, and interpretability.

The following figure displays the training dynamics of the baseline and topology-aware models.

Figure 5. Training dynamics of baseline and topology-aware models

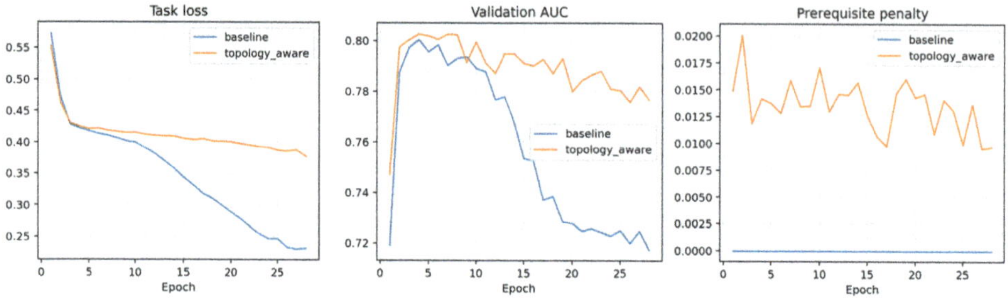

Training reading. Figure 5 shows that the topology-aware model gains structural discipline without unstable optimisation. Validation AUC remains close to or slightly above the baseline at the best epochs, while the prerequisite penalty is shaped during training rather than added as a post hoc explanation. In educational terms, the constraint participates in learning itself; the model is not trained first and justified later.

Topological reading. Figure 6 plots Betti curves, which count connected components and cycles as the scale of analysis changes. The topology-aware model shows lower and shorter-lived H1 activity, indicating fewer persistent loops and a smoother learner space that supports more stable educational explanations. This matters because a representation with unnecessary loops may send similar learners through inconsistent recommendations, whereas a smoother space makes local comparisons easier to defend.

The following figure displays the Betti curves for the baseline and topology-aware learner spaces.

Figure 6. Betti curves of baseline and topology-aware learner spaces

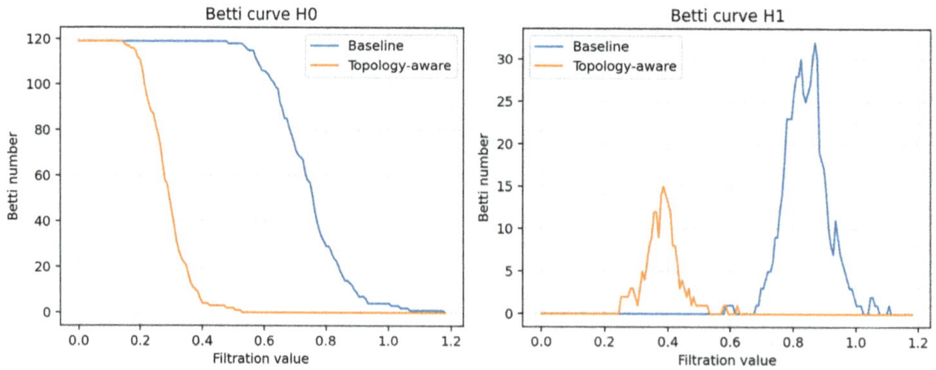

Topological reading. Figure 6 plots Betti curves, which count connected components and cycles as the scale of analysis changes. The topology-aware model shows lower and shorter-lived H1 activity, indicating fewer persistent loops and a smoother learner space that supports more stable educational explanations. This matters because a representation with unnecessary loops may send similar learners through inconsistent recommendations, whereas a smoother space makes local comparisons easier to defend.

Homological reading. Figure 7 compares persistent homology, which measures components and loops that remain visible across geometric scales. The topology-aware model reduces H0 total lifetime from 88.033 to 34.017 and H1 total lifetime from 4.591 to 1.477, suggesting less fragmentation and fewer redundant holes in the learner representation. The interpretation is not that all complexity should disappear, but that unnecessary fragmentation is being replaced by a more pedagogically continuous organization.

The following figure displays the persistent homology of the learner latent representations.

Figure 7. Persistent homology of learner latent representations

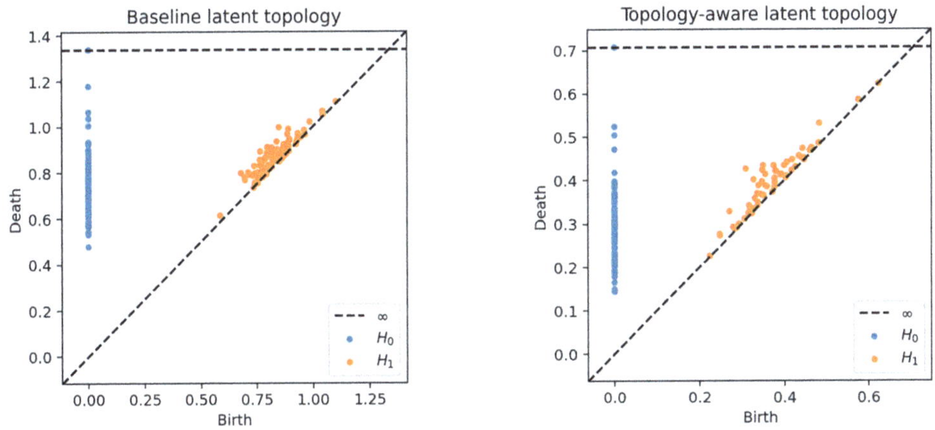

Homological reading. Figure 7 compares persistent homology, which measures components and loops that remain visible across geometric scales. The topology-aware model reduces H0 total lifetime from 88.033 to 34.017 and H1 total lifetime from 4.591 to 1.477, suggesting less fragmentation and fewer redundant holes in the learner representation. The interpretation is not that all complexity should disappear, but that unnecessary fragmentation is being replaced by a more pedagogically continuous organization.

Geometric reading. Figure 8 compares the latent manifold, understood here as the learned geometric organization of learner states. The topology-aware space is more compact and organized than the baseline while preserving learner heterogeneity, a property that supports more stable recommendations and more defensible explanations. The compactness is therefore not a loss of learner diversity; it is a reduction of arbitrary geometric noise around curricular progression.

The following figure displays the learner manifolds before and after topology-aware regularisation.

Figure 8. Latent learner manifolds before and after topology-aware regularisation

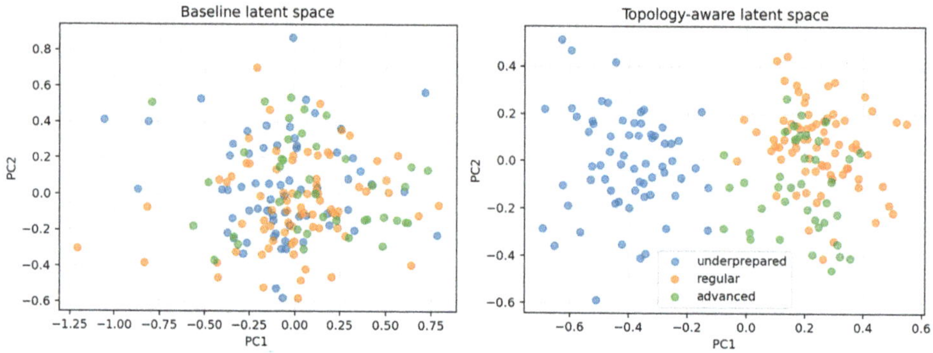

Geometric reading. Figure 8 compares the latent manifold, understood here as the learned geometric organization of learner states. The topology-aware space is more compact and organized than the baseline while preserving learner heterogeneity, a property that supports more stable recommendations and more defensible explanations. The compactness is therefore not a loss of learner diversity; it is a reduction of arbitrary geometric noise around curricular progression.

Table 3 condenses the homological comparison into a compact audit. The topology-aware model preserves the same number of H0 generators because the learner sample size is unchanged, but the total lifetime of those components declines sharply, and the H1 count drops from 110 to 57. The pattern is the signature expected from a representation that is becoming more connected, more stable, and less burdened by topological artefacts. For reporting purposes, these values translate geometric intuition into auditable indicators that can be read by technical and non-technical stakeholders alike.

Audit Summary

Table 3 summarizes the persistent-homology profile of the baseline and topology-aware latent spaces.

Table 3. Persistent-homology summary of the latent learner spaces.

Model	H0 count	H0 total lifetime	H0 Max lifetime	H1 count	H1 total lifetime	H1 Max lifetime	Wasserstein H1 distance	Landscape distance
baseline	120.0	88.033	1.179	110.0	4.591	0.15	4.291	N/A
topology_ aware	120.0	34.017	0.524	57.0	1.477	0.118	4.291	N/A

Table 4 compares the ranking behaviour of the three principal policies. Relative to baseline_plain, topology_constrained raises Recall@K from 0.198 to 0.253 and NDCG@K from 0.093 to 0.104, while reducing mean step size from 0.384 to 0.311. The topology_plain policy, by contrast, is weaker in retrieval utility despite sharing the same reduced H0 total lifetime. This contrast shows that representation learning alone is not sufficient; the final decision policy determines whether structural information becomes pedagogically useful. The objectives are met by the joint behaviour of topology-aware learning and topology-constrained recommendation.

Policy Summary

Table 4 compares the principal ranking metrics of the baseline, topology-aware, and constrained topology-aware policies.

Table 4. Offline policy comparison for ranking quality, coherence, and stability

Policy	Recall@K	NDCG@K	MRR@K	Violation rate	Mean step size	Support share	Stability (Jaccard)	Mean H0 total lifetime
baseline_plain	0.198	0.093	0.062	0.0	0.384	1.0	0.99	88.033
topology_constrained	0.253	0.104	0.06	0.0	0.311	0.926	0.971	34.017
topology_plain	0.155	0.06	0.033	0.0	0.443	1.0	0.98	34.017

5.3. Decision-Level Coherence, Subgroup Audit, and Governance-Ready Verifier Reports

The third layer of evidence concerns decision making under explicit structural constraints. The aim is not merely to maximise instantaneous ranking performance, but to determine whether a topology-aware policy can deliver recommendations and tutoring actions that remain educationally coherent under realistic operational conditions. The constrained policy improves Recall@K from 0.198 to 0.253 and NDCG@K from 0.093 to 0.104 relative to the plain baseline while simultaneously reducing mean step size from 0.384 to 0.311. In other words, the policy becomes both more accurate and more pedagogically disciplined.

These results indicate that structural governance need not sacrifice educational intelligence. The constrained policy maintains high ranking stability, with a Jaccard overlap of 0.971 under perturbation, while discouraging abrupt curricular jumps. This decision-oriented interpretation is consistent with decision-curve reasoning, where a model is judged by whether thresholded action improves practical benefit rather than by discrimination alone (Vickers & Holland, 2021). For teachers, programme coordinators, and student-support teams, stability provides a defensible basis for scrutiny.

Section 5.3 offers evidence of practical feasibility: the constrained policy performs better when quality is measured by coherent retrieval and stable recommendation, and it behaves more responsibly when quality is measured by drift robustness, subgroup visibility, and structural transparency.

The following figure displays example tutoring trajectories under the two policies.

Figure 9. Example tutoring trajectories under two policies

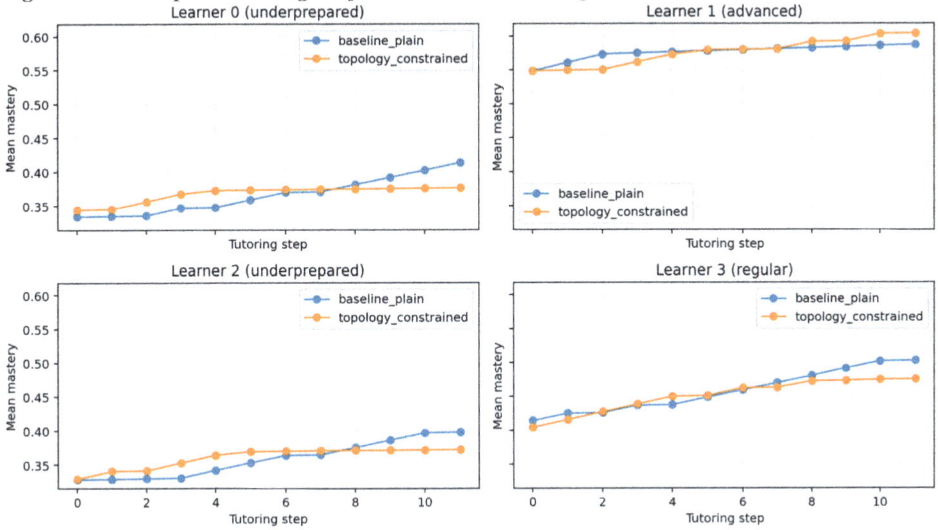

Trajectory reading. Figure 9 translates the policy comparison into individual tutoring paths. The topology-constrained policy tends to produce smoother mastery accumulation with fewer abrupt oscillations, making the results more legible for teachers, programme coordinators, and student-support teams. This view is useful because educational stakeholders often need to inspect a concrete path of support, not only an aggregate ranking score.

The following figure displays the one-skeleton of the learning simplicial complex.

Figure 10. One-skeleton of the learning simplicial complex

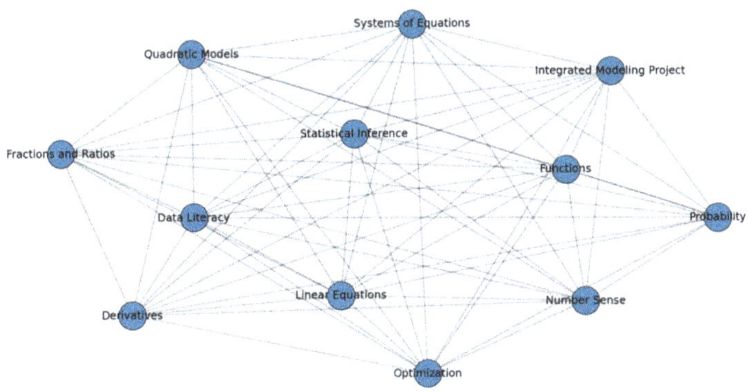

Higher-order reading. Figure 10 shows the 1-skeleton of a simplicial complex, which extends a graph by representing higher-order relations among concepts or trajectories rather than only pairwise links. The presence of 217 two-simplices indicates that the prototype preserves recurrent concept neighbourhoods in learner trajectories. This is educationally important because several concepts often operate together in practice; a responsible model should preserve those bundles rather than only isolated edges.

Mapper reading. Figure 11 reports a Mapper graph, a compact network summary of the shape of a dataset. Its single dominant node indicates that the concept-level feature space remains globally integrated, which helps governance reviewers inspect a coherent audit region instead of fragmented local patterns. The result should not be read as absence of information; it shows that the synthetic concept system forms one reviewable core.

The following figure displays the Mapper governance graph over concept-level educational features.

Figure 11. Mapper governance graph over concept-level educational features

Mapper reading. Figure 11 reports a Mapper graph, a compact network summary of the shape of a dataset. Its single dominant node indicates that the concept-level feature space remains globally integrated, which helps governance reviewers inspect a coherent audit region instead of fragmented local patterns. The result should not be read as absence of information; it shows that the synthetic concept system forms one reviewable core.

The following figure displays the subgroup audit across learner preparation profiles.

Figure 12. Subgroup audit across learner preparation profiles

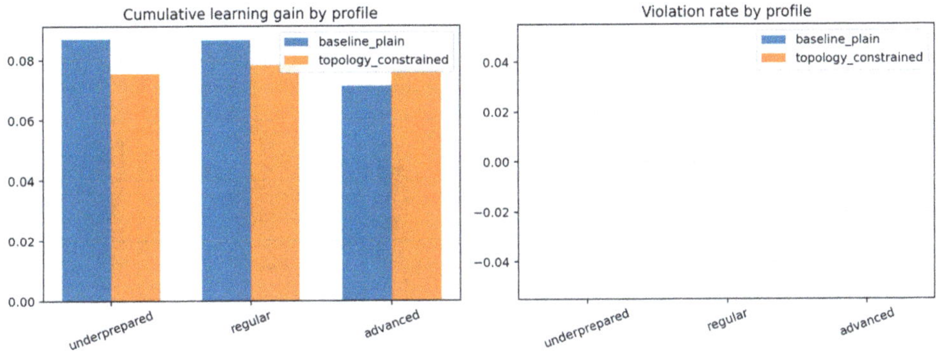

Subgroup reading. Figure 12 shows that policy effects differ across preparation profiles. The advanced and regular groups benefit from lower or eliminated looping under the constrained policy, while underprepared learners gain success but require monitoring for repeated review. The value of the audit is that this tension is visible rather than hidden. For an institutional reader, this is the main fairness-style lesson: global improvement is not enough unless subgroup trade-offs remain inspectable.

The following figure displays the robustness of tutoring policies under scenario shift.

Figure 13. Robustness of tutoring policies under scenario shift

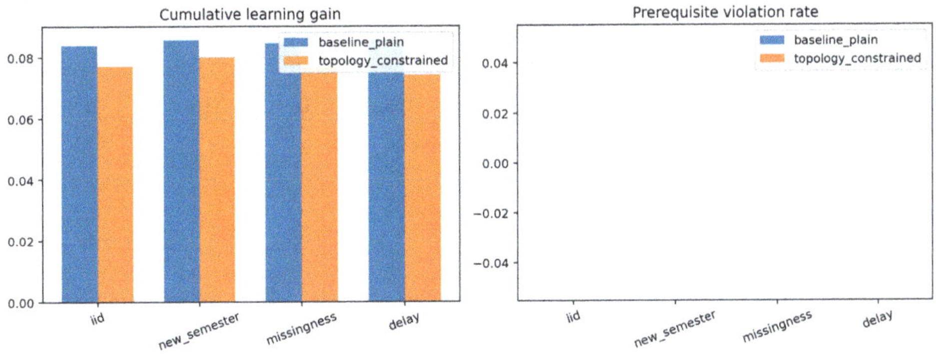

Robustness reading. Figure 13 shows that the topology-constrained policy remains robust under i.i.d. evaluation, new-semester shift, missingness, and delayed information. It consistently increases success and lowers loop rates, even when cumulative gain is marginally lower than the baseline. This is a defensible educational trade-off, because a support system should prefer stable, explainable, and high-success trajectories over fragile short-term gains.

The following figure displays offline ranking quality, coherence, and stability by policy.

Figure 14. Offline ranking quality, coherence, and stability by policy

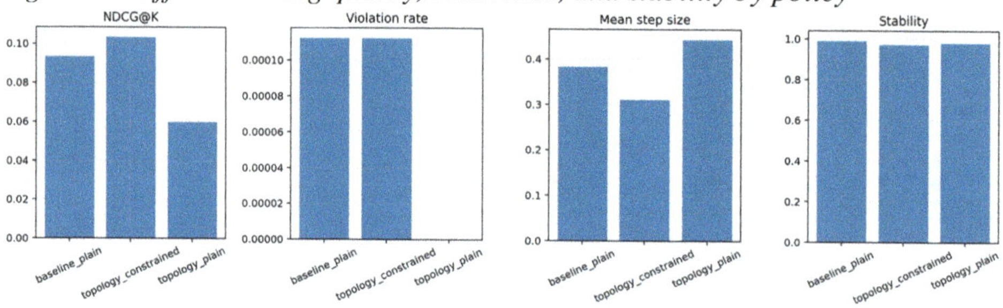

Decision-level reading. Figure 14 condenses ranking quality, curricular coherence, and stability. The constrained topology-aware policy achieves the strongest ranking profile among the principal alternatives while reducing curricular jump size, so the policy appears disciplined rather than fragile. Its slight loss in nominal perturbation stability remains small relative to the gain in curricular coherence, which is the more relevant criterion for supervised educational use.

Table 5 brings together the two global topology summaries used for governance interpretation. The simplicial-complex statistics show that the learning process generates rich higher-order neighbourhoods, while the Mapper summary indicates that these neighbourhoods remain organised around a compact connected audit region. Together these results strengthen the chapter's objective of producing governance-ready educational analytics. They show that the system can be summarized not only by raw performance metrics but also by interpretable structural artefacts that describe the shape of learning itself.

Governance Summary

Table 5 summarizes the higher-order topology and Mapper-based governance view of the educational environment.

Table 5. Higher-order topological and Mapper governance summary.

0-simplices	1-simplices	2-simplices	Complex dimension	Harmonic 1-cycles	Smallest positive Hodge eigenvalue	Mapper nodes	Mapper edges	Connected components	Largest component size	Mean mapper node size
12	66	217	2	0	9.0	1	0	1	1	3.0

Table 6 clarifies that policy effects are not uniform across learner groups. The constrained policy increases advanced learners' cumulative gain from 0.071 to 0.076 while eliminating loops, and it raises regular learners' success rate from 0.792 to 0.860 with a strong reduction in looping. For underprepared learners, however, the same policy increases success from 0.662 to 0.902 and lowers mean step size from 0.276 to 0.179, but loop rate rises. This substantive finding shows why a governance-ready system should not report only average performance; it must also identify where structural caution begins to turn into pedagogical over-review. Responsible educational AI advances when such subgroup-specific tensions become visible rather than hidden inside a global score.

Table 6 reports subgroup outcomes for the principal tutoring policies.

Table 6. Subgroup audit across learner preparation profiles.

Profile	Policy	Cumulative learning gain	Final mean mastery	Success rate	Violation rate	Mean step size	Loop rate
advanced	baseline_plain	0.071	0.595	0.893	0.0	0.092	0.471
advanced	topology_ constrained	0.076	0.6	0.802	0.0	0.66	0.0
regular	baseline_plain	0.087	0.517	0.792	0.0	0.12	0.265
regular	topology_ constrained	0.078	0.509	0.86	0.0	0.463	0.025
underprepared	baseline_plain	0.087	0.421	0.662	0.0	0.276	0.038
underprepared	topology_ constrained	0.075	0.41	0.902	0.0	0.179	0.225

Table 7 confirms that the constrained policy is operationally robust. Across all four scenarios, it yields success rates above the baseline by approximately nine to thirteen percentage points, and it does so with zero prerequisite violations. The baseline policy obtains slightly larger cumulative learning gain in the aggregate, but this advantage is accompanied by substantially higher loop rates in most scenarios and less disciplined step-size control. For institutional use, the constrained profile is easier to justify: it produces fewer structurally questionable transitions while maintaining strong learning progress. An educational support system must be defendable not only when it works, but also when its recommendations are scrutinised by teachers and programme coordinators.

Table 7 summarizes the rollout performance of the two principal tutoring policies under multiple scenarios.

Table 7. Sequential tutoring outcomes under multiple robustness scenarios.

Scenario	Policy	Cumulative learning gain	Final mean mastery	Success rate	Violation rate	Mean step size	Loop rate
delay	baseline_plain	0.086	0.489	0.755	0.0	0.158	0.209
delay	topology_ constrained	0.074	0.478	0.876	0.0	0.357	0.115
iid	baseline_plain	0.084	0.488	0.772	0.0	0.175	0.234
iid	topology_ constrained	0.077	0.481	0.862	0.0	0.385	0.097
missingness	baseline_plain	0.085	0.488	0.741	0.0	0.2	0.162
missingness	topology_ constrained	0.077	0.48	0.865	0.0	0.362	0.11
new_ semester	baseline_plain	0.086	0.489	0.743	0.0	0.179	0.193
new_ semester	topology_ constrained	0.08	0.484	0.876	0.0	0.393	0.078

6. DISCUSSION AND CONCLUSIONS

6.1. Theoretical, Pedagogical, and Governance Implications

The integrated evidence from Sections 5.1-5.3 allows the chapter to move from a conceptual proposal to a defensible empirical argument. The theoretical implication is that explainable educational AI should not be reduced to a narrow question of post hoc explanation. The present results show that explanation quality is inseparable from representational geometry, curricular coherence, and decision regularity. When the learning architecture is constrained by educational topology, the resulting system does not merely produce different scores; it reorganizes the latent manifold, reduces structural fragmentation, and yields recommendations that can be interpreted as better aligned with the logic of progression through a curriculum. This strengthens the chapter's core proposition that trustworthy educational analytics must be modelled as a socio-technical system in which data structure, geometric organization, and decision policy are jointly audited.

The pedagogical implication is equally significant. The results demonstrate that a constrained policy can produce safer and more interpretable tutoring trajectories, by managing curricular transitions, reducing loop behaviour in most scenarios, and sustaining high success rates under scenario shift. This does not imply that the most conservative policy is always the best. Indeed, the subgroup analysis shows that underprepared learners may experience more review loops under a strongly constrained policy, which means that educational safety must be balanced against stagnation. However, this very tension confirms rather than weakens the chapter's argument. It shows that governance-ready educational AI requires interpretable diagnostics capable of revealing when a policy is becoming over-cautious for certain learner groups. In that sense, the chapter's aim is not merely to optimize automated action, but to support human judgement with evidence that is pedagogically legible.

6.2. Conclusions, Limitations, and Responsible Use

The chapter closes with a focused conclusion. Within a controlled synthetic prototype, the results support the main claim that educational analytics become more defensible when structural constraints are embedded in the modelling pipeline. The prototype shows that topology-aware regularisation compresses fragmented latent structure, preserves ranking quality, reduces incoherent curricular jumps, and produces robust tutoring behaviour across several operational scenarios. These findings provide methodological evidence for explainability, structural preservation, governance readiness, and ethically interpretable decision support, while leaving institutional dropout validation for future work.

The evidence also defines the responsible-use boundary. First, the prototype is controlled rather than a live institutional deployment, so the metrics should be read as methodological validation, not as a final production claim. Second, the experiment is strong on structural and decision-coherence criteria, but it does not fully implement the privacy and fairness battery envisioned in the broader framework. Third, the underprepared subgroup results show that caution can produce local looping, making human-in-the-loop review indispensable. Release notes should state intended uses, checked populations, uncertain subgroup results, verified privacy evidence, and decisions that remain under human authority.

Release boundary. Here, governance-ready means that the report documents evidence, omissions, subgroup cautions, and intended-use limits; it does not authorize automated dropout intervention.

Operational adoption should follow a staged release model: first, code testing and reproducibility checks; second, model comparison only when TSTR, calibration, and privacy stress tests remain within thresholds; third, any real-plus-synthetic augmentation only after human review of subgroup diagnostics, alert-budget behaviour, and explanation stability. The generator proposes candidate data, the verifier produces validity evidence, and institutional reviewers decide whether the artefact is appropriate for educational action.

A further conclusion follows from the combined evidence. The strongest contribution of the computational prototype is not any single metric in isolation, but the consistency of the pattern across multiple levels of analysis. Structural summaries, graph visualizations, latent-space topology, ranking metrics, rollout scenarios, subgroup audits, and higher-order summaries all point in the same direction: educational intelligence becomes more dependable when learning states and decisions are constrained by curricular topology. This convergence of evidence allows the chapter to claim fulfilment of its objectives with credibility. The final value of the work lies in transforming an abstract call for responsible educational AI into a reproducible analytical pipeline whose outputs can be reviewed, challenged, and improved.

From a governance standpoint, the verifier-style logic is strengthened because the reporting layer can combine structural density, latent compactness, retrieval quality, loop behaviour, subgroup sensitivity, privacy notes, and higher-order topology in one dossier. Such a dossier is more informative than an accuracy table because it helps institutions examine whether the system succeeds for educationally defensible reasons and whether release conditions remain appropriate after cohort or policy change.

7. FUTURE WORK

7.1. Toward Explainable, Adaptive, and Privacy-Preserving Synthetic Ecosystems for STEAM Personalization

Future work should extend verifier-guided synthesis beyond static tabular settings. One promising direction is multimodal synthesis integrating event logs, assessment trajectories, textual learner support data, laboratory interaction traces, and sensor-rich smart-space evidence. Another is online verification, where the verifier monitors drift and recalibrates acceptance thresholds as cohorts evolve. Further work is also needed on causal fairness, subgroup-conditional explanation stability, and federated or institution-local verification protocols that allow cross-site comparison without raw-data exchange.

A longer-term direction is the development of synthetic educational ecosystems that support adaptive simulation, scenario testing, and safe evaluation of personalization strategies before they are deployed to real students. Such work would connect synthetic generation more directly with explainable tutoring systems, ethical automated assessment, and intelligent STEAM infrastructure. The present chapter is intended as a foundation for that broader research agenda.

The code generated to obtain all the results in this chapter can be found at the following URL:

https://github.com/JAIME6609/EDUCATION/blob/main/CODE-BOOK-15-ART-03.py

Reproducibility. Synthetic-data prototype for topology-aware tutoring/recommendation; no institutional records. Dependencies: numpy, pandas, matplotlib, networkx, scipy, scikit-learn, torch, ripser, persim, kmapper, toponetx. Default seed exports 5.1–5.3 outputs; dropout TSTR/TATR remains future work.

REFERENCES

Berg, A. M., Mol, S. T., Kismihók, G., & Sclater, N. (2016). The role of a reference synthetic data generator within the field of learning analytics. *Journal of Learning Analytics*, *3*(1), 107–128. DOI: 10.18608/jla.2016.31.7

Chouldechova, A. (2017). Fair prediction with disparate impact: A study of bias in recidivism prediction instruments. *Big Data*, *5*(2), 153–163. DOI: 10.1089/big.2016.0047 PMID: 28632438

Deho, O. B., Zhan, C., Li, J., Liu, J., Liu, L., & Duy Le, T. (2022). How do the existing fairness metrics and unfairness mitigation algorithms contribute to ethical learning analytics? *British Journal of Educational Technology*, *53*(4), 822–843. DOI: 10.1111/bjet.13217

El Emam, K., Mosquera, L., & Bass, J. (2020). Evaluating identity disclosure risk in fully synthetic health data: Model development and validation. *Journal of Medical Internet Research*, *22*(11), e23139. Advance online publication. DOI: 10.2196/23139 PMID: 33196453

Ferguson, R. (2012). Learning analytics: Drivers, developments and challenges. *International Journal of Technology Enhanced Learning*, *4*(5/6), 304–317. DOI: 10.1504/IJTEL.2012.051816

Gebru, T., Morgenstern, J., Vecchione, B., Vaughan, J. W., Wallach, H., Daumé, H.III, & Crawford, K. (2021). Datasheets for datasets. *Communications of the ACM*, *64*(12), 86–92. DOI: 10.1145/3458723

Goncalves, A., Ray, P., Soper, B., Stevens, J., Coyle, L., & Sales, A. P. (2020). Generation and evaluation of synthetic patient data. *BMC Medical Research Methodology*, *20*(1), 108. Advance online publication. DOI: 10.1186/s12874-020-00977-1 PMID: 32381039

Hardt, M., Price, E., & Srebro, N. (2016). Equality of opportunity in supervised learning. In *Advances in Neural Information Processing Systems 29*. NeurIPS. https://papers.nips.cc/paper/6374-equality-of-opportunity-in-supervised-learning

Joksimović, S., Marshall, R., Rakotoarivelo, T., Ladjal, D., Zhan, C., & Pardo, A. (2022). Privacy-driven learning analytics. In McKay, E. (Ed.), *Manage your own learning analytics: Implement a Rasch modelling approach* (pp. 1–22). Springer., DOI: 10.1007/978-3-030-86316-6_1

Khalil, M., Vadiee, F., Shakya, R., & Liu, Q. (2025). Creating artificial students that never existed: Leveraging large language models and CTGANs for synthetic data generation. In *LAK '25: Proceedings of the 15th International Learning Analytics and Knowledge Conference* (pp. 439–450). Association for Computing Machinery. DOI: 10.1145/3706468.3706523

Kotelnikov, A., Baranchuk, D., Rubachev, I., & Babenko, A. (2023). TabDDPM: Modelling tabular data with diffusion models. In A. Krause, E. Brunskill, K. Cho, B. Engelhardt, S. Sabato, & J. Scarlett (Eds.), *Proceedings of the 40th International Conference on Machine Learning* (*Proceedings of Machine Learning Research*, Vol. 202, pp. 17564–17579). PMLR. https://proceedings.mlr.press/v202/kotelnikov23a.html

Liu, Q., Khalil, M., Shakya, R., & Jovanović, J. (2024). Scaling while privacy preserving: A comprehensive synthetic tabular data generation and evaluation in learning analytics. In *LAK '24: Proceedings of the 14th International Learning Analytics and Knowledge Conference* (pp. 620–631). Association for Computing Machinery. DOI: 10.1145/3636555.3636921

Liu, Q., Shakya, R., Jovanović, J., Khalil, M., & de la Hoz-Ruiz, J. (2025). Ensuring privacy through synthetic data generation in education. *British Journal of Educational Technology*, *56*(3), 1053–1073. DOI: 10.1111/bjet.13576

Macfadyen, L. P., & Dawson, S. (2010). Mining LMS data to develop an "early warning system" for educators: A proof of concept. *Computers & Education*, *54*(2), 588–599. DOI: 10.1016/j.compedu.2009.09.008

Marshall, R., Pardo, A., Smith, D., & Watson, T. (2022). Implementing next generation privacy and ethics research in education technology. *British Journal of Educational Technology*, *53*(4), 737–755. DOI: 10.1111/bjet.13224

Mitchell, M., Wu, S., Zaldivar, A., Barnes, P., Vasserman, L., Hutchinson, B., Spitzer, E., Raji, I. D., & Gebru, T. (2019). Model cards for model reporting. In *Proceedings of the Conference on Fairness, Accountability, and Transparency* (pp. 220–229). Association for Computing Machinery. DOI: 10.1145/3287560.3287596

Pham, N., Pham Ngoc, H., & Nguyen-Duc, A. (2025). Fairness for machine learning software in education: A systematic mapping study. *Journal of Systems and Software*, *219*, 112244. Advance online publication. DOI: 10.1016/j.jss.2024.112244

Riley, R. D., Archer, L., Snell, K. I. E., Ensor, J., Dhiman, P., Martin, G. P., Bonnett, L. J., & Collins, G. S. (2024). Evaluation of clinical prediction models (part 2): How to undertake an external validation study. *BMJ (Clinical Research Ed.)*, *384*, e074820. Advance online publication. DOI: 10.1136/bmj-2023-074820 PMID: 38224968

Siemens, G. (2013). Learning analytics: The emergence of a discipline. *The American Behavioral Scientist*, *57*(10), 1380–1400. DOI: 10.1177/0002764213498851

Slade, S., & Prinsloo, P. (2013). Learning analytics: Ethical issues and dilemmas. *The American Behavioral Scientist*, *57*(10), 1509–1528. DOI: 10.1177/0002764213479366

van Breugel, B., Qian, Z., & van der Schaar, M. (2023). Synthetic data, real errors: How (not) to publish and use synthetic data. In *Proceedings of the 40th International Conference on Machine Learning* (*Proceedings of Machine Learning Research*, Vol. 202, pp. 34793–34808). PMLR. https://proceedings.mlr.press/v202/van-breugel23a.html

van Breugel, B., Sun, H., Qian, Z., & van der Schaar, M. (2023). Membership inference attacks against synthetic data through overfitting detection. In *Proceedings of the 26th International Conference on Artificial Intelligence and Statistics* (*Proceedings of Machine Learning Research*, Vol. 206, pp. 3493–3514). PMLR. https://proceedings.mlr.press/v206/breugel23a.html

van Calster, B., McLernon, D. J., van Smeden, M., Wynants, L., Steyerberg, E. W., Bossuyt, P., Collins, G. S., Macaskill, P., Moons, K. G. M., & Vickers, A. J. (2019). Calibration: The Achilles heel of predictive analytics. *BMC Medicine*, *17*(1), 230. Advance online publication. DOI: 10.1186/s12916-019-1466-7 PMID: 31842878

Vickers, A. J., & Holland, F. (2021). Decision curve analysis to evaluate the clinical benefit of prediction models. *The Spine Journal*, *21*(10), 1643–1648. DOI: 10.1016/j.spinee.2021.02.024 PMID: 33676020

Xu, L., Skoularidou, M., Cuesta-Infante, A., & Veeramachaneni, K. (2019). Modeling tabular data using conditional GAN. In *Advances in Neural Information Processing Systems 32* (pp. 7333–7343). NeurIPS. https://papers.nips.cc/paper/8953-modeling-tabular-data-using-conditional-gan

Yale, A., Dash, S., Dutta, R., Guyon, I., Pavao, A., & Bennett, K. P. (2020). Generation and evaluation of privacy preserving synthetic health data. *Neurocomputing*, *416*, 244–255. DOI: 10.1016/j.neucom.2019.12.136

Yan, L., Martinez-Maldonado, R., & Gašević, D. (2024). Generative artificial intelligence in learning analytics: Contextualising opportunities and challenges through the learning analytics cycle. In *LAK '24: Proceedings of the 14th International Learning Analytics and Knowledge Conference* (pp. 101–111). Association for Computing Machinery. DOI: 10.1145/3636555.3636856

Zhan, C., Joksimović, S., Ladjal, D., Rakotoarivelo, T., Marshall, R., & Pardo, A. (2024). Preserving both privacy and utility in learning analytics. *IEEE Transactions on Learning Technologies*, *17*, 1655–1667. DOI: 10.1109/TLT.2024.3393766

Compilation of References

Abulibdeh, A., Zaidan, E., & Abulibdeh, R. (2024). Navigating the confluence of artificial intelligence and education for sustainable development in the era of industry 4.0: Challenges, opportunities, and ethical dimensions. *Journal of Cleaner Production*, *437*, 140527. Advance online publication. DOI: 10.1016/j.jclepro.2023.140527

Adadi, A., & Berrada, M. (2018). Peeking Inside the Black-Box: A Survey on Explainable Artificial Intelligence (XAI). *IEEE Access : Practical Innovations, Open Solutions*, *6*, 52138–52160. DOI: 10.1109/ACCESS.2018.2870052

Adel, A. (2024). The convergence of intelligent tutoring, robotics, and IoT in smart education for the transition from industry 4.0 to 5.0. *Smart Cities*, *7*(1), 325–369. DOI: 10.3390/smartcities7010014

Aeni, N., Muhalim, M., Ganteng, H., Tahir, M., & Talib, A. (2025). English Education Students' Perceptions of Automated vs Human Assessment in Spoken English Proficiency. AL-ISHLAH. *Jurnal Pendidikan*, *17*(3), 5615–5625.

Afzaal, M., Nouri, J., Zia, A., Papapetrou, P., Fors, U., Wu, Y., Li, X., & Weegar, R. (2021). Explainable AI for data-driven feedback and intelligent action recommendations to support students self-regulation. *Frontiers in Artificial Intelligence*, *4*, 723447. Advance online publication. DOI: 10.3389/frai.2021.723447

Akgun, S., & Greenhow, C. (2022). Artificial intelligence in education: Addressing ethical challenges in K-12 settings. *AI and Ethics*, *2*(3), 431–440. DOI: 10.1007/s43681-021-00096-7 PMID: 34790956

Albugami, S., Almaghrabi, H., & Wali, A. (2024). From data to decision: Machine learning and explainable AI in student dropout prediction. *The Journal of Learning in Higher Education*, *2024*, 246301. Advance online publication. DOI: 10.5171/2024.246301

Ali, D., Asaad, A., Jimenez, M.-J., Nanda, V., Paluzo-Hidalgo, E., & Soriano-Trigueros, M. (2023). A survey of vectorization methods in topological data analysis. *IEEE Transactions on Pattern Analysis and Machine Intelligence*, *45*(12), 14069–14080. DOI: 10.1109/TPAMI.2023.3308391 PMID: 37647183

Aljamaan, A., Alsaber, A., Emmanuel, C., & Alkandari, A. (2025). Leveling up learning effectiveness in STEM education through gamification: An empirical study on behavioral intention and digital literacy among undergraduate students in Kuwait. *Frontiers in Education*, *10*, 1586466. Advance online publication. DOI: 10.3389/feduc.2025.1586466

Alkhabra, Y. A., Ibrahem, U. M., & Alkhabra, S. A. (2023). Augmented reality technology in enhancing learning retention and critical thinking according to STEAM program. *Humanities & Social Sciences Communications*, *10*(1), 174. Advance online publication. DOI: 10.1057/s41599-023-01650-w

Alshareef, N. (2022). Investment opportunity of blockchain technology in the education sector of Saudi Arabia: A systematic literature review. *Frontiers in Education*, *7*, 911126. Advance online publication. DOI: 10.3389/feduc.2022.911126

Altukhi, Z. M., & Pradhan, S. (2024). Systematic literature review: Explainable AI definitions and challenges in education. In *Proceedings of the 45th International Conference on Information Systems (ICIS 2024), 11*. Association for Information Systems. https://aisel.aisnet.org/icis2024/lit_review/lit_review/11

Altukhi, Z. M., Pradhan, S., & Aljohani, N. (2025). A systematic literature review of the latest advancements in XAI. *Technologies*, *13*(3), 93. Advance online publication. DOI: 10.3390/technologies13030093

Al-Zahrani, A., Khalil, I., Awaji, B., & Mohsen, M. (2024). AI technologies in STEAM education for students: Systematic literature review. *Journal of Ecohumanism*, *3*(4), 3380–3394. DOI: 10.62754/joe.v3i4.4041

Amato, F., Galli, A., Gravina, M., Marassi, L., Marrone, S., & Sansone, C. (2023, May). AI-Powered Learning: Personalizing Education for each Student. In Ital-IA (pp. 478-483).

Amershi, S., Cakmak, M., Knox, W. B., & Kulesza, T. (2014). Power to the people: The role of humans in interactive machine learning. *AI Magazine*, *35*(4), 105–120. DOI: 10.1609/aimag.v35i4.2513

Anđelić, N., & Baressi Šegota, S. (2024). Achieving high accuracy in Android malware detection through genetic programming symbolic classifier. *Computers*, *13*(8), 197. Advance online publication. DOI: 10.3390/computers13080197

Anđelić, N., Baressi Šegota, S., Glučina, M., & Lorencin, I. (2023). Classification of wall following robot movements using genetic programming symbolic classifier. *Machines (Basel), 11*(1), 105. Advance online publication. DOI: 10.3390/machines11010105

Anđelić, N., Baressi Šegota, S., & Mrzljak, V. (2025). Hybrid explainable AI for machine predictive maintenance: From symbolic expressions to meta-ensembles. *Processes (Basel, Switzerland), 13*(7), 2180. Advance online publication. DOI: 10.3390/pr13072180

Apoki, Y., Railean, J., & Elci, A. (2022). The role of pedagogical agents in personalised adaptive learning. *Sustainability (Basel), 14*(11), 6442. DOI: 10.3390/su14116442

Asmussen, G., Rodemer, M., & Bernholt, S. (2025). Stepping stones to success: A qualitative investigation of the effectiveness of adaptive stepped supporting tools for problem-solving in organic chemistry to design an intelligent tutoring system. *International Journal of Science Education, 47*(10), 1252–1274. Advance online publication. DOI: 10.1080/09500693.2024.2361933

Ayeni, O. O., Al Hamad, N. M., Chisom, O. N., Osawaru, B., & Adewusi, O. E. (2024). AI in education: A review of personalized learning and educational technology. *GSC Advanced Research and Reviews, 18*(2), 261–271. DOI: 10.30574/gscarr.2024.18.2.0062

Baidoo-Anu, D., & Owusu Ansah, L. (2023). Education in the era of generative artificial intelligence (AI): Understanding the potential benefits of ChatGPT in promoting teaching and learning. *Journal of AI, 7*(1), 52–62. DOI: 10.61969/jai.1337500

Baker, R. S. J. d., & Inventado, P. S. (2014). Educational data mining and learning analytics. In Larusson, J. A., & White, B. (Eds.), *Learning analytics: From research to practice* (pp. 61–75). Springer., DOI: 10.1007/978-1-4614-3305-7_4

Baker, R. S., & Hawn, A. (2022). Algorithmic bias in education. *International Journal of Artificial Intelligence in Education, 32*(4), 1052–1092. DOI: 10.1007/s40593-021-00285-9

Baker, R. S., Martin, T., & Rossi, L. M. (2016). Educational data mining and learning analytics. In Rupp, A. A., & Leighton, J. P. (Eds.), *The Wiley handbook of cognition and assessment: Frameworks, methodologies, and applications* (pp. 379–396). Wiley., DOI: 10.1002/9781118956588.ch16

Baldinger, I., Seifried, C., & Rummer, D. (2026). Digital adaptive learning in secondary mathematics: A mixed-methods study of the antecedents of students' motivational and learning outcomes. *Journal of Computer Assisted Learning*. Advance online publication. DOI: 10.1002/jcal.70178

Barocas, S., & Selbst, A. D. (2016). Big data's disparate impact. *SSRN*, *104*(3), 671–732. DOI: 10.2139/ssrn.2477899

Barredo Arrieta, A., Díaz-Rodríguez, N., Del Ser, J., Bennetot, A., Tabik, S., Barbado, A., Garcia, S., Gil-Lopez, S., Molina, D., Benjamins, R., Chatila, R., & Herrera, F. (2020). Explainable Artificial Intelligence (XAI): Concepts, taxonomies, opportunities and challenges toward responsible AI. *Information Fusion*, *58*, 82–115. DOI: 10.1016/j.inffus.2019.12.012

Barros, C. D. T., Mendonça, M. R. F., Vieira, A. B., & Ziviani, A. (2021). A survey on embedding dynamic graphs. *ACM Computing Surveys*, *55*(1), 10. Advance online publication. DOI: 10.1145/3483595

Bas, C., & Kiraz, A. (2025). Primary school teachers' needs for AI-supported STEM education. *Sustainability (Basel)*, *17*(15), 7044. Advance online publication. DOI: 10.3390/su17157044

Belbase, S., Mainali, B. R., Kasemsukpipat, W., Tairab, H., Gochoo, M., & Jarrah, A. (2022). At the dawn of science, technology, engineering, arts, and mathematics (STEAM) education: Prospects, priorities, processes, and problems. *International Journal of Mathematical Education in Science and Technology*, *53*(11), 2919–2955. DOI: 10.1080/0020739X.2021.1922943

Berg, A. M., Mol, S. T., Kismihók, G., & Sclater, N. (2016). The role of a reference synthetic data generator within the field of learning analytics. *Journal of Learning Analytics*, *3*(1), 107–128. DOI: 10.18608/jla.2016.31.7

Bertolini, R., Finch, S. J., & Nehm, R. H. (2023). An application of Bayesian inference to examine student retention and attrition in the STEM classroom. *Frontiers in Education*, *8*, 1073829. Advance online publication. DOI: 10.3389/feduc.2023.1073829

Bertrand, M. G., & Namukasa, I. K. (2023). A pedagogical model for STEAM education. *Journal of Research in Innovative Teaching & Learning*, *16*(2), 169–191. DOI: 10.1108/JRIT-12-2021-0081

Bhati, D., Amiruzzaman, M., Zhao, Y., Guercio, A., & Le, T. (2025). A survey of post-hoc xai methods from a visualization perspective: Challenges and opportunities. *IEEE Access : Practical Innovations, Open Solutions*, *13*, 120785–120806. DOI: 10.1109/ACCESS.2025.3581136

Bhattacharjya, M. (2025). Future-proofing education: Developing transdisciplinary STEAM models to prepare learners for a workforce in the forthcoming era of automation. *Transdisciplinary Journal of Engineering & Science*, *16*(6), 67–97. DOI: 10.22545/2025/00271

Bhutoria, A. (2022). Personalized education and artificial intelligence in the United States, China, and India: A systematic review using a human-in-the-loop model. *Computers and Education: Artificial Intelligence*, *3*, 100068. Advance online publication. DOI: 10.1016/j.caeai.2022.100068

Bin Qushem, U., Christopoulos, A., Kaliisa, R., Khalil, M., Salakoski, T., & Laakso, M.-J. (2025). Technology-enhanced learning and learning analytics for personalised STEM learning: A scoping review. *International Journal of Educational Research*, *134*, 102827. Advance online publication. DOI: 10.1016/j.ijer.2025.102827

Bird, K. A., Castleman, B. L., & Song, Y. (2025). Are algorithms biased in education? Exploring racial bias in predicting community college student success. *Journal of Policy Analysis and Management*, *44*(2), 379–402. DOI: 10.1002/pam.22569

Bond, M., Khosravi, H., De Laat, M., Bergdahl, N., Negrea, V., Oxley, E., Pham, P., Chong, S. W., & Siemens, G. (2024). A meta systematic review of artificial intelligence in higher education: A call for increased ethics, collaboration, and rigour. *International Journal of Educational Technology in Higher Education*, *21*(1), 4. Advance online publication. DOI: 10.1186/s41239-023-00436-z

Brown, T. B., Mann, B., Ryder, N., Subbiah, M., Kaplan, J. D., Dhariwal, P., Neelakantan, A., Shyam, P., Sastry, G., Askell, A., Agarwal, S., Herbert-Voss, A., Krueger, G., Henighan, T., Child, R., Ramesh, A., Ziegler, D. M., Wu, J., Winter, C., & Amodei, D. (2020). Language models are few-shot learners. *Advances in Neural Information Processing Systems*, *33*, 1877–1901.

Brunke, L., Greeff, M., Hall, A. W., Yuan, Z., Zhou, S., Panerati, J., & Schoellig, A. P. (2022). Safe learning in robotics: From learning-based control to safe reinforcement learning. *Annual Review of Control, Robotics, and Autonomous Systems*, *5*(1), 411–444. DOI: 10.1146/annurev-control-042920-020211

Bulathwela, S., Pérez-Ortiz, M., Holloway, C., Cukurova, M., & Shawe-Taylor, J. (2024). Artificial intelligence alone will not democratise education: On educational inequality, techno-solutionism and inclusive tools. *Sustainability (Basel)*, *16*(2), 781. DOI: 10.3390/su16020781

Cai, C., Zhu, G., & Ma, M. (2025). A systemic review of AI for interdisciplinary learning: Application contexts, roles, and influences. *Education and Information Technologies*, *30*(7), 9641–9687. DOI: 10.1007/s10639-024-13193-x

Chan, C. K. Y. (2023). A comprehensive AI policy education framework for university teaching and learning. *International Journal of Educational Technology in Higher Education, 20*(1), 38. Advance online publication. DOI: 10.1186/s41239-023-00408-3

Chang, C. H., & Kidman, G. (2025). Interdisciplinary learning and pedagogical content knowledge in sustainability education–implications for STEAM education. *International Research in Geographical and Environmental Education, 34*(2), 95–99. DOI: 10.1080/10382046.2025.2476805

Chazal, F., & Michel, B. (2021). An introduction to topological data analysis: Fundamental and practical aspects for data scientists. *Frontiers in Artificial Intelligence, 4*, 667963. Advance online publication. DOI: 10.3389/frai.2021.667963 PMID: 34661095

Chen, M., Wang, D., Feng, S., & Zhang, Y. (2023). Topological regularization for representation learning via persistent homology. *Mathematics, 11*(4), 1008. Advance online publication. DOI: 10.3390/math11041008

Chen, T., & Guestrin, C. (2016, August). Xgboost: A scalable tree boosting system. In *Proceedings of the 22nd acm sigkdd international conference on knowledge discovery and data mining* (pp. 785-794).

Chen, X. (2013). *STEM Attrition: College Students' Paths into and out of STEM Fields. Statistical Analysis Report. NCES 2014-001*. National Center for Education Statistics.

Chigbu, B. I., & Makapela, S. L. (2025). AI in education, sustainability, and the future of work: An integrative review of industry 5.0, education 5.0, and work 5.0. *Journal of Open Innovation, 11*(4), 100645. Advance online publication. DOI: 10.1016/j.joitmc.2025.100645

Chi, M. T., & Wylie, R. (2014). The ICAP framework: Linking cognitive engagement to active learning outcomes. *Educational Psychologist, 49*(4), 219–243. DOI: 10.1080/00461520.2014.965823

Chouldechova, A. (2017). Fair prediction with disparate impact: A study of bias in recidivism prediction instruments. *Big Data, 5*(2), 153–163. DOI: 10.1089/big.2016.0047 PMID: 28632438

Conati, C., Barral, O., Putnam, V., & Rieger, L. (2021). Toward personalized XAI: A case study in intelligent tutoring systems. *Artificial Intelligence, 298*, 103503. Advance online publication. DOI: 10.1016/j.artint.2021.103503

Contrino, M. F., Reyes-Millán, M., Vázquez-Villegas, P., & Membrillo-Hernández, J. (2024). Using an adaptive learning tool to improve student performance and satisfaction in online and face-to-face education for a more personalized approach. *Smart Learning Environments*, *11*(1), 6. Advance online publication. DOI: 10.1186/s40561-024-00292-y

Credé, M., Roch, S. G., & Kieszczynka, U. M. (2010). Class attendance in college: A meta-analytic review of the relationship of class attendance with grades and student characteristics. *Review of Educational Research*, *80*(2), 272–295. DOI: 10.3102/0034654310362998

Cuba, M. J., Taylor, J. P., Tariq, A. R., Lee, J. Y., & Avellone, L. (2026). Disproportionate Representation of Multilingual Learners With Intellectual and Developmental Disabilities: A Systematic Literature Review. *Review of Educational Research*, •••, 00346543261426579. DOI: 10.3102/00346543261426579

da Silva, F. L., Slodkowski, B. K., da Silva, K. K. A., & Cazella, S. C. (2023). A systematic literature review on educational recommender systems for teaching and learning: Research trends, limitations and opportunities. *Education and Information Technologies*, *28*(3), 3289–3328. DOI: 10.1007/s10639-022-11341-9 PMID: 36124004

De Bruijn, H., Warnier, M., & Janssen, M. (2022). The perils and pitfalls of explainable AI: Strategies for explaining algorithmic decision-making. *Government Information Quarterly*, *39*(2), 101666. DOI: 10.1016/j.giq.2021.101666

Deho, O. B., Zhan, C., Li, J., Liu, J., Liu, L., & Duy Le, T. (2022). How do the existing fairness metrics and unfairness mitigation algorithms contribute to ethical learning analytics? *British Journal of Educational Technology*, *53*(4), 822–843. DOI: 10.1111/bjet.13217

Dembe, A. (2024). Advancing personalized learning through educational artificial intelligence: Challenges, opportunities, and future directions. *Res Invent J Eng Phys Sci*, *3*(1), 89–101.

DeWallace-Marenholz, J. L. (2025). High-Quality Instruction in Practice: Empowering Teachers Through a Co-Created STEAM Learning Lab (Doctoral dissertation, Northeastern University).

Dignam, C., Smith, C. M., & Kelly, A. L. (2025). The heart and art of robotics: From AI to artificial emotional intelligence in STEM education. *Journal of Education in Science, Environment and Health*, *11*(2), 151–169. DOI: 10.55549/jeseh.813

Doroudi, S. (2023). The intertwined histories of artificial intelligence and education. *International Journal of Artificial Intelligence in Education, 33*(4), 885–928. DOI: 10.1007/s40593-022-00313-2

Doshi-Velez, F., & Kim, B. (2017). *Towards A Rigorous Science of Interpretable Machine Learning*. arXiv. /arXiv.1702.08608DOI: 10.48550

du Plooy, M., Casteleijn, E., & Franzsen, R. (2024). Personalized adaptive learning in higher education: A scoping review of key characteristics and impact on academic performance and engagement. *Heliyon, 10*(21), e39630. DOI: 10.1016/j.heliyon.2024.e39630 PMID: 39524879

Duan, X., Pei, B., Ambrose, G. A., Hershkovitz, A., Cheng, Y., & Wang, C. (2024). Towards transparent and trustworthy prediction of student learning achievement by including instructors as co-designers: A case study. *Education and Information Technologies, 29*(3), 3075–3096. DOI: 10.1007/s10639-023-11954-8

Ducange, P., Marcelloni, F., & Pecori, R. (2021). Fuzzy Hoeffding decision tree for data stream classification. *International Journal of Computational Intelligence Systems, 14*(1), 946–964. DOI: 10.2991/ijcis.d.210212.001

Dutta, A., & Chauhan, S. (2025). Artificial intelligence in student privacy and data security. *International Journal of Advanced Research in Computer Science, 16*(3), 146–151. DOI: 10.26483/ijarcs.v16i3.7261

Dwivedi, R., Dave, D., Naik, H., Singhal, S., Omer, R., Patel, P., Qian, B., Wen, Z., Shah, T., Morgan, G., & Ranjan, R. (2023). Explainable AI (XAI): Core ideas, techniques, and solutions. *ACM Computing Surveys, 55*(9), 1–33. DOI: 10.1145/3561048

El Emam, K., Mosquera, L., & Bass, J. (2020). Evaluating identity disclosure risk in fully synthetic health data: Model development and validation. *Journal of Medical Internet Research, 22*(11), e23139. Advance online publication. DOI: 10.2196/23139 PMID: 33196453

Eldrandaly, K. A., Abdel-Basset, M., Ibrahim, M., & Abdel-Aziz, N. M. (2023). Explainable and secure artificial intelligence: Taxonomy, cases of study, learned lessons, challenges and future directions. *Enterprise Information Systems, 17*(9), 2098537. DOI: 10.1080/17517575.2022.2098537

Esteves, B., Asgarinia, H., Penedo, A. C., Mutiro, B., & Lewis, D. (2022, December). Fostering trust with transparency in the data economy era: An integrated ethical, legal, and knowledge engineering approach. In *Proceedings of the 1st International Workshop on Data Economy* (pp. 57-63). DOI: 10.1145/3565011.3569061

European Commission: Directorate-General for Education, Youth, Sport and Culture. (2022). *Ethical guidelines on the use of artificial intelligence (AI) and data in teaching and learning for educators*. Publications Office of the European Union. DOI: 10.2766/153756

European Education and Culture Executive Agency. (2025). *Explainable AI in education: Fostering human oversight and shared responsibility*. Publications Office of the European Union., DOI: 10.2797/6780469

European Parliament and Council of the European Union. (2024). *Regulation (EU) 2024/1689 of the European Parliament and of the Council of 13 June 2024 laying down harmonised rules on artificial intelligence and amending Regulations (EC) No 300/2008, (EU) No 167/2013, (EU) No 168/2013, (EU) 2018/858, (EU) 2018/1139 and (EU) 2019/2144 and Directives 2014/90/EU, (EU) 2016/797 and (EU) 2020/1828 (Artificial Intelligence Act). Official Journal of the European Union, L 2024/1689.* https://data.europa.eu/eli/reg/2024/1689/oj

Fasco, P. S. (2025). Cognitive Architecture for Adaptive Problem-Solving and Computational Models of Expert Knowledge Acquisition in Computer Science Education.

Feldman, M., Friedler, S. A., Moeller, J., Scheidegger, C., & Venkatasubramanian, S. (2015). Certifying and removing disparate impact. In *Proceedings of the 21st ACM SIGKDD International Conference on Knowledge Discovery and Data Mining* (pp. 259–268). Association for Computing Machinery. https://doi.org/DOI: 10.1145/2783258.2783311

Feldman-Maggor, Y., Cukurova, M., Kent, C., & Alexandron, G. (2025). The impact of explainable AI on teachers' trust and acceptance of AI EdTech recommendations: The power of domain-specific explanations. *International Journal of Artificial Intelligence in Education*, *35*(5), 2889–2922. DOI: 10.1007/s40593-025-00486-6

Ferguson, R. (2012). Learning analytics: Drivers, developments and challenges. *International Journal of Technology Enhanced Learning*, *4*(5/6), 304–317. DOI: 10.1504/IJTEL.2012.051816

Filgueiras, F. (2024). Artificial intelligence and education governance. *Education, Citizenship and Social Justice*, *19*(3), 349–361. DOI: 10.1177/17461979231160674

Fiok, K., Farahani, F. V., Karwowski, W., & Ahram, T. (2022). Explainable artificial intelligence for education and training. *The Journal of Defense Modeling and Simulation*, *19*(2), 133–144. DOI: 10.1177/15485129211028651

Fischer, C., Pardos, Z. A., Baker, R. S., Williams, J. J., Smyth, P., Yu, R., & Warschauer, M. (2020). Mining big data in education: Affordances and challenges. *Review of Research in Education, 44*(1), 130–160. DOI: 10.3102/0091732X20903304

Floridi, L., Cowls, J., Beltrametti, M., Chatila, R., Chazerand, P., Dignum, V., Luetge, C., Madelin, R., Pagallo, U., Rossi, F., Schafer, B., Valcke, P., & Vayena, E. (2018). AI4People—An Ethical Framework for a Good AI Society: Opportunities, Risks, Principles, and Recommendations. *Minds and Machines, 28*(4), 689–707. DOI: 10.1007/s11023-018-9482-5 PMID: 30930541

Fodouop Kouam, A. W. (2024). The effectiveness of intelligent tutoring systems in supporting students with varying levels of programming experience. *Discover Education, 3*(1), 278. Advance online publication. DOI: 10.1007/s44217-024-00385-3

Freeman, S., Eddy, S. L., McDonough, M., Smith, M. K., Okoroafor, N., Jordt, H., & Wenderoth, M. P. (2014). Active learning increases student performance in science, engineering, and mathematics. *Proceedings of the National Academy of Sciences of the United States of America, 111*(23), 8410–8415. DOI: 10.1073/pnas.1319030111 PMID: 24821756

Fregosi, C. (2025). How to Explain in XAI?-Investigating Explanation Protocols in Decision Support Systems.

Galés, N. L. (2024). Trust and connection in the artificial intelligence educational ecosystem: From algorithmism to algoritharism. *Revista Catalana de Pedagogia, 26*, 4–37.

Galindo Domínguez, H., Perines, H., Verde Trabada, A., & Valero Esteban, J. M. (2022). Understanding the pedagogical gap between the educational research and the reality of teachers: an analisis of the difficulties and proposals.

Gao, N. (2025). Design and application of an intelligent teaching platform integrating international Chinese education and STEAM education. In *Proceedings of the 2025 2nd International Conference on Artificial Intelligence and Future Education* (pp. 316–320). Association for Computing Machinery. https://doi.org/ DOI: 10.1145/3785987.3786039

García, J., & Fernández, F. (2015). A comprehensive survey on safe reinforcement learning. *Journal of Machine Learning Research, 16*, 1437–1480. https://jmlr.org/papers/v16/garcia15a.html

García-Senín, S., Arguedas, M., & Daradoumis, T. (2022). Using learning analytics to support STEAM students' academic achievement and self-regulated learning. *Research on Education and Media, 14*(1), 36–45. DOI: 10.2478/rem-2022-0005

Garzón, J., Pavón, J., & Baldiris, S. (2019). Systematic review and meta-analysis of augmented reality in educational settings. *Virtual Reality (Waltham Cross)*, *23*(4), 447–459. DOI: 10.1007/s10055-019-00379-9

Gašević, D., Dawson, S., & Siemens, G. (2015). Let's not forget: Learning analytics are about learning. *TechTrends*, *59*(1), 64–71. DOI: 10.1007/s11528-014-0822-x

Gebru, T., Morgenstern, J., Vecchione, B., Vaughan, J. W., Wallach, H., Daumé, H.III, & Crawford, K. (2021). Datasheets for datasets. *Communications of the ACM*, *64*(12), 86–92. DOI: 10.1145/3458723

Gee, K., Ryndak, D. L., Fisher, M., & Walker, V. L. (2024). Access to the general education curriculum for students with extensive support needs: Experts' perspectives. *Research and Practice for Persons with Severe Disabilities : the Journal of TASH*, *49*(1), 3–19. DOI: 10.1177/15407969231219027

George, B., & Wooden, O. (2023). Managing the strategic transformation of higher education through artificial intelligence. *Administrative Sciences*, *13*(9), 196. Advance online publication. DOI: 10.3390/admsci13090196

George, E. B., Senthilkumar, R., Al-Junaibi, F., & Al-Shuaibi, Z.E. Ben George. (2025). Explainable AI methods for predicting student grades and improving academic success. *Journal of Information Systems Engineering & Management*, *10*(23s), 117–126. DOI: 10.52783/jisem.v10i23s.3680

Gjoka, A., & Pireva Nuci, K. (2025). Exploring the role of augmented reality in STEAM learning environments: Evidence from geometry education. *Information (Basel)*, *16*(12), 1113. Advance online publication. DOI: 10.3390/info16121113

Gligorea, A. M., Cioca, M., Oancea, R., Gorski, A.-T., Gorski, O. D., & Tudorache, A. A. (2023). Adaptive learning using artificial intelligence in e-learning: A literature review. *Education Sciences*, *13*(12), 1216. DOI: 10.3390/educsci13121216

Gómez, E., Zhang, C. S., Boratto, L., Salamó, M., & Ramos, G. (2022). Enabling cross-continent provider fairness in educational recommender systems. *Future Generation Computer Systems*, *127*, 435–447. DOI: 10.1016/j.future.2021.08.025

Goncalves, A., Ray, P., Soper, B., Stevens, J., Coyle, L., & Sales, A. P. (2020). Generation and evaluation of synthetic patient data. *BMC Medical Research Methodology*, *20*(1), 108. Advance online publication. DOI: 10.1186/s12874-020-00977-1 PMID: 32381039

González-Calatayud, V., Prendes-Espinosa, P., & Roig-Vila, R. (2021). Artificial intelligence for student assessment: A systematic review. *Applied Sciences (Basel, Switzerland)*, *11*(12), 5467. Advance online publication. DOI: 10.3390/app11125467

Grant, D. G., Behrends, J., & Basl, J. (2025). What we owe to decision-subjects: Beyond transparency and explanation in automated decision-making. *Philosophical Studies*, *182*(1), 55–85. DOI: 10.1007/s11098-023-02013-6

Griffiths, D., Hoel, T., & Cooper, A. (2016). *Learning analytics interoperability: Requirements, specifications and adoption*. LACE Project.

Grinsztajn, L., Oyallon, E., & Varoquaux, G. (2022). Why do tree-based models still outperform deep learning on typical tabular data? *Advances in Neural Information Processing Systems*, *35*, 507–520. DOI: 10.52202/068431-0037

Guan, Q., Cheng, X., Xiao, F., Li, Z., He, C., Fang, L., Chen, G., Gong, Z., & Luo, W. (2025). Explainable exercise recommendation with knowledge graph. *Neural Networks*, *183*, 106954. Advance online publication. DOI: 10.1016/j.neunet.2024.106954 PMID: 39667214

Guidotti, R., Monreale, A., Ruggieri, S., Turini, F., Giannotti, F., & Pedreschi, D. (2018). A survey of methods for explaining black box models. *ACM Computing Surveys*, *51*(5), 93. Advance online publication. DOI: 10.1145/3236009

Gunasekara, S. V. S., & Saarela, M. (2025). Systematic literature review on explainable learning analytics and educational data mining. *IEEE Access : Practical Innovations, Open Solutions*, *13*, 214387–214408. DOI: 10.1109/ACCESS.2025.3643645

Gunasekara, S., & Saarela, M. (2025). Explainable AI in education: Techniques and qualitative assessment. *Applied Sciences (Basel, Switzerland)*, *15*(3), 1239. DOI: 10.3390/app15031239

Gunning, D., Stefik, M., Choi, J., Miller, T., Stumpf, S., & Yang, G. Z. (2019). XAI—Explainable artificial intelligence. *Science Robotics*, *4*(37), eaay7120. DOI: 10.1126/scirobotics.aay7120 PMID: 33137719

Han, S.-I., Nakamura, K., & Hong, B.-W. (2024). Splitting of composite neural networks via proximal operator with information bottleneck. *IEEE Access : Practical Innovations, Open Solutions*, *12*, 157–167. DOI: 10.1109/ACCESS.2023.3346697

Hardt, M., Price, E., & Srebro, N. (2016). Equality of opportunity in supervised learning. In *Advances in Neural Information Processing Systems 29*. NeurIPS. https://papers.nips.cc/paper/6374-equality-of-opportunity-in-supervised-learning

Heiser, R., Underhill, G., & Stritto, M. E. D. (2026). Power, Privacy, and Transparency in Communicating Learning Analytics in Higher Education: A Critical Discourse Analysis. *American Journal of Qualitative Research*, *10*(1), 246–265. DOI: 10.29333/ajqr/17463

Holmes, W., Bialik, M., & Fadel, C. (2019). *Artificial intelligence in education: Promises and implications for teaching and learning*. Center for Curriculum Redesign.

Holmes, W., Porayska-Pomsta, K., Holstein, K., Sutherland, E., Baker, T., Shum, S. B., Santos, O. C., Rodrigo, M. T., Cukurova, M., Bittencourt, I. I., & Koedinger, K. R. (2022). Ethics of AI in education: Towards a community-wide framework. *International Journal of Artificial Intelligence in Education, 32*(3), 504–526. DOI: 10.1007/s40593-021-00239-1

Honke, N., & Becker-Genschow, S. (2025). Adaptive learning in bionics: Transforming science education. *Frontiers in Education, 10*, 1427083. Advance online publication. DOI: 10.3389/feduc.2025.1427083

How, M.-L., & Hung, W. L. D. (2019). Educing AI-thinking in science, technology, engineering, arts, and mathematics (STEAM) education. *Education Sciences, 9*(3), 184. Advance online publication. DOI: 10.3390/educsci9030184

Hsiao, H.-S., Chen, J.-H., Tsai, H.-W., & Chung, G.-H. (2025). Investigating the effectiveness of VR technology on hands-on STEAM learning activities for junior high school students. *Interactive Learning Environments*, 1–19. Advance online publication. DOI: 10.1080/10494820.2025.2580984

Huang, Q., Wang, Z., Yang, J., Wu, L., & Hung, W. L. D. (2025). The Influencing Factors of Integrating Artificial Intelligence in Teaching for STEAM Teachers in Primary and Secondary Schools: A Qualitative Study. In International Handbook of Research on STEAM Curriculum and Practice (pp. 432-449). Routledge. DOI: 10.4324/9781003435488-27

Huang, A. Y. Q., Lu, O. H. T., & Yang, S. J. H. (2023). Effects of artificial intelligence-enabled personalized recommendations on learners' learning engagement, motivation, and outcomes in a flipped classroom. *Computers & Education, 194*, 104684. Advance online publication. DOI: 10.1016/j.compedu.2022.104684

Hughes, B. S., Corrigan, M. W., Grove, D., Andersen, S. B., & Wong, J. T. (2022). Integrating arts with STEM and leading with STEAM to increase science learning with equity for emerging bilingual learners in the United States. *International Journal of STEM Education, 9*(1), 58. DOI: 10.1186/s40594-022-00375-7

Hwang, G.-J., Xie, H., Wah, B. W., & Gašević, D. (2020). Vision, challenges, roles and research issues of artificial intelligence in education. *Computers and Education: Artificial Intelligence, 1*, 100001. Advance online publication. DOI: 10.1016/j.caeai.2020.100001

Idrizi, E. (2024, May). Exploring the role of explainable artificial intelligence (XAI) in adaptive learning systems. In *Proceedings of the Cognitive Models and Artificial Intelligence Conference* (pp. 100-105). DOI: 10.1145/3660853.3660877

International Organization for Standardization. (2020). *Information technology for learning, education and training—Learning analytics interoperability—Part 3: Guidelines for data interoperability* (ISO/IEC TS 20748-3:2020). ISO.

Ismail, I. A., & Aloshi, J. M. (2025). Data privacy in AI-driven education: An in-depth exploration into the data privacy concerns and potential solutions. In Keeley, K. L. (Ed.), *AI applications and strategies in teacher education* (pp. 223–252). IGI Global Scientific Publishing., DOI: 10.4018/979-8-3693-5443-8.ch008

Ito, T., Campbell, M., Horesh, L., Klinger, T., & Ram, P. (2025). Quantifying artificial intelligence through algorithmic generalization. *Nature Machine Intelligence*, *7*(8), 1195–1205. DOI: 10.1038/s42256-025-01092-w

Jang, Y., Choi, S.-H., Jung, H., & Kim, H. (2022). Practical early prediction of students' performance using machine learning and eXplainable AI. *Education and Information Technologies*, *27*(9), 12855–12889. DOI: 10.1007/s10639-022-11120-6

Jia, Z. (2022). Designing an intelligent teaching system of Chinese as a foreign language under the internet background. *Scientific Programming*, *2022*, 3610081. Advance online publication. DOI: 10.1155/2022/3610081

Jing, H., Zhao, L., Zhu, M., Wang, C., Wang, H., & Xia, Y. (2023). The influence of AI adaptive learning systems on learning attitude and learning performance: The moderating effect of learning style. *Sustainability*, *15*(4), 3115. DOI: 10.3390/su15043115

Joksimović, S., Marshall, R., Rakotoarivelo, T., Ladjal, D., Zhan, C., & Pardo, A. (2022). Privacy-driven learning analytics. In McKay, E. (Ed.), *Manage your own learning analytics: Implement a Rasch modelling approach* (pp. 1–22). Springer., DOI: 10.1007/978-3-030-86316-6_1

Ju, W., Fang, Z., Gu, Y., Liu, Z., Long, Q., Qiao, Z., Qin, Y., Shen, J., Sun, F., Xiao, Z., Yang, J., Yuan, J., Zhao, Y., Wang, Y., Luo, X., & Zhang, M. (2024). A comprehensive survey on deep graph representation learning. *Neural Networks*, *173*, 106207. Advance online publication. DOI: 10.1016/j.neunet.2024.106207 PMID: 38442651

Kabudi, T., Pappas, I., & Olsen, D. H. (2021). AI-enabled adaptive learning systems: A systematic mapping of the literature. *Computers and Education: Artificial Intelligence*, *2*, 100017. Advance online publication. DOI: 10.1016/j.caeai.2021.100017

KANAROS, D. (2025). STEAM Education and Technological Innovation: New Models of Creative Learning. ISPEC JOURNAL OF SCIENCE INSTITUTE, 4(2), 93-103.

Karpicke, J. D. (2009). Metacognitive control and strategy selection: Deciding to practise retrieval during learning. *Journal of Experimental Psychology. General*, *138*(4), 469–486. DOI: 10.1037/a0017341 PMID: 19883131

Kasneci, E., Seßler, K., Küchemann, S., Bannert, M., Dementieva, D., Fischer, F., Gasser, U., Groh, G., Günnemann, S., Hüllermeier, E., Krusche, S., Kutyniok, G., Michaeli, T., Nerdel, C., Pfeffer, J., Poquet, O., Sailer, M., Schmidt, A., Seidel, T., & Kasneci, G. (2023). ChatGPT for good? On opportunities and challenges of large language models for education. *Learning and Individual Differences*, *103*, 102274. Advance online publication. DOI: 10.1016/j.lindif.2023.102274

Katona, G., & Gyonyoru, K. I. K. (2025). AI-based adaptive programming education for socially disadvantaged students. *TechTrends*, *69*(5), 925–942. Advance online publication. DOI: 10.1007/s11528-025-01088-8

Katz, S., Albacete, P., Chounta, I. A., Jordan, P., McLaren, B. M., & Zapata-Rivera, D. (2021). Linking dialogue with student modelling to create an adaptive tutoring system for conceptual physics. *International Journal of Artificial Intelligence in Education*, *31*(3), 397–445. DOI: 10.1007/s40593-020-00226-y

Kayama, M., Nagai, T., Tachi, N., Asuke, T., Taguchi, N., & Futagami, T. (2021). IoT-based learning material and its management system for STEAM in primary and secondary education. In Daniela, L. (Ed.), *The Internet of Things for education: A new actor on the stage* (pp. 145–163). Springer., DOI: 10.1007/978-3-030-85720-2_9

Kayyali, M. (2025). The impact of personalized learning on student engagement and achievement in STEAM. In *Integrating personalized learning methods into STEAM education* (pp. 51–78). IGI Global Scientific Publishing. DOI: 10.4018/979-8-3693-7718-5.ch003

Ke, G., Meng, Q., Finley, T., Wang, T., Chen, W., Ma, W., Ye, Q., & Liu, T.-Y. (2017). LightGBM: A highly efficient gradient boosting decision tree. *Advances in Neural Information Processing Systems*, *30*, 3146–3154.

Khalil, M., Vadiee, F., Shakya, R., & Liu, Q. (2025). Creating artificial students that never existed: Leveraging large language models and CTGANs for synthetic data generation. In *LAK '25: Proceedings of the 15th International Learning Analytics and Knowledge Conference* (pp. 439–450). Association for Computing Machinery. DOI: 10.1145/3706468.3706523

Khosravi, H., Shum, S. B., Chen, G., Conati, C., Tsai, Y.-S., Kay, J., Knight, S., Martinez-Maldonado, R., Sadiq, S., & Gašević, D. (2022). Explainable artificial intelligence in education. *Computers and Education: Artificial Intelligence, 3*, 100074. Advance online publication. DOI: 10.1016/j.caeai.2022.100074

Kim, S., Oh, J., Lee, S., Yu, S., Do, J., & Taghavi, T. (2023). Grounding counterfactual explanation of image classifiers to textual concept space. In *Proceedings of the IEEE/CVF Conference on Computer Vision and Pattern Recognition (CVPR)* (pp. 10942–10950). IEEE. https://doi.org/DOI: 10.1109/CVPR52729.2023.01053

Kizilcec, R. F., & Lee, H. (2022). Algorithmic fairness in education. In Holmes, W., & Porayska-Pomsta, K. (Eds.), *The ethics of artificial intelligence in education* (pp. 174–202). Routledge., DOI: 10.4324/9780429329067-10

Kohnke, S., & Zaugg, T. (2025). Artificial intelligence: An untapped opportunity for equity and access in STEM education. *Education Sciences, 15*(1), 68. Advance online publication. DOI: 10.3390/educsci15010068

Kotelnikov, A., Baranchuk, D., Rubachev, I., & Babenko, A. (2023). TabDDPM: Modelling tabular data with diffusion models. In A. Krause, E. Brunskill, K. Cho, B. Engelhardt, S. Sabato, & J. Scarlett (Eds.), *Proceedings of the 40th International Conference on Machine Learning* (*Proceedings of Machine Learning Research*, Vol. 202, pp. 17564–17579). PMLR. https://proceedings.mlr.press/v202/kotelnikov23a.html

Koutsantonis, G., Gronseth, J., & Surry, P. (2022). A bibliometric literature review of adaptive learning systems. *Sustainability (Basel), 14*(19), 12684. DOI: 10.3390/su141912684

Lai, J.-L., Chiu, P.-S., & Chou, T.-H. (2025). A case study of intelligent tutoring system for coding and learning (ITS-CAL) for learning effectiveness analysis. *Applied Sciences (Basel, Switzerland), 15*(4), 1922. DOI: 10.3390/app15041922

Leavy, A., Dick, L., Meletiou-Mavrotheris, M., Paparistodemou, E., & Stylianou, E. (2023). The prevalence and use of emerging technologies in STEAM education: A systematic review of the literature. *Journal of Computer Assisted Learning, 39*(4), 1061–1082. DOI: 10.1111/jcal.12806

Lee, H., Mojica, G., Thrasher, E., & Baumgartner, P. (2022). Investigating data like a data scientist: Key practices and processes. *Statistics Education Research Journal, 21*(2), 3–3. DOI: 10.52041/serj.v21i2.41

Le, N., & Taherdoost, H. (2025, February). Pervasive AI and IoT in STEAM Education: Advancing Future Learning Through Intelligent Systems and Computational Technologies. In *2025 International Conference on Pervasive Computational Technologies (ICPCT)* (pp. 736-741). IEEE. DOI: 10.1109/ICPCT64145.2025.10940569

Lewis, M., & Crawford, C. (2024). Towards blockchain-based incentives for STEM education. In Stephanidis, C., Antona, M., Ntoa, S., & Salvendy, G. (Eds.), *HCI International 2024 Posters* (Vol. 2117, pp. 123–134). Springer., DOI: 10.1007/978-3-031-61953-3_15

Lewis, P., Perez, E., Piktus, A., Petroni, F., Karpukhin, V., Goyal, N., & Kiela, D. (2020). Retrieval-augmented generation for knowledge-intensive nlp tasks. *Advances in Neural Information Processing Systems*, *33*, 9459–9474.

Liang, X., Xiong, W., Lou, S., Lin, J., & Chan, C.-K. (2026). Design and implementation of an AI-powered adaptive learning system for university students. *International Journal of Data Science and Analytics*, *22*(1), 118. Advance online publication. DOI: 10.1007/s41060-026-01045-5

Li, B., Qi, P., Liu, B., Di, S., Liu, J., Pei, J., Yi, J., & Zhou, B. (2023). Trustworthy AI: From principles to practices. *ACM Computing Surveys*, *55*(9), 177. Advance online publication. DOI: 10.1145/3555803

Li, M.-J., Li, S.-T., Yang, A. C. M., Huang, A. Y. Q., & Yang, S. J. H. (2024). Trustworthy and Explainable AI for Learning Analytics. *CEUR Workshop Proceedings*, *3667*, 3–12. https://ceur-ws.org/Vol-3667/DC-LAK24-paper-1.pdf

Lin, C.-C., Huang, A. Y. Q., & Lu, O. H. T. (2023). Artificial intelligence in intelligent tutoring systems toward sustainable education: A systematic review. *Smart Learning Environments*, *10*(1), 41. Advance online publication. DOI: 10.1186/s40561-023-00260-y

Lin, M. P.-C., & Chang, D. (2023). CHAT-ACTS: A pedagogical framework for personalised chatbot to enhance active learning and self-regulated learning. *Computers and Education: Artificial Intelligence*, *5*, 100167. Advance online publication. DOI: 10.1016/j.caeai.2023.100167

Lin, Y.-T., Hsu, Y.-S., & Tsai, I.-C. (2025). The impact of Taiwan Adaptive Learning Platform (TALP) on self-regulated learning and mathematics achievement. *Educational Psychology*. Advance online publication. DOI: 10.1080/01443410.2025.2561028

Liu, C. (2022). A case study of the adaptive learning platform in a Taiwanese elementary school: Precision education from teachers' perspectives. *Education and Information Technologies*, *27*(5), 6295–6316. DOI: 10.1007/s10639-021-10851-2 PMID: 35013667

Liu, Q., Khalil, M., Shakya, R., & Jovanović, J. (2024). Scaling while privacy preserving: A comprehensive synthetic tabular data generation and evaluation in learning analytics. In *LAK '24: Proceedings of the 14th International Learning Analytics and Knowledge Conference* (pp. 620–631). Association for Computing Machinery. DOI: 10.1145/3636555.3636921

Liu, Q., Shakya, R., Jovanović, J., Khalil, M., & de la Hoz-Ruiz, J. (2025). Ensuring privacy through synthetic data generation in education. *British Journal of Educational Technology*, *56*(3), 1053–1073. DOI: 10.1111/bjet.13576

Li, Y., Shan, Z., Raković, M., Guan, Q., Gašević, D., & Chen, G. (2025). When AI explains in natural language: Unveiling the impact of generative AI explanations on educators' grading and feedback practices. *Education and Information Technologies*, *30*(17), 24931–24964. DOI: 10.1007/s10639-025-13741-z

López-Pernas, S., Oliveira, E., Song, Y., & Saqr, M. (2026). AI, explainable AI and evaluative AI: Informed data-driven decision-making in education. In Saqr, M., & López-Pernas, S. (Eds.), *Advanced learning analytics methods: AI, precision and complexity* (pp. 17–39). Springer., DOI: 10.1007/978-3-031-95365-1_2

Love, P. E., Fang, W., Matthews, J., Porter, S., Luo, H., & Ding, L. (2023). Explainable artificial intelligence (XAI): Precepts, models, and opportunities for research in construction. *Advanced Engineering Informatics*, *57*, 102024. DOI: 10.1016/j.aei.2023.102024

Luckin, R., Holmes, W., Griffiths, M., & Forcier, L. B. (2016). *Intelligence unleashed: An argument for AI in education*. Pearson.

Lundberg, S. M., & Lee, S.-I. (2017). A Unified Approach to Interpreting Model Predictions. *Advances in Neural Information Processing Systems, 30*, 4765-4774. arXiv. DOI: 10.48550/arXiv.1705.07874

Lundberg, S. M., Erion, G., Chen, H., DeGrave, A., Prutkin, J. M., Nair, B., Katz, R., Himmelfarb, J., Bansal, N., & Lee, S. I. (2020). From local explanations to global understanding with explainable AI for trees. *Nature Machine Intelligence*, *2*(1), 56–67. DOI: 10.1038/s42256-019-0138-9 PMID: 32607472

Lundberg, S. M., & Lee, S.-I. (2017). A unified approach to interpreting model predictions. *Advances in Neural Information Processing Systems*, *30*, 4765–4774.

Luo, Z., & Tahir, R. (2025). ChatGPT-assisted lesson planning for children's STEAM arts education: An experimental study on benefits, challenges, methods, and a prompt framework. *International Journal of Artificial Intelligence in Education, 35*(6), 3696–3745. DOI: 10.1007/s40593-025-00513-6

Lyu, W., Wang, Y., Yue, M., Sun, Y., Suh, J., Kier, M., & Zhang, Y. (2026, April). Designing AI Peers for Collaborative Mathematical Problem Solving with Middle School Students: A Participatory Design Study. In *Proceedings of the 2026 CHI Conference on Human Factors in Computing Systems* (pp. 1-21). DOI: 10.1145/3772318.3791138

Ma, S. (2024). Towards Human-centered Design of Explainable Artificial Intelligence (XAI): A Survey of Empirical Studies. arXiv preprint arXiv:2410.21183.

Macfadyen, L. P., & Dawson, S. (2010). Mining LMS data to develop an "early warning system" for educators: A proof of concept. *Computers & Education, 54*(2), 588–599. DOI: 10.1016/j.compedu.2009.09.008

Mahamad, S., Chin, Y. H., Zulmuksah, N. I. N., Haque, M. M., Shaheen, M., & Nisar, K. (2025). Technical review: Architecting an AI-driven decision support system for enhanced online learning and assessment. *Future Internet, 17*(9), 383. Advance online publication. DOI: 10.3390/fi17090383

Marín Díaz, G. (2025). Integrating exploratory data analysis and explainable AI into astronomy education: A fuzzy approach to data-literate learning. *Education Sciences, 15*(12), 1688. Advance online publication. DOI: 10.3390/educsci15121688

Marras, M., Boratto, L., Ramos, G., & Fenu, G. (2022). Equality of learning opportunity via individual fairness in personalized recommendations. *International Journal of Artificial Intelligence in Education, 32*(3), 636–684. DOI: 10.1007/s40593-021-00271-1

Marshall, R., Pardo, A., Smith, D., & Watson, T. (2022). Implementing next generation privacy and ethics research in education technology. *British Journal of Educational Technology, 53*(4), 737–755. DOI: 10.1111/bjet.13224

Martinez-Maldonado, R., Echeverria, V., Santos, O. C., Santos, A. D. P., & Yacef, K. (2018). Physical learning analytics: A multimodal perspective. In *Proceedings of the 8th International Conference on Learning Analytics and Knowledge* (pp. 375–379). ACM. https://doi.org/DOI: 10.1145/3170358.3170379

Mastour, H., Dehghani, T., Moradi, E., & Eslami, S. (2025). Explainable artificial intelligence for predicting medical students' performance in comprehensive assessments. *Scientific Reports*, *15*(1), 23752. Advance online publication. DOI: 10.1038/s41598-025-07460-1

Matcha, W., Ahmad Uzir, N. A., Gašević, D., & Pardo, A. (2020). A systematic review of empirical studies on learning analytics dashboards: A self-regulated learning perspective. *IEEE Transactions on Learning Technologies*, *13*(2), 226–245. DOI: 10.1109/TLT.2019.2916802

Matta, S. S., & Bolli, M. (2023). Trustworthy ai: Explainability & fairness in large-scale decision systems. *Review of Applied Science and Technology*, *2*(04), 54–93. DOI: 10.63125/3w9v5e52

Memarian, B., & Doleck, T. (2024). Human-in-the-loop in artificial intelligence in education: A review and entity-relationship (ER) analysis. *Computers in Human Behavior: Artificial Humans, 2*, Article 100053.

Méndez-Parra, C., & Conde-Carmona, R. J. (2025). Integración del enfoque STEAM y la realidad aumentada en la enseñanza de la traslación de figuras geométricas. *Revista Virtual Universidad Católica del Norte*, (74), 69–92. DOI: 10.35575/rvucn.n74a4

Meylani, R. (2025). Rethinking explainability in educational artificial intelligence: A critical systematic review of models, applications, and ethical dimensions. *Veredas do Direito*, *22*(3), e223553. Advance online publication. DOI: 10.18623/rvd.v22.n3.3553

Miah, M. N. I., Uddin, M. J., & Ahmed, M. W. (2025). Regulating artificial intelligence in education: Analyzing legal and ethical frameworks for the deployment of AI and machine learning models in U.S. educational institutions. *Journal of Computer Science and Technology Studies*, *7*(11), 387–404. DOI: 10.32996/jcsts.2025.7.11.37

Minh, D., Wang, H. X., Li, Y. F., & Nguyen, T. N. (2022). Explainable artificial intelligence: A comprehensive review. *Artificial Intelligence Review*, *55*(5), 3503–3568. DOI: 10.1007/s10462-021-10088-y

Mishra, A., & Motta, F. C. (2023). Stability and machine learning applications of persistent homology using the Delaunay-Rips complex. *Frontiers in Applied Mathematics and Statistics*, *9*, 1179301. Advance online publication. DOI: 10.3389/fams.2023.1179301

Mitchell, M., Wu, S., Zaldivar, A., Barnes, P., Vasserman, L., Hutchinson, B., Spitzer, E., Raji, I. D., & Gebru, T. (2019). Model cards for model reporting. In *Proceedings of the Conference on Fairness, Accountability, and Transparency* (pp. 220–229). Association for Computing Machinery. DOI: 10.1145/3287560.3287596

Moore, M. G. (2013). The theory of transactional distance. In Moore, M. G. (Ed.), *Handbook of distance education* (3rd ed., pp. 66–85). Routledge. DOI: 10.4324/9780203803738.ch5

Moraliyage, H., Kulawardana, G., De Silva, D., Issadeen, Z., Manic, M., & Katsura, S. (2025). Explainable artificial intelligence with integrated gradients for the detection of adversarial attacks on text classifiers. *Applied System Innovation*, *8*(1), 17. Advance online publication. DOI: 10.3390/asi8010017

Müller, R. (2025). How explainable AI affects human performance: A systematic review of the behavioural consequences of saliency maps. *International Journal of Human-Computer Interaction*, *41*(4), 2020–2051. DOI: 10.1080/10447318.2024.2381929

Mulwa, M. M., Mwangi, R. W., & Mindila, A. (2024). GMM-LIME explainable machine learning model for interpreting sensor-based human gait. *Engineering Reports*, *6*(10), e12864. Advance online publication. DOI: 10.1002/eng2.12864

Na Nongkhai, R., Boonjing, V., & Jantakoon, P. (2025). Development and evaluation of adaptive learning support system for computer programming based on an ontology approach. *Education Sciences*, *15*(6), 724. DOI: 10.3390/educsci15060724

Nagy, M., & Molontay, R. (2024). Interpretable dropout prediction: Towards XAI-based personalized intervention. *International Journal of Artificial Intelligence in Education*, *34*(2), 274–300. DOI: 10.1007/s40593-023-00331-8

Nakagawa, H., Iwasawa, Y., & Matsuo, Y. (2021). Graph-based knowledge tracing: Modeling student proficiency using graph neural networks. *Web Intelligence*, *19*(1–2), 87–102. DOI: 10.3233/WEB-210458

Nartey, E. K. (2026). *Generative AI in Higher Education: Ethical Governance, Skills, and Employability* (Vol. 2). CRC Press. DOI: 10.1201/9781003502517

Naveenkumar, R. (2025). Advancing Modern Education through Explainable Artificial Intelligence: Enhancing Learning Outcomes and Teaching with Transparent AI Systems. *Journal of Computer Based Parallel Programming*, *10*(3), 37–49. https://matjournals.net/engineering/index.php/JoCPP/article/view/2821

Nemorin, S. (2026). Towards decolonising the ethics of AI in education. *Globalisation, Societies and Education*, *24*(4), 1260–1272. DOI: 10.1080/14767724.2024.2333821

Neshaei, S. P., Tolzin, A., Berkle, Y., Leuchter, M., Leimeister, J. M., Janson, A., & Wambsganss, T. (2025). Leveraging Learner Errors in Digital Argumentation Learning: How ALure Helps Students Learn from their Mistakes and Write Better Arguments. *Proceedings of the ACM on Human-Computer Interaction*, *9*(2), 1–32. DOI: 10.1145/3711023

Ng, D. T. K., Leung, J. K. L., Su, J., Ng, R. C. W., & Chu, S. K. W. (2023). Teachers' AI digital competencies and twenty-first century skills in the post-pandemic world. *Educational Technology Research and Development*, *71*(1), 137–161. DOI: 10.1007/s11423-023-10203-6 PMID: 36844361

Ngoc, D. N. T. (2025). Artificial Intelligence Plays a Crucial Role in Integrating Personalized Learning Methods Into STEAM Education. In *Integrating Personalized Learning Methods Into STEAM Education* (pp. 189–210). IGI Global Scientific Publishing. DOI: 10.4018/979-8-3693-7718-5.ch009

Nguyen, A., Ngo, H. N., Hong, Y., Dang, B., & Nguyen, B.-P. T. (2023). Ethical principles for artificial intelligence in education. *Education and Information Technologies*, *28*(4), 4221–4241. DOI: 10.1007/s10639-022-11316-w

Nikolova, N., Kirilova, B., Mihnev, P., Zafirova-Malcheva, T., & Petkova, M. (2026). From Formal to Operational: A Triangulated Analysis of Policy, Practice, and Perception Regarding Digital Competence Development in Mathematics and IT Teacher Education. *Education Sciences*, *16*(2), 272. DOI: 10.3390/educsci16020272

Niu, T., Liu, T., Luo, Y. T., Pang, P. C.-I., Huang, S., & Xiang, A. (2025). Decoding student cognitive abilities: A comparative study of explainable AI algorithms in educational data mining. *Scientific Reports*, *15*(1), 26862. Advance online publication. DOI: 10.1038/s41598-025-12514-5

Nokes, C. (2022). Effective learning in the modern classroom. Journal for Learning through the Arts, 18(1).

Ocen, S., Elasu, J., Aarakit, S. M., & Olupot, C. (2025). Artificial intelligence in higher education institutions: Review of innovations, opportunities and challenges. *Frontiers in Education*, *10*, 1530247. Advance online publication. DOI: 10.3389/feduc.2025.1530247

Ochoa, X., & Wise, A. F. (2021). Supporting the shift to digital with student-centered learning analytics. *Educational Technology Research and Development*, *69*(1), 357–361. DOI: 10.1007/s11423-020-09882-2 PMID: 33250614

Ojetunde, S. M., & Ramnarain, U. (2026). Enhancing STEM and STEAM education at the grade level through mixed reality applications: A meta-analytical study. *Canadian Journal of Science, Mathematics and Technology Education = Revue Canadienne de l'Enseignement des Sciences, des Mathématiques et de la Technologie, 26*(2), 19. Advance online publication. DOI: 10.1007/s42330-026-00456-7

Oliva-Córdova, L. M., Tohom, M. F. V., Salazar de la Cruz, R. C., & Martín-Núñez, J. L. (2025). Application of learning analytics in medical education: Enhancing student digital competences within the STEAM framework. *International Journal of Educational Research Open, 9*, 100511. Advance online publication. DOI: 10.1016/j.ijedro.2025.100511

Omirali, A., Kozhakhmet, K., & Zhumaliyeva, R. (2025). Digital Trust in Transition: Student Perceptions of AI-Enhanced Learning for Sustainable Educational Futures. *Sustainability (Basel), 17*(17), 7567. DOI: 10.3390/su17177567

Organisation for Economic Co-operation and Development. (2019). *OECD skills outlook 2019: Thriving in a digital world.* OECD Publishing., DOI: 10.1787/df80bc12-

Organisation for Economic Co-operation and Development. (2023). *Education at a glance 2023: OECD indicators.* OECD Publishing., DOI: 10.1787/e13bef63-

Osborne, J. B., & Lang, A. S. I. D. (2023). Predictive identification of at-risk students: Using learning management system data. *Journal of Postsecondary Student Success, 2*(4), 108–126. DOI: 10.33009/fsop_jpss132082

Otaru, B. E. (2025). Leveraging Artificial Intelligence (AI) for personalized and inclusive STEAM education: Strategies for bridging learning gaps among diverse learners. *KONTAGORA JOURNAL OF SCIENCE AND TECHNOLOGY, 18*(1-2), 94–99.

Pachouly, S., & Bormane, D. S. (2025). Explainable Artificial Intelligence in Education: Transforming Teaching and Learning – A review. *TPM. Testing, Psychometrics, Methodology in Applied Psychology, 32*(S8), 1571–1584. DOI: 10.5281/zenodo.17866084

Patil, H. Y., Assumption, M., & Latha, G. H. (2025). Smart Education: A Need of the Hour Using Explainable Artificial Intelligence (XAI). In Personalized Learning Through Adaptive Systems and Intelligent Tutoring (pp. 1-72). IGI Global Scientific Publishing.

Paulsen, L., & Lindsay, E. (2024). Learning analytics dashboards are increasingly becoming about learning and not just analytics—A systematic review. *Education and Information Technologies*, *29*(11), 14279–14308. Advance online publication. DOI: 10.1007/s10639-023-12401-4

Penn, M. (2025). Creating adaptive learning pathways for inquiry-based science teaching using generative AI tools. *International Journal of Science Education*. Advance online publication. DOI: 10.1080/09500693.2025.2574519

Perrotta, C., & Selwyn, N. (2020). Deep learning goes to school: Toward a relational understanding of AI in education. *Learning, Media and Technology*, *45*(3), 251–269. DOI: 10.1080/17439884.2020.1686017

Peters, M. A., Jackson, L., Papastephanou, M., Jandrić, P., Lazaroiu, G., Evers, C. W., Cope, B., Kalantzis, M., Araya, D., Tesar, M., Mika, C., Chen, L., Wang, C., Sturm, S., Rider, S., & Fuller, S. (2024). AI and the future of humanity: ChatGPT-4, philosophy and education–Critical responses. *Educational Philosophy and Theory*, *56*(9), 828–862. DOI: 10.1080/00131857.2023.2213437

Pham, N., Pham Ngoc, H., & Nguyen-Duc, A. (2025). Fairness for machine learning software in education: A systematic mapping study. *Journal of Systems and Software*, *219*, 112244. Advance online publication. DOI: 10.1016/j.jss.2024.112244

Phillips, P. J., Hahn, C. A., Fontana, P. C., Yates, A. N., Greene, K. K., Broniatowski, D. A., & Przybocki, M. A. (2021). *Four principles of explainable artificial intelligence* (NIST Interagency/Internal Report No. NIST.IR.8312). National Institute of Standards and Technology. https://doi.org/DOI: 10.6028/NIST.IR.8312

Piccarozzi, M., Silvestri, L., Silvestri, C., & Ruggieri, A. (2024). Roadmap to Industry 5.0: Enabling technologies, challenges, and opportunities towards a holistic definition in management studies. *Technological Forecasting and Social Change*, *205*, 123467. Advance online publication. DOI: 10.1016/j.techfore.2024.123467

Popenici, S. A., & Kerr, S. (2017). Exploring the impact of artificial intelligence on teaching and learning in higher education. *Research and Practice in Technology Enhanced Learning*, *12*(1), 22. DOI: 10.1186/s41039-017-0062-8 PMID: 30595727

Prinsloo, P., & Slade, S. (2014). Educational triage in open distance learning: Walking a moral tightrope. *International Review of Research in Open and Distance Learning*, *15*(4), 306–331. DOI: 10.19173/irrodl.v15i4.1881

Prinsloo, P., & Slade, S. (2016). Student vulnerability, agency and learning analytics: An exploration. *Journal of Learning Analytics*, *3*(1), 159–182. DOI: 10.18608/jla.2016.31.10

Prinsloo, P., & Slade, S. (2017). An elephant in the learning analytics room: The obligation to act. In *Proceedings of the Seventh International Learning Analytics & Knowledge Conference* (pp. 46–55). ACM. https://doi.org/DOI: 10.1145/3027385.3027406

Prokhorenkova, L., Gusev, G., Vorobev, A., Dorogush, A. V., & Gulin, A. (2018). CatBoost: Unbiased boosting with categorical features. *Advances in Neural Information Processing Systems*, •••, 31.

Purwandari, E. P., Winarni, E. W., Junus, K., & Soraya, S. (2025). An adaptive learning system integrated with fuzzy logic to improve higher-order thinking skills. *Engineering. Technology and Applied Science Research*, *15*(5), 28150–28156. DOI: 10.48084/etasr.12751

Quevedo Piratova, D. A., Sánchez Duarte, M. M., Chiappe, A., & Sáez Delgado, F. M. (2025). Intelligent classrooms: How Ai and Iot can reshape learning spaces. *European Journal of Education*, *60*(1), e70000. DOI: 10.1111/ejed.70000

Radvila, V., Bredelytė, A., & Lekutienė, K. (2025). Empowering STEAM educators through AI: A conceptual framework for adaptive, inclusive professional development. *Social Welfare: Interdisciplinary Approach*, *15*, 160–174. DOI: 10.15388/SW.2025.15.9

Reinhardt, K. (2023). Trust and trustworthiness in AI ethics. *AI and Ethics*, *3*(3), 735–744. DOI: 10.1007/s43681-022-00200-5

Relmasira, S. C., Lai, Y. C., & Donaldson, J. P. (2023). Fostering AI literacy in elementary science, technology, engineering, art, and mathematics (STEAM) education in the age of generative AI. *Sustainability (Basel)*, *15*(18), 13595. Advance online publication. DOI: 10.3390/su151813595

Ribeiro, M. T., Singh, S., & Guestrin, C. (2016). "Why Should I Trust You?": Explaining the Predictions of Any Classifier. *Proceedings of the 22nd ACM SIGKDD International Conference on Knowledge Discovery and Data Mining*, 1135–1144. DOI: 10.1145/2939672.2939778

Riley, R. D., Archer, L., Snell, K. I. E., Ensor, J., Dhiman, P., Martin, G. P., Bonnett, L. J., & Collins, G. S. (2024). Evaluation of clinical prediction models (part 2): How to undertake an external validation study. *BMJ (Clinical Research Ed.)*, *384*, e074820. Advance online publication. DOI: 10.1136/bmj-2023-074820 PMID: 38224968

Romero, C., & Ventura, S. (2010). Educational Data Mining: A Review of the State of the Art. *IEEE Transactions on Systems, Man, and Cybernetics. Part C, Applications and Reviews*, *40*(6), 601–618. DOI: 10.1109/TSMCC.2010.2053532

Romero, C., & Ventura, S. (2020). Educational data mining and learning analytics: An updated survey. *Wiley Interdisciplinary Reviews. Data Mining and Knowledge Discovery*, *10*(3), e1355. DOI: 10.1002/widm.1355

Rudin, C. (2019). Stop explaining black box machine learning models for high stakes decisions and use interpretable models instead. *Nature Machine Intelligence*, *1*(5), 206–215. DOI: 10.1038/s42256-019-0048-x PMID: 35603010

Sajja, R., Sermet, Y., & Demir, I. (2025). End-to-end deployment of the Educational AI Hub for personalized learning and engagement: A case study on environmental science education. *IEEE Access : Practical Innovations, Open Solutions*, *13*, 55169–55186. DOI: 10.1109/ACCESS.2025.3554222

Salas-Pilco, S. Z., Xiao, K., & Oshima, J. (2022). Artificial intelligence and new technologies in inclusive education for minority students: A systematic review. *Sustainability (Basel)*, *14*(20), 13572. Advance online publication. DOI: 10.3390/su142013572

Santos, A., Martins, J., Pestana, P. D., Gonçalves, R., Mamede, H. S., & Branco, F. (2024). Factors affecting cloud computing adoption in the education context: Systematic literature review. *IEEE Access : Practical Innovations, Open Solutions*, *12*, 71641–71674. DOI: 10.1109/ACCESS.2024.3400862

Saqr, M., & López-Pernas, S. (Eds.). (2024). *Learning analytics methods and tutorials: A practical guide using R*. Springer., DOI: 10.1007/978-3-031-54464-4

Saseendran, A., & Thomas, M. V. (2025). Design thinking in science and integrated STEM/STEAM education: Trends, challenges, and future directions from a systematic review. *STEM Education*, *5*(6), 1058–1101. DOI: 10.3934/steme.2025046

Schiff, D. (2022). Education for AI, not AI for education: The role of education and ethics in national AI policy strategies. *International Journal of Artificial Intelligence in Education*, *32*(3), 527–563. DOI: 10.1007/s40593-021-00270-2

Schwartz, R. (2025). Improving Instructional Practices in Algebra I Classrooms by Facilitating a Professional Learning Community and Providing Instructional Performance Feedback (Doctoral dissertation, Fordham University).

Sein, Y. M. (2022). AI-assisted knowledge assessment techniques for adaptive learning environments. *Computers and Education: Artificial Intelligence*, *3*, 100050. DOI: 10.1016/j.caeai.2022.100050

Selwyn, N. (2019). *Should robots replace teachers? AI and the future of education*. Polity Press.

Shalabi, E., Khedr, W., Rushdy, E., & Salah, A. (2025). A comparative study of privacy-preserving techniques in federated learning: A performance and security analysis. *Information (Basel)*, *16*(3), 244. Advance online publication. DOI: 10.3390/info16030244

Shapley, L. S. (1953). A value for n-person games. In Kuhn, H. W., & Tucker, A. W. (Eds.), *Contributions to the theory of games II* (pp. 307–317). Princeton University Press., DOI: 10.1515/9781400881970-018

Shermis, M. D., & Burstein, J. (Eds.). (2013). *Handbook of automated essay evaluation: Current applications and new directions*. Routledge. DOI: 10.4324/9780203122761

Shernoff, D. J. (2024). Computer science, artificial intelligence (ai), and machine learning in STEM/STEAM education. In *Integrative STEM and STEAM Education for Real-Life Learning* (pp. 197–222). Springer International Publishing. DOI: 10.1007/978-3-031-69824-8_9

Shoaib, M., Sayed, N., Singh, J., Shafi, J., Khan, S., & Ali, F. (2024). AI student success predictor: Enhancing personalized learning in campus management systems. *Computers in Human Behavior*, *158*, 108301. Advance online publication. DOI: 10.1016/j.chb.2024.108301

Siemens, G. (2013). Learning analytics: The emergence of a discipline. *The American Behavioral Scientist*, *57*(10), 1380–1400. DOI: 10.1177/0002764213498851

Siemens, G., & Baker, R. S. J. D. (2012). Learning analytics and educational data mining: Towards communication and collaboration. *Proceedings of the 2nd International Conference on Learning Analytics and Knowledge*, 252–254. DOI: 10.1145/2330601.2330661

Silva-Díaz, F., Marfil-Carmona, R., Narváez, R., Silva Fuentes, A., & Carrillo-Rosúa, J. (2023). Introducing virtual reality and emerging technologies in a teacher training STEM course. *Education Sciences*, *13*(10), 1044. Advance online publication. DOI: 10.3390/educsci13101044

Skittou, M., Merrouchi, M., & Gadi, T. (2024). Development of an early warning system to support educational planning process by identifying at-risk students. *IEEE Access : Practical Innovations, Open Solutions*, *12*, 2260–2271. DOI: 10.1109/ACCESS.2023.3348091

Slade, S., & Prinsloo, P. (2013). Learning analytics: Ethical issues and dilemmas. *The American Behavioral Scientist*, *57*(10), 1509–1528. DOI: 10.1177/0002764213479366

Son, T. (2024). Intelligent tutoring systems in mathematics education: A systematic literature review using the substitution, augmentation, modification, redefinition model. *Computers*, *13*(10), 270. Advance online publication. DOI: 10.3390/computers13100270

Soroko, N. (2024). Features of organizing STEAM educational projects using immersive technologies. *Physical and Mathematical Education*, *39*(2), 51–59. DOI: 10.31110/fmo2024.v39i2-07

Spyropoulou, N., & Kameas, A. (2025). AI and the future of teaching in STEAM: Competences, challenges, and opportunities. INTED2025 Proceedings, 4421-4427.

Suaza-Medina, M., Peñabaena-Niebles, R., & Jubiz-Diaz, M. (2024). A model for predicting academic performance on standardised tests for lagging regions based on machine learning and Shapley additive explanations. *Scientific Reports*, *14*(1), 25306. Advance online publication. DOI: 10.1038/s41598-024-76596-3

Subramanian, M., Portia, R., Mishra, B. R., & Selvakumar, P. PV, R., & TC, M. (2025). Assessment and evaluation in personalized STEAM education. In Integrating Personalized Learning Methods Into STEAM Education (pp. 103-122). IGI Global Scientific Publishing.

Svensson, Å., & Warne, M. (2024). Staff perspectives on poor mental health in secondary school students: An increasing problem handled with insufficient resources. *Frontiers in Public Health*, *12*, 1292520. DOI: 10.3389/fpubh.2024.1292520 PMID: 38496395

Sweller, J. (2011). Cognitive load theory. In Ross, B. H. (Ed.), *Psychology of learning and motivation* (Vol. 55, pp. 37–76). Academic Press., DOI: 10.1016/B978-0-12-387691-1.00002-8

Swiecki, Z., Khosravi, H., Chen, G., Martinez-Maldonado, R., Lodge, J. M., Milligan, S., Selwyn, N., & Gašević, D. (2022). Assessment in the age of artificial intelligence. *Computers and Education: Artificial Intelligence*, *3*, 100075. Advance online publication. DOI: 10.1016/j.caeai.2022.100075

Tan, S., Chong, C., Wei, Z., & Tang, X. (2025). Artificial intelligence-enabled adaptive learning platforms: A review of technologies, impact, and future directions. *Computers and Education: Artificial Intelligence*, *7*, 100258. DOI: 10.1016/j.caeai.2025.100258

Tan, X., Cheng, K. S., & Ling, M. H. A. (2025). Artificial intelligence in teaching and teacher professional development: A systematic review. *Computers and Education: Artificial Intelligence*, *8*, 100355. Advance online publication. DOI: 10.1016/j.caeai.2024.100355

Tariq, M. U. (Ed.). (2024). *AI-driven learning and engagement in higher education*. IGI Global. DOI: 10.4018/979-8-3693-4074-5

Terzieva, V., Ivanova, M., Djambazova, E., & Ilchev, S. (2025). The role of internet of things and security aspects in STEM education. *Information (Basel)*, *16*(7), 533. Advance online publication. DOI: 10.3390/info16070533

Tınmaz, H. (2025). From Transparency to Trust: A Literature Review on Explainable AI in Educational Systems. *Mersin Üniversitesi Eğitim Fakültesi Dergisi*, *21*(3), 999–1018. DOI: 10.17860/mersinefd.1739347

Tlili, A., Shehata, B., Adarkwah, M. A., Bozkurt, A., Hickey, D. T., Huang, R., & Agyemang, B. (2023). What if the devil is my guardian angel: ChatGPT as a case study of using chatbots in education. *Smart Learning Environments*, *10*(1), 15. Advance online publication. DOI: 10.1186/s40561-023-00237-x

Tolman, A. O., & Kremling, J. (Eds.). (2023). *Why students resist learning: A practical model for understanding and helping students*. Taylor & Francis.

Tong, C., & Ren, C. (2025). Deep knowledge tracing and cognitive load estimation for personalized learning path generation using neural network architecture. *Scientific Reports*, *15*(1), 24925. Advance online publication. DOI: 10.1038/s41598-025-10497-x PMID: 40640459

Topuz, K., Davazdahemami, B., & Delen, D. (2024). A Bayesian belief network-based analytics methodology for early-stage risk detection of novel diseases. *Annals of Operations Research*, *341*(1), 673–697. DOI: 10.1007/s10479-023-05377-4

Torres-Rivera, A. D., Rendón Peña, A. A., Díaz-Torres, S. T., & Díaz-Torres, L. A. (2025). Ethical integration of AI and STEAM pedagogies in higher education: A sustainable learning model for society 5.0. *Sustainability (Basel)*, *17*(19), 8525. DOI: 10.3390/su17198525

Tretow-Fish, T. A. B., & Khalid, M. S. (2023). Methods for Evaluating Learning Analytics and Learning Analytics Dashboards in Adaptive Learning Platforms: A Systematic Review. *Electronic Journal of e-Learning*, *21*(5), 430–449. DOI: 10.34190/ejel.21.5.3088

Türkmen, G. (2025). The review of studies on explainable artificial intelligence in educational research. *Journal of Educational Computing Research*, *63*(2), 277–310. DOI: 10.1177/07356331241310915

Tursunalieva, A., Alexander, D. L. J., Dunne, R., Li, J., Riera, L., & Zhao, Y. (2024). Making sense of machine learning: A review of interpretation techniques and their applications. *Applied Sciences (Basel, Switzerland)*, *14*(2), 496. Advance online publication. DOI: 10.3390/app14020496

UNESCO. (2022). *Recommendation on the ethics of artificial intelligence*. https://unesdoc.unesco.org/ark:/48223/pf0000381137

UNESCO. (2023). *Global education monitoring report 2023: Technology in education: A tool on whose terms?* UNESCO., DOI: 10.54676/UZQV8501

Valenzuela-Domínguez, F. A., Munguía-Martínez, L. F., Meléndez-Tiznado, S., Guzmán-Limón, Z., Benitez, V. H., & Félix-Herrán, L. C. (2024). Design of a two-degrees-of-freedom robotic arm for monitoring applications for teaching robotics and artificial intelligence technology. *Computer Applications in Engineering Education*, *32*(6), e22786. Advance online publication. DOI: 10.1002/cae.22786

van Breugel, B., Qian, Z., & van der Schaar, M. (2023). Synthetic data, real errors: How (not) to publish and use synthetic data. In *Proceedings of the 40th International Conference on Machine Learning* (*Proceedings of Machine Learning Research*, Vol. 202, pp. 34793–34808). PMLR. https://proceedings.mlr.press/v202/van-breugel23a.html

van Breugel, B., Sun, H., Qian, Z., & van der Schaar, M. (2023). Membership inference attacks against synthetic data through overfitting detection. In *Proceedings of the 26th International Conference on Artificial Intelligence and Statistics* (*Proceedings of Machine Learning Research*, Vol. 206, pp. 3493–3514). PMLR. https://proceedings.mlr.press/v206/breugel23a.html

Van Busum, K., & Fang, S. (2025). Interactive mitigation of biases in machine learning models for undergraduate student admissions. *AI*, *6*(7), 152. Advance online publication. DOI: 10.3390/ai6070152

Van Calster, B., McLernon, D. J., van Smeden, M., Wynants, L., & Steyerberg, E. W. (2019). Calibration: The Achilles heel of predictive analytics. *BMC Medicine*, *17*(1), 230. Advance online publication. DOI: 10.1186/s12916-019-1466-7 PMID: 31842878

Vasconcelos, L., de Castro Filho, J. A., Barreto, D., de Castro, J. B., de Souza, M. D. F. C., de Barros Cardoso, L. A., & Maia, D. (2025). Design guidelines for integrating artificial intelligence into preservice teacher EFL and STEAM education. *Journal of Technology and Teacher Education, 33*(4), 753–784. DOI: 10.70725/195498ziigzw

Velarde-Camaqui, D., Celaya-Ramírez, R., Contreras-Fuentes, Y., & Sanabria-Z, J. (2024). Enhancing STEAM education through augmented reality: The EduAR open platform experience. *Frontiers in Education, 9*, 1391803. Advance online publication. DOI: 10.3389/feduc.2024.1391803

Verbert, K., Duval, E., Klerkx, J., Govaerts, S., & Santos, J. L. (2013). Learning analytics dashboard applications. *The American Behavioral Scientist, 57*(10), 1500–1509. DOI: 10.1177/0002764213479363

Verbert, K., Ochoa, X., De Croon, R., Dourado, R., & De Laet, T. (2020). Learning analytics dashboards: The past, the present and the future. In *Proceedings of the Tenth International Conference on Learning Analytics & Knowledge* (pp. 35–40). ACM. https://doi.org/DOI: 10.1145/3375462.3375504

Vickers, A. J., & Holland, F. (2021). Decision curve analysis to evaluate the clinical benefit of prediction models. *The Spine Journal, 21*(10), 1643–1648. DOI: 10.1016/j.spinee.2021.02.024 PMID: 33676020

Villegas-Ch, W., Buenano-Fernandez, D., Navarro, A. M., & Mera-Navarrete, A. (2025). Adaptive intelligent tutoring systems for STEM education: Analysis of the learning impact and effectiveness of personalized feedback. *Smart Learning Environments, 12*(1), 41. Advance online publication. DOI: 10.1186/s40561-025-00389-y

Viswan, V., Shaffi, N., Mahmud, M., Subramanian, K., & Hajamohideen, F. (2024). Explainable artificial intelligence in Alzheimer's disease classification: A systematic review. *Cognitive Computation, 16*(1), 1–44. DOI: 10.1007/s12559-023-10192-x

Vonen, M. N. (2024). Teachers' management of students' incorrect answers in oral examinations. *Linguistics and Education, 80*, 101266. DOI: 10.1016/j.linged.2023.101266

Wang, T., Xu, Y., & Wu, J. (2023). When adaptive learning is effective learning: Comparison of an adaptive learning system to teacher-led instruction. *Interactive Learning Environments, 31*(2), 793–803. Advance online publication. DOI: 10.1080/10494820.2020.1808794

Wang, X., Younas, M., Jiang, Y., Imran, M., & Almusharraf, N. (2025). Transforming education through blockchain: A systematic review of applications, projects, and challenges. *IEEE Access : Practical Innovations, Open Solutions*, *13*, 13264–13284. DOI: 10.1109/ACCESS.2024.3519350

Watkins, J. (2023). "That is Still STEM": Appropriating the Engineering Design Process to Challenge Dominant Narratives of Engineering and STEM. *Cognition and Instruction*, *41*(4), 405–435. DOI: 10.1080/07370008.2022.2156512

Williamson, B., & Eynon, R. (2020). Historical threads, missing links, and future directions in AI in education. *Learning, Media and Technology*, *45*(3), 223–235. DOI: 10.1080/17439884.2020.1798995

Winkelmes, M. A. (2023). Why it works: Understanding the concepts behind transparency in learning and teaching. Transparent design in higher education teaching and leadership, 17-35.

Wolpert, D. H. (1992). Stacked generalization. *Neural Networks*, *5*(2), 241–259. DOI: 10.1016/S0893-6080(05)80023-1 PMID: 18276425

Wu, E., Lee, H., Wang, W.-S., Lin, C.-J., & Huang, Y.-M. (2023). Leveraging computer vision for adaptive learning in STEM education: Effect of engagement and self-efficacy. *International Journal of Educational Technology in Higher Education*, *20*(1), 53. Advance online publication. DOI: 10.1186/s41239-023-00422-5

Xu, L., Skoularidou, M., Cuesta-Infante, A., & Veeramachaneni, K. (2019). Modeling tabular data using conditional GAN. In *Advances in Neural Information Processing Systems 32* (pp. 7333–7343). NeurIPS. https://papers.nips.cc/paper/8953-modeling-tabular-data-using-conditional-gan

Xu, W., & Ouyang, F. (2022). The application of artificial intelligence technologies in STEM education: A systematic review from 2011 to 2021. *International Journal of STEM Education*, *9*, 59. DOI: 10.1186/s40594-022-00377-5

Yadegaridehkordi, E., Noor, N. F. B. M., Ayub, M. N. B., Affal, H. B., & Hussin, N. B. (2019). Affective computing in education: A systematic review and future research. *Computers & Education*, *142*, 103649. Advance online publication. DOI: 10.1016/j.compedu.2019.103649

Yale, A., Dash, S., Dutta, R., Guyon, I., Pavao, A., & Bennett, K. P. (2020). Generation and evaluation of privacy preserving synthetic health data. *Neurocomputing*, *416*, 244–255. DOI: 10.1016/j.neucom.2019.12.136

Yang, S. J. H., Ogata, H., Matsui, T., & Chen, N. S. (2021). Human-centered artificial intelligence in education: Seeing the invisible through the visible. *Computers and Education: Artificial Intelligence*, *2*, 100008. Advance online publication. DOI: 10.1016/j.caeai.2021.100008

Yang, Z., Shen, J., Xiao, T., & Huang, H. (2024). Enhancing python learning with PyTutor: Efficacy of a ChatGPT-based intelligent tutoring system for computer programming. *Computers and Education: Artificial Intelligence*, *6*, 100212. DOI: 10.1016/j.caeai.2024.100309

Yan, L., Martinez-Maldonado, R., & Gašević, D. (2024). Generative artificial intelligence in learning analytics: Contextualising opportunities and challenges through the learning analytics cycle. In *LAK '24: Proceedings of the 14th International Learning Analytics and Knowledge Conference* (pp. 101–111). Association for Computing Machinery. DOI: 10.1145/3636555.3636856

Yan, P., Javorcik, T., Ghamat, S., & Milligan, M. (2024). Adaptive practicing design to facilitate self-regulated learning with an online adaptive learning system. *Canadian Journal of Learning and Technology*, *50*(2), 1–22. Advance online publication. DOI: 10.21432/cjlt28768

Yılmaz, O. I. (2025). AI, ethical stress, and emotional labor in educational leadership: Toward a human-centered framework. The New DNA of Education: Innovation, Technology, Equity, and the Cognitive Turn, 77.

Yun, S.-J., Kwon, J.-W., Lee, Y.-H., Kim, J.-H., & Kim, W.-T. (2024). A learner-centric explainable educational metaverse for cyber–physical systems engineering. *Electronics (Basel)*, *13*(17), 3359. Advance online publication. DOI: 10.3390/electronics13173359

Zawacki-Richter, O., Marín, V. I., Bond, M., & Gouverneur, F. (2019). Systematic review of research on artificial intelligence applications in higher education—Where are the educators? *International Journal of Educational Technology in Higher Education*, *16*(1), 39. Advance online publication. DOI: 10.1186/s41239-019-0171-0

Zhai, X., Chu, X., Chai, C. S., Jong, M. S.-Y., Istenic, A., Spector, M., Liu, J.-B., Yuan, J., & Li, Y. (2021). A review of artificial intelligence (AI) in education from 2010 to 2020. *Complexity*, *2021*(1), 8812542. Advance online publication. DOI: 10.1155/2021/8812542

Zhan, C., Joksimović, S., Ladjal, D., Rakotoarivelo, T., Marshall, R., & Pardo, A. (2024). Preserving both privacy and utility in learning analytics. *IEEE Transactions on Learning Technologies*, *17*, 1655–1667. DOI: 10.1109/TLT.2024.3393766

Zhang, J. (2025). Ethics of Artificial Intelligence in Education: Balancing Automation and Human-Centered Learning. *Applied Mathematics and Nonlinear Sciences, 10*(1), 1–15. DOI: 10.2478/amns-2025-0843

Zhang, Q., Li, J., & Liang, Y. (2023). A recommendation system based on an adaptive learning cognitive map model and its effects. *Interactive Learning Environments*. Advance online publication. DOI: 10.1080/10494820.2023.2232841

Zhang, X. (2024). Innovation of teaching methods of international Chinese language education in universities based on artificial intelligence analysis technology. *Applied Mathematics and Nonlinear Sciences*, *9*(1), 20230336. Advance online publication. DOI: 10.2478/amns.2023.2.00336

Zheng, Y., Li, G., Li, Y., Shan, C., & Cheng, R. (2017). Truth inference in crowdsourcing: Is the problem solved? *Proceedings of the VLDB Endowment International Conference on Very Large Data Bases*, *10*(5), 541–552. DOI: 10.14778/3055540.3055547

Zhilmagambetova, R., Mazhenov, G., Tazhibayeva, G., Kerimbayev, N., & Assanov, U. (2023). Stepik as a tool for teaching mathematics: An adaptive personalized online course in higher education. *Education Sciences*, *13*(9), 895. DOI: 10.3390/educsci13090895

Zhu, Q., & Wang, M. (2023). Team-based mobile learning supported by an intelligent system: Case study of STEM students. In Wang, M., Ryoo, J., & Winkelmann, K. (Eds.), *Cross Reality (XR) and immersive learning environments (ILEs) in education* (pp. 5–21). Routledge., DOI: 10.4324/9781003457121-2

Zimmerman, B. J. (2002). Becoming a self-regulated learner: An overview. *Theory into Practice*, *41*(2), 64–70. DOI: 10.1207/s15430421tip4102_2

About the Contributors

Jorge Ruiz Vanoye is a Professor and Researcher at Universidad Politécnica de Pachuca (UPP), a National Researcher under the Secretaria de Ciencia, Humanidades, Tecnología e Innovación program, and an Adjunct Researcher at the National Laboratory of Autonomous Vehicles and Exoskeletons (LANAVEX). Additionally, he holds the title of Lecturer-level Researcher for the Agency for the Quality of the University System of Catalonia (Generalitat de Catalunya). His research interests include Smart Cities, Smart Water, Smart Education, Smart Government, Smart Healthcare, Smart Farming, Smart Energy, Smart Sports, Smart Food, Smart Tourism, Algorithmic Finance, Algorithmic Portfolio Management, Applications and Theory of Algorithms, Bio-inspired Algorithms, Combinatorial Optimization Problems, Compilers, Computational Intelligence, Computational Complexity Theory, Computational Financial Intelligence, Complexity of Algorithms, Complexity of Instances, Computational Statistics, Computer Networks, Computer Science Security, Cybercrimes, Data Mining, Education, Evolutionary Computation, Heuristic Optimization Techniques in Bioinformatics, Hybrid Evolutionary Algorithms, Hybrid Optimization Algorithms, Machine Learning, Meta-heuristics, Operations Research, Operations Management, Parallel & Distributed Computing, Production Planning and Logistics Optimization, Project Scheduling Problems, Software Engineering, and Transgenic Algorithms.

Francisco R. Trejo-Macotela received the PhD degree in Electronics from the National Institute of Astrophysics, Optics and Electronics (INAOE), Puebla, Mexico. He is a Certified LabVIEW Associate Developer (CLAD) accredited by National Instruments and holds professional competence certifications in the EC0477 and EC0217 standards issued by the National Council for Standardisation and Certification of Competencies (CONOCER). He is currently Professor and Researcher in the Master's programmes in Mechatronics and Information and Communication Technologies, and the PhD programme in Advanced Science and

Technology, at the Polytechnic University of Pachuca (UPP), Mexico. During his academic career at UPP, he has held several leadership positions, including Director of Mechatronics Engineering (2007–2009), Director of Research, Innovation and Postgraduate Studies (2015–2023), and Coordinator of the Master's Programme in Information and Communication Technologies (2023–2024). He also served as Professor and Researcher in the Departments of Mechatronics (2006–2007) and Telematics (2009–2015). He has contributed to numerous research and innovation projects and has participated in more than eight evaluation processes for master's and doctoral programmes within the National Postgraduate System (SNP) of the Secretariat of Science, Humanities, Technology and Innovation (SECIHTI). He is an Adjunct Researcher at the SECIHTI National Laboratory for Autonomous Vehicles and Exoskeletons (LANAVEX). He currently serves as an evaluator for the Interinstitutional Committees for the Evaluation of Higher Education (CIEES), the Engineering Education Accreditation Council (CACEI–COPAES), and the Higher Education Evaluation and Accreditation System (SEAES) through the Peer Registry for Diagnostic and Formative Evaluation (REPEV) of the Mexican Ministry of Public Education (SEP). In 2019, he served as an External Peer Evaluator for the accreditation of Ecuadorian universities and polytechnic institutions under the Higher Education Quality Assurance Council (CACES). He has also acted as a peer evaluator for postgraduate programmes within the National Postgraduate System (SNP) and as a project evaluator for the Innovation Incentives Programme (PEI) of SECIHTI. He is currently a Level 1 member of the National System of Researchers (SNI) of SECIHTI. His research interests include Integrated Circuit Design, Analogue and Digital Electronics, Automation, Embedded Systems, Cyber-physical Systems, Internet of Things, Telecommunications, Smart Cities, Smart Water, Precision Agriculture, Educational Technology, Artificial Intelligence, Machine Learning, Autonomous Navigation, and Optimisation.

***

Jaime Aguilar-Ortiz holds a Ph.D. in Mathematical Sciences (CINVESTAV–IPN, Mexico) and serves as a professor and researcher in the fields of Mathematics, Artificial Intelligence, and Project Management, with academic involvement also extending to the Universidad Politécnica Metropolitana de Hidalgo. He additionally leads innovation-driven initiatives as Director General of CICAINTE and TEDNOVA GROUP, bridging rigorous academic work with applied technological development and institutional impact. His prior scholarly and editorial contributions include the preparation and/or editing of a substantial body of books and educational resources spanning mathematics education, financial mathematics, programming, and technology-based learning, complemented by the creation of audiovisual materials, educational platforms, and serious-game applications aimed at strengthening learning outcomes. His academic production further includes dozens of peer-reviewed articles and book chapters addressing themes at the intersection of smart cities, education, and AI, together with sustained experience in research mentoring, curriculum development, and interdisciplinary collaboration. These achievements, combined with recognized academic credentials and a consistent record of knowledge dissemination and capacity building, position him as a strong editor for a high-impact scholarly volume with methodological rigor, cross-sector relevance, and measurable educational and societal value.

Arturo Austria Cornejo is a professor and researcher at Universidad Politécnica de Pachuca, Mexico. His research focuses on artificial intelligence, computer vision, intelligent systems, Internet of Things (IoT), and smart education technologies. He has participated in multiple research projects related to intelligent transportation systems, pattern recognition, and AI-driven educational environments. His current work explores explainable artificial intelligence, human-centered AI systems, and the integration of intelligent technologies in smart learning ecosystems.

Ricardo Barrera-Cámara has a Ph.D. in Computer Systems from the Universidad del Sur. Master in Informatics from the Universidad Autónoma of Carmen. Research professor at the Autonomous University of Carmen in Mexico. National System of Researchers level 1. Leader of the academic group of scientific and technological computing. Leader of the Academy of Administration and information processing. His research areas are Scientific Computing, Data Science, Optimization, Quality and Information Technology, Sustainable Development Goals.

Lakshmi D is presently designated as a Senior Associate Professor in the School of Computing Science and Engineering (SCSE) & Assistant Director, at the Centre for Innovation in Teaching & Learning (CITL) at VIT Bhopal. She has 17 international conference presentations, and 21 international journal papers inclusive of SCOPUS & SCI (cumulative impact factor 31). 3 SCOPUS inee book chapters. A total of 24 patents are in various states and 18 patents have been granted at both national and international levels. One Edited book with Taylor & Francis (SCOPUS Indexed). She has won two Best Paper awards at international conferences, one at the IEEE conference and another one at EAMMIS 2021. She received two awards in the year 2022. She received two awards in the year 2022. She has addressed innumerable guest lectures, acted as a session chair, and was invited as a keynote speaker at several international conferences. She has conducted FDPs that cover approximately ~80,000 plus faculty members including JNTU, TEQIP, SERB,

SWAYAM, DST, AICTE, MHRD, ATAL, ISTE, Madhya Pradesh Government-sponsored, and self-financed workshops across India on various titles.

Ocotlan Diaz-Parra is a Professor and Researcher at Universidad Politécnica de Pachuca (UPP), a National Researcher under the Secretaria de Ciencia, Humanidades, Tecnología e Innovación program, and an Adjunct Researcher at the National Laboratory of Autonomous Vehicles and Exoskeletons (LANAVEX). His research interests include Smart Cities, Smart Water, Smart Education, Smart Government, Smart Healthcare, Smart Farming, Smart Energy, Smart Sports, Smart Food, Smart Tourism, Algorithmic Finance, Algorithmic Portfolio Management, Applications and Theory of Algorithms, Bio-inspired Algorithms, Combinatorial Optimization Problems, Compilers, Computational Intelligence, Computational Complexity Theory, Computational Financial Intelligence, Complexity of Algorithms, Complexity of Instances, Computational Statistics, Computer Networks, Computer Science Security, Cybercrimes, Data Mining, Education, Evolutionary Computation, Heuristic Optimization Techniques in Bioinformatics, Hybrid Evolutionary Algorithms, Hybrid Optimization Algorithms, Machine Learning, Meta-heuristics, Operations Research, Operations Management, Parallel & Distributed Computing, Production Planning and Logistics Optimization, Project Scheduling Problems, Software Engineering, and Transgenic Algorithms.

Carlos Domínguez-Mayorga holds a Ph.D. in Sciences specializing in Artificial Intelligence, with a foundational background in Physics and Mathematics. His research focuses on Deep Learning, NLP, neural networks, and the development of predictive models. He has an extensive track record in scientific publications and graduate program management, applying cutting-edge data science techniques to engineering and sustainability projects.

Alejandro Fuentes-Penna is a mexican academic and researcher specializing in strategic planning, artificial intelligence, and educational technology. He earned his Ph.D. in Strategic Planning and Technology Management from the Universidad Popular Autónoma del Estado de Puebla (UPAEP) in 2012. Prior to that, he completed a Master's degree in Computer Science at the Instituto Tecnológico y de Estudios Superiores de Monterrey (ITESM), where he published two articles in international conferences and secured first place in the Technology category of the Third Banamex Award for Internet Evolution. Dr. Fuentes Penna has held various academic positions, including serving as a Full-Time Research Professor at the Escuela Superior de Tlahuelilpan of the Universidad Autónoma del Estado de Hidalgo (UAEH). His research interests encompass educational management, educational technology, complexity in social sciences, and bio-inspired intelligent scientific computing. He has contributed to multiple publications, including articles indexed in JCR and Scopus, as well as books in his areas of expertise. Throughout his career, Dr. Fuentes Penna has received numerous national and international recognitions for academic and research excellence. He has been awarded the PRODEP Profile (formerly PROMEP) three times, is a member of the State System of Researchers in Morelos, and was recently included in the National System of Researchers at the Candidate level. Additionally, he has collaborated with various universities and research institutes, including the Universidad Nacional Autónoma de México (UNAM) and the Mexican Institute of Transportation. Dr. Fuentes Penna has extensive experience in teaching at both undergraduate and graduate levels, in both face-to-face and online modalities. He has supervised theses, coordinated educational programs, and organized significant academic events such as the International Space Week and the National Science and Technology Week.

David H. Fuque-Ehuanc is a professor of Information Technology at Universidad Autónoma del Carmen. Develops technology solutions for enterprise and institutional process optimization, with research focus on Machine Learning, Database Systems, Computer Vision, and Internet of Things (IoT). Background includes graduate studies in Education.

Marco Antonio García Márquez is a computer scientist, AI researcher, and professor with extensive experience in machine learning, computer vision, and data science. He holds a Master's degree in Computer Science and a PhD in Applied Engineering. With over 20 years of experience in higher education and academic leadership, he has played a key role in curriculum design, program accreditation, and student success strategies for universities and public institutions. His work focuses on the implementation of information systems, deep learning, image processing, and artificial intelligence, with practical applications in automated decision-making, pattern recognition, and IoT systems. He has developed and implemented AI-powered algorithms using Python, Keras, OpenCV, PyTorch, and Pandas, as well as real-time embedded systems with OpenCV, OpenGL, PHP, JavaScript, C, C++, Python, MicroPython, and Arduino. García Márquez is an active contributor to scientific research, academic quality assessment, and AI-powered solutions for education and industry. His commitment to interdisciplinary collaboration and technological advancements has positioned him as a key figure in Science computer...

Marcos Yamir Gómez Ramos is an experienced professor and researcher specialising in artificial intelligence, machine learning, higher education and science outreach. His academic work has centred on developing interdisciplinary projects related to social inclusion, gender equity, and providing access to science and technology for vulnerable populations. He has contributed to the design and review of theses, academic reports and research projects related to artificial intelligence, digital transformation, educational methodologies and community development. Dr. Gómez Ramos has also promoted initiatives aimed at STEM education, educational innovation, and the social appropriation of knowledge, combining the use of emerging technologies with a humanistic and socially impactful approach.

Laura Araceli Guerrero Herrera holds a Ph.D. in Economic and Administrative Sciences from the Autonomous University of the State of Hidalgo (UAEH), awarded with Honors in March 2025. She also earned a Master's in Innovation for Business Development with Highest Honors from the Monterrey Institute of Technology and Higher Education (ITESM), and a Bachelor's degree in Economics from UAEH, where she was recognized for Academic Merit. Currently, she serves as a Professor in both the Financial Engineering undergraduate program and the Master's in Finance and Management at the Polytechnic University of Pachuca (UPP). Her research explores the intersection of technology and human capital, specializing in labor market competency analysis. By leveraging Artificial Intelligence and Natural Language Processing tools, her work aims to bridge the gap between educational outcomes and workforce demands.

Shashi Kant Gupta is a distinguished academic and researcher in the field of Computer Science and Engineering, with a prolific career spanning over a decade. His extensive contributions to academia and industry are marked by his roles in various prestigious institutions and his leadership in innovative research projects. Prof. Gupta's work primarily focuses on Cloud Computing, Big Data Analytics, IoT, and Computational Intelligence with multidisciplinary areas in which he has made significant advancements. Prof. Gupta is currently serving as a Post-Doctoral Fellow and Researcher at Eudoxia Research University, USA, where he is involved in cutting-edge research in Computer Science and Engineering. In addition, he holds the position of Adjunct Faculty, Faculty of Information Technology, Victorian Institute of Technology, Level 14,123 Queen Street, Melbourne VIC 3000, Australia. And an Adjunct Professor at Lincoln University College, Malaysia, contributing to the academic development of students in the region. His role as a Research Fellow at Inti International University, Malaysia, further underscores his commitment to fostering research and innovation.

Vishal Jain currently serves as a Professor and Dean of Accreditation, Statutory Compliances & Institutional Development at the School of Engineering & Technology, Vivekananda Institute of Professional Studies - Technical Campus, New Delhi. His previous roles include Professor at Sharda University, Greater Noida, and Associate Professor at Bharati Vidyapeeth's Institute of Computer Applications and Management (BVICAM), New Delhi. Dr. Jain has actively participated in various academic governance bodies, including the Faculty Board, Board of Planning and Management, Executive Council, Academic Council, Curriculum Development and Review Committee, and Academic Audit across multiple higher education institutions. He collaborates with Kuala Lumpur University of Science and Technology (KLUST), Malaysia, Lincoln University College, Malaysia and the Research Institute of IoT Cybersecurity at National Kaohsiung University of Science and Technology in Taiwan for research initiatives. He has supervised three Ph.D. candidates, with two additional scholars currently pursuing their degrees under his guidance.

Mustafa Kayyali is an ardent advocate for excellence in higher education, driven by a relentless pursuit of quality, recognition, and innovation. Their journey in academia started with a Master's in Quality Management and Evaluation in Higher Education from Universitat Oberta de Catalunya, followed by a Ph.D. in Quality Management from Azteca University. These academic pursuits have laid a strong foundation for their expertise in Accreditation, Quality Assurance, and Higher Education Rankings. As an entrepreneur, researcher, translator, and publisher, they are deeply involved in various facets of the academic world. Their diverse interests encompass Management, Translation, Interpretation, and Academic consulting, contributing to a well-rounded understanding of the industry. Throughout their career, they have made significant contributions to academic literature, with more than 40 published papers and 30 book chapters to my name. Additionally, they take pride in having translated 6 books, bridging language gaps, and promoting knowledge exchange on a global scale. They are committed to fostering positive change in higher education and contributing to its continuous improvement.

Archan Mitra is an Assistant Professor at School of Media Studies (SOMS) at Presidency University, Bangalore. He is the author of two book "Cases for Classroom Media and Entertainment Business" and "Multiverse and Media", he also has other several edited books to his credit. He has done his doctorate from Visva-Bharati Santiniketan, West Bengal in the field of "environmental informatics and communication for sustainability". In addition to that he is a certified Science Communicator and Journalism from Indian Science Communication Society (ISCOS), certified Corporate Trainer with Amity Institute of Training and Development, Certified Social Media Network Analyst. He has a strong interest in environmental communication. He was awarded certificate of merit by PRSI, Kolkata Chapter and Medal of Honor by Journalistic Club of Kolkata. He was working as a research assistant with the World Bank's "Environmental Capacity Building in

Southeast Asia" project at IIM Kashipur. He was instrumental in launching the World Bank's Green MBA MOOC, he has also assisted in the research project on Uttarakhand disaster mitigation by ICSSR, the leading research on Uttarakhand disaster.

Supratim Mukherjee is an academician and media education professional with expertise in communication studies, journalism, animation, VFX, media research, and academic administration. He is actively engaged in teaching, curriculum development, student mentoring, and research, focusing on digital media, creative technologies, industry-oriented education, and innovative learning practices in higher education.

Fernando Sánchez-Martínez is a professor at the Universidad Autónoma del Carmen, with 25 years' experience in teaching, research and academic management. He has collaborated in the design of curricula and the management of educational programmes, contributing to the strengthening of education in Information Technology and Computer Science. He is a member of the Academic Body of Scientific Computing, where he develops projects focused on solving organizational problems through technological applications. Throughout his career, he has been involved in educational innovation projects and the development of strategies to improve students' academic performance. His work has been presented at conferences and published in peer-reviewed journals, reinforcing his commitment to applied research in computing and technology.

Index

A

E

F

G

V

X

www.ingramcontent.com/pod-product-compliance
Lightning Source LLC
LaVergne TN
LVHW080905300926
849162LV00003B/559